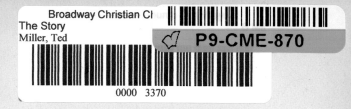

Broadway Christian Ch...
The Story
Miller, Ted

0000 3370

P9-CME-870

We are pleased to offer "The Story," adapted from THE LIVING BIBLE. This unusual book can be read through in a few days. It captures the full sweep of God's Word in an abridged, chronological form.

Thank you for your loyal support of our ministry. Your contribution makes it possible for our Team to continue spreading the Gospel of Jesus Christ around the world.

Billy Graham

BILLY GRAHAM

EVANGELISTIC ASSOCIATION
Minneapolis, Minnesota 55440

THE STORY

ADAPTED BY TED MILLER FROM
THE BOOK

PROPERTY OF
BROADWAY CHRISTIAN CHURCH LIBRARY
910 BROADWAY
FORT WAYNE, IN 46802

Tyndale House Publishers, Inc.
Wheaton, Illinois

This special edition is published
with permission from the original
publisher, Tyndale House Publishers,
336 Gunderson Drive, Wheaton, IL 60187.

Second printing, November 1986
The Story, copyright © 1986 by
E. Theodore Miller.
All rights reserved.
Adapted from *The Book,* an
edition of *The Living Bible,* a
compilation of the Scripture
portions previously published by
Tyndale House Publishers under
the following titles: *Living
Letters,* 1962; *Living
Prophecies,* 1965; *Living
Gospels,* 1966; *Living Psalms
and Proverbs,* 1967; *Living
Lessons of Life and Love,* 1968;
Living Books of Moses, 1969;
Living History of Israel, 1970.
Copyright © 1971 by Tyndale
House Publishers, Wheaton,
Illinois 60187. All rights
reserved.

Library of Congress Catalog
Card Number 86-050774
ISBN 0-8423-6677-6 paper

Printed in the United States of
America

PROPERTY OF
BROADWAY CHRISTIAN CHURCH LIBRARY
910 BROADWAY
FORT WAYNE, IN 46

CONTENTS

THE STORY OF LIFE

This is the story of life on Planet Earth, a story recorded by prophets, priests, and scribes across a span of 1,500 years. It celebrates the first man—Adam—in the dawn of life, chronicles the rise of the Jewish nation and the Christian church, and culminates in history's climactic battle—Armageddon—predicted in these writings.

No other book among the world's millions of volumes so plausibly describes the origin of Planet Earth and foretells its dramatic future. No other book is so bold yet discreet, terrifying but reassuring, graphic while veiled in mystery, stern and still gracious. It is a drama of love and murder, heroes and villains, majesty and depravity, saints and tyrants, miracles and tragedies, angels and demons, heaven and hell.

Most of all, it is an epic of the loving God who moves heaven and earth to restore searching humans to his presence and eternal pleasures. This story is fully told in the Holy Bible, the sacred book of a billion Christians, which has been translated at least partially into nearly 2,000 languages and dialects.

The first Bible writer, Moses the prophet, told Israel: "Jehovah is our God . . . you must love him with all your heart . . . think constantly about these commandments . . . teach them to your children." The last writer of the Bible, John the apostle, promised readers: "Those who listen and do what it says will be blessed." Jesus Christ, the sublime personality of the Bible, declared: "Heaven and earth will disappear, but my words remain forever."

Since its first printing in 1456, the Bible has been the world's most widely circulated book. It is more than a single book, however. It is a library—and comparatively few readers have absorbed this library of life.

To help readers connect the end with the beginning and correlate main events with the full panorama of biblical history, this abridgment selects, condenses, and chronologically rearranges Bible portions into a coherent, compelling story. The text is from *The Book,* an edition of the best-selling *Living Bible,* paraphrased for contemporary readers by Kenneth N. Taylor. The abridgment is by Ted Miller, a digest magazine editor for many years.

Only a few words have been changed in this abridgment to ease transition steps in thought. Twelve division headings indicate the major periods of human history on earth. Sectional headings identify episodes in the developing narrative, and sectional footnotes list the specific Bible sources of the text in sequential order. Passages from the Psalms—the songs of Israel—appear in italic print at appropriate places in the story. Gaps in story action and time progression usually reflect the absence of details and terseness of style characteristic of the Bible.

Jeremiah, the prophet who survived Jerusalem's destruction in 586 B.C. and heralded God's promise to resurrect the holy city, spoke to every generation when he wrote: "The Lord says, 'Let not the wise bask in wisdom, nor the mighty in might, nor the rich in riches. Let them boast in this alone: that they truly know me, the Lord of justice and righteousness whose love is steadfast.'"

This story is, truly, God's story.

The Compiler

PART
1
PARADISE
LOST

DAWN When God began creating the heavens and the earth, the earth was a shapeless, chaotic mass, with the Spirit of God brooding over the dark vapors. Then God said, "Let there be light," and light appeared. God was pleased with it, and divided the light from the darkness. He called the light "daytime," and the darkness "nighttime." Together they formed the first day.

And God said, "Let the vapors separate to form the sky above and the oceans below." This happened on the second day.

Then God said, "Let the water beneath the sky be gathered into oceans so that dry land will emerge." God named the land "earth" and the water "seas." And he said, "Let the earth burst forth with every sort of grass, seed-bearing plant, and fruit trees with seeds inside the fruit, so the seeds will produce the kinds of plants and fruits they came from." And so it was on the third day.

God said, "Let bright lights appear in the sky to give light to the earth and to identify the day and the night; they shall bring about seasons on the earth, and mark days and years." And so it was, for God had made two huge lights, the sun and moon, to shine upon the earth—the larger one to preside over the day and the smaller one through the night. He also made the stars. And God was pleased. This happened on the fourth day.

Then God said, "Let the waters teem with fish and other life, and let the skies be filled with birds of every kind." God looked at them with pleasure and blessed them all. "Multiply and stock the oceans," he told them; and to the birds he said, "Let your numbers increase." That ended the fifth day.

And God said, "Let the earth bring forth every kind of animal—cattle and reptiles and wildlife of every kind." And so it was.

Then God said, "Let us make a man—someone like ourselves—to be the master of all life on the earth and in the skies and in the seas." The Lord God formed a man's body from the dust of the ground and breathed into it the breath of life, and man became a living person.[1]

ADAM Then the Lord planted a garden in Eden, to the east, and placed in the garden the man he had formed. God planted all sorts of beautiful trees there, trees producing the choicest fruit. At the center of the garden he placed the Tree of Life, and also the Tree of Conscience giving knowledge of good and bad.

A river from the land of Eden flowed through the garden to water it; afterward the river divided into four branches. One of these was named the Pishon; it winds across the entire length of the land of Havilah where nuggets of pure gold are found, also beautiful bdellium and lapis lazuli. The second branch is the Gihon, crossing the entire length of the land of Cush. The third branch is the Tigris, which flows to the east of the city of Asher. And the fourth is the Euphrates.

God placed the man in the Garden of Eden to tend and care for it. But the Lord gave the man this warning: "You may eat any fruit in the garden except fruit from the Tree of Conscience—for its fruit will make you aware of right and wrong, good and bad. If you eat its fruit, you will be doomed to die."

And the Lord said, "It isn't good for man to be alone; I will make a companion for him, a helper suited to his needs." Then the Lord caused the man to fall into a deep sleep, took one of his ribs and closed up the place from which he had removed it, and made the rib into a woman and brought her to the man.

"This is it!" Adam exclaimed; "she is part of my own bone and flesh! Her name is 'woman' because she was taken out of a man." Although the man and his wife were naked, neither of them was ashamed.

So God made man like his Maker: man and maid he made them. And God told them, "Multiply and fill the earth and subdue it; you are masters of the fish and birds and all the animals. I have given you the seed-bearing plants throughout the earth and all the fruit trees for your food. And I've given all the grass and plants as food for the animals and birds." Then God looked over all he had made, and it was excellent in every way. This ended the sixth day.

Now at last the heavens and earth were completed, with all they contained. Having finished his task, God blessed the seventh day and declared it holy because it was the day when he ceased his work of creation.[2]

ALLELUIA *"Can't you hear the voice of wisdom? "'I, Wisdom, give good advice and common sense. I love all who love me. Those who search for me shall surely find me. Unending riches, honor, justice, and righteousness are mine to distribute. My gifts are better than the purest gold or sterling silver! My paths are those of justice and right. Those who love and follow me are indeed wealthy. I fill their treasuries.*

"'The Lord formed me in the beginning, before he created anything else. From ages past, I am. I lived before the oceans were created, before the springs bubbled forth their waters onto the earth, before the mountains and the hills were made. I was there when he made the blueprint for the earth and oceans. Whoever finds me finds life and wins approval from the Lord. Those who refuse me show that they love death.'"

"The earth belongs to God! Everything in all the world is his!"

"O Lord, what a variety you have made! And in wisdom you have made them all! The earth is full of your riches.

*You send your Spirit and new life is born to replenish
all the living of the earth. You have reigned from prehistoric
times, from the everlasting past. The mighty oceans thunder
your praise."*

*"Bless the Lord, you mighty angels of his who carry
out his orders, listening for each of his commands. Yes,
bless the Lord, you armies of his angels who serve him
constantly. Let everything bless the Lord."*[3]

DOOM The serpent was the craftiest of all the creatures the Lord had made. The serpent came
to the woman. "Really?" he asked. "None of
the fruit in the garden? God says you mustn't eat any of
it?"

"Of course we may eat it," the woman told him. "It's
only the fruit from the tree at the center of the garden
that we are not to eat. God says we mustn't eat it or
even touch it, or we will die."

"That's a lie!" the serpent hissed. "You'll not die! God
knows very well that the instant you eat it you will become
like him, for your eyes will be opened—you will be able
to distinguish good from evil!"

The woman was convinced. How lovely and fresh looking
it was! And it would make her wise! So she ate the fruit
and gave some to her husband, and he ate it too. And as
they ate it, suddenly they became aware of their nakedness
and were embarrassed. So they strung fig leaves together
to cover themselves around the hips.

That evening they heard the sound of the Lord walking
in the garden, and they hid themselves among the trees.
The Lord called to Adam, "Why are you hiding?"

Adam replied, "I heard you coming and didn't want you
to see me naked."

"Who told you you were naked?" the Lord asked. "Have
you eaten fruit from the tree I warned you about?"

"Yes," Adam admitted, "but it was the woman you gave
me who brought me some, and I ate it."

Then the Lord asked the woman, "How could you do
such a thing?"

"The serpent tricked me," she replied.

So the Lord said to the serpent, "This is your punishment: you are singled out from all the domestic and wild animals of the whole earth—to be cursed. You shall grovel in the dust as long as you live, crawling along on your belly. From now on, you and the woman will be enemies, as will your offspring and hers. You will strike his heel, but he will crush your head."

Then God said to the woman, "You shall bear children in pain, yet you shall welcome your husband's affections, and he shall be your master."

To Adam God said, "Because you listened to your wife and ate the fruit when I told you not to, I have placed a curse upon the soil. You will struggle to extract a living from it; it will grow thorns and thistles, and you shall eat its grasses. All your life you will sweat to master it, then you will return to the ground from which you came."

The man named his wife Eve (meaning "The life-giving one"), for he said, "She shall become the mother of all mankind."

And God clothed Adam and his wife with garments made from skins of animals.

Then the Lord said, "Now that the man has become as we are, knowing good from bad, what if he eats the fruit of the Tree of Life and lives forever?" So the Lord banished him forever from the Garden of Eden, and sent him out to farm the ground from which he had been taken. God placed mighty angels at the east of the garden with a flaming sword to guard the entrance to the Tree of Life [4]

DEVIL "How you are fallen from heaven, O Lucifer, son of the morning! You said to yourself, 'I will ascend to heaven and rule the angels. I will take the highest throne. I will preside on the Mount of Assembly far away in the north. I will climb to the highest heavens and be like the Most High.' But instead, you will be brought down to the pit of hell, down to its lowest depths.

"You were the perfection of wisdom and beauty. Your clothing was bejeweled with every precious stone—ruby, topaz, diamond, chrysolite, onyx, jasper, sapphire, carbuncle, and emerald—all in beautiful settings of finest gold. They were given to you on the day you were created. I appointed you to be the anointed Guardian Angel. You had access to the holy mountain of God. You were perfect in all you did from the day you were created until that time when wrong was found in you. Your great wealth filled you with internal turmoil and you sinned. Therefore, I cast you out of the mountain of God like a common sinner."[5]

FAMILY Adam had sexual intercourse with his wife and she conceived and gave birth to a son, Cain (meaning "I have created"). For, as she said, "With God's help, I have created a man!" Her next child was his brother, Abel.

Abel became a shepherd, while Cain was a farmer. At harvest time Cain brought the Lord a gift of his farm produce, and Abel brought cuts of meat from his best lambs and presented them to the Lord. The Lord accepted Abel's offering, but not Cain's. This made Cain very angry.

The Lord asked him, "Why is your face dark with rage? It can be bright with joy if you do what you should! But if you refuse to obey, watch out: sin is waiting to attack you, longing to destroy you. But you can conquer it!"

One day Cain suggested to his brother, "Let's go out to the fields"—and while they were there, Cain attacked and killed his brother.

Afterwards the Lord asked Cain, "Where is your brother?"

"How should I know?" Cain retorted. "Am I supposed to keep track of him?"

The Lord said, "Your brother's blood calls to me from the ground. You are hereby banished from this ground which you have defiled with your brother's blood. No longer will it yield crops for you. From now on you will be a fugitive upon the earth, wandering from place to place."

Cain replied, "My punishment is greater than I can bear. You have banished me from my farm and made me a tramp; and everyone who sees me will try to kill me."

"They won't kill you," the Lord replied. Then the Lord

put an identifying mark on Cain as a warning not to kill him. So Cain went out from the presence of the Lord and settled in the Land of Nod, east of Eden.

Cain's wife conceived, and presented him with a baby son named Enoch. When Cain founded a city, he named it Enoch. Enoch was the father of Irad, the father of Mehujael, the father of Methusael, the father of Lamech.

Lamech married two wives—Adah and Zillah. To Adah was born Jabal. He became the first of the cattlemen and those living in tents. His brother was Jubal, the first musician. To Lamech's other wife, Zillah, was born Tubal-Cain. He opened the first foundry forging instruments of bronze and iron.

Later on Eve gave birth to another son and named him Seth. When Seth grew up, he had a son and named him Enosh. During his lifetime men first began to call themselves "the Lord's people."

Here is a list of some of the descendants of Adam. Adam was 130 years old when his son Seth was born. Adam lived another 800 years, producing sons and daughters, and died at the age of 930.

Seth was 105 years old when Enosh was born. Afterwards he lived another 807 years, producing sons and daughters, and died at the age of 912.

Enosh was ninety years old when his son Kenan was born. He lived another 815 years, producing sons and daughters, and died at the age of 905.

Kenan was seventy years old when his son Mahalalel was born. He lived another 840 years.

Mahalalel was sixty-five years old when his son Jared was born. Afterwards he lived 830 years.

Jared was 162 years old when his son Enoch was born. He lived another 800 years.

Enoch was sixty-five years old when his son Methuselah was born. He lived another 300 years in fellowship with God, then he disappeared, for God took him!

Methuselah was 187 years old when his son Lamech was born; he lived another 782 years and died at the age of 969.

Lamech was 182 years old when his son Noah was born. Afterwards Lamech lived 595 years, and died at the age of 777.

Noah was 500 years old and had three sons: Shem, Ham, and Japheth.[6]

CATACLYSM Now a population explosion took place on the earth. At this time, beings from the spirit world looked upon the beautiful earth women and took any they desired to be their wives.

Then Jehovah said, "My Spirit must not forever be disgraced in man, wholly evil as he is. I will give him 120 years to mend his ways."

When the evil beings were sexually involved with human women, their children became giants of whom so many legends are told. God saw the extent of human wickedness and said, "I will blot out from the earth all mankind that I created. Yes, the animals too and the reptiles and the birds."

But Noah was a pleasure to the Lord. The only righteous man at that time, he tried to conduct his affairs according to God's will.

As God saw that all mankind was vicious and depraved, he said to Noah, "I have decided to destroy mankind, for the earth is filled with crime. Make a boat from resinous wood, sealing it with tar; and construct decks and stalls throughout the ship. Make it 450 feet long, 75 feet wide, and 45 feet high. Construct a skylight all the way around the ship, eighteen inches below the roof; and make three decks inside the boat—a bottom, middle, and upper deck—and put a door in the side.

"I am going to cover the earth with a flood. But I promise to keep you safe in the ship with your wife and your sons and their wives. Bring a pair of every animal—a male and a female—into the boat with you, to keep them alive through the flood. Store away in the boat all the food that they and you will need."

Noah did everything as God commanded him. Finally the day came when the Lord said to Noah, "Go into the boat with all your family. Bring in the animals, too—a pair of each, except those kinds I have chosen for eating and for sacrifice: take seven pairs of each of them, and seven pairs of every kind of bird. One week from today I will begin forty days and nights of rain."

Noah did everything the Lord commanded. He was 600 years old when the flood came. Rain came down in mighty torrents from the sky, and the subterranean waters burst forth upon the earth for forty days and nights.

As the water rose higher and higher, the boat floated safely upon it until finally the water covered all the high mountains under the whole heaven. All living things upon the earth perished—birds, domestic and wild animals, reptiles, and all mankind. God destroyed them all, leaving only Noah alive and those with him in the boat. And the water covered the earth 150 days.

God sent a wind to blow across the waters and the flood gradually receded until the boat came to rest upon the mountains of Ararat. Three months later, as the waters continued to go down, other mountain peaks appeared.

At last the earth was dry. God told Noah, "You may go out; release the animals, birds, and reptiles so that they will reproduce in great numbers." Noah, his wife, and his sons and their wives disembarked along with the animals, reptiles, and birds. Noah built an altar and sacrificed on it some of the animals and birds God had designated for that purpose. Then God told Noah and his sons, "I will never again send another flood to destroy the earth. And I seal this promise with this sign: I have placed my rainbow in the clouds as a sign of my promise until the end of time, to you and to all the earth."[7]

DYNASTIES

God blessed Noah and his sons and told them to repopulate the earth.

"All wild animals and birds and fish will be afraid of you," God told him, "for I have placed them in your power, and they are yours to use for food in addition to grain and vegetables. But never eat animals unless their life-blood has been drained off. And murder is forbidden. Man-killing animals must die, and any man who murders shall be killed; for to kill a man is to kill one made like God."

These are the families of Shem, Ham, and Japheth, the three sons of Noah. The sons of Japheth were: Gomer, Magog, Madai, Javan, Tubal, Meshech, Tiras. The sons of Gomer: Ashkenaz, Riphath, Togarmah. The sons of Javan: Elishah, Tarshish, Kittim, Dodanim. Their descendants became the maritime nations in various lands.

The sons of Ham were Cush, Mizraim, Put, Canaan. One of the descendants of Cush was Nimrod, who became the first of the kings. He was a mighty hunter. The heart of his empire included Babel, Erech, Accad, and Calneh in the land of Shinar. From there he extended his reign to Assyria; he built Nineveh.

Canaan's oldest son was Sidon. From Canaan descended these nations: Jebusites, Amorites, Girgashites, Hivites. The descendants of Canaan spread from Sidon to Gerar in the Gaza strip, and to Sodom.

Eber descended from Shem, the oldest brother of Japheth. Here is a list of Shem's other descendants: Elam, Asshur, Arpachshad, Lud, Aram. Arpachshad's son was Shelah, and Shelah's son was Eber. Two sons were born to Eber: Peleg (meaning "Division," for during his lifetime the people of the world were dispersed), and Joktan.

All of the men descended from Noah, through many generations, living in various nations that developed after the flood.[8]

BABEL

As the population grew and spread eastward, a plain was discovered in the land of Babylon and was soon thickly populated. The people who lived there began to talk about building a great city, with a temple-tower reaching to the skies—a proud, eternal monument to themselves.

"This will weld us together," they said, "and keep us from scattering all over the world." So they made great piles of hardburned brick and collected bitumen to use as mortar.

God said, "If they are able to accomplish all this when

they have just begun to exploit their linguistic and political unity, nothing will be unattainable for them! Let us give them different languages so that they won't understand each other's words!"

In that way, God scattered them over the earth, and that ended the building of the city. That is why the city was called Babel, meaning "confusion."[9]

WORLDS' WAR

There lived in the land of Uz a man named Job—a man who feared God. He had a family of seven sons and three daughters and was immensely wealthy. Every year when each of Job's sons had a birthday, he invited the brothers and sisters to his home for a celebration. When these parties ended, Job would summon his children to him and sanctify them, offering a burnt offering for each of them. For Job said, "Perhaps my sons have sinned and turned away from God in their hearts." This was Job's regular practice.

One day as angels came to present themselves before the Lord, Satan—the Accuser—came with them.

"Where have you come from?" the Lord asked Satan.

"From patrolling the earth."

"Have you noticed my servant Job? He is the finest man in all the earth—a man who fears God and will have nothing to do with evil."

"Why shouldn't he?" Satan scoffed. "You have always protected him and his home and his property from harm. You have prospered everything he does. But just take away his wealth and you'll see him curse you to your face!"

The Lord replied, "You may do anything you like with his wealth, but don't harm him physically."

Satan went away; and not long afterwards tragedy struck. A messenger rushed to Job's home with this news: "Your oxen were plowing, with the donkeys feeding beside them, when the Sabeans raided us, drove away the animals, and killed all the farmhands except me."

While this messenger was speaking, another arrived with more bad news: "Fire has fallen from heaven and burned up your sheep and all the herdsmen."

Before this man finished, another rushed in: "Three bands of Chaldeans have driven off your camels and killed your servants."

As he was speaking, another arrived to say, "Your sons and daughters were feasting in their oldest brother's home when a mighty wind swept in from the desert and engulfed the house so that the roof fell in on them and all are dead; I alone escaped to tell you."

Job stood up, tore his robe in grief, and fell down to the ground before God. "The Lord gave me everything I had, and they were his to take away. Blessed be the name of the Lord."

The angels came again to present themselves before the Lord, and Satan with them.

"Well, have you noticed my servant Job?" the Lord asked. "He has kept his faith in me despite the fact that you persuaded me to let you harm him without any cause."

"Skin for skin," Satan replied. "A man will give anything to save his life. Touch his body with sickness and he will curse you to your face!"

"Do with him as you please," the Lord replied; "only spare his life."

So Satan went from the presence of the Lord and struck Job with terrible boils from head to foot. Job took a broken piece of pottery to scrape himself, and sat among ashes.

His wife said to him, "Are you still trying to be godly when God has done all this to you? Curse him and die."

He replied, "Shall we receive only pleasant things from the hand of God?"

When three of Job's friends heard of the tragedy, they traveled from their homes to comfort him. Their names were Eliphaz, Bildad, and Zophar. Job was so changed that they could scarcely recognize him. They sat upon the ground with him seven days and nights, no one speaking a word; for they saw that his suffering was too great for words.

At last Job spoke and cursed the day of his birth. "Let that day be forever forgotten. Curse it for its failure to shut my mother's womb, for letting me be born to come to all this trouble. Why is a man allowed to be born if

God is going to give him a hopeless life of uselessness?"

A reply to Job from Eliphaz: "In the past you have told many a troubled soul to trust in God, and have encouraged those who are weak. But now, when trouble strikes, you are broken.

"Stop and think Have you ever known a truly good person who was punished? It is those who sow sin and trouble who harvest the same. Misery comes upon them to punish them for sowing seeds of sin. Mankind heads for sin and misery as predictably as flames shoot upwards from a fire. My advice to you is: go to God and confess your sins to him."

Bildad replies to Job: "Does God twist justice? If your children sinned against him and he punished them and you begged Almighty God for them—if you were pure, he would hear your prayer and answer you and bless you with a happy home.

"The wisdom of the past will teach you: those who forget God have no hope. God will not cast away a good man, nor prosper evildoers. He will yet fill your mouth with laughter and your lips with shouts of joy"

Zophar replies to Job: "Listen! God is doubtless punishing you far less than you deserve! Before you turn to God and stretch out your hands to him, get rid of your sins and leave all iniquity behind you. Only then can you walk steadily forward to God without fear. Only then can you forget your misery. It will all be in the past."

Job's reply: "Be silent now that I may speak—and I am willing to face the consequences. God may kill me for saying this—in fact, I expect him to. Nevertheless I am going to argue my case with him.

"This is my case: I know that I am righteous. If you could prove me wrong, I would stop defending myself and die.

"O God, there are two things I beg you not to do to me: don't abandon me; and don't terrify me with your awesome presence. Call to me to come—how quickly I will answer!

"If a man dies, shall he live again? This thought gives

me hope, so that in all my anguish I eagerly await sweet death! You would call and I would come, and you would reward all I do.

"O God, you have turned me to skin and bones—as a proof, they say, of my sins. These 'comforters' have gaping jaws to swallow me. My enemies gather themselves against me. My eyes are dim with weeping and I am but a shadow of my former self. Fair-minded men are astonished when they see me.

"The fact of the matter is that God has overthrown me. God has blocked my path and turned my light to darkness. My relatives have failed me; my friends have forsaken me. Even my servants regard me as a stranger. I call my servant, but he doesn't come. Young children despise me; when I stand to speak, they mock. I am skin and bones and have escaped death by the skin of my teeth.

"But, as for me, I know that my Redeemer lives, and that he will stand upon the earth at last. And I know that after this body has decayed, this body shall see God. Yes, I shall see him, not as a stranger but as a friend! What a glorious hope!

"Oh, that I knew where to find God—that I could go to his throne and talk with him there. I would tell him my side of this argument, and listen to his reply. But I search in vain. I seek him here, I seek him there, and cannot find him.

"Oh, for the years gone by when God took care of me, when he lighted the way before me and I walked safely through the darkness, when the friendship of God was felt in my home, when my children were around me, when my projects prospered. Those were the days when I went out to the city gate and took my place among the honored elders. All rejoiced at what I said.

"For I, as an honest judge, helped the poor in their need and the fatherless who had no one to help them. I served as eyes for the blind and feet for the lame. I was as a father to the poor, and saw to it that even strangers received a fair trial. I thought, 'Surely I shall die quietly in my nest after a long, good life.'

"Depression haunts my days; my weary nights are filled with pain as though something were relentlessly gnawing at my bones. I have become as dust and ashes. My skin is black and peeling. My bones burn with fever. The voice of joy has turned to mourning."

The three men refused to reply further to Job because he kept insisting on his innocence. Then Elihu, son of Barachel, became angry because Job refused to admit he had sinned. He said, "I am young and you are old, so I did not dare to tell you what I think. But it is not mere age that makes men wise. Please listen, Job, to what I have to say.

"You have said 'I am pure; I am innocent; I have not sinned.' You say God is using a fine-toothed comb to try to find a single fault, and so to count you as his enemy. You have sinned by speaking of God that way. For God is greater than man. Why should you fight against him just because he does not give account to you of what he does?

"Listen to me, you wise men. First of all, we must define what is good. For Job has said, 'I am innocent but God says I'm not. I am horribly punished even though I have not sinned.' Who is as arrogant as Job?

"Surely everyone knows that God doesn't sin! Rather, he punishes the sinners. He alone has authority over the earth and dispenses justice. If God were to withdraw his Spirit, all life would disappear and mankind would turn again to dust.

"Why don't people exclaim to their God, 'We have sinned, but we will stop'? Or, 'We know not what evil we have done; only tell us, and we will cease'?

"Must God tailor his justice to your demands? Must he change the order of the universe to suit your whims? The answer must be obvious.

"The oppressed may shriek beneath their wrongs and the power of the rich, yet none of them cry to God, asking, 'Where is God, my Maker?' When anyone does cry out this question, he never replies by instant punishments of the tyrants; but it is false to say he doesn't hear those cries, and it is even more false to say that he doesn't see what is going on. He does bring about justice at last, if you will only wait.

"God is all powerful. Who can say that what he does is absurd or evil? Instead, glorify him for his mighty works for which he is so famous.

"As we cannot look at the sun for its brightness when the winds have cleared away the clouds, neither can we gaze at the terrible majesty of God breaking forth upon us from heaven, clothed in dazzling splendor. We cannot imagine the power of the Almighty, and yet he is so just and merciful that he does not destroy us. No wonder men everywhere fear him!"

Then the Lord answered Job from the whirlwind: "Why are you using your ignorance to deny my providence? I am going to demand some answers from you.

"Where were you when I laid the foundations of the earth? Do you know how its dimensions were determined? Who decreed the boundaries of the seas when they gushed from the depths?

"Have you once caused the dawn to rise in the east? Have you ever robed the dawn in red?

"Has the location of the gates of death been revealed to you? Tell me about it if you know. Or tell me about the darkness: can you find its boundaries, or go to its source?

"Who dug the valleys for the torrents of rain? Who laid out the path for the lightning, causing the rain to fall upon the barren deserts so that the parched and barren ground is satisfied with water?

"Can you restrain Orion or Pleiades? Can you ensure the proper sequence of the seasons, or guide the constellation of the Bear with her satellites across the heavens?

"Do you still want to argue with the Almighty? Do you—God's critic—have the answers?"

Then Job replied: "I am nothing—how could I ever find the answers? I lay my hand upon my mouth in silence. I have said too much already."

The Lord spoke to Job again: "Stand up like a man and prepare yourself for battle. Are you going to discredit my justice and condemn me so you can say you are right?

Are you as strong as God? Then put on your majesty and splendor. Humiliate the haughty with a glance; tread down the wicked where they stand. If you can do that, then I'll agree with you that your own strength can save you."

Then Job replied to God: "I know that you can do anything and that no one can stop you. You ask who has so foolishly denied your providence. It is I; I was talking about things I knew nothing about, things far too wonderful for me. I had heard about you before, but now I have seen you, and I repent in dust and ashes."

After the Lord finished speaking with Job, he said to Eliphaz, "I am angry with you and with your two friends, for you have not been right in what you said about me. Now take seven bulls and seven rams and offer a burnt offering for yourselves; and my servant Job will pray for you, and I will accept his prayer on your behalf."

Eliphaz and Bildad and Zophar did as the Lord commanded, and the Lord accepted Job's prayer. When Job prayed for his friends, the Lord restored his wealth and happiness. In fact, the Lord gave him twice as much as before. His brothers, sisters, and former friends arrived and feasted with him, comforting him because of all the trials the Lord had brought upon him.

The Lord blessed Job at the end of his life more than at the beginning. For now he had 14,000 sheep, 6,000 camels, 1,000 teams of oxen, and 1,000 female donkeys.

God also gave him seven more sons and three more daughters. And in all the land there were no other girls as lovely as the daughters of Job; and their father put them into his will along with their brothers.

Job lived 140 years after that, living to see his grandchildren and great-grandchildren too. At last he died, after a long, good life.[10]

PART
2
COVENANT
PEOPLE

ABRAM Shem's descendants included Arpachshad—born two years after the flood—Shelah, Eber, Peleg, Reu, Serug, Nahor, Terah. By the time Terah was seventy years old, he had three sons: Abram, Nahor, and Haran. And Haran had a son named Lot. But Haran died young, in the land where he was born—Ur of the Chaldeans—and was survived by his father.

Abram married his half-sister Sarai, while his brother Nahor married their orphaned niece Milcah, the daughter of Haran. Then Terah took Abram, Lot, and Sarai to go to the land of Canaan, but they stopped instead at the city of Haran and settled there.

God had told Abram, "Leave your country and go to the land I will guide you to. I will cause you to become the father of a great nation; I will bless you and make your name famous, and you will be a blessing to many others. I will bless those who bless you and curse those who curse you; and the entire world will be blessed because of you."

So Abram left Haran as the Lord instructed him. He took Sarai, Lot, and all the wealth he had gotten in Haran and finally arrived in Canaan. They came to a place near Shechem and set up camp beside the oak at Moreh.

Then Jehovah appeared to Abram and said, "I am going to give this land to your descendants." And Abram built an altar there to commemorate Jehovah's visit. Afterwards Abram traveled southward to the hilly country between Bethel and Ai. There he made camp, and made an altar to the Lord and prayed to him. Thus he continued slowly southward to the Negeb, pausing frequently.

There was at that time a famine in the land, so Abram went on to Egypt to live. As he was approaching Egypt, he asked Sarai to tell everyone that she was his sister. "You are very beautiful, and when the Egyptians see you they will say, 'This is his wife; let's kill him and then we can have her!' But if you say you are my sister, the Egyptians will treat me well because of you."

Sure enough, in Egypt everyone spoke of her beauty. When the palace aides saw her, they praised her to their king, the Pharaoh, and she was taken into his harem. Pharaoh gave Abram many gifts because of her—sheep, oxen, donkeys, men and women slaves, and camels.

But the Lord sent a plague upon Pharaoh's household on account of her being there. Then Pharaoh called Abram before him and accused him sharply: "Why didn't you tell me she was your wife? Here, take her and be gone!" And Pharaoh sent them out of the country.

So they left Egypt and traveled north into the Negeb. They continued northward toward Bethel where he had camped before, to the place where he had built the altar. And there he again worshiped the Lord.

Lot too was wealthy, with sheep and cattle and many servants. The land could not support both Abram and Lot with all of their flocks and herds; fights broke out between the herdsmen of Abram and Lot despite the danger they all faced from the Canaanites in the land. Abram talked it over with Lot. "This fighting has to stop. I'll tell you what we'll do: take your choice of any section of the land you want, and we will separate."

Lot took a long look at the fertile plains of the Jordan River; the whole section was like the beautiful country in Egypt. That is what Lot chose. Abram stayed in the land of Canaan, while Lot lived near the city of Sodom.

After Lot was gone, the Lord said to Abram, "Look as

far as you can see in every direction, for I am going to give it all to you and your descendants. And I am going to give you so many descendants that they can't be counted!" Then Abram moved his tent to the oaks of Mamre, near Hebron, and built an altar to Jehovah there.

Now war filled the land—Amraphel, Arioch, Ched-or-laomer, and Tidal fought against Bera, Birsha, Shinab, Shemeber, and the king of Bela. For twelve years they had been subject to King Ched-or-laomer, but now they rebelled.

The army unsuccessfully attacked Ched-or-laomer in the Salt Valley. The victors plundered Sodom and Gomorrah and carried off their wealth and food, taking with them Lot, Abram's nephew. One of the men who escaped came and told Abram.

Abram called together the men born into his household, 318 in all, and chased after the retiring army. That night he successfully attacked and pursued the fleeing army to Hobah, north of Damascus, and recovered everything—including women and other captives.

As Abram returned from his strike, Melchizedek, the king of Salem (Jerusalem), a priest of the God of Highest Heaven, brought him bread and wine. Then Melchizedek blessed him: "The blessing of the supreme God, Creator of heaven and earth, be upon you, Abram; and blessed be God, who has delivered your enemies to you." Then Abram gave Melchizedek a tenth of the spoils.[1]

PROPERTY OF
BROADWAY CHRISTIAN CHURCH LIBRARY
910 BROADWAY
FORT WAYNE, IN 46802

ISHMAEL
Sarai and Abram had no children, so Sarai took her maid, an Egyptian girl named Hagar, and gave her to Abram to be his second wife. "Since the Lord has given me no children," Sarai said, "you may sleep with my servant girl, and her children shall be mine."

Abram agreed. Hagar conceived, and when she realized she was pregnant, she became very arrogant toward her mistress.

Sarai said to Abram, "Now this servant girl despises me, though I gave her the privilege of being your wife."

"You have my permission to punish the girl," Abram

replied. So Sarai beat her—and she ran away. The Angel of the Lord found her beside a desert spring along the road to Shur.

"Hagar, where are you going?"

"I am running away from my mistress."

"Return to your mistress, for I will make you into a great nation. Your baby will be a son, and you are to name him Ishmael ('God hears'), because God has heard your woes."

Thereafter Hagar spoke of Jehovah as "the God who looked upon me." So Hagar gave Abram a son, and Abram named him Ishmael. Abram was 86 years old at this time.[2]

ISAAC When Abram was ninety-nine years old, God appeared and told him, "I am the Almighty; I will prepare a contract between us, guaranteeing you shall be the father of a multitude of nations." Abram fell face downward in the dust as God talked with him.

"I am changing your name. It is no longer 'Abram,' but 'Abraham'—'Father of nations.' I will continue this agreement between us generation after generation forever; I shall be your God and the God of your posterity. And I will give all this land of Canaan to you and them forever. You personally and all your posterity have this continual responsibility: that every male among you shall be circumcised. Your bodies will thus be marked as participants in my everlasting covenant."

God added: "Regarding Sarai, her name is 'Sarah' ('Princess'). I will bless her and give you a son from her. You are to name him Isaac ('Laughter'), and I will sign my covenant with him forever, and with his descendants. As for Ishmael, I will cause him to multiply and become a great nation. Twelve princes shall be among his posterity. But my contract is with Isaac, who will be born to you and Sarah next year at about this time."

That very day, Abraham took Ishmael and every other male and cut off their foreskins, as God told him.[3]

SODOM   The Lord appeared again to Abraham while he was living at Mamre. "The people of Sodom and Gomorrah are utterly evil. I am going down."

Abraham said, "Suppose you find fifty godly people in the city—will you destroy it?"

God replied, "If I find fifty godly people there, I will spare the entire city for their sake."

"Suppose there are only forty-five? Will you destroy the city for lack of five?"

"I will not destroy it if I find forty-five."

"Suppose there are only forty?"

"I won't destroy it if there are forty."

"Suppose only thirty are found there?"

"I won't do it if there are thirty there."

"Since I have dared to speak, suppose there are only twenty?"

"Then I won't destroy it."

Finally Abraham said, "Suppose only ten are found?"

And God said, "For the sake of the ten, I won't destroy it."

The Lord went on his way, and Abraham returned to his tent.

That evening two angels came to the entrance of Sodom. Lot saw them; he stood up to meet them. "Sirs," he said, "come to my home as my guests for the night. You can get up as early as you like and be on your way again."

They went home with him and he set a feast before them. After the meal, as they were preparing to retire for the night, the men of the city—young and old from all over the city—surrounded the house and shouted to Lot, "Bring out those men to us so we can rape them."

Lot stepped outside, shutting the door behind him. "Please," he begged, "don't do such a wicked thing. Leave these men alone, for they are under my protection."

"Stand back," they yelled. "We'll deal with you far worse than with those men." And they lunged at Lot and began breaking down the door.

But the two men pulled Lot in, bolted the door, and temporarily blinded the men of Sodom.

"What relatives do you have here in the city?" the men asked. "Get them out of this place—for we will destroy the city completely. The stench of this place has reached to heaven and God has sent us to destroy it."

Lot rushed out to tell his daughters' fiancés, "Quick, get out of the city, for the Lord is going to destroy it." But the young men looked at him as though he had lost his senses.

At dawn the angels became urgent. "Hurry," they said to Lot. "Take your wife and two daughters to the mountains or you will die."

"Sirs, please," Lot begged, "let me flee to that little village instead of into the mountains, for I fear disaster in the mountains."

"All right," the angel said; "I won't destroy that little city. But hurry! For I can do nothing until you are there." (From that time on, that village was named Zoar, meaning "Little City.")

The sun was rising as Lot reached the village. Then the Lord rained down fire and flaming tar from heaven upon Sodom and Gomorrah and utterly destroyed them along with the other cities and villages of the plain, eliminating all life—people, plants, and animals alike. But Lot's wife looked back as she was following along behind him, and became a pillar of salt.

Afterwards Lot left Zoar, fearful of the people there, and went to live in a cave in the mountains with his two daughters. One day the older girl said to her sister, "There isn't a man anywhere in this area that our father would let us marry. And our father will soon be too old for having children. Come, let's fill him with wine and then we will sleep with him, so our clan will not come to an end."

So they got him drunk that night, and the older girl had sexual intercourse with her father; but he was unaware of her lying down or getting up again.

The next morning she said to her younger sister, "I slept with my father last night. Let's fill him with wine again tonight, and you go in and lie with him, so that our family line will continue."

They got him drunk again that night and the younger

girl went in and lay with him. And so both girls became pregnant from their father. The older girl's baby was named Moab; he became the ancestor of the nation of the Moabites. The name of the younger girl's baby was Benammi; he became the ancestor of the Ammonites.[4]

COWARDICE

Abraham moved south to the Negeb and settled between Kadesh and Shur. One day when visiting the city of Gerar he remarked that Sarah was his sister! King Abimelech sent for her and had her brought to him at his palace. That night God came to him in a dream and told him, "You are a dead man, for that woman you took is married."

But Abimelech hadn't slept with her yet, so he said, "Lord, will you slay an innocent man? He told me, 'She is my sister.' I hadn't the slightest intention of doing wrong."

"I know," the Lord replied. "Now restore her to her husband and you shall live. If you don't, you are doomed."

The king was up early the next morning, and called for Abraham. "What have I done that deserves treatment like this, to make me and my kingdom guilty of this great sin? Whatever made you think of this vile deed?"

"Well," Abraham said, "I figured they will want my wife and will kill me to get her. Besides, she is my sister, or at least a half-sister—we both have the same father—and I married her. And I told her, 'Have the kindness to mention that you are my sister.'"

Then King Abimelech returned Sarah to him. "Look my kingdom over and choose the place where you want to live," the king told him.[5]

HEIR

Then God did as he had promised: Sarah became pregnant and gave Abraham a baby son in his old age. Abraham named him Isaac, meaning "Laughter." And Sarah declared, "God has brought me laughter! For who would have dreamed that I would ever have a baby?"

Time went by and the child was weaned, and Abraham gave a party to celebrate the occasion. But when Sarah noticed Ishmael—the son of Abraham and Hagar—mocking

Isaac, she turned upon Abraham and demanded, "Get rid of that slave girl and her son. He is not going to share your property with my son."

This upset Abraham very much. But God told Abraham, "Don't be upset over the boy or your slave-girl wife; do as Sarah says, for Isaac is the son through whom my promise will be fulfilled. And I will make a nation of the descendants of the slave-girl's son, too, because he also is yours."

So Abraham the next morning prepared food for the journey, strapped a canteen of water to Hagar's shoulders, and sent her away with their son. She hiked into the wilderness of Beer-sheba. When the water was gone, she left the child beneath a bush and went off and sat down a hundred yards away. "I don't want to watch him die," she said, and burst into tears.

Then the Angel of God called to Hagar from the sky, "Hagar, don't be afraid! For God has heard the lad's cries. Get the boy and comfort him, for I will make a great nation from his descendants."

Then she saw a well, so she refilled the canteen and gave the lad a drink. God blessed the boy, and he grew up in the wilderness of Paran and became an expert archer. His mother arranged a marriage for him with a girl from Egypt.

About this time King Abimelech came to Abraham and said, "It is evident that God helps you in everything you do. Swear to me by God's name that you won't defraud me or my son or my grandson, but that you will be on friendly terms with my country, as I have been toward you."

"All right, I swear to it!" Abraham replied. Then Abraham complained to the king about a well the king's servants had taken away from Abraham's servants.

"This is the first I've heard of it," the king exclaimed. "Why didn't you tell me before?"

Abraham gave sheep and oxen to the king as sacrifices to seal their pact. When he took seven ewe lambs and set them off by themselves, the king inquired, "Why are you doing that?"

Abraham replied, "They are my gift to you as a public

confirmation that this well is mine." From that time on, the well was called Beer-sheba ("Well of the Oath"). And Abraham lived in the Philistine country for a long time.[6]

SACRIFICE

Later on, God tested Abraham's faith and obedience. "Abraham," God called. "Yes, Lord," he replied.

"Take your only son—yes, Isaac whom you love so much—and go to the land of Moriah and sacrifice him there as a burnt offering upon one of the mountains which I'll point out to you!"

The next morning Abraham got up early, chopped wood for a fire upon the altar, saddled his donkey, and took his son Isaac and two young servants to the place God had told him to go. On the third day of the journey, Abraham saw the place in the distance. "Stay here with the donkey," Abraham told the young men, "and the lad and I will travel yonder and worship and then come right back."

Abraham placed the wood for the burnt offering upon Isaac's shoulders, while he carried the knife and the flint for striking a fire.

"Father," Isaac asked, "we have the wood and the flint to make the fire, but where is the lamb for the sacrifice?"

"God will see to it, my son," Abraham replied.

When they arrived at the place where God had told Abraham to go, he built an altar and placed the wood in order—then tied Isaac and laid him on the altar over the wood. Abraham took the knife and lifted it up to plunge it into his son.

At that moment the Angel of God shouted from heaven, "Abraham! Lay down the knife; don't hurt the lad. For I know that God is first in your life—you have not withheld even your beloved son from me."

Then Abraham noticed a ram caught by its horns in a bush. He took the ram and sacrificed it as a burnt offering on the altar. Abraham named the place "Jehovah Provides."

Then the Angel of God called again to Abraham: "I the Lord have sworn that because you obeyed me and have not withheld your son from me, I will bless you with incredible blessings and multiply your descendants into countless thousands and millions, like the stars above you in the sky and like the sands along the seashore. These descendants will conquer their enemies and be a blessing to all the nations of the earth—all because you have obeyed me."

So they returned to his young men and traveled home again to Beer-sheba.

When Sarah was 127 years old, she died in Hebron. Abraham mourned and wept for her. He said to the men of Heth: "Here I am, a visitor in a foreign land, with no place to bury my wife. Please sell me a piece of ground for this purpose."

"Certainly," the men replied, "for you are an honored prince of God among us. Choose the finest of our sepulchres so you can bury her there."

Abraham bowed and said, "Be so kind as to ask Ephron, Zohar's son, to sell me the cave of Mach-pelah, at the end of his field. I will pay whatever is publicly agreed upon, and it will become a permanent cemetery for my family."

Ephron was there among the others, and he spoke up: "The land is worth 400 pieces of silver, but what is that between friends? Go ahead and bury your dead."

So Abraham paid Ephron 400 pieces of silver. Ephron's field at Mach-pelah, the cave at the end of the field, and all the trees in the field became his permanent possession. So Abraham buried Sarah there.[7]

REBEKAH

Abraham, now very old, said to his oldest servant, "Swear by Jehovah, the God of heaven and earth, that you will not let my son marry one of these local girls, these Canaanites. Go instead to my relatives and find a wife for him there."

"But suppose I can't find a girl who will come so far from home?" the servant asked. "Then shall I take Isaac there to live among your relatives?"

"No!" Abraham warned. "For the Lord God told me to leave that land, and promised to give me and my children this land. He will send his angel ahead of you and he will see to it that you will find a girl there to be my son's wife."

The servant vowed to follow Abraham's instructions.

He took ten of Abraham's camels loaded with samples of the best of everything his master owned, and journeyed to Iraq to Nahor's village. There he made the camels kneel outside the town beside a spring. It was evening, and the women of the village were coming to draw water.

"O Jehovah, God of my master," he prayed, "help me to accomplish the purpose of my journey. The girls of the village are coming to draw water; when I ask one of them for a drink and she says, 'Yes, certainly, and I will water your camels too!'—let her be the one you have appointed as Isaac's wife. That is how I will know."

As he was speaking to the Lord, a beautiful girl arrived with a water jug on her shoulder and filled it at the spring. Running over to her, the servant asked her for a drink.

"Certainly, sir," she said, and quickly lowered the jug for him to drink. Then she said, "I'll draw water for your camels, too, until they have enough."

She emptied the jug into the watering trough and ran down to the spring again and kept carrying water to the camels until they had enough. When the camels had finished drinking, he produced a quarter-ounce gold earring and two five-ounce golden bracelets for her wrists.

"Whose daughter are you, miss?" he asked. "Would your father have any room to put us up for the night?"

"My father is Bethuel, the son of Milcah the wife of Nahor," she replied. "Yes, we have plenty of straw and food for the camels, and a guest room."

The man stood there a moment with head bowed, worshiping Jehovah. "Thank you, Lord God of my master. Thank you for being so kind and true to him, and for leading me straight to the family of my master's relatives."

The girl ran home to tell her folks, and when her brother Laban saw the ring and bracelets and heard her story, he rushed out to the spring where the man was still standing beside his camels. "Come and stay with us; we have a room all ready for you, and a place prepared for the camels."

So the man went home with Laban. Supper was served, but the old man said, "I don't want to eat until I have told you why I am here."

"All right," Laban said, "tell us your errand."

"I am Abraham's servant," he explained. "And Jehovah has overwhelmed my master with blessings so that he is a great man among the people of the land. When Sarah, my master's wife, was very old, she gave birth to my master's son, and my master has given him everything he owns. My master made me promise to come to his relatives in this far-off land and to bring back a girl from here to marry his son.

"Well, this afternoon I prayed, 'O Jehovah, please guide me in this way: I will say to some girl who comes out to draw water, "Please give me a drink." And she will reply, "Certainly. And I'll water your camels too." Let that girl be the one you have selected.' While I was speaking these words, Rebekah was coming along. I said to her, 'Please give me a drink.' She told me, 'Certainly, sir, and I will water your camels too.' Then I asked her, 'Whose family are you from?' And she told me, 'Nahor's.' So I gave her the ring and the bracelets. Tell me, will you be kind to my master?"

Laban and Bethuel replied, "The Lord has obviously brought you here. Yes, let her be the wife of your master's son, as Jehovah has directed."

At this, Abraham's servant brought out jewels set in solid gold and silver for Rebekah, and lovely clothing; and he gave many valuable presents to her mother and brother. Then they had supper, and the servant and the men with him stayed there overnight.

Early the next morning he said, "Send me back to my master."

"But we want Rebekah here at least another ten days," her mother and brother exclaimed.

"Don't hinder my return," he pleaded. "The Lord has made my mission successful and I want to report back to my master."

"Well," they said, "we'll call the girl and ask her what she thinks."

So they called Rebekah. "Are you willing to go with this man?" they asked. She replied, "Yes, I will go."

So Rebekah and her servant girls mounted the camels and went with him.

Meanwhile Isaac, whose home was in the Negeb, had returned to Beer-lahai-roi. One evening as he was taking a walk in the fields, he looked up and saw the camels coming. Rebekah noticed him. "Who is that man walking through the fields?" she asked the servant.

"It is my master's son," he replied. So she covered her face with her veil.

The servant told Isaac the whole story. And Isaac brought Rebekah into his mother's tent and she became his wife. He loved her very much.

Abraham deeded everything he owned to Isaac, then Abraham died at the age of 175. His sons Isaac and Ishmael buried him in the cave of Mach-pelah near Mamre where Sarah was buried.

The descendants of Ishmael—Nebaioth, Kedar, Abdeel, Mibsam, Mishma, Dumah, Massa, Hadad, Tema, Jetur, Naphish, Kedeman—became the founders of twelve tribes. Ishmael died at the age of 137, and these descendants were scattered across the country from Havilah to Shur (which is a little to the northeast of the Egyptian border).[8]

RIVALS

Isaac was forty years old when he married Rebekah. Isaac pleaded with Jehovah to give Rebekah a child, for after many years of marriage she had no children. At last she became pregnant, and it seemed as though children were fighting inside her.

She asked the Lord about it, and he told her, "The sons in your womb shall become two rival nations, and the older shall be a servant of the younger!"

Sure enough, she had twins. The first was so covered with reddish hair that one would think he was wearing a fur coat! So they called him Esau. The other twin was born with his hand on Esau's heel! They called him Jacob, meaning "Grabber."

As the boys grew, Esau became a skillful hunter while Jacob was a quiet sort who liked to stay at home. Isaac's favorite was Esau because of the venison he brought home, and Rebekah's favorite was Jacob.

One day Jacob was cooking stew when Esau arrived home exhausted from the hunt. "Boy, am I starved! Give me a bite of that red stuff there!" (From this came his nickname "Edom," which means "red stuff.")

Jacob: "All right; trade me your birthright for it!"

Esau: "When a man is dying of starvation, what good is his birthright?"

Jacob: "Well, then, vow to God that it is mine!"

And Esau vowed, thereby selling all his eldest-son rights to his younger brother. Then he ate and drank and went on about his business, indifferent to the loss of the rights.

A severe famine shadowed the land, as had happened in Abraham's time, so Isaac moved to Gerar where Abimelech, king of the Philistines, lived. Jehovah appeared to him there and told him, "Don't go to Egypt. I will be with you and I will give all this land to you and your descendants, just as I promised Abraham. They shall be a blessing to all the nations of the earth. I will do this because Abraham obeyed my commandments."

So Isaac stayed in Gerar. That year Isaac's crops were tremendous—100 times the grain he sowed. He was soon a man of great wealth: he had large flocks of sheep and goats, herds of cattle, and many servants. The Philistines became jealous of him, so King Abimelech asked Isaac to leave the country. "You have become too rich and powerful for us."

Isaac moved to Gerar Valley and redug the wells of Abraham, ones the Philistines had filled after his father's death, and gave them the same names his father had named them.

When he went to Beer-sheba, Jehovah appeared to him on the night of his arrival. "I am the God of Abraham," he said. "I am with you and will bless you, and will give you so many descendants they will become a great nation— because of my promise to Abraham." Then Isaac built an altar and worshiped Jehovah, and he settled there.

One day Isaac had visitors from Gerar. King Abimelech arrived with his advisor and his army commander. They said, "We can plainly see that Jehovah is blessing you. We've decided to ask for a treaty: promise that you will not harm us, just as we have done only good to you; we bless you in the name of the Lord."

So Isaac prepared a feast for them. In the morning they

each took solemn oaths to a nonaggression pact, then Isaac sent them happily home.

That day Isaac's servants came to tell him, "We have found water." So he named the well, "The Well of the Oath," and the city that grew up there was named Beersheba.

Esau, at the age of forty, married Judith, the Hethite. He also married Basemath, the Hethite. Isaac and Rebekah were bitter about his marrying them.

One day in Isaac's old age, when he was almost blind, he called for Esau. "I am old and expect to die any day. Take your bow and arrows and get me some venison; prepare it just the way I like it, and I will give you the blessings that belong to my first-born son."

Rebekah overheard the conversation, so when Esau left to hunt for the venison she called Jacob and told him what his father had said. "Now do exactly as I tell you. Go out to the flocks and bring me two young goats, and I'll prepare your father's favorite dish from them. Then take it to your father, and after he has enjoyed it he will bless you instead of Esau."

"But mother! He won't be fooled. Think how hairy Esau is, and how smooth my skin is! He'll think I'm making a fool of him, and curse me instead of blessing me!"

"Let his curse be on me, dear son. Just do what I tell you."

So Jacob followed his mother's instructions. Then she took Esau's best clothes and instructed Jacob to put them on. She made him a pair of gloves from the hairy skin of the young goats and fastened a strip of hide around his neck. Then she gave him the meat with its rich aroma and some fresh-baked bread. Jacob carried the food into the room where his father was lying.

"Father?"

"Yes? Who is it, my son—Esau or Jacob?"

"It's Esau. I've done as you told me. Here is the delicious venison you wanted. Sit up and eat it, so that you will bless me."

"How were you able to find it so quickly, my son?"

"Because Jehovah your God put it in my path!"

"Come over here. I want to feel you, and be sure it is really Esau. The voice is Jacob's, but the hands are Esau's! Bring me the venison and I will eat it, and bless you with all my heart. The smell of my son is the good smell of the earth that Jehovah has blessed. May God always give you plenty of rain for your crops, and good harvest of grain, and new wine. Be the master of your brothers. Cursed are all who curse you, and blessed are all who bless you."

As soon as Isaac blessed Jacob—almost before Jacob left—Esau arrived from his hunting.

"Here I am, father, with the venison. Eat it so that you can give me your finest blessings!"

"Who is it?"

"Why, it's Esau, your oldest son!"

"Then who was just here with venison, and I have already eaten it and blessed him with irrevocable blessing? . . . Your brother tricked me and has carried away your blessing!"

"No wonder they call him 'The Cheater.' He took my birthright, and now he has stolen my blessing. Haven't you saved even one blessing for me?"

"I have made him your master; I have guaranteed him abundance of grain and wine—what more is there left?"

"O my father, bless me too."

"Yours will be no life of ease and luxury, but you shall hew your way with your sword. For a time you will serve your brother, but you will finally shake loose and be free."

Esau hated Jacob because of what he had done. He said to himself, "My father will soon be gone, and then I will kill Jacob."

But someone got wind of what he was planning and reported it to Rebekah. She sent for Jacob and told him that his life was being threatened by Esau. "Flee to your Uncle Laban in Haran. Stay there until your brother's fury is spent, then I will send for you."

Rebekah said to Isaac, "I'm tired of these local girls; I'd rather die than see Jacob marry one of them."

So Isaac called for Jacob and said to him, "Go to the house of your grandfather Bethuel, and marry one of your cousins. May you become a great nation of many tribes!

May God pass on to you and your descendants the mighty blessings promised to Abraham."

Esau realized that his father and mother had sent Jacob to Paddan-aram to get a wife. They had strictly warned him against marrying a Canaanite girl. So Esau went to his Uncle Ishmael's family and married two additional wives from there. One was Mahalath, the daughter of Ishmael, Abraham's son.[9]

_____

RACHEL, LEAH

Jacob journeyed toward Haran. When he stopped to camp at sundown, he lay down to sleep and dreamed that a staircase reached from earth to heaven. At the top of the stairs stood the Lord.

"I am Jehovah," he said, "the God of Abraham and of your father Isaac. The ground you are lying on I will give to you and your descendants. I am with you, and will protect you wherever you go, and will bring you back safely to this land."

Jacob woke up. "God lives here!" he exclaimed. "This is the awesome entrance to heaven!" He got up very early and set his stone headrest upright as a memorial pillar, and poured olive oil over it. He named the place Bethel ("House of God") and vowed, "If God will help and protect me on this journey and will bring me back safely, then I will choose Jehovah as my God! This memorial pillar shall become a place for worship, and I will give you back a tenth of everything you give me!"

Jacob traveled on. He saw in the distance three flocks of sheep lying beside a well. Jacob went over to the shepherds and asked where they lived.

"At Haran," they said.

"Do you know Laban, the son of Nahor?"

"We sure do."

"How is he?"

"He's well and prosperous. Look—there comes his daughter Rachel with the sheep."

Rachel arrived with her father's sheep, and because she was his cousin Jacob went over to the well and rolled away the stone and watered his uncle's flock. Then Jacob kissed

Rachel and explained that he was her Aunt Rebekah's son.

She quickly ran and told her father, and he rushed out to meet him and brought him home. Then Jacob told his story. "My own flesh and blood!" Laban exclaimed.

After Jacob had been there about a month, Laban said, "Just because we are relatives is no reason for you to work without pay. How much do you want?"

Laban had two daughters—Leah, the older, and Rachel. Leah had lovely eyes, but Rachel was in every way a beauty. Jacob was in love with Rachel, so he told her father, "I'll work for you seven years if you'll give me Rachel as my wife."

"Agreed!" Laban replied.

So Jacob spent the next seven years working to pay for Rachel. They seemed but a few days, he was so much in love.

"I have fulfilled my contract," Jacob said to Laban. "Now give me my wife."

Laban invited all the men of the settlement to celebrate with Jacob at a big party. Afterwards, when it was dark, Laban took Leah to Jacob, and he slept with her.

In the morning Jacob raged at Laban: "I worked for seven years for Rachel; what do you mean by this trickery?"

"It's not our custom to marry off a younger daughter ahead of her sister," Laban replied smoothly. "Wait until the bridal week is over and you can have Rachel, too—if you promise to work for me another seven years!"

Jacob agreed, then Laban gave him Rachel. Jacob loved her more than Leah, and stayed and worked the additional seven years.

Because Jacob was slighting Leah, Jehovah let her have a son, Reuben. She soon became pregnant again and had another son, Simeon. Again she became pregnant and had a son, Levi. Once again she was pregnant and had a son, Judah. Then she stopped having children.

Rachel became envious. "Give me children or I'll die," she exclaimed to Jacob.

"Am I God?" he flared. "He is the one who is responsible for your barrenness."

Then Rachel told him, "Sleep with my servant-girl, Bilhah,

and her children will be mine." So she gave him Bilhah to be his wife, and he slept with her. She became pregnant and presented him with a son. Rachel named him Dan. Bilhah became pregnant again and gave Jacob a second son; Rachel named him Naphtali.

When Leah realized she wasn't getting pregnant anymore, she gave her servant-girl Zilpah to Jacob to be his wife. Soon Zilpah presented him with a son; Leah named him Gad. Then Zilpah produced a second son, and Leah named him Asher.

One day during the wheat harvest, Reuben found some mandrakes growing in a field and brought them to his mother, Leah. That evening as Jacob was coming home from the fields, Leah went out to meet him. "You must sleep with me tonight," she said. He did, and she became pregnant again and gave birth to her fifth son, Issachar. Once again she became pregnant with a sixth son; she named him Zebulun. Afterwards she gave birth to a daughter, Dinah.

Then God remembered Rachel's plight and answered her prayers. She became pregnant and gave birth to a son; she named him Joseph.

Soon after the birth of Joseph, Jacob said to Laban, "I want to go back home."

"Please don't leave," Laban replied, "for a fortune-teller that I consulted told me the many blessings I've been enjoying are because of your being here. How much of a raise do you need to stay? Whatever it is, I'll pay it."

Jacob replied, "If you'll do one thing, I'll work for you. Let me go among your flocks and remove all the goats that are speckled or spotted, and all the black sheep. Give them to me as my wages."

"All right," Jacob replied. "It shall be as you have said."

That day Laban formed a flock for Jacob of all the male goats that were ringed and spotted, and the females that were speckled and spotted with any white patches, and all of the black sheep. He gave them to Jacob's sons to take them three days' distance, and Jacob stayed and cared for Laban's flock. Then Jacob divided out the ewes from Laban's flock and let them mate only with Jacob's black rams. Thus he built his flock from Laban's. Jacob's flocks increased rapidly and he became very wealthy, with many servants, camels, and donkeys.

Jacob learned that Laban's sons were grumbling. "He owes everything to our father. All his wealth is at our father's expense." Soon Jacob noticed a cooling in Laban's attitude towards him.

Jehovah now spoke to Jacob and told him, "Return to the land of your fathers, and I will be with you."

So one day while Laban was out shearing sheep, Jacob set his wives and sons on camels and took everything he owned to return to his father Isaac in the land of Canaan. Jacob sent messengers to his brother Esau with this message: "Hello from Jacob! I have been living with Uncle Laban, and now I own oxen, donkeys, sheep, and many servants. I have sent these messengers to inform you of my coming, hoping that you will be friendly to us."

The messengers returned with the news that Esau was on the way to meet Jacob—with an army of 400 men! Jacob was frantic. He divided his household, along with the flocks and herds and camels, into two groups; for he said, "If Esau attacks one group, perhaps the other can escape."

Then Jacob prayed, "O God of Abraham my grandfather and of my father Isaac—O Jehovah who told me to return to the land of my relatives and said that you would do me good—I am not worthy of your loving kindnesses shown me again and again as you promised. O Lord, please deliver me from destruction at the hand of Esau. You promised to do me good and to multiply my descendants until they become as the sands along the shores—too many to count."

Jacob stayed where he was for the night, and prepared a present for his brother: 200 female goats, 200 male goats, 200 ewes, 20 rams, 30 milk camels with their colts, 40 cows, 10 bulls, 20 female donkeys, 10 male donkeys. He instructed his servants to drive them on ahead, each group of animals separated by a distance between. He told the men driving the first group that when they met Esau and he asked, "Whose animals are these?" they should reply:

"These belong to your servant Jacob. They are a present for his master Esau!" Jacob gave the same instructions to each driver. So the presents were sent on ahead, and Jacob spent that night in the camp.

But during the night he got up and wakened his two wives and two concubines and eleven children, and took them across the Jordan River at the Jabbok ford, then returned to the camp alone.[10]

_____ And a Man wrestled with him until dawn.
ISRAEL   When the Man saw he couldn't win, he
_____ struck Jacob's hip and knocked it out of joint. Then the Man said, "Let me go, for it is dawn."

Jacob panted, "I will not let you go until you bless me."

"What is your name?" the Man asked.

"Jacob," was the reply.

"It isn't anymore!" the Man told him. "It is Israel—one who has power with God. Because you have been strong with God, you shall prevail with men."

"What is your name?" Jacob asked.

"You mustn't ask," the Man told him. And he blessed him there.

Jacob named the place Peniel ("The Face of God"). The sun rose as he started on, and he was limping because of his hip. Then, far in the distance, Jacob saw Esau coming with his 400 men. Jacob arranged his family into a column, then went on ahead.

As he approached his brother he bowed low seven times, and Esau ran to meet him and embraced him affectionately. Both were in tears.

Esau looked at the women and children and asked, "Who are these people with you?"

"My children," Jacob replied. Then the concubines came forward with their children, next came Leah with her children, and finally Rachel and Joseph.

"And what were all the flocks and herds I met as I came?" Esau asked.

"They are my gifts to you."

"Brother, I have plenty. Keep what you have."

"No, please accept them," Jacob said. "For God has been very generous to me." So Esau accepted them.

"Well, let's get going," Esau said. "My men and I will lead the way."

Jacob replied, "Some of the children are small, and the flocks and herds have their young, so you go on ahead of us and we'll follow at our own pace."

So Esau started back. Jacob and his household went as far as Succoth; there he built a camp, with pens for his flocks and herds. Then they arrived at Shechem, in Canaan, and camped outside the city. He bought the land he camped on from the family of Hamor, and there he erected an altar and called it El-Elohe-Israel—"The Altar to the God of Israel."

"Move on to Bethel," God said to Jacob, "and build an altar to worship the God who appeared to you when you fled from your brother Esau." Then they started on again.

Upon Jacob's arrival at Bethel, God appeared to him again. "I am God Almighty, and I will cause you to multiply and become a great nation. I will pass on to you the land I gave to Abraham and Isaac; I will give it to you and to your descendants."

Afterwards Jacob built a stone pillar at the place where God had appeared to him; he poured wine over it as an offering and anointed the pillar with olive oil.

Leaving Bethel, he and his household traveled on toward Ephrath. But Rachel's pains of childbirth began while they were still a long way away. After a very hard delivery, the midwife exclaimed, "Another boy!" And with Rachel's last breath—for she died—she named him Ben-oni ("Son of my sorrow"), but his father called him Benjamin ("Son of my right hand").

Rachel was buried near the road to Ephrath (also called Bethlehem), and Jacob set up a monument of stones upon her grave.

Israel journeyed on and came to Isaac his father at Mamre in Kiriath-arba (now called Hebron), where Abraham too had lived. Isaac died soon afterwards, at the age of 180. His sons Esau and Jacob buried him.[11]

THE DREAMER Jacob settled again in the land of Canaan where his father had lived.

Joseph was now seventeen years old. His job, along with his half-brothers, was to shepherd his father's flocks. As it happened, Israel loved Joseph more than any of his other children. One day Jacob gave him a special gift—a brightly colored coat. His brothers noticed their father's partiality, and consequently hated Joseph.

One night Joseph had a dream and promptly reported the details to his brothers, causing even deeper hatred. "Listen to this," he announced. "We were out in the field binding sheaves, and my sheaf stood up and your sheaves all gathered around and bowed before it!"

"So you want to be our king, do you?" his brothers derided. And they hated him both for the dream and for his cocky attitude.

One day Joseph's brothers took their father's flocks to Shechem to graze. A few days later Israel called for Joseph and told him, "Your brothers are over in Shechem. Go and see how they are getting along, and bring me word."

So he traveled to Shechem from his home at Hebron Valley. A man noticed him wandering in the fields. "Who are you looking for?"

"For my brothers and their flocks; have you seen them?"

"Yes, I heard your brothers say they were going to Dothan."

So Joseph followed them to Dothan.

When they saw him coming, they decided to kill him! "Here comes that master-dreamer," they exclaimed. "Let's kill him and tell Father a wild animal has eaten him—then we'll see what will become of his dreams!"

But Reuben hoped to spare Joseph's life. "Let's not kill him; let's throw him into this well here—he'll die without our touching him!" Reuben was planning to get him out later and return him to his father.

When Joseph got there, they pulled off his brightly-colored robe and threw him into an empty well. Then they sat down for supper. Suddenly they noticed a string of camels coming toward them, probably Ishmaelite traders who were taking gum, spices, and herbs from Gilead to Egypt.

"Look," Judah said, "here come some Ishmaelites. Let's sell Joseph to them! Let's not be responsible for his death, for after all, he is our brother."

His brothers agreed. When the traders came by, his brothers pulled Joseph out of the well and sold him for twenty pieces of silver, and they took him along to Egypt.

Sometime later, Reuben—who was away when the traders came—returned to get Joseph out of the well. When Joseph wasn't there, he ripped his clothes in anguish. "The child is gone," he wept to his brothers.

The brothers killed a goat and spattered its blood on Joseph's coat and took the coat to their father. "We found this in the field," they told him. "Is it Joseph's coat or not?"

Their father recognized it at once. "Yes," he sobbed, "it is my son's coat. Joseph is without doubt torn in pieces."

Then Israel put on sackcloth and mourned for his son for many weeks. His family tried to comfort him, but it was no use.

When Joseph arrived in Egypt he was purchased by Potiphar, a member of the personal staff of Pharaoh, the king of Egypt. The Lord blessed Joseph in the home of his master, so that everything he did succeeded. Soon he was put in charge of the administration of Potiphar's household and business affairs. Crops flourished and flocks multiplied, so Potiphar gave Joseph complete administrative responsibility over everything he owned.

One day Potiphar's wife began making eyes at Joseph and suggested that he come and sleep with her.

"My master trusts me with everything; he has held back nothing from me except yourself. How can I do such a wicked thing as this? It would be a great sin against God."

But she kept on with her suggestions, day after day. Then one day as he was going about his work, she grabbed him by the sleeve, demanding, "Sleep with me." He tore himself away, but his jacket slipped off and she was left holding it as he fled from the house. When she saw that she had his jacket and he had fled, she began screaming. Men came running to see what had happened. "My husband had to bring in this Hebrew slave to insult us!" she sobbed. "He tried to rape me, but when I screamed he ran." When her husband came home that night, she told him her story.

Furious, he threw Joseph into prison, where prisoners were kept in chains.

But the Lord was with Joseph there, too, by granting him favor with the chief jailer. The jailer soon handed over prison administration to Joseph so that all the other prisoners were responsible to him.

Sometime later the king of Egypt became angry with his chief baker and his wine taster, so he jailed them both in the prison where Joseph was. They remained under arrest for quite some time. One night each of them had a dream. The next morning Joseph noticed that they looked dejected. "What is the matter?" he asked.

"We both had dreams last night, but there is no one here to tell us what they mean."

"Tell me what you saw."

The wine taster told his dream first. "I saw a vine with three branches that began to bud and blossom, and soon there were clusters of ripe grapes. I was holding Pharaoh's cup in my hand, so I took the grapes and squeezed the juice into it, and gave it to him to drink."

"I know what the dream means," Joseph said. "The three branches mean three days. Within three days Pharaoh is going to take you out of prison and give you back your job. Please have pity on me when you are back in his favor and ask him to let me out of here. For I am in jail when I did nothing to deserve it."

The chief baker told his dream to Joseph, too. "There were three baskets of pastries on my head. In the top basket were all kinds of bakery goods for Pharaoh, but the birds came and ate them."

"The three baskets mean three days," Joseph told him. "Three days from now Pharaoh will take off your head and impale your body, and birds will come and pick off your flesh!"

Pharaoh's birthday came three days later and he held a

party for his officials. He sent for his wine taster and chief baker, and they were brought to him from the prison. He restored the wine taster to his former position, but he sentenced the baker to be impaled, just as Joseph had predicted. Pharaoh's wine taster promptly forgot about Joseph.

Later Pharaoh dreamed he was standing on the bank of the Nile River when seven sleek, fat cows came out of the river and began grazing in the grass. Then seven other cows came from the river, but they were very skinny. They went over and stood beside the fat cows. Then the skinny cows ate the fat ones! At that point, Pharaoh woke up.

Next morning as he thought about it, he became very concerned as to what the dreams might mean. He called for all the magicians and sages of Egypt and told them about it, but not one could suggest what his dreams meant.

Then the king's wine taster spoke up. "Today I remember; some time ago when you put me and the chief baker in jail, the baker and I each had a dream. We told the dreams to a young Hebrew who was a slave of the captain of the guard, and he told us what our dreams meant. And everything happened just as he said."

Pharaoh sent at once for Joseph. He was brought hastily from the dungeon and came before Pharaoh.

"I had a dream last night," Pharaoh told him, "and none of these men can tell me what it means. But I have heard that you can interpret dreams."

"I can't do it by myself," Joseph replied, "but God will tell you what it means!"

So Pharaoh told him the dream.

Joseph told Pharaoh, "God was telling you what he is going to do here in the land of Egypt. The seven fat cows mean there are seven years of prosperity ahead. The seven skinny cows indicate there will be seven years of famine following the prosperity. The famine will be so terrible that even the memory of the good years will be erased.

"My suggestion is that you find the wisest man in Egypt and put him in charge of administering a nationwide farm program. Let Pharaoh divide Egypt into five administrative districts, and let the officials gather into the royal storehouses all the excess crops of the next seven years so there will be enough to eat when the seven years of famine come."

Joseph's suggestions were well received by Pharaoh and his assistants. As they discussed who should be appointed for the job, Pharaoh said, "Who could do it better than Joseph?" Turning to Joseph, Pharaoh said, "Since God has revealed the meaning of the dreams to you, you are the wisest man in the country! I am appointing you to be in charge of this entire project. I alone will outrank you."

Pharaoh placed his own signet ring on Joseph's finger as a token of his authority, dressed him in beautiful clothing, and placed the royal golden chain about his neck and declared, "I have placed you in charge of all the land of Egypt."

Pharaoh gave him a name meaning, "He has the godlike power of life and death." And he gave him a wife named Asenath. So Joseph became famous throughout Egypt. He was thirty years old as he entered the service of the king.

Sure enough, for the next seven years there were bumper crops everywhere. Joseph requisitioned for the government a portion of all the crops, storing them in nearby cities. After seven years the granaries were overflowing.

Before the arrival of the famine years, two sons were born to Joseph, Manasseh (meaning "Made to Forget"— God had made up to him for the anguish of his youth and the loss of his father's home); the second boy was named Ephraim (meaning "Fruitful"—"For God has made me fruitful in this land of my slavery," he said).

Then the seven years of famine began. There were crop failures in the surrounding countries, too, but in Egypt there was plenty of grain in the storehouses. Joseph opened the storehouses and sold grain to the Egyptians and to those from other lands who came to Egypt to buy grain.[12]

REUNION When Jacob heard there was grain available in Egypt, he said to his sons, "Go down and buy some before we all starve." Jacob wouldn't let Joseph's younger brother Benjamin go with them, for fear some harm might happen to him.

Israel's sons arrived in Egypt along with others from many lands to buy food. Since Joseph was in charge of the sale of grain, it was to him that his brothers came. Joseph recognized them instantly but pretended he didn't.

"Where are you from?" he demanded roughly.

"Canaan," they replied. "We have come to buy grain."

Then Joseph remembered the dream of long ago! But he said to them, "You are spies! You have come to see how destitute the famine has made our land."

"No, no," they exclaimed. "We are all brothers and honest men, sir! There are twelve of us brothers; our youngest brother is with our father, and one of our brothers is dead."

Joseph said to them, "I am a God-fearing man and I'm going to give you an opportunity to prove yourselves. One of you shall remain in chains in jail, and the rest may go home with grain for your families; but bring your youngest brother back to me. In this way I will know whether you are telling me the truth."

Speaking among themselves, they said, "This has happened because of what we did to Joseph long ago. We saw his terror and heard his pleadings but we wouldn't listen."

"Didn't I tell you not to do it?" Reuben asked. "But you wouldn't listen."

They didn't know that Joseph understood them, for he had been speaking to them through an interpreter. He left the room and found a place where he could weep. Returning, he selected Simeon from among them and had him bound. Joseph then ordered his servants to fill the men's sacks with grain.

They loaded up their donkeys with the grain and started for home. So they came to their father Jacob in Canaan and told him all that had happened.

Jacob exclaimed, "You have bereaved me of my children—Joseph didn't come back, Simeon is gone, and now you want to take Benjamin too! My son shall not go down with you, for he alone is left of his mother's children. If anything should happen to him, I would die."

But there was no relief from the terrible famine. When the grain was almost gone, Israel finally said, "If it can't be avoided, load your donkeys with the best products of the land, take them to the man as gifts—balm, honey, spices, myrhh, pistachio nuts, and almonds—and take your brother and go. May God Almighty give you mercy before the man."

So they took the gifts to Egypt and stood before Joseph. Joseph said to the manager of his household, "These men will eat with me this noon. Take them home and prepare a big feast."

They were conducted into the palace, and their donkeys were fed. Then they got their presents ready for Joseph's arrival. When Joseph came home they gave him their presents, bowing low before him.

He asked, "And how is your father—is he still alive?"

"Yes," they replied, "he is well."

Looking at his brother Benjamin, he asked, "Is this your youngest brother, the one you told me about?" Then Joseph made a hasty exit, for he was overcome with love for his brother. He washed his face and came out, keeping himself under control. "Let's eat," he said.

Joseph seated them in the order of their ages, to their amazement. They had a wonderful time bantering back and forth.

When his brothers were ready to leave, Joseph ordered his household manager to fill each of their sacks with as much grain as they could carry—and to put Joseph's own silver cup at the top of Benjamin's sack. The manager did as he was told.

The brothers were up at dawn and on their way with their loaded donkeys. When they were barely out of the city, Joseph said to his manager, "Chase after them and ask them, 'What do you mean by stealing my lord's personal cup?' "

He caught up with them and spoke the line he had been instructed.

"What are you talking about?" they demanded. "If you find his cup with any of us, let that one die. And all the rest of us will be slaves forever to your master."

"Fair enough," the man replied, "except that only the one who stole it will be a slave, and the rest of you can go free."

They quickly took down their sacks and opened them.

He began searching the oldest brother's sack, going on down the line to the youngest. And the cup was found in Benjamin's. They ripped their clothing in despair, loaded the donkeys again, and returned to the city.

Joseph was still home when Judah and his brothers arrived, and they fell to the ground before him. Judah said, "What shall we say to my lord? How can we prove our innocence? God is punishing us for our sins. Sir, we have all returned to be your slaves."

"No," Joseph said. "Only the man who stole the cup shall be my slave. The rest of you can go home to your father."

Judah stepped forward and said, "O sir, if I go back to my father and the lad is not with us, our father will die; and we will be responsible for bringing down his gray hairs with sorrow to the grave. Sir, I pledged my father that I would take care of the lad. Please, let me stay here as a slave instead of the lad. I cannot bear to see what this would do to him."

Joseph could stand it no longer. "Out!" he cried to his attendants, and he was left alone with his brothers. Then he wept aloud.

"I am Joseph!" he said. His brothers were stunned with surprise.

"Come here," he said. They came closer. And he said again, "I am Joseph, your brother whom you sold into Egypt! But don't be angry with yourselves, for God sent me here ahead of you to preserve your lives, so that you will become a great nation. And he has made me a counselor to Pharaoh and manager of this entire nation. Hurry, return to my father and tell him, 'Your son Joseph says, "God has made me chief of the land of Egypt. Come down right away! You shall live in the land of Goshen so that you can be near me with all your children, grandchildren, flocks and herds, and all that you have." ' "

Then, weeping with joy, he embraced Benjamin and did the same with each of his brothers. Joseph gave them wagons and provisions for the journey and new clothes for each of them.

They returned to Jacob. "Joseph is alive!" they shouted to him. "And he is ruler over the land of Egypt!"

Jacob couldn't take it in. But when they had given him Joseph's messages his spirit revived. "I will go and see him before I die."

Israel set out with his possessions and came to Beersheba, and offered sacrifices there to God. During the night God spoke to him in a vision.

"I am God, the God of your father. Don't be afraid to go to Egypt, for I will see to it that you become a great nation there. And I will bring your descendants back again, but you shall die in Egypt with Joseph at your side."

The total number of those going to Egypt, not counting the wives of Jacob's sons, was sixty-six. With Joseph's two sons, Jacob's household in Egypt totaled seventy.

Jacob sent Judah ahead to tell Joseph they were on the way. Joseph jumped into his chariot and journeyed to Goshen to meet his father, and they fell into each other's arms and wept. Israel said, "Now let me die, for I have seen you again!"

Upon their arrival, Joseph took five of his brothers and presented them to Pharaoh. Pharaoh asked, "What is your occupation?"

They replied, "We are shepherds like our ancestors. There is no pasture for our flocks in Canaan. We request permission to live in the land of Goshen."

The people of Israel began to prosper and there was a veritable population explosion among them. Jacob lived seventeen years after his arrival, so he was 147 years old at the time of his death. As the time drew near for him to die, he called together all his sons and said, "I will tell you what is going to happen to you in the days to come.

"Reuben, you are my oldest son, the head of the list in rank and honor. But you are unruly as the wild waves of the sea, and you shall be first no longer.

"Simeon and Levi are two of a kind, men of violence and injustice. In their anger they murdered a man, and maimed oxen for fun. Cursed be their anger, for it is fierce and cruel. Therefore I will scatter their descendents throughout Israel.

"Judah, your brothers shall praise you. You shall destroy your enemies. Judah is a young lion—who will dare to rouse him? The scepter shall not depart from Judah until Shiloh comes, whom all people shall obey.

"Zebulun shall dwell on the shores of the sea and be a harbor for ships, with his borders extending to Sidon.

"Issachar is a strong beast of burden; when he saw how good the countryside was, he bent his shoulder to the task and served his masters with vigor.

"Dan shall be a serpent in the path that bites the horses' heels, so that the rider falls off.

"A marauding band shall stamp upon Gad, but he shall rob and pursue them!

"Asher shall produce rich foods, fit for kings.

"Naphtali is a deer let loose, producing lovely fawns.

"Joseph is a fruitful tree beside a fountain. He has been severely injured by those who persecuted him, but their weapons were shattered by the Mighty One of Jacob, the Shepherd, the Rock of Israel. May the God of your fathers, the Almighty, bless you with blessings of heaven above and of the earth beneath, blessings reaching to the utmost bounds of the everlasting hills.

"Benjamin is a wolf that prowls. He devours his enemies in the morning and in the evening divides the loot.

"Soon I will die. You must bury me with my fathers in Canaan, in the cave of Mach-pelah—the field Abraham bought from Ephron the Hethite."

When Jacob had finished his prophecies to his sons, he lay back in the bed and died.

His sons did as Israel commanded them and carried his body into Canaan and buried it in the cave of Mach-pelah. Then Joseph returned to Egypt with his brothers and all who had accompanied him to the funeral of his father.

Joseph and his brothers and their families continued to live in Egypt. Joseph lived to see the birth of his son Ephraim's children and the children of Machir, Manasseh's son.

"Soon I will die," Joseph told his brothers. "God will

surely take you back to the land he promised to the descendents of Abraham, Isaac, and Jacob." Then Joseph made his brothers promise they would take his body back with them when they returned to Canaan. Joseph died at the age of 110; they embalmed him and his body was placed in a coffin in Egypt.[13]

PART
3
CHOSEN
NATION

SLAVES

Eventually a king came to the throne of Egypt who felt no obligation to the descendants of Joseph. He told his people:

"These Israelis are becoming dangerous because there are so many of them. Let's figure out a way to put an end to this. If we don't and war breaks out, they will join our enemies, fight against us, and escape out of the country."

So the Egyptians made slaves of them and put brutal taskmasters over them while building the store-cities Pithom and Raamses. But the more the Egyptians oppressed them, the more the Israelis seemed to multiply.

Then the king of Egypt instructed the Hebrew midwives, Shiphrah and Puah, to kill all Hebrew boys as soon as they were born but to let the girls live. But the midwives feared God and didn't obey the king. So the people of Israel continued to multiply.

Then Pharaoh commanded his people to throw the newborn Hebrew boys into the Nile River. The girls, he said, could live.[1]

MOSES

At this time a Hebrew fellow and girl of the tribe of Levi married and had a family, and a baby son was born to them. The baby's mother hid him at home for three months, and when she could no longer hide him she made a little boat from papyrus reeds along the river's edge. The baby's sister watched from a distance to see what would happen to him.

One of Pharaoh's daughters came to the river, and as she and her maids were walking along the bank she spied the little boat among the reeds and sent one of the maids to bring it to her. When she opened it, there was a baby, crying. "He must be one of the Hebrew children," she said.

The baby's sister approached the princess and asked, "Shall I go and find one of the Hebrew women to nurse the baby for you?"

"Yes, do," the princess replied. The girl rushed home and called her mother.

"Take this child and nurse him for me," the princess instructed, "and I will pay you well." So she took him home and nursed him.

When he was older, she brought him back to the princess and he became her son. She named him Moses, meaning "to draw out," because she had drawn him out of the water.

Many years later Moses, grown up, went out to visit his fellow Hebrews and saw the terrible conditions they were under. During his visit he saw an Egyptian knock a Hebrew to the ground. Moses looked to be sure no one was watching, then killed the Egyptian and hid his body in the sand.

The next day as he was visiting the Hebrews again he saw two of them fighting. "What are you doing, hitting your own Hebrew brother?" he said.

"And who are you?" the man demanded. "I suppose you think you are our prince! And do you plan to kill me as you did that Egyptian yesterday?"

When Moses realized his deed was known, he was frightened. And when Pharaoh heard about it he ordered Moses arrested and executed.

Moses ran away into the land of Midian. As he was sitting beside a well, seven daughters of the priest of Midian came to draw water and fill water troughs for their father's flocks, but shepherds chased the girls away. Moses came to their aid and watered their flocks.

When they returned to their father, Reuel, he asked, "How did you get the flocks watered so quickly today?"

"An Egyptian defended us against the shepherds," they told him. "He drew water for us and watered the flocks."

"Well, where is he? Did you just leave him there? Invite him for supper."

Moses eventually decided to accept Reuel's invitation to live with them, and Reuel gave him one of the girls, Zipporah, as his wife. They had a baby, Gershom, meaning "foreigner," for he said, "I am in a foreign land."[2]

JEHOVAH One day as Moses was tending the flock of his father-in-law at the edge of the desert near Horeb, suddenly the Angel of Jehovah appeared as a flame of fire in a bush. When Moses saw the bush was on fire and it didn't burn up, he went over to investigate. Then God called out, "Moses!"

"Who is it?" Moses asked.

"I am the God of Abraham, Isaac, and Jacob. I have seen the sorrows of my people in Egypt and heard their pleas for freedom from their taskmasters. I am going to send you to Pharaoh to demand that he let you lead my people out of Egypt."

"But I'm not the person for a job like that!" Moses exclaimed.

God told him: "I will certainly be with you, and this is the proof that I am the one who is sending you—when you have led the people out of Egypt you shall worship God here upon this mountain!"

"If I go to the people of Israel and tell them their fathers' God has sent me, they will ask, 'Which God are you talking about?' What shall I tell them?"

"The Sovereign God," was the reply. "Just say, 'I Am has sent me!' Tell them, 'Jehovah, the God of Abraham, Isaac, and Jacob, has sent me to you.' This is my eternal name, to be used throughout all generations. I promise to rescue them from the drudgery and humiliation they are undergoing and to take them to the land now occupied by the Canaanites, a land flowing with milk and honey."

But Moses said, "They won't believe me. They'll say, 'Jehovah never appeared to you!'"

"What do you have in your hand?" the Lord asked him.

"A shepherd's rod."

"Throw it down," the Lord told him. So he threw it down—and it became a serpent! Moses ran from it.

Then the Lord told him, "Grab it by the tail!" He did, and it became a rod in his hand again!

"Do that, and they will believe you!" the Lord told him. "Then they will realize that Jehovah has really appeared to you."

But Moses pleaded, "O Lord, I'm just not a good speaker; I have a speech impediment."

"Who makes mouths?" Jehovah asked. "Isn't it I, the Lord? I will help you to speak well, and I will tell you what to say."

But Moses said, "Lord, please, send someone else."

"Your brother Aaron is a good speaker. He is coming here to look for you. I will tell you what to tell him, and he will be your spokesman to the people."

Aaron traveled to Mount Horeb and met Moses there. They greeted each other warmly. Moses told Aaron what God had said they must do, so Moses and Aaron returned to Egypt and summoned the elders of the people of Israel to a council meeting. Aaron told them what Jehovah had said to Moses, and Moses performed miracles as they watched. The elders rejoiced, bowed their heads, and worshiped.[3]

LIBERATED After this, Moses and Aaron went to see Pharaoh. They told him, "We bring you a message from Jehovah, the God of Israel. He says, 'Let my people go, for they must make a holy pilgrimage into the wilderness for a religious feast, to worship me there.'"

"Is that so?" retorted Pharaoh. "And who is Jehovah, that I should listen to him? I don't know Jehovah, and I will not let Israel go."

But Aaron and Moses persisted. "The God of the Hebrews has met with us. We must take a three days' trip into the wilderness and sacrifice there to Jehovah."

"Who do you think you are," Pharaoh shouted, "distracting the people from their work? Get back to your jobs!"

That same day Pharaoh sent this order to the officers over Israel: "Don't give the people any more straw for making bricks. However, don't reduce their production quotas by a single brick, for they obviously don't have enough to do. Load them with work; that will teach them to listen to Moses' and Aaron's lies!"

The taskmasters were brutal. "Fulfill your daily quota as before," they kept demanding. They whipped the Israeli work-crew bosses. "Why haven't you fulfilled your quotas?" they roared.

Then Moses went back to the Lord. "Ever since I gave Pharaoh your message, he has been more and more brutal, and you have not delivered them at all!"

"Now you will see what I shall do to Pharaoh," the Lord told Moses. "I am Jehovah, the Almighty who appeared to Abraham, Isaac, and Jacob—though I did not reveal my name Jehovah to them. And I entered into a solemn covenant to give them the land of Canaan. Tell the descendants of Israel that I will perform great miracles to deliver them from slavery. And I will accept them as my people and be their God. I will bring them into the land I promised. The Egyptians will find out that I am indeed God when I force them to let my people go."

Moses was eighty years old and Aaron eighty-three at this time of confrontation. The Lord said, "Pharaoh will demand that you show him a miracle as Jehovah had instructed."

Aaron threw down his rod and it became a serpent! Pharaoh called in his sorcerers—the magicians of Egypt—and they were able to do the same thing with their magical arts—their rods became serpents, too! But Aaron's serpent swallowed their serpents! Pharaoh's heart was still stubborn, and he wouldn't listen.

Next the Lord told Moses, "Early in the morning meet Pharaoh as he comes to the river to bathe, and say to him, 'Jehovah says, Let my people go and worship me. If you refuse I will send swarms of flies throughout Egypt. Your homes will be filled with them, but in Goshen, where the Israelis live, there will be no flies.'"

And Jehovah did as he said, so there were terrible swarms of flies in Pharaoh's palace and in every home.

Pharaoh hastily summoned Moses and said, "All right, sacrifice to your God, but do it here in the land."

Moses replied, "Our sacrifices to God are hated by the Egyptians, and if we do this here they will kill us. We must make a three-day trip into the wilderness and sacrifice there to Jehovah as he commanded."

"All right," Pharaoh replied. "Now plead with God for me."

"Yes," Moses said, "but I warn you never again to lie by promising to let the people go and then changing your mind."

So Moses asked the Lord to get rid of the flies. The Lord did as Moses asked so that not one remained. But Pharaoh hardened his heart again and did not let the people go.

Then the Lord said to Moses, "Stand before Pharaoh and tell him, 'This time I am going to send a plague that will prove to you there is no other God in all the earth. Tomorrow I will send a hailstorm such as there has never been since Egypt was founded. Bring in your cattle from the fields, for every man and animal left in the fields will die beneath the hail!'"

Some Egyptians, terrified by this threat, brought their cattle and slaves in from the fields but those who had no regard for the word of Jehovah left them out in the storm.

Then Jehovah said to Moses, "Point your hand toward heaven and cause the hail to fall." Moses held out his hand, and the Lord sent thunder and hail and lightning. It was terrible. Everything in the fields, men and animals alike, was killed, and trees were shattered and crops destroyed.

Pharaoh sent for Moses and Aaron. "I finally see my fault," he confessed. "Jehovah is right. Beg God to end this terrifying thunder and hail, and I will let you go at once."

Moses left Pharaoh and lifted his hands to heaven, to the Lord, and the thunder and hail stopped. When Pharaoh saw this, he and his officials sinned yet more by refusal to do what they had promised.

Then Jehovah said to Moses, "Lift your hands to heaven, and darkness will descend upon the land." Moses did, and there was thick darkness for three days. During that time the people scarcely moved.

Pharaoh called for Moses and said, "Go and worship Jehovah—but let your flocks and herds stay here; you can even take your children with you."

"No," Moses said, "we must take our flocks and herds for sacrifices for the Lord, and we do not know what he will choose until we get there."

"Get out and don't let me ever see you again," Pharaoh shouted at Moses.

"Very well," Moses replied.

Then the Lord said to Moses, "I will send one more disaster on Pharaoh and his land, and after that he will let you go. From now on, this month will be the first and most important month of the Jewish calendar. Annually, on the tenth day of this month each family shall get a lamb—a year-old male, either a sheep or a goat without any defects; on the evening of the fourteenth day of this month all these lambs shall be killed and their blood placed on the two side-frames of the door of every home and on the panel above the door. Everyone shall eat roast lamb that night, with unleavened bread and bitter herbs. If all is not eaten that night, burn what is left. Eat it with your traveling clothes on, prepared for a long journey. This observance shall be called the Lord's Passover. For I will pass through the land of Egypt tonight and kill all the oldest sons and firstborn male animals in the land of Egypt, and execute judgment upon all the gods of Egypt. You shall celebrate this event each year to remind you of this day when I brought you out of the land of Egypt."

Moses called for the elders of Israel and said, "Go and get lambs from your flocks, a lamb for one or more families depending upon the number of persons in the families, and kill the lamb. Drain the lamb's blood and take a cluster of hyssop branches and dip them into the blood and strike the hyssop against the lintel above the door and the two side panels, and none of you shall go outside all night. For Jehovah will pass through the land and kill the Egyptians; but when he sees the blood upon the door he will pass over that home and not permit the Destroyer to enter."

That night at midnight, Jehovah killed the firstborn sons in Egypt, from Pharaoh's oldest son to the oldest son of the captive in the dungeon, also the firstborn of the cattle. Pharaoh and his officials and the people of Egypt got up in the night and there was bitter crying throughout the land.

Pharaoh summoned Moses and said, "Leave us, all of you; go and serve Jehovah. Take your flocks and herds and be gone!"

That night the people of Israel left Rameses for Succoth; there were six hundred thousand of them, besides women and children. The sons of Jacob and their descendants had lived in Egypt 430 years, and it was on the last day of the 430th year that all of Jehovah's people left the land.

Moses said to the people, "This is a day to remember forever—the day of leaving your slavery. In the future when your children ask you, 'What is this all about?' you shall tell them, 'With mighty miracles Jehovah brought us out of Egypt.' This celebration shall identify you as God's people."

Moses took the bones of Joseph with them, for Joseph had made the sons of Israel vow that they would take his bones with them when God led them out of Egypt— as he was sure God would.

Leaving Succoth, they camped in Etham at the edge of the wilderness. The Lord guided them by a pillar of cloud during the daytime and by a pillar of fire at night, so they could travel either by day or by night. The cloud and fire were never out of sight.

Jehovah instructed Moses, "Tell the people to turn toward Pihahiroth between Migdol and the sea, and to camp there along the shore. Pharaoh will think, 'Those Israelites are trapped now, and he will chase after you. I have planned this to gain honor over Pharaoh and all his armies. The

Egyptians shall know that I am the Lord."

When word reached the king of Egypt that the Israelis were not planning to return after three days, Pharaoh became bold again. "What is this we have done, letting all these slaves get away?" So Pharaoh led the chase in his chariot, followed by Egypt's chariot corps—600 in all. Pharaoh's cavalry overtook Israel as they were camped beside the shore. They were terribly frightened and cried out to the Lord to help them.

Moses told the people, "Don't be afraid. You will see the wonderful way the Lord will rescue you today. You won't need to lift a finger!"

The Angel of God who was leading Israel moved the cloud behind them, and it stood between Israel and the Egyptians. That night, as it changed to a pillar of fire, it gave darkness to the Egyptians but light to Israel!

Meanwhile, Moses stretched his rod over the sea and the Lord opened up a path through the sea, with walls of water on each side, and a strong east wind blew all that night, drying the sea bottom. So Israel walked through the sea on dry ground!

Then the Egyptians followed them between the walls of water. When all the Israelites were on the other side, the Lord said to Moses, "Stretch out your hand again over the sea, so that the waters will come back." Moses did, and the sea returned. The Egyptians tried to flee, but the water covered the path and the chariots and horsemen. Of all the army that chased after Israel through the sea, not one remained alive.

When the people of Israel saw the mighty miracle, they revered the Lord and believed in him and in his servant Moses.

"O Lord, through all the generations you have been our home!

Before the mountains were created, you are God, without beginning or end.

You speak, and man turns back to dust.

A thousand years are but as yesterday to you!

We glide along the tides of time as swiftly as a racing

river, and vanish as quickly as a dream.

We are like grass that is green in the morning but mowed down and withered before the evening shadows fall.

We die beneath your anger.

You spread out our sins before you—our secret sins— and see them all.

Seventy years are given us!

And some may even live to eighty.

But even the best of these years are often emptiness and pain; soon they disappear, and we are gone.

Which of us can fear you as we should?

Teach us to number our days and recognize how few they are; help us to spend them as we should.

O Jehovah, bless us!

Satisfy us in our earliest youth with your loving kindness. Give us gladness in proportion to our former misery! Replace the evil years with good.

Let us see your miracles again; let our children see glorious things, and let the Lord our God favor us and give us success."

Moses led the people on from the Red Sea into the wilderness of Shur and they came to Elim. There were twelve springs and seventy palm trees, and they camped there.

They left Elim and journeyed into the Sihn Wilderness, between Elim and Mount Sinai. There the people spoke bitterly: "Oh, that we were back in Egypt for there we had plenty to eat. You have brought us into this wilderness to kill us with starvation."

The Lord said to Moses, "I'm going to rain down food from heaven. Everyone can go out each day and gather as much food as he needs. Tell them to gather twice as much as usual on the sixth day of the week."

Moses and Aaron called a meeting of the people and told them, "This evening you will realize that it was the Lord who brought you out of Egypt. The Lord will give you meat to eat in the evening, and bread in the morning."

That evening vast numbers of quail arrived and covered the camp; and in the morning the desert around the camp

was wet with dew, and when the dew disappeared it left
tiny flakes of something as small as hoarfrost on the ground.
The people asked each other, "What is it?"

Moses told them, "It is the food Jehovah has given you.
Gather as much as is needed for each person. Don't leave
it overnight."

So they gathered the food morning by morning, each
home according to its need. When the sun became hot,
the food melted and disappeared. On the sixth day they
gathered twice as much as usual; then the leaders asked
Moses why this had been commanded.

He told them, "The Lord has appointed tomorrow as a
day of rest, a holy Sabbath to the Lord when we must
refrain from doing our daily tasks. So cook as much as
you want today, and keep what is left overnight." And
the next morning the food was wholesome and good.

Some of the people went out to gather food even though
it was the Sabbath, but there wasn't any.

The food became known as manna, meaning "What is
it?" It was white, like coriander seed, and flat, and tasted
like honey bread. The people of Israel ate the manna forty
years until they arrived in Canaan where there were crops
to eat.[4]

SINAI The Israelis arrived in the Sinai peninsula three
months after their departure from Egypt. They
came to the base of Mount Sinai and set up
camp there.

Moses climbed the rugged mountain, and from some-
where in the mountain God called to him:

"Give these instructions to the people of Israel—'You
have seen what I did to the Egyptians, and how I brought
you to myself. Now if you will obey me and keep your
part of my contract with you, you shall be my own flock
from among all the nations of the earth, and you shall be
a kingdom of priests to God, a holy nation.' "

Moses returned from the mountain and called together
the leaders of the people and told them what the Lord
had said. They all responded in unison, "We will do every·
thing he asks of us."

Moses reported the words of the people to the Lord, then he said to Moses, "I am going to come to you in the form of a dark cloud, so the people can hear me when I talk with you. See that the people are ready for my visit: sanctify them today and tomorrow, and have them wash their clothes. Set boundary lines the people may not pass, and tell them, 'Stay away from the mountain entirely until you hear a ram's horn sounding one long blast, then gather at the foot of the mountain.'"

So Moses sanctified them and told them, "Get ready for God's appearance two days from now."

On the morning of the third day there was a terrific thunder and lightning storm, and a huge cloud came down upon the mountain. There was a long, loud blast as from a ram's horn, and all the people trembled. Moses led them out from the camp to meet God at the foot of the mountain. All Mount Sinai was covered with smoke, and the mountain shook with a violent earthquake. As the trumpet blast grew louder, Moses spoke and God thundered his reply. So the Lord called Moses up to the top of the mountain, and Moses ascended to God.

Then God issued this edict:

"You may worship no other god than me.

"You shall not make yourselves any idols—any images resembling animals, birds, or fish. You must never bow to an image or worship it in any way; for I the Lord will not share your affection with any other god!

"You shall not use the name of Jehovah your God irreverently, nor use it to swear to a falsehood.

"Remember to observe the Sabbath as a holy day. Six days a week are for your daily duties and your regular work, but the seventh day is a day of Sabbath rest before the Lord your God. For in six days the Lord made the heaven, earth, and sea, and everything in them, and rested the seventh day; so he blessed the Sabbath day and set it aside for rest.

"Honor your father and mother, that you may have a long, good life in the land your God will give you.

"You must not murder.

"You must not commit adultery.

"You must not steal.

"You must not lie.

"You must not be envious of your neighbor's house, or his wife, or his slaves, oxen, donkeys, or anything else he has."

Moses announced to the people all the laws and regulations God had given him, and the people answered, "We will obey them all."

Moses wrote down the laws; and early the next morning he built an altar at the foot of the mountain, with twelve pillars around the altar because there were twelve tribes of Israel. Then he sent some of the young men to sacrifice offerings to the Lord. Moses took half the blood of these animals in basins; the other half he splashed against the altar. And he read to the people the Book he had written containing God's directions and laws. The people said again, "We solemnly promise to obey every one of these rules."

Then Moses threw the blood from the basins towards the people and said, "This blood confirms and seals the covenant the Lord has made with you in giving you these laws."

The Lord said to Moses, "Come up to me into the mountain, and remain until I give you the laws and commandments I have written on tablets of stone, so that you can teach the people from them."

So Moses and Joshua, his assistant, went up to the mountain. He told the elders, "Stay here and wait for us; if there are any problems while I am gone, consult with Aaron and Hur."

Then Moses went up the mountain and disappeared into the cloud at the top. And the glory of the Lord rested upon Mount Sinai six days; the seventh day he called to Moses from the cloud. Those at the bottom of the mountain saw the awesome sight: the glory of the Lord looked like a raging fire. And Moses was there for forty days and forty nights.

HOLY PLACE Jehovah said to Moses, "Tell the people that everyone who wants to may bring me an offering, for I want Israel to make me a sacred Temple where I can live among them. This home of mine shall be a tent pavilion—a Tabernacle. I will give you the construction plan and details of each furnishing.

"Using acacia wood, make an Ark 3¾ feet long, 2¼ feet wide, and 2¼ feet high. Overlay it inside and outside with pure gold; cast four rings of gold for it and attach them to the four lower corners. Make poles from acacia wood overlaid with gold, and fit the poles into the rings at the sides of the Ark to carry it. When the Ark is finished, place inside it the tablets of stone I will give you, with the Ten Commandments engraved on them.

"And make a lid of pure gold; this is the place of mercy for your sins. Make images of angels, using beaten gold, at the ends of the lid. One at each end, the cherubim— the angels—shall be facing each other, looking down upon the place of mercy, and shall have wings spread out above the gold lid. And I will meet you there and talk with you from above the place of mercy.

"Then make a table of acacia wood 3 feet long, 1½ feet wide, and 2¼ feet high. Overlay it with pure gold. And make golden dishes, spoons, pitchers, and flagons; and always keep the special Bread of the Presence on the table before me.

"Make a lampstand of pure, beaten gold. The lampstand will have three branches going out from each side of the center shaft, each branch decorated with three almond flowers. Then make seven lamps for the lampstand, and set them so that they reflect their light forward. Be sure everything follows the pattern I am showing you.

"Make the Tabernacle-tent from ten colored sheets of fine-twined linen, forty-two feet long and six feet wide, dyed blue, purple, and scarlet, with figures of Guardian Angels embroidered on them. Join five sheets end to end for each side of the tent. Use loops at the edges to join these two long pieces, then make golden clasps to fasten the loops so that the Tabernacle becomes a single unit.

"The roof of the Tabernacle is made of goat's hair tarpaulins. There are to be eleven of these; connect five into one wide section, and use the other six for another wide section. The sixth tarpaulin will hang down to form a curtain across the front of the sacred tent.

"The framework of the tent shall be made from acacia wood, each frame piece being fifteen feet high and 2¼ feet wide, with grooves on each side to mortise into the next piece. Make bars of acacia wood to run across the frames, five bars on each side. Overlay the frames with gold and make gold rings to hold the bars; and also overlay the bars with gold.

"Inside the Tabernacle, make a veil from blue, purple, and scarlet cloth, the fine-twined linen, with cherubim embroidered into the cloth. Behind this curtain, place the Ark containing the stone tablets engraved with God's laws. The curtain will separate the Holy Place from the Most Holy Place. Place the table and lampstand across the room from each other on the outer side of the veil, the lampstand on the south side and the table on the north.

"As a screen for the door of the sacred tent, make another curtain from skillfully embroidered blue, purple, and scarlet fine-twined linen. Hang this curtain on gold hooks set into posts made from acacia wood. The posts are to rest on bronze bases.

"Using acacia wood, make a square altar 7½ feet wide and three feet high. Make horns for the four corners of the altar, attach them firmly, and overlay everything with bronze. Ash buckets, shovels, basins, carcass hooks, and fire pans are all to be made of bronze. Make a bronze grating, and fit the grating halfway down into the fire box. For moving the altar, make poles from acacia wood overlaid with bronze. To carry it, put the poles into the rings at each side of the altar.

"Then make a courtyard for the Tabernacle, enclosed with curtains made from fine-twined linen. On the south side, the curtains will stretch for 150 feet, and be held up by twenty posts, fitting into twenty bronze post holders. It will be the same on the north side. The west side will be seventy-five feet wide, the east side also.

"The entrance to the court will be a thirty-foot-wide curtain, made of beautifully embroidered blue, purple, and scarlet fine-twined linen. All the posts around the court are to be connected to silver rods, using silver hooks, the posts being imbedded in solid bronze bases.

"Instruct the people to bring you pure olive oil to use in the lamps of the Tabernacle, to burn there continually. Aaron and his sons shall place this eternal flame in the outer holy room, tending it day and night before the Lord.

"Consecrate Aaron, your brother, and his sons, Nadab, Abihu, Eleazer, and Ithamar, to be priests to minister to me. Make special clothes for Aaron, to indicate his separation to God. Instruct those to whom I have given special skill as tailors to make the wardrobe: a chestpiece, an ephod, a robe, a checkered tunic, a turban, and a sash. They shall also make special garments for Aaron's sons.

"The ephod shall be made by the most skilled of the workmen, using blue, purple, and scarlet threads of fine-twined linen. It will consist of two pieces, front and back, joined at the shoulders. And the sash shall be made of the same material. Take two onyx stones, and engrave on them the names of the tribes of Israel. Fasten the stones on the shoulders of the ephod; Aaron will carry their names before the Lord as a constant reminder.

"Using the most careful workmanship, make a chestpiece to be used as God's oracle; use the same gold, blue, purple, and scarlet threads of fine-twined linen as in the ephod. This chestpiece is to be of two folds of cloth, forming a pouch. Attach to it four rows of stones: a ruby, a topaz, and an emerald in the first row; the second row will be an carbuncle, a sapphire, and a diamond; the third an amber, an agate, and an amethyst; the fourth an onyx, a beryl, and a jasper—all set in gold settings. Each stone will represent one of the tribes of Israel.

"Attach the top of the chestpiece to the ephod by means of two twisted cords of pure gold. In this way Aaron shall carry the names of the tribes over his heart when he goes into the Holy Place. The bottom edge of the ephod shall be embroidered with blue, purple, and scarlet pomegranates, alternated with gold bells. Aaron shall wear the ephod whenever he goes in to minister to the Lord; the bells will tinkle as he goes in and out of the presence of the Lord in the Holy Place.

"Make a plate of pure gold and engrave on it: 'Consecrated to Jehovah.' This plate is to be attached to the front of Aaron's turban.

"Weave Aaron's tunic from fine-twined linen, using a checkerboard pattern; make the turban, too, of this linen; and make him an embroidered sash.

"For Aaron's sons, make robes, sashes, and turbans to give them honor and respect. Clothe Aaron and his sons with these garments, then dedicate these men to their ministry by anointing their heads with olive oil.

"Each day offer two yearling lambs upon the altar, one in the morning and the other in the evening. This shall be a perpetual daily offering at the door of the Tabernacle, where I will meet with the people of Israel. And the Tabernacle shall be sanctified by my glory.

"Make a small altar for incense from acacia wood. It is to be eighteen inches square and three feet high, with horns carved from the wood of the altar. Overlay the top, sides, and horns of the altar with pure gold. Place the altar just outside the veil, near the place of mercy that is above the Ark.

"Every morning when Aaron trims the lamps, he shall burn sweet spices on the altar, and each evening when he lights the lamps he shall burn the incense before the Lord, and this shall go on from generation to generation.

"Make a bronze basin with a bronze pedestal. Put it between the Tabernacle and the altar, and fill it with water. Aaron and his sons shall wash their hands and feet there when they approach the altar to burn offerings to the Lord. They must always wash before doing so, or they will die.

"I have appointed Bezalel, son of Uri and grandson of Hur, of the tribe of Judah, and have filled him with the Spirit of God, giving him great wisdom, ability, and skill in constructing the Tabernacle and everything it contains. And I have appointed Oholiab to be his assistant. Moreover, I have given special skill to all who are known as experts, so that they can make all the things I have instructed you to make. They are to follow exactly the directions I gave you."

As God finished speaking with Moses on Mount Sinai, he gave him the two tablets of stone on which the Ten Commandments were written with the finger of God.[6]

LAW BREAKERS

When Moses didn't come back down the mountain right away, the people went to Aaron. "Look," they said, "make us a god to lead us, for this fellow Moses who brought us here from Egypt has disappeared; something must have happened to him."

"Give me your golden earrings," Aaron replied.

So they all did. Aaron melted the gold, then molded and tooled it into the form of a calf. The people exclaimed, "O Israel, this is the god that brought you out of Egypt!"

When Aaron saw how happy the people were about it, he built an altar before the calf and announced, "Tomorrow there will be a feast to Jehovah!"

They were up early the next morning and began offering burnt offerings and peace offerings to the calf-idol; afterwards they sat down to feast and drink at a wild party.

The Lord told Moses, "Quick! Go down, for your people have defiled themselves and have abandoned my laws. What a rebellious lot these people are. My anger shall blaze out against them and destroy them all. I will make you, Moses, into a great nation instead of them."

But Moses begged: "Lord, why is your anger so hot against your people whom you brought from Egypt? Do you want the Egyptians to say, 'God tricked them into coming to the mountains so that he could destroy them from the earth'? Turn back from your fierce wrath. Remember your promise to Abraham, Isaac, and Israel."

So the Lord spared them. Moses went down the mountain, holding the Ten Commandments on stone tablets. When Moses saw the calf and the dancing, in terrible anger he threw the tablets to the ground, and they broke. He took the calf and melted it in the fire, and when the metal cooled he ground it into powder and spread it upon the water and made the people drink it.

The next day Moses said to the people, "You have sinned a great sin, but I will return to the Lord on the mountain—perhaps I will be able to obtain his forgiveness for you."

Moses returned to the Lord and said, "These people have made themselves gods of gold, yet now if you will only forgive their sin—and if not, then blot me out of the Book you have written."

The Lord replied, "Whoever has sinned against me will be blotted out of my Book." And the Lord sent a great plague upon the people because they had worshiped Aaron's calf.

The Lord told Moses, "Prepare two stone tablets like the first ones, and I will write upon them the same commands that were on the tablets you broke."

Moses took two tablets and climbed Mount Sinai. Then the Lord descended in the form of a pillar of cloud and announced the meaning of his name. "I am Jehovah, the merciful and gracious God, slow to anger and rich in steadfast love and truth. I show this love by forgiving sins, or else I refuse to clear the guilty."

Moses fell down before the Lord and worshiped. "If it is true that I have found favor in your sight, O Lord, please go with us to the Promised Land; pardon our iniquity; and accept us as your own."

The Lord replied, "All right, this is the contract I make with you. I will do miracles such as have never been done before, and Israel shall see the power of the Lord. Your part of the agreement is to obey my commandments; then I will drive out from before you the Canaanites.

"Be very, very careful never to compromise with the people in the land where you are going, for if you do you will soon be following their evil ways. Instead, break down their heathen altars, smash the obelisks they worship, and cut down their shameful idols. For you must worship only Jehovah, a God who claims absolute loyalty."[7]

OWNERSHIP

On Mount Sinai the Lord gave these instructions for the people:

"When you come into the land I am going to give you, you must let the land rest every seventh year. For six years you may sow your field and prune your vineyards and harvest your crops, but during the seventh year the land is to lie before the Lord uncultivated. Don't even reap for yourself the volunteer crops that come up. Any crops that do grow that year shall be free to your servants, slaves, and any foreigners living among you. Cattle and wild animals alike shall be allowed to graze there.

"Every fiftieth year, on the Day of Atonement, let the trumpets blow loud and long throughout the land. For the fiftieth year shall be holy, a time to proclaim liberty to all enslaved debtors, and a time for the canceling of all public and private debts. All the family estates sold to others shall be returned to the original owners or their heirs.

"If the land is sold or bought during the preceding forty-nine years, a fair price shall be arrived at by counting the number of years until the Jubilee. If the Jubilee is many years away, the price will be high; if few years, the price will be low; for what you are really doing is selling the number of crops the new owner will get from the land before it is returned to you.

"You must fear your God and not overcharge! Obey my laws if you want to live safely in the land. When you obey, the land will yield bumper crops.

"But you will ask, 'What shall we eat the seventh year?' I will bless you with bumper crops the sixth year that will last you until the crops of the eighth year are harvested. And remember, the land is mine, so you may not sell it permanently. You are merely my tenants and sharecroppers.

"In every contract of sale there must be a stipulation that the land can be redeemed at any time by the seller. If anyone becomes poor and sells some of his land, then his nearest relatives may redeem it. If he himself gets together enough money, he may buy it back at a price proportionate to the number of harvests until the Jubilee.

"If a man sells a house in the city, he has up to one year to redeem it. But if it is not redeemed within the year, then it does not return to the original owner in the Year of Jubilee. But village houses—a village is a settlement without fortifying walls—are like farmland, redeemable at any time, and are always returned to the original owner in the Year of Jubilee.

"If your brother becomes poor, you are responsible to help him; invite him to live as a guest in your home. And don't charge him interest on the money you lend him.

"If a fellow Israelite becomes poor and sells himself to you, you must not treat him as an ordinary slave, but rather as a hired servant or as a guest; and he shall serve you only until the Year of Jubilee. At that time he can leave with his children and return to his family and possessions.

"If you obey all of my commandments, I will give you regular rains and the land will yield bumper crops; I will give you peace, and you will go to sleep without fear. I will chase away the dangerous animals. You will chase your enemies; they will die beneath your swords. I will look after you, and multiply you, and fulfill my covenant with you. I will walk among you, and be your God, and you shall be my people. I have broken your chains and will make you walk with dignity.

"But if you will not listen or obey me, but reject my laws, I will punish you with sudden terrors and panic, with tuberculosis and burning fever; your eyes shall be consumed and your life shall ebb away; you will sow your crops in vain, for your enemies will eat them. You will flee before your attackers; those who hate you will rule you.

"And if you still won't obey me, I will send you seven times greater punishment for your sins. And I will destroy the altars on the hills where you worship your idols, leaving your dead bodies to rot among your idols. I will make your cities desolate, and I will scatter you among the nations. Then the land will rest and make up for the rest you didn't give it every seventh year when you lived upon it.

"But at last they shall confess their sins and their fathers' sins of treachery against me. When their hearts are humbled and they accept the punishment I send for their sins, then I will remember again my promises to Abraham, Isaac, and Jacob, and I will remember the land. Despite all they have done, I will not utterly destroy them and my covenant with them, for I am Jehovah their God."

Moses was up on the mountain forty days and forty

nights, and all that time he neither ate nor drank. At that time God wrote out the Covenant—the Ten Commandments—on the stone tablets. Moses didn't realize as he came down the mountain that his face glowed from being in the presence of God.[8]

BUILDERS Moses called a meeting of the people and told them, "All of you who wish to may bring these offerings to Jehovah: gold, silver, and bronze; blue, purple, and scarlet cloth made of fine-twined linen or of goat's hair; tanned rams' skins and specially treated goatskins; acacia wood; olive oil for the lamps; spices for the anointing oil and for the incense; onyx stones and stones to be used for the ephod and chestpiece.

"All of you who are skilled craftsmen, construct what God has commanded us: the Tabernacle, the Ark, the veil, the table, the Bread of the Presence, lamp holders, the incense altar, the anointing oil and sweet incense, the curtain for the door, the altar for burnt offerings, the holy garments for Aaron and his sons."

So the people went to their tents to prepare their gifts. Those whose hearts were stirred returned with their offerings for the Tabernacle, its equipment, and the holy garments.

Moses told Bezalel and Oholiab and all others who felt called to the work to begin. Moses gave them the materials donated by the people, and additional gifts were received each morning. Finally the workmen left their task to meet with Moses and told him, "We have more than enough materials on hand now to complete the job!" So Moses sent a message throughout the camp announcing that no more donations were needed.

The people brought gifts of 3,140 pounds of gold. The amount of silver used was 9,575 pounds. The people brought 7,540 pounds of bronze.

Then the Lord said to Moses, "Summon the tribe of Levi and present them to Aaron as his assistants. They will follow his instructions and perform the sacred duties at the Tabernacle on behalf of all the people. They are in charge of all the furnishings and maintenance of the Tabernacle. However, only Aaron and his sons may carry out the duties of the priesthood."

And the Lord said, "I have accepted the Levites in substitution for all the oldest sons of the people of Israel. From the day I killed the oldest sons of the Egyptians, I took for myself all the firstborn in Israel of both men and animals! They are mine; I am Jehovah."

At last the Tabernacle was finished, following all the Lord's instructions. On the first day of the first month, in the second year, the Tabernacle was put together. Moses placed the outside altar for the burnt offerings near the entrance, and offered upon it a burnt offering and a meal offering, as the Lord had commanded. Then he erected the enclosure surrounding the tent and the altar, and set up the curtain-door at the entrance to the enclosure. At last Moses finished the work. Then the cloud covered the Tabernacle, and the glory of the Lord filled it.

Whenever the cloud lifted and moved, the people journeyed onward, following it; if the cloud stayed, they stayed. This continued throughout all their journeys.[9]

WORSHIP; MARCH

The Lord now spoke to Moses from the Tabernacle and commanded him to give the following instructions to the people.

"When you sacrifice to the Lord, use animals from your herds and flocks. Bring the animal to the entrance of the Tabernacle where the priests will accept your gift for the Lord. The person bringing it is to lay his hand upon its head, and it then becomes his substitute: the death of the animal will be accepted by God instead of the death of the man who brings it, as the penalty for his sins. The man shall then kill the animal there before the Lord, and Aaron's sons, the priests, will present the blood before the Lord, sprinkling it upon all sides of the altar at the entrance of the Tabernacle. Then the priests will skin the animal and quarter it, build a wood fire upon the altar, and put the sections of the animal upon the wood. The priests will burn them upon the altar, and they will be an acceptable burnt offering.

"If anyone wishes to use a bird as his burnt offering, he may choose either turtle doves or young pigeons.

"Anyone who wishes to sacrifice a grain offering is to bring fine flour and pour olive oil and incense upon it. He is to take a handful, representing the entire amount, to one of the priests to burn, and the Lord will be fully pleased. The remainder of the flour is to be given to Aaron and his sons as their food.

"Every offering must be seasoned with salt, because the salt is a reminder of God's covenant.

"When anyone wants to give an offering of thanksgiving, he may use either a bull or a cow, but the animal must be entirely without defect. If a goat or sheep is used, it must have no defect and may be either a male or female.

"These are instructions concerning the sin offering:

"This sacrifice is most holy, and shall be killed before the Lord at the place where the burnt offerings are killed. The priest who performs the ceremony shall eat it in the courtyard of the Tabernacle. No sin offering may be eaten by the priests if any of its blood is taken into the Tabernacle to make atonement in the Holy Place. That carcass must be entirely burned before the Lord.

"If anyone sins by unintentionally defiling what is holy, then he shall bring a ram without defect.

"Here are instructions concerning the most holy offering for guilt:

"The sacrificial animal shall be killed at the place where the burnt offering sacrifices are slain, and its blood shall be sprinkled back and forth upon the altar. The priest will offer upon the altar all its fat. The carcass shall be given to the priest who is in charge of the atonement ceremony for his food.

"Here are instructions concerning sacrifices given as special peace offerings:

"Unleavened shortbread shall be included with the sacrifice, along with unleavened wafers spread with olive oil and loaves from a batter of flour mixed with olive oil. This thanksgiving peace offering shall be accompanied with loaves of leavened bread."

Then the Lord said to Moses, "Tell the people never to eat fat, whether from oxen, sheep, or goats. Never eat blood, whether of birds or animals. Anyone who does shall be excommunicated from his people."

The Lord instructed Aaron, "Never drink wine or strong drink when you go into the Tabernacle, lest you die; and this rule applies to your sons and to all your descendants from generation to generation. Your duties will be to arbitrate for the people, to teach them the difference between what is holy and what is ordinary, what is pure and what is impure; and to teach them all the laws Jehovah has given through Moses."

The Lord then told Moses to tell the people:

"I am Jehovah your God, so don't act like the people of Egypt where you lived so long, or the people of Canaan where I am going to take you.

"None of you shall marry a near relative.

"You shall not give any of your children to Molech, burning them upon his altar.

"Homosexuality is absolutely forbidden, for it is an enormous sin.

"Do not defile yourselves in any of these ways, for these are the things the heathen do; and because they do them I am going to cast them out from the land into which you are going.

"You must be holy because I, the Lord your God, am holy.

"When you harvest your crops, don't reap the corners of your fields, and don't pick up stray grains of wheat from the ground. Leave them for the poor and for those traveling through.

"You shall not oppress anyone, and you shall pay your hired workers promptly.

"Judges must always be just in their sentences, not noticing whether a person is poor or rich.

"Don't gossip. Don't falsely accuse your neighbor of some crime.

"Don't hate your brother.

"Don't seek vengeance. Don't bear a grudge; but love your neighbor as yourself.

"Do not defile yourselves by consulting mediums and wizards.

"Give due honor and respect to the elderly, in the fear of God.

"Do not take advantage of foreigners in your land; love them as yourself, for remember that you too were foreigners in Egypt.

"Use accurate measurements—lengths, weights, and volumes—and give full measure."

The Lord said to Moses, "Announce to the people that they are to celebrate several annual festivals of the Lord— times when all Israel will assemble and worship me.

"The Passover of the Lord: this is to be celebrated at the end of March.

"The Festival of Unleavened Bread: to be celebrated the day following the Passover; on the first day of this festival you shall gather the people for worship and all ordinary work shall cease. You shall do the same on the seventh day of the festival. On each of the intervening days you shall make an offering by fire to the Lord.

"The Festival of First Fruits: when you arrive in the land I will give you, bring the first sheaf of the harvest to the priest on the day after the Sabbath. He shall wave it before the Lord in a gesture of offering, and it will be accepted by the Lord as your gift. That same day you shall sacrifice to the Lord a male yearling lamb without defect as a burnt offering. A grain offering shall accompany it, consisting of a fifth of a bushel of finely ground flour mixed with olive oil, to be offered by fire to the Lord. Also offer a drink offering consisting of three pints of wine. Until this is done, you must not eat any of the harvest for yourselves.

"The Festival of Pentecost: fifty days later you shall bring to the Lord an offering of a sample of the new grain of your later crops. This shall consist of two loaves of bread from your homes to be waved before the Lord in a gesture of offering. Bake this bread from a fifth of a bushel of fine flour containing yeast. Along with the bread and the wine, you shall sacrifice as burnt offerings seven yearling lambs without defects, one young bull, and two rams. And you shall offer one male goat for a sin offering, and two male yearling lambs for a peace offering.

"The Festival of Trumpets: mid-September is a solemn time for all the people to meet together for worship; it is to be announced by loud blowing of trumpets. Don't do any work on the day of the celebration, but offer a sacrifice by fire to the Lord.

"The Day of Atonement follows nine days later. All the people, saddened by their sin, shall offer sacrifices by fire to the Lord. Anyone who does not spend the day in repentance and sorrow for sin shall be excommunicated from his people.

"The Festival of Tabernacles: five days later is the Festival of Shelters to be celebrated for seven days. On the first day there will be a sacred assembly of all the people. On each of the seven days you are to sacrifice an offering by fire to the Lord. The eighth day requires another sacred convocation of all the people, at which time there will be again an offering by fire. It is a joyous celebration. On the first day take boughs of fruit trees laden with fruit, and palm fronds, and the boughs of leafy trees, and build shelters with them, rejoicing before the Lord for seven days. The purpose of this is to remind Israel, generation after generation, that I rescued you from Egypt and caused you to live in shelters."

So Moses announced these annual festivals of the Lord to the people of Israel.

On the fifteenth day of April of the second year after the Israelis left Egypt, the Lord issued the following instructions to Moses.

"Take a census of all the men twenty years old and older who are able to go to war, indicating their tribe and family. You and Aaron are to direct the project, assisted by leaders from each tribe."

Moses and Aaron and the leaders summoned all the men twenty years old and older to come and register. Here is the tabulation:

Reuben, 46,500; Simeon, 59,300; Gad, 45,650; Judah,

74,600; Issachar, 54,400; Zebulun, 57,400; Ephraim, 40,500; Manasseh, 32,200; Benjamin, 35,400; Dan, 62,700; Asher, 41,500; Naphtali, 53,400; grand total—603,550.

This total did not include the Levites, for the Levites were assigned for work with the Tabernacle and its transportation. Each tribe had a separate camping area with its own flag.

The Lord said to Moses, "Make two trumpets of silver to summon the people to assemble and for signaling the breaking of camp. When both trumpets are blown, the people will know they are to gather at the entrance of the Tabernacle. If only one is blown, only the chiefs of the tribes shall come to you. Only the priests are permitted to blow the trumpets.

"When you arrive in the Promised Land and go to war against your enemies, God will hear you and save you from your enemies when you sound the alarm with these trumpets. Use the trumpets in times of gladness, too, blowing them at your annual festivals and at the beginning of each month to rejoice over your burnt offerings and peace offerings. And God will be reminded of his covenant with you."

The cloud lifted from the Tabernacle on the twentieth day of the second month of the second year of Israel's leaving Egypt, so the Israelites left the Sinai wilderness and followed the Cloud until it stopped in the wilderness of Paran.

At the head of the march was the tribe of Judah behind its flag. Next came the tribe of Issachar and the tribe of Zebulun. The men of the Gershon and Merari divisions of the tribe of Levi were next in line, carrying the Tabernacle upon their shoulders. Then came the flag of Reuben. Next were Simeon and Gad. Next came the Kohathites carrying the items from the inner sanctuary. Next in line was the tribe of Ephraim and of Manasseh and of Benjamin. Last were the tribes of Dan, Asher, and Naphtali.

They traveled for three days after leaving Mount Sinai, with the Ark at the front of the column. Egyptians who had come with them began to long for the good things of Egypt. This added to the discontent of the people of Israel.

"Oh, that we had some of the delicious fish we enjoyed so much in Egypt, and the wonderful cucumbers and melons, leeks, onions, and garlic. But now day after day we have to face this manna!"

Manna looked like droplets of gum from the bark of a tree. The people gathered it from the ground and crushed it into flour or pounded it in mortars, boiled it, and then made pancakes from it.

Moses, highly displeased, said to the Lord, "Where am I supposed to get meat for all these people? Let me out of this impossible situation!"

The Lord said, "Summon seventy of the leaders of Israel; bring them to the Tabernacle to stand there with you. I will take of the Spirit which is on you and will put it upon them also; they shall bear the burden along with you, so that you will not have the task alone. And tell the people:

" 'The Lord has heard your complaints about all you left behind in Egypt, and he is going to give you meat. You shall eat it, not for just a day or two or five or ten or even twenty! For one month you will have meat until you vomit it; you have rejected the Lord who is here among you and have wept for Egypt.' "

Moses left the Tabernacle and reported Jehovah's words to the people; and he gathered the seventy elders and placed them around the Tabernacle. The Lord came down in the Cloud and took of the Spirit that was upon Moses and put it upon the elders, and they prophesied for some time. Then Moses returned to the camp with the elders.

The Lord sent a wind that brought quail from the sea and let them fall into the camp and all around it! As far as one could walk in a day in any direction, there were quail flying three or four feet above the ground. So the people caught and killed quail all that day and through the night and all the next day! But the anger of the Lord rose against the people, and he killed large numbers of them with a plague. So the name of that place was called, "The Place of the Graves Caused by Lust," because they buried the people there who had lusted for meat and for Egypt. From that place, they journeyed to Hazeroth where they stayed awhile. Afterwards they left and camped in the wilderness of Paran.[10]

RECONNOITER

Jehovah now instructed Moses, "Send spies into the land of Canaan—the land I am giving to Israel; send one leader from each tribe." Moses sent these twelve: Shammu-a, Shaphat, Caleb, Igal, Hoshea, Palti, Gaddiel, Gaddi, Ammiel, Sethur, Nahbi, Geuel (it was at this time Moses changed Hoshea's name to Joshua).

Moses sent them with these instructions: "Go northward into the hill country of the Negeb and see what the land is like; see also what the people are like, whether they are strong or weak, many or few; and what cities there are, and whether they are fortified. Bring back samples of the crops you see."

So they spied out the land from the wilderness of Zin to Rehob near Hamath. Going northward, they passed through the Negeb and arrived at Hebron. Then they came to what is now known as the Valley of Eshcol where they cut down a single cluster of grapes so large that it took two of them to carry it on a pole between them! They also took samples of the pomegranates and figs.

Forty days later they returned from their tour. "The land you sent us to see is indeed a magnificent country—here is some fruit we have brought as proof. But the people living there are powerful, and their cities are fortified and very large; what's more, we saw Anakim giants there! The Amalekites live in the south, while in the hill country are Hittites, Jebusites, and Amorites; along the coast of the Mediterranean Sea and in the Jordan River Valley are Canaanites."

But Caleb reassured the people. "Let us go up at once and possess it, for we are well able to conquer it!"

"Not against people as strong as they are!" the other spies said. "They would crush us."

So the majority report of the spies was negative: "The land is full of warriors, and we saw some descendants of the ancient race of giants. We felt like grasshoppers before them!"

The people rose in a chorus of complaint. "We wish we had died in Egypt, or even here in the wilderness, rather than be taken into this country ahead of us. Let's elect a leader to take us back to Egypt!"

Two of the spies, Joshua and Caleb, said, "It's a wonderful country ahead, and the Lord loves us. He will bring us safely into the land and give it to us. It is a land flowing with milk and honey. Do not rebel against the Lord, and do not fear the people of the land. The Lord has promised his protection from them."

But the response of the people was to talk of stoning them![11]

WANDERERS

Then the Lord said to Moses, "How long will these people despise me? Will they never believe even after the miracles I have done among them?" But I vow that no one of the men who has seen my glory and the miracles I did in Egypt and the wilderness—and refused to trust and obey me—shall see the land I promised to this people's ancestors. Only Caleb and Joshua are permitted to enter it. You must wander in the desert like nomads."

One day Korah, a descendant of Levi, conspired with Dathan and Abiram and On, all from the tribe of Reuben, to incite a rebellion against Moses. Two hundred and fifty leaders were involved. They went to Moses and Aaron and said, "We have had enough of your presumption; everyone in Israel has been chosen of the Lord; what right do you have to claim that we must obey you?"

Moses said, "In the morning the Lord will show you who are his, and who is holy, and whom he has chosen as his priest. You, Korah, and all those with you, take censers tomorrow and light them and put incense upon them before the Lord, and we will find out whom the Lord has chosen."

So they came with their censers and stood at the entrance of the Tabernacle with Moses and Aaron. Korah had stirred up the entire nation against Moses and Aaron, and they all assembled to watch.

Then the glory of Jehovah appeared, and Jehovah said

to Moses and Aaron, "Get away from these people so I may destroy them!"

Moses and Aaron fell face downward to the ground. "O God," they pleaded, "must you be angry with all the people when one man sins?"

The Lord said, "Then tell the people to get away from the tents of Korah, Dathan, and Abiram."

Moses rushed to the tents of Dathan and Abiram. "Quick!" he told the people, "get away from the tents of these wicked men lest you be destroyed with them."

The people stood back, and Moses said, "By this you shall know that Jehovah has sent me to do all these things I have done; if these men die a natural death, then Jehovah has not sent me. But if the Lord does a miracle, then you will know these men have despised the Lord."

He had hardly finished speaking when the ground split open and a great fissure swallowed them up, along with their tents and families and the friends who were standing with them. Then fire came forth from Jehovah and burned up the 250 men who were offering incense. Thus the Lord's directions to Moses were carried out.

Then the Lord said to Moses, "Tell the people that each of their tribal chiefs is to bring you a wooden rod with his name inscribed on it. Aaron's name is to be on the rod of the tribe of Levi. Put these rods in the inner room of the Tabernacle where I meet with you, in front of the Ark. I will use these rods to identify the man I have chosen: for buds will grow on his rod! Then this murmuring against you will stop."

Moses gave the instructions to the people, and each of the twelve chiefs brought him a rod. He put them before the Lord in the inner room of the Tabernacle.

When he went in the next day, he found that Aaron's rod, representing the tribe of Levi, had budded and was blossoming, and had ripe almonds hanging from it! When Moses brought them out to show the others, they stared in disbelief!

The Lord told Moses to place Aaron's rod permanently beside the Ark as a reminder of this rebellion. He was to

bring it out and show it to the people again if there were
any further complaints about Aaron's authority.

Israel arrived in the wilderness of Zin and camped at
Kadesh. There was not enough water to drink at that place,
so the people again held a protest meeting. "Would that
we had died with our brothers the Lord killed!" they shouted
at Moses. "You have brought us into this wilderness to
get rid of us—there isn't even water enough to drink!"

Moses and Aaron turned away and went to the entrance
of the Tabernacle where they fell down before the Lord;
and the glory of Jehovah appeared to them. He said to
Moses, "Get Aaron's rod, then you and Aaron summon
the people. As they watch, speak to that rock over there
and tell it to pour out its water! You will give them water
enough for all the people and all their cattle."

Moses took the rod, then summoned the people to gather
at the rock. He said, "Listen, you rebels! Must we bring
you water from this rock?" Moses lifted the rod and struck
the rock twice, and water gushed out.

But the Lord said to Moses and Aaron, "Because you
did not sanctify me in the eyes of the people, you shall
not bring them into the land I have promised them!"[12]

ON THE MOVE   At Kadesh Moses sent messengers to the king of Edom. "We
are the descendants of your
brother Jacob," he declared. "You know how our ancestors
went down to visit Egypt and became slaves. But the Lord
brought us out, and now we are camped on the border
of your land. Please let us pass through your country. We
will not go through your planted fields nor your vineyards,
but will stay on the main road until we have crossed your
border on the other side."

But the king said, "Stay out! If you attempt to enter
my land I will meet you with an army!" And mobilizing
his army, he marched to the frontier. Israel turned back
and journeyed to Mount Hor.

Then the Lord said to Moses and Aaron, "The time
has come for Aaron to die. Take Aaron and his son Eleazar

and lead them up onto Mount Hor. There you shall remove
Aaron's priestly garments and put them on Eleazar; and
Aaron shall die there."

So the three of them went up Mount Hor as all the
people watched. When they reached the summit, Moses
removed the priestly garments from Aaron and put them
on Eleazar. Aaron died on the top of the mountain, and
Moses and the people mourned for him thirty days. Then
Israel continued south along the road to the Red Sea in
order to go around Edom. Israel journeyed next to Oboth,
then to Iyeabarim, a short distance east of Moab. From
there they traveled to the brook Zared, then moved to
the far side of the Arnon River near the borders of the
Amorites. Israel traveled to Beer, then left the desert and
proceeded through Mattanah, Nahaliel, and Bamoth, then
to the valley in the plateau of Moab which overlooks the
desert with Mount Pisgah in the distance.

Israel now sent ambassadors to King Sihon of the Amorites. "Let us travel through your land," they requested.
"We will not leave the road until we have passed beyond
your borders."

King Sihon refused. Instead, he mobilized his army and
attacked. But Israel slaughtered them and occupied their
land to the Jabbok River.

Israel next turned to the city of Bashan, but King Og
met them with his army. The Lord told Moses, "The same
thing will happen to King Og as happened to King Sihon."
And Israel was victorious and occupied the land.

When Israel arrived in Gilead, the tribes of Reuben and
Gad noticed what wonderful sheep country it was. They
came to Moses and other leaders and said, "This countryside is ideal for our flocks. Let us have this as our portion
instead of land on the other side of the Jordan River."

"You mean you want to sit here while your brothers
go across and do all the fighting?" Moses demanded. "If
you turn away from God like this, he will make the people
stay even longer in the wilderness."

"Not at all!" they explained. "We will build sheepfolds
for our flocks and cities for our little ones, but we will

go over armed, ahead of the rest of Israel, until we have brought them safely to their inheritance."

Moses gave approval and assigned the territory of King Sihon and of King Og to the tribes of Gad, Reuben, and the half-tribe of Manasseh, son of Joseph.

One day the Lord said to Moses, "Go up Mount Abarim and look across the river to the land I have given to Israel. After you have seen it, you shall die as Aaron your brother did."

Moses said, "O Jehovah, the God of the spirits of all mankind, before I am taken away please appoint a new leader who will lead them into battle and care for them."

The Lord replied, "Go and get Joshua, who has the Spirit in him, and take him to Eleazar. As all the people watch, charge him with the responsibility of leading the people. He shall consult with Eleazar the priest to get directions. The Lord will speak to Eleazar through the Urim, and Eleazar will pass on these instructions to Joshua and the people."

Moses took Joshua to Eleazar, laid his hands upon him, and dedicated him to his responsibilities as the Lord commanded.[13]

MOSES' BENEDICTION

This records Moses' address to Israel when they were camped in the wilderness of Moab, east of the Jordan River. The speech was given on February 15, forty years after Israel left Mount Horeb.

"In all history, going back to the time when God created man upon the earth, search from one end of the heavens to the other to see if you can find anything like this: an entire nation heard the voice of God speaking to it from fire, as you did, and lived! Where else will you ever find another example of God's removing a nation from its slavery by sending terrible plagues, mighty miracles, war, and terror? That is what the Lord did for you in Egypt. He did these things so you would realize that Jehovah is God, and there is no one else like him.

"O Israel, listen: Jehovah is our God, Jehovah alone.

You must love him with all your heart, soul, and might. And you must think constantly about these commandments I am giving you today. You must teach them to your children and talk about them when you are at home or out for a walk, at bedtime and the first thing in the morning.

"When the Lord has brought you into the land he promised your ancestors, Abraham, Isaac, and Jacob, and when he has given you great cities full of good things—cities you didn't build, wells you didn't dig, and vineyards and olive trees you didn't plant—then beware lest you forget the Lord who brought you out of slavery.

"When the Lord brings you into the Promised Land, he will destroy seven nations all mightier than you are: the Hittites, Girgashites, Amorites, Canaanites, Perizzites, Hivites, Jebusites. When God delivers them to you, don't make any treaties or show mercy. Do not intermarry with them; that would surely result in your young people's beginning to worship their gods.

"You must break down the heathen altars and shatter the obelisks and cut up the shameful images and burn the idols. For you are dedicated to the Lord. He didn't choose you because you were a larger nation than any other; it was just because he loves you.

"Do not be afraid of those nations, for the Lord is among you. He will cast them out a little at a time, not all at once, for the wild animals would multiply too quickly and become dangerous.

"Do you remember how the Lord led you through the wilderness, testing you to find out how you would respond? He humbled you by letting you go hungry and then feeding you with manna, a food previously unknown to you. He did it to help you realize that food isn't everything, and that real life comes by obeying every command of God. For all these years your clothes haven't grown old, and your feet haven't been blistered or swollen. So you should realize that, as a man punishes his son, the Lord punishes you to help you.

"The Lord is bringing you into a land of brooks, pools, gushing springs, valleys, and hills; it is a land of wheat and barley, of grape vines, fig trees, pomegranates, olives, and honey; it is a land where iron is as common as stone, and copper is abundant in the hills.

"When you have become full and prosperous and have built fine homes, when your flocks and herds have become very large and your silver and gold have multiplied, that is the time to watch out you don't become proud and forget the Lord. He gave you water from the rock! He fed you with manna so that your trust in him would grow. Remember that it is the Lord who gives you power to become rich, and he does it to fulfill his promise to your ancestors.

"But if you forget about the Lord and worship other gods instead, you shall certainly perish, just as the Lord has caused other nations in the past to perish.

"Jehovah is God of gods and Lord of lords. He is the God who shows no partiality. He gives justice to the fatherless and widows. He loves foreigners; you too must love foreigners.

"If a prophet among you claims to foretell the future by dreams, and if his predictions come true but he says, 'Come, let us worship the gods of the other nations,' don't listen to him. For the Lord is testing you to find out whether or not you really love him.

"When you begin to think, 'We ought to have a king like the other nations around us,' be sure that you select as king the man the Lord shall choose. Be sure that he doesn't build up a large stable of horses for himself, nor send his men to Egypt to raise horses for him there. He must not have many wives, lest his heart be turned away from the Lord; neither shall he be excessively rich.

"And when he has been crowned he must copy these laws from the book kept by the Levite-priests. He must read from it every day of his life so that he will learn to respect the Lord by obeying his commands. It will also ensure his having a long, good reign. His sons will then follow him upon the throne.

"When you arrive in the Promised Land you must be very careful lest you be corrupted by the horrible customs of the nations now living there. For example, any Israeli who presents his child to be burned to death as a sacrifice to heathen gods must be killed. No Israeli may practice black magic; or call on the evil spirits for aid; or be a fortune teller, serpent charmer, medium, or wizard; or call forth the spirits of the dead. Anyone doing these things is an object of horror to the Lord, and it is because the nations do these things that your God will displace them. The Lord will not permit you to do such things.

"Instead, he will raise up for you a Prophet like me, a man whom you must obey. The Lord said, 'I will personally deal with anyone who will not listen to him and heed his messages from me.'

"Never convict anyone on the testimony of one witness. There must be at least two, and three is even better. If anyone gives false witness, his penalty shall be the punishment he thought the other man would get. Then those who hear about it will be afraid to tell lies on the witness stand.

"When you cross into the Promised Land, the tribes of Simeon, Levi, Judah, Issachar, Joseph, and Benjamin shall stand upon Mount Gerizim to proclaim a blessing; and the tribes of Reuben, Gad, Asher, Zebulun, Dan, and Naphtali shall stand upon Mount Ebal to proclaim a curse. Then the Levites standing between them shall shout to all Israel:

" 'The curse of God be upon anyone who makes and worships an idol, even in secret, whether carved of wood or made from molten metal—for these handmade gods are hated by the Lord.' And all the people shall reply, 'Amen.'

" 'Cursed is anyone who despises his father or mother.' And all the people shall reply, 'Amen.'

" 'Cursed is anyone who moves the boundary marker between his land and his neighbor's.' And all the people shall reply, 'Amen.'

" 'Cursed is he who takes advantage of a blind man.' And all the people shall reply, 'Amen.'

" 'Cursed is he who is unjust to the foreigner, the orphan, and the widow.' And all the people shall reply, 'Amen.'

" 'Cursed is he who commits adultery with one of his father's wives, for she belongs to his father.' And all the people shall reply, 'Amen.'

" 'Cursed is he who has sexual intercourse with an animal.' And all the people shall reply, 'Amen.'

" 'Cursed is he who has sexual intercourse with his sister.' And all the people shall reply, 'Amen.'

" 'Cursed is he who has sexual intercourse with his widowed mother-in-law.' And all the people shall reply, 'Amen.'

" 'Cursed is he who secretly slays another.' And all the people shall reply, 'Amen.'

" 'Cursed is he who accepts a bribe to kill an innocent person.' And all the people shall reply, 'Amen.'

" 'Cursed is anyone who does not obey these laws.' And all the people shall reply, 'Amen.'

"If you won't listen to the Lord your God and won't obey these laws, these curses shall come upon you:

"The Lord will send tuberculosis, fever, infections, plague, and war. He will blight your crops, covering them with mildew. The heavens above you will be as unyielding as bronze, and the earth beneath will become as dry as dust for lack of rain.

"You will march out to battle gloriously but flee before your enemies in confusion. You will watch as your sons and daughters are taken away as slaves. Your heart will break with longing for them, but you will not be able to help them. A foreign nation you have not heard of will eat the crops you will have worked so hard to grow.

"The Lord will exile you and the king you choose to a nation to whom neither you nor your ancestors gave a second thought. You will become an object of horror, a byword among the nations, for the Lord will thrust you away.

"These curses shall pursue you until you are destroyed—all because you refuse to listen to the Lord your God.

"When all these things have happened to you—the blessings and the curses I have listed—you will meditate upon them as you are living among the nations where the Lord will have driven you. If at that time you want to return to the Lord, and you and your children have begun wholeheartedly to obey the commandments I have given you, then the Lord will rescue you from your captivity! He will gather you out of all the nations and bring you back again to the land of your ancestors. You shall possess the land again, and he will bless you more than he did your ancestors!

He will cleanse your hearts and the hearts of your children
and of your children's children so that you will love the
Lord your God with all your hearts and souls, and Israel
shall come alive again!

"I call heaven and earth to witness against you that today
I have set before you life or death, blessing or curse. Oh,
that you would choose life; that you and your children might
live! Choose to love the Lord your God and to obey him
and to cling to him, for he is your life."

After Moses had said these things to the people, he
told them, "I am now 120 years old! I am no longer able
to lead you, for the Lord has told me that I shall not cross
the Jordan River. Joshua is your new commander, as the
Lord has instructed. Be strong! Do not be afraid, for the
Lord your God will be with you. He will neither fail you
nor forsake you."

Then Moses climbed from the plains of Moab to Pisgah
Peak in Mount Nebo, across from Jericho. And the Lord
pointed out to him the Promised Land, as they gazed out
across Gilead as far as Dan:

"There is Naphtali; and there is Ephraim and Manasseh;
and across there, Judah, extending to the Mediterranean
Sea; there is the Negeb; and the Jordan Valley; and Jericho,
the city of palm trees; and Zoar," the Lord told him.

"It is the Promised Land," the Lord told Moses. "I promised Abraham, Isaac, and Jacob that I would give it to their
descendants. Now you have seen it, but you will not enter
it."

So Moses, the disciple of the Lord, died in the land of
Moab. The Lord buried him in a valley near Beth-Peor,
but no one knows the exact place. The people of Israel
mourned for him for thirty days. There has never been
another prophet like Moses, for the Lord talked to him
face to face. And at God's command he performed amazing
miracles which have never been equaled.[14]

PART
4
PROMISED
LAND

JOSHUA After the death of Moses, God spoke to Moses' assistant, Joshua, and said,

"Now that my disciple is dead, you lead my people across the Jordan River into the Promised Land. Wherever you go will be part of the land of Israel—all the way from Negeb desert in the south to the Lebanon mountains in the north, and from the Mediterranean Sea in the west to the Euphrates River in the east. No one will be able to oppose you as long as you live, for I will be with you just as I was with Moses.

"You need only to be strong and courageous and to obey every law Moses gave you. Constantly remind the people about these laws, and you yourself think about them every day and every night. Only then will you succeed."

Then Joshua issued instructions to the leaders to tell the people to get ready to cross the Jordan River. "In three days we will conquer and live in the land which God has given us!" he told them.[1]

INVASION Joshua sent two spies from the Israeli camp at Acacia to cross the river and check out the other side, especially Jericho. They arrived at an inn operated by a woman named Rahab, who was a prostitute. Someone informed the king of Jericho that two Israelis suspected of being spies had arrived in the city. He dispatched a police squadron to Rahab's home.

She told the officer in charge, "The men were here, but they left the city as the city gates were about to close. If you hurry you can probably catch them!"

Actually she had taken them up to the roof and hidden them beneath piles of flax drying there. Rahab went up to talk to the men.

"I know that your God is going to give my country to you," she told them. "Everyone is terrified if the word Israel is even mentioned, for we have heard how the Lord made a path through the Red Sea for you. And we know what you did to Sihon and Og, the Amorite kings. Your God is the supreme God, not an ordinary god. I beg for this one thing: swear to me that when Jericho is conquered you will let me live, along with my father and mother, my brothers and sisters, and all their families. This is fair after the way I have helped you."

The men agreed. "If you won't betray us, we'll see that you and your family aren't harmed." Since her house was on top of the city wall, she let them down by a rope from a window. Before they left, the men said, "We cannot be responsible for what happens to you unless this rope is hanging from this window and all your relatives are here inside the house."

The spies went up into the mountains and stayed there until the men who were chasing them had returned to the city after searching everywhere along the road without success. Then the spies crossed the river and reported to Joshua all that had happened. "The Lord will certainly give us the land," they said, "for the people are scared to death of us."

Early the next morning Joshua and the people of Israel left Acacia, and arrived that evening at the banks of the Jordan where they camped. On the third day, officers went through the camp giving these instructions: "When you see the priests carrying the Ark of God, follow them. Stay about a half mile behind." Joshua told the people to perform the purification ceremony for themselves. "Tomorrow," he said, "the Lord will do a great miracle."

In the morning Joshua ordered the priests, "Take up the Ark and lead us across the river!" So they started out. Joshua summoned all the people and told them, "Today you are going to know that the living God will drive out the people who live in the land you will soon occupy."

It was harvest season and the Jordan was overflowing its banks; but as the feet of the priests touched the water at the river's edge, suddenly, far up the river, the water began piling up as though against a dam! And the water below that point flowed on to the Salt Sea until the riverbed was empty. Then all the people crossed at a spot close to the city of Jericho.

When all the people were safely across, the Lord said to Joshua, "Tell twelve men, one from each tribe, to take a stone from the middle of the Jordan and to pile them up as a monument where you camp tonight."

Joshua summoned the twelve men, and the men did as Joshua told them.

The water poured down again as usual and overflowed the banks of the river as before! That day the entire nation crossed the Jordan River and camped in Gilgal at the eastern edge of Jericho; and there the twelve stones from the Jordan were piled up as a monument.

Joshua explained the purpose of the stones: "In the future when your children ask you why these stones are here, tell them these stones are a reminder of this amazing miracle—the Lord dried up the river before our eyes and kept it dry until we were all across! It is the same thing the Lord did forty years ago at the Red Sea! He did this so all nations will realize that Jehovah is the mighty God."

Camped on the plains of Jericho, they celebrated the Passover during the evening of April first. The next day they began to eat from the gardens and grain fields which they invaded. The following day no manna fell, and it was never seen again![2]

JERICHO   As Joshua was sizing up the city of Jericho, a man appeared nearby with a drawn sword. Joshua strode over to him and demanded, "Are you friend or foe?"

"I am the Commander-in-Chief of the Lord's army," he replied.

Joshua fell to the ground and worshiped him and said, "Give me your commands."

"Jericho and its king and all its mighty warriors are already defeated, for I have given them to you! Your entire army is to walk around the city once a day for six days, followed by seven priests walking ahead of the Ark, each carrying a trumpet made from a ram's horn. On the seventh day you are to walk around the city seven times, with the priests blowing their trumpets. Then when they give one long, loud blast, all the people are to give a mighty shout, and the walls of the city will fall down."

Joshua summoned the priests and gave them their instructions. The Ark was carried around the city once that day, after which everyone returned to the camp. At dawn the next morning they went around again, and returned again to camp. They followed this pattern for six days. At dawn of the seventh day, they started out again, but this time they went around the city seven times. As the priests blew a long, loud trumpet blast, Joshua yelled to the people, "Shout! The Lord has given us the city!"

He had told them previously, "Kill everyone except Rahab and anyone in her house, for she protected our spies. Don't take any loot, for everything is to be destroyed."

The people shouted as loud as they could, and suddenly the walls of Jericho crumbled and fell before them, and the people of Israel poured into the city from every side and captured it!

Then Joshua said to the two spies, "Go and rescue the prostitute and everyone with her." The young men found her and rescued her, along with her father, mother, brothers, and other relatives who were with her. Arrangements were made for them to live outside the camp of Israel. Then the Israelis burned the city and everything in it except the silver and gold and the bronze and iron utensils kept for the Lord's treasury.

When the kings of the surrounding area heard what had happened to Jericho, they combined their armies to fight—

these were the kings of the Hittites, Amorites, Canaanites, Perizzites, Hivites, and Jebusites.

But the people of Gibeon sent ambassadors to Joshua wearing worn-out clothing, as though from a long journey. They told the men of Israel, "We have come from a distant land to ask for a peace treaty."

The Israelis replied, "How do we know you don't live nearby?"

"Who are you?" Joshua demanded.

They told him, "We are from a very distant country; we have heard of the might of your God, so our people instructed us, 'Prepare for a long journey; go to the people of Israel and declare our nation to be their servants, and ask for peace.'"

Joshua and the other leaders finally believed them and signed a peace treaty.

Three days later the facts came out—these men were close neighbors. Joshua summoned their leaders and demanded, "Why have you lied to us? Now a curse shall be upon you! From this moment you must always furnish us with servants to chop wood and carry water for the service of our God."

They replied, "We did it because we feared for our lives. Now you may do with us as you wish."

Joshua would not allow the people of Israel to kill them, but they became wood-choppers and water-carriers for the people of Israel and for the altar of the Lord—wherever it would be built.

When Adoni-zedek, king of Jerusalem, heard how the people of Gibeon had made peace with Israel, he was frightened. For Gibeon was a great city and its men were known as hard fighters. Adoni-zedek sent messengers to several other kings:

"Come and help me destroy Gibeon, for they have made peace with Joshua and Israel."

Five Amorite kings combined their armies for an attack on Gibeon. The men of Gibeon sent messengers to Joshua: "Come quickly and save us! The kings of the Amorites are here with their armies."

Joshua and the Israeli army left Gilgal and went to rescue Gibeon. "Don't be afraid of them," the Lord said to Joshua, "for they are already defeated! Not a single one will be able to stand up to you."

Joshua traveled all night and took the enemy armies by surprise. The army of Israel slaughtered great numbers at Gibeon and chased the others to Beth-horon. As the enemy was racing down the hill to Beth-horon, the Lord destroyed them with a great hailstorm; in fact, more men died from the hail than by the swords of the Israelis.

As the men of Israel were pursuing the foe, Joshua prayed aloud: "Let the sun stand still over Gibeon, and let the moon stand in its place over the valley." And the sun and the moon didn't move until the Israeli army had finished the destruction of its enemies! There had never been such a day before.

So Joshua and his army conquered the nations and kings of the hill country, the Negeb, the lowlands, and the mountain slopes. Then Joshua and his army returned to their camp at Gilgal.

When King Jabin of Hazor heard what had happened, he sent urgent messages to the kings of Madon, Shimron, Achshaph, the northern hill country, the Arabah, the lowland, the mountain areas of Dor, Canaan both east and west, the Amorites, the Hittites, the Perizzites, the Jebusite hill country, the cities on the slopes of Mount Hermon in the land of Mizpah. All these kings responded by mobilizing to crush Israel. Their combined troops, along with a vast array of horses and chariots, covered the landscape around the Springs of Merom.

But the Lord said to Joshua, "Don't be afraid of them, for by this time tomorrow they will all be dead!"

Joshua and his troops arrived suddenly at the Springs of Merom and attacked. The Israelis chased them as far as Great Sidon and a place called the Salt Pits and eastward into the valley of Mizpah; not one enemy troop survived the battle.

On the way back Joshua captured Hazor, at one time the capital of the federation of all those kingdoms. Then he attacked and destroyed all the other cities of those kings.

So the Israeli territory extended all the way from Mount Halak, near Seir, to Baal-gad at the foot of Mount Hermon. It took seven years of war to accomplish this. In all, thirty-one kings and their cities were destroyed.[3]

CONQUEROR

Joshua was now old. The Lord said to him, "There are still many nations to be conquered. I am ready to drive these people out from before Israel, so include all this territory when you divide the land among the nine tribes and the half-tribe of Manasseh as I have commanded you." The other half of the tribe of Manasseh, and the tribes of Reuben and Gad, had already received their inheritance on the east side of the Jordan.

After the conquest—though seven of the tribes had not yet conquered the land God had given them—all Israel gathered at Shiloh to set up the Tabernacle.

Joshua asked them, "How long are you going to wait before clearing out the people living in the land which the Lord has given to you? Select three men from each tribe and I will send them to scout the unconquered territory and bring back a report of its size and natural divisions so that I can divide it for you."

The men did as they were told and divided the territory into seven sections, listing the cities in each section. Then they returned to Joshua at Shiloh. There at the Tabernacle Eleazar the priest, Joshua, and the leaders of the tribes supervised the sacred lottery to divide the land among the tribes in the Lord's presence.

The Lord said to Joshua, "Tell the people to designate now the Cities of Refuge, as I instructed Moses. If a man is guilty of killing someone unintentionally, he can run to one of these cities and be protected from the relatives of the dead man who may try to kill him in revenge. The innocent killer will meet with the city council and explain what happened, and they must give him a place to live among them. The man must stay in that city until he has been tried by the judges, and until the death of the High

Priest who was in office at the time of the accident. Then he is free to return to his own city."

The cities chosen as Cities of Refuge were Kedesh of Galilee; Shechem, in the hill country of Ephraim; and Kiriath-arba (also known as Hebron) in the hill country of Judah. The Lord also instructed that three cities be set aside for this purpose on the east side of the Jordan River, across from Jericho: Bezer, Ramoth, and Golan. These Cities of Refuge were for foreigners living in Israel as well as for the Israelis.

Leaders of the tribe of Levi came to Shiloh to consult with Eleazar, Joshua, and leaders of the various tribes. "The Lord instructed Moses to give cities to us Levites for our homes, and pastureland for our cattle," they said. So they were given some of the recently conquered cities with their pasturelands.

When the Lord had given success to Israel against their enemies and when Joshua was very old, he called for the leaders—elders, judges, and officers—and said, "I am old now, and you have seen all that the Lord God has done for you during my lifetime. I have divided to you the land of the nations yet unconquered as well as the land of those you have already destroyed. All the land from the Jordan River to the Mediterranean Sea shall be yours, and you will live there just as he has promised you.

"But be very sure to follow the instructions written in the book of Moses. Be sure that you do not mix with the heathen people still remaining in the land. Follow the Lord just as you have until now. Each one of you has put to flight a thousand of the enemy, for the Lord fights for you.

"If you begin to intermarry with the nations around you, know for a certainty that the Lord will no longer chase those nations from your land. Instead, they will be a snare to you, and you will disappear from this good land.

"You know very well that God's promises to you have all come true. But as certainly as the Lord has given you the good things he promised, just as certainly he will bring evil upon you if you disobey him. If you worship other gods, he will wipe you out from this good land."

Then Joshua summoned all the people to Shechem. He addressed them as follows:

"The God of Israel says, 'Your ancestors, including Terah the father of Abraham and Nahor, lived east of the Euphrates River; and they worshiped other gods. But I took Abraham from that land across the river and led him to Canaan and gave him many descendants through Isaac. Isaac's children were Jacob and Esau; to Esau I gave the area around Mount Seir, while Jacob and his children went into Egypt.

" 'Then I sent Moses and Aaron to bring terrible plagues upon Egypt; and I brought my people out as free men. Israel lived in the wilderness for many years. I brought you into the land of the Amorites on the other side of the Jordan; and they fought against you, but I destroyed them.

" 'Then you crossed the Jordan River and came to Jericho. The men of Jericho fought against you, and so did many others. It was not your swords or bows that brought you victory! I gave you land you had not worked for and cities you did not build—these cities where you are now living.'

"So revere Jehovah and serve him. Put away forever the idols which your ancestors worshiped beyond the Euphrates River and in Egypt. Decide today whom you will obey. As for me and my family, we will serve the Lord."

The people replied, "We would never forsake the Lord and worship other gods! For our God did mighty miracles. Yes, we choose the Lord; he alone is our God."

So Joshua made a covenant at Shechem, committing them to a permanent contract between themselves and God. Joshua recorded the people's reply in the book of the laws of God, and took a huge stone as a reminder and rolled it beneath the oak tree that was beside the Tabernacle. Then Joshua sent the people away to their own sections of the country.

Soon after this, he died at the age of 110. He was buried on his own estate at Timnath-serah, in the hill country of Ephraim.

The bones of Joseph, which the people had brought with them when they left Egypt, were buried in Shechem in the parcel of ground which Jacob had bought from the sons of Hamor. Eleazar, the son of Aaron, also died; he was buried in the hill country of Ephraim, at Gibe-ah, the city which had been given to his son Phinehas.[4]

PART
5
HEROES;
HUMILIATIONS

OTHNI-EL; EHUD

After Joshua died, the nation went to the Lord to receive his instructions. "Which of our tribes should be the first to go to war against the Canaanites?" they inquired.

God's answer came: "Judah; and I will give them a great victory." And the Lord helped them defeat the Canaanites and Perizzites.

Judah conquered Jerusalem, setting the city on fire. Afterward the army fought Canaanites in the hill country and in the Negeb, as well as on the coastal plains. Then Judah marched against the Canaanites in Hebron. The army also conquered the cities of Gaza, Ashkelon, and Ekron. The city of Hebron was given to Caleb as the Lord had promised.

The tribe of Benjamin failed to exterminate the Jebusites living in Jerusalem, so they still mingled with the Israelis.

As for the tribe of Joseph, they attacked the city of Bethel, formerly known as Luz, and the Lord was with them.

The tribe of Manasseh failed to drive out the people living in Megiddo, with their surrounding towns; so the Canaanites stayed there. And the tribe of Zebulun did not massacre the people of Kitron, but made them their slaves; nor did the tribe of Asher drive out the residents of Acco, Sidon, or Rehob. And the tribe of Naphtali did not drive out the people of Beth-shemesh. As for the tribe of Dan, the Amorites forced them into the hill country.

The people had remained true to the Lord throughout Joshua's lifetime and as long afterward as the men of his generation were living. But all that generation died—and the next generation did not worship Jehovah. They did many things which the Lord had forbidden, including worshiping heathen gods.

Israel lived among the Canaanites, Hittites, Hivites, Perizzites, Amorites, and Jebusites instead of destroying them. The young men of Israel took their girls as wives, and Israeli girls married their men. Soon Israel was worshiping Baal and the Asheroth idols.

Then the anger of the Lord flamed against Israel, and he let King Cushan-rishathaim of eastern Syria conquer them. They were under his rule for eight years. When Israel cried out to the Lord, he gave them Caleb's nephew, Othni-el, to save them. The Spirit of the Lord took control of him and he reformed Israel so that when he led Israel against the army of King Cushan-rishathaim, the Lord helped Israel conquer him completely.

For forty years under Othni-el, there was peace in the land. But when Othni-el died, Israel turned once again to their sinful ways. So God helped King Eglon of Moab conquer part of Israel. Allied with him were armies of the Ammonites and Amalekites. These forces took possession of Jericho, "The City of Palm Trees." For the next eighteen years the people of Israel were required to pay crushing taxes to King Eglon.

When they cried to the Lord, he sent them a savior, Ehud, a Benjaminite. Ehud was chosen to carry Israel's annual tax money to the Moabite capital. Before this journey, he made a double-edged dagger and hid it in his clothing, strapped against his thigh. After delivering the money to King Eglon, he started home again. But outside the city, at the quarries of Gilgal, he sent his companions on and returned alone to the king.

"I have a secret message for you," he told him.

The king dismissed all those with him so he could have a private interview. Ehud walked over to him and said,

"It is a message from God!" King Eglon stood up to receive it, whereupon Ehud reached beneath his robe, pulled out the dagger, and plunged it deep into the king's belly. Leaving the dagger there, Ehud locked the doors behind him and escaped across an upstairs porch.

Ehud escaped past the quarries. When he arrived in the hill country of Ephraim, he blew a trumpet as a call to arms and mustered an army. "Follow me," he told them, "for the Lord has put the Moabites at your mercy!"

The army proceeded to seize the fords of the Jordan River near Moab, preventing anyone from crossing. Then they attacked the Moabites, letting not one escape. So Moab was conquered, and the land was at peace for the next eighty years.[1]

DEBORAH

After Ehud's death the people again sinned against the Lord, so the Lord let them be conquered by King Jabin of Hazor. The commander-in-chief of his army was Sisera, who had nine hundred iron chariots and made life unbearable for the Israelis for twenty years. Finally they begged the Lord for help. Israel's leader at that time was Deborah, a prophetess. She held court at a place now called "Deborah's Palm Tree," between Ramah and Bethel. Israelites came to her to decide their disputes.

One day she summoned Barak, who lived in Kedesh in the land of Naphtali, and said to him, "God has commanded you to mobilize ten thousand men from the tribes of Naphtali and Zebulun. Lead them to Mount Tabor to fight King Jabin's army. The Lord says, 'I will draw them to the Kishon River, and you will defeat them there.' "

"I'll go if you go with me!" Barak told her.

"All right," she replied, "but the honor of conquering Sisera will go to a woman instead of to you!"

When Barak summoned the men to mobilize at Kedesh, ten thousand volunteered. And Deborah marched with them. Heber the Kenite—the Kenites were descendants of Moses' father-in-law Hobab—had moved away from the rest of his clan and had been living in places as far away as Kedesh.

When General Sisera was told that Barak and his army

were camped at Mount Tabor, he mobilized his army and marched to the Kishon River.

Then Deborah said to Barak, "Now is the time for action! The Lord leads on! He has already delivered Sisera into your hand!"

Barak led his men down the slopes of Mount Tabor into battle, then the Lord threw the enemy into a panic, both the soldiers and the charioteers, and Sisera leaped from his chariot and escaped on foot. Barak and his men chased the enemy until all of Sisera's army was destroyed.

Meanwhile Sisera had escaped to the tent of Jael, the wife of Heber the Kenite, for there was a mutual-assistance agreement between King Jabin and the clan of Heber.

"Stand in the door of the tent," he told her, "and if anyone comes by looking for me, tell them no one is here."

Jael took a sharp tent peg and a hammer and, quietly creeping up to him as he slept, she drove the peg through his temples, and so he died. After that there was peace in the land for forty years.[2]

GIDEON   Israel began once again to worship other gods, and again the Lord let their enemies harass them. The Midianites were so cruel that the Israelis took to the mountains, living in caves and dens. When they planted their seed, marauders from Midian, Amalek, and other neighboring nations came and destroyed their crops and plundered the countryside, leaving nothing to eat and taking away their sheep, oxen, and donkeys. Israel was reduced to poverty. At last the people began to cry out to the Lord for help.

One day the Angel of the Lord came and sat beneath the oak tree on the farm of Joash. Joash's son, Gideon, had been threshing wheat in the bottom of a pit where grapes were pressed, hiding from the Midianites. The Angel appeared to him and said, "Mighty soldier, the Lord is with you!"

"Stranger," Gideon replied, "if the Lord is with us, why has all this happened to us? And where are the miracles our ancestors have told us about? The Lord let the Midianites ruin us."

The Lord said, "I will make you strong! Go and save Israel from the Midianites!"

Gideon replied, "Sir, how can I save Israel? My family is the poorest in the tribe of Manasseh, and I am the least in the entire family!"

"But Jehovah will be with you! And you shall quickly destroy the Midianite hordes!"

"If it is really true that you are going to help me like that, do some miracle to prove it! But stay here until I go and get a present for you."

"All right," the Angel agreed.

Gideon hurried home and roasted a young goat, baked some unleavened bread, then, carrying the meat in a basket and broth in a pot, he took it to the Angel.

The Angel said, "Place the meat and the bread upon that rock over there, and pour the broth over it."

When Gideon had followed these instructions, the Angel touched the meat and bread with his staff and fire flamed up from the rock and consumed them! And suddenly the Angel was gone!

When Gideon realized that it had indeed been the Angel of the Lord, he cried out, "I have seen the Angel of the Lord face to face!"

And Gideon built an altar there and named it, "The Altar of Peace with Jehovah."

Soon afterwards the armies of Midian, Amalek, and other neighboring nations united against Israel. They crossed the Jordan and camped in the valley of Jezreel. Then the Spirit of the Lord came upon Gideon, and he sent messengers throughout Manasseh, Asher, Zebulun, and Naphtali, summoning their fighting forces.

Gideon said to God, "If you are really going to use me to save Israel, prove it to me in this way: I'll put some wool on the threshing floor tonight, and if in the morning the fleece is wet and the ground is dry, I will know you are going to help me!"

And it happened just that way! When he got up the next morning he pressed the fleece together and wrung out a bowlful of water!

Gideon and his army got an early start and went as far

as the spring of Harod. The Lord then said, "There are too many of you! Send home any of your men who are frightened."

Twenty-two thousand left, and ten thousand remained. But the Lord told Gideon, "There are still too many! Bring them down to the spring and I'll show you which ones shall go with you."

At the water the Lord told him, "Divide them into two groups decided by the way they drink: the men who cup the water in their hands to get it to their mouths; and those who kneel, with their mouths in the stream."

Only three hundred of the men drank from their hands. "I'll conquer the Midianites with these three hundred!" the Lord told Gideon. "Send the others home!"

So after Gideon had collected all the clay jars and trumpets they had among them, he sent them home.

During the night, with the Midianites camped in the valley just below, the Lord said to Gideon, "Take your troops and attack the Midianites, for I will cause you to defeat them!"

He divided the three hundred men into three groups and gave each man a trumpet and a clay jar with a torch in it. Then he explained his plan.

"When we arrive at the outer guardposts of the camp, do just as I do. As soon as I and the men in my group blow our trumpets, you blow yours on all sides of the camp and shout, 'We fight for God and for Gideon!' "

Just after midnight and the change of guards, Gideon and the hundred men with him crept to the outer edge of the camp of Midian. Suddenly they blew their trumpets and broke their clay jars so that their torches blazed into the night. Then the other two hundred men did the same, blowing the trumpets in their right hands and holding the flaming torches in their left hands, all yelling, "For the Lord and for Gideon!"

They stood and watched as the enemy army began rushing around in panic. In the confusion troops began fighting and killing each other from one end of the camp to the other, and they fled into the night. Then Gideon sent for the troops of Naphtali, Asher, and Manasseh to chase and destroy the fleeing army.

That is how Midian was subdued. Midian never recovered, and the land was at peace for forty years—all during Gideon's lifetime. Gideon finally died, an old, old man, and was buried in the sepulcher of his father Joash in Ophrah.

Once again Israel sinned by worshiping other gods, so the Lord let them be conquered by the Philistines, who kept them in subjection for forty years.[3]

SAMSON One day the Angel of the Lord appeared to the wife of Manoah, of the tribe of Dan. The Angel said, "Though you have been barren so long, you will soon conceive and have a son! Don't drink any wine and don't eat any food that isn't kosher. Your son's hair must never be cut, for he shall be a Nazirite, a special servant of God from the time of his birth; and he will begin to rescue Israel from the Philistines."

When her son was born, they named him Samson, and the Lord blessed him as he grew up.

One day when Samson was in Timnah, he noticed a certain Philistine girl, and when he got home he told his father and mother that he wanted to marry her. They objected strenuously. "Why don't you marry a Jewish girl?" they asked.

His father and mother didn't realize that the Lord was behind the request, for God was setting a trap for the Philistines.

As Samson and his parents were going to Timnah, a young lion attacked Samson on the outskirts of the town. The Spirit of the Lord came mightily upon him, and he ripped the lion's jaws apart as though it were a young goat! Upon arriving at Timnah, he talked with the girl and found her to be just what he wanted, so the arrangements were made.

When he returned for the wedding, he turned off the path to look at the carcass of the lion. He found a swarm of bees in it, and some honey! He took some of the honey with him, eating as he went.

Samson threw a party for thirty young men of the village, as was the custom. When Samson asked if they would like to hear a riddle they replied they would.

"If you solve my riddle during these seven days of the celebration," he said, "I'll give you thirty plain robes and thirty fancy robes. But if you can't solve it, then you must give robes to me!"

"All right," they agreed.

This was his riddle: "Food came out of the eater, and sweetness from the strong!" Three days later they were still trying to figure it out.

On the fourth day they said to his new wife, "Get the answer from your husband, or we'll burn down your father's house with you in it."

So Samson's wife broke down in tears and said, "You don't love me at all; for you have told a riddle to my people and haven't told me the answer!"

"I haven't even told it to my father or mother; why should I tell you?" he replied.

So she cried whenever she was with him. At last, on the seventh day, he told her the answer, and she gave the answer to the young men. Before sunset of the seventh day they gave him their reply.

"What is sweeter than honey?" they asked, "and what is stronger than a lion?"

"If you hadn't plowed with my heifer, you wouldn't have found the answer to my riddle!" he retorted.

Then he went to the city of Ashkelon, killed thirty men, took their clothing, and gave it to the young men who had told him the answer to his riddle. But he was furious about it, and abandoned his wife and went back home to live with his father and mother.

Later Samson took a young goat as a present to his wife, but her father wouldn't let him in.

"I thought you hated her," he explained, "so I married her to your best man."

Samson was furious. He went out and caught three hundred foxes and tied their tails together in pairs with a torch between each pair. Then he lit the torches and let the foxes run through the fields of the Philistines, burning the grain to the ground and destroying the olive trees.

"Who did this?" the Philistines demanded.

"Samson," was the reply, "because his wife's father gave her to another man." So the Philistines came and got the girl and her father and burned them alive.

"Now my vengeance will strike again!" Samson vowed. So he attacked them and killed many. Then he went to live in a cave. The Philistines in turn sent a huge posse to Judah.

"Why have you come here?" the men of Judah asked.

"To capture Samson and do to him as he has done to us."

So three thousand men of Judah went to get Samson at the cave in the rock. They demanded, "Don't you realize that the Philistines are our rulers? We have come to take you to the Philistines."

"All right," Samson said, "but promise me that you won't kill me yourselves."

"No," they replied, "we won't do that."

So they tied him with two new ropes and led him away. As Samson and his captors arrived, the Philistines shouted with glee. But then the strength of the Lord came upon Samson, and the ropes with which he was tied snapped like thread. He picked up a donkey's jawbone that was lying on the ground and killed a thousand Philistines with it.

Samson was Israel's judge for the next twenty years, but the Philistines still controlled the land.

Samson fell in love with a girl named Delilah in the valley of Sorek. The five heads of the Philistine nation went to her and demanded she find out from Samson what made him so strong so they would know how to overpower him.

"Each of us will give you a thousand dollars for this job," they promised.

So Delilah begged Samson, "Please tell me, Samson, why you are so strong. I don't think anyone could ever capture you!" She nagged at him every day until he couldn't stand it any longer.

"My hair has never been cut," he confessed, "for I've been a Nazirite to God since before my birth. If my hair were cut, my strength would leave me."

Delilah realized he had told her the truth, so she sent for the five Philistine leaders.

She lulled him to sleep with his head in her lap, and they brought in a barber and cut off his hair. Then she screamed, "The Philistines are here to capture you, Samson!"

He woke up and thought, "I will do as before; I'll just shake myself free." But he didn't realize that the Lord had left him.

So the Philistines captured him, gouged out his eyes, and took him to Gaza where he was bound with chains and made to grind grain in the prison.

The Philistine leaders declared a great festival to celebrate the capture. The people made sacrifices to their god Dagon and excitedly praised him. "Our god has delivered Samson to us!" they gloated. "The scourge of our nation is now in our power!" Half drunk, the people demanded, "Bring out Samson so we can have some fun with him!"

So he was brought from the prison and made to stand at the center of the temple between two pillars supporting the roof. Samson said to the boy who was leading him by the hand, "Place my hands against the two pillars."

By then the temple was filled with people. The five Philistine leaders were there as well as three thousand people in the balconies who were watching Samson and making fun of him.

Then Samson prayed to the Lord, "O Lord Jehovah, remember me again—please strengthen me one more time, so that I may pay back the Philistines for the loss of my eyes."

Then Samson pushed against the pillars with all his might. "Let me die with the Philistines," he prayed.

And the temple crashed down upon the Philistine leaders and all the people. Those he killed at the moment of his death were more than those he had killed during his entire lifetime. Later, his brothers and other relatives came to get his body, and they brought him back home and buried him where his father, Manoah, was buried. He had judged Israel for twenty years.[4]

RUTH   When judges ruled in Israel, a man named Elimelech from Bethlehem left the country because of a famine and moved to the land of Moab. With him were his wife, Naomi, and his two sons, Mahlon and Chilion. During their residence there, Elimelech died and Naomi was left with her two sons.

These young men married girls of Moab, Orpah and Ruth. But later both men died, so that Naomi was left alone, without her husband or sons. She decided to return to Israel with her daughters-in-law, for she had heard that the Lord had blessed his people by giving them good crops again.

But after they had begun their journey, she changed her mind and said to her daughters-in-law, "Why don't you return to your parents' homes instead of coming with me? And may the Lord reward you for your faithfulness to your husbands and to me."

"No," they said, "we want to go with you to your people."

But Naomi replied, "It is better for you to return to your own people. Oh, how I grieve for you that the Lord has punished me in a way that injures you."

They cried together, and Orpah kissed her mother-in-law good-bye and returned to her childhood home. But Ruth insisted on staying with Naomi. "Don't make me leave you, for I want to go wherever you go and live wherever you live; your people shall be my people, and your God shall be my God."

When Naomi saw that Ruth could not be persuaded otherwise, she stopped urging her. So they both came to Bethlehem, and the entire village was stirred by their arrival.

"Is it really Naomi?" the women asked.

She told them, "Don't call me Naomi. Call me Mara," (Naomi means "pleasant"; Mara means "bitter") "for Almighty God has dealt me bitter blows."

Naomi had an in-law in Bethlehem who was very wealthy. His name was Boaz.

One day Ruth said to Naomi, "Perhaps I can go into the fields of some kind man to glean the free grain behind his reapers."

Naomi said, "All right, dear daughter. Go ahead."

As it happened, the field where she found herself belonged to Boaz, this relative of Naomi's husband.

Boaz arrived from the city while she was there. After exchanging greetings with the reapers he said to his foreman, "Who's that girl over there?"

"It's that girl from Moab who came back with Naomi. She asked me if she could pick up the grains dropped by the reapers."

Boaz went over and talked to her. "Listen, my child," he said. "Stay here with us to glean; stay right behind my women workers. When you are thirsty, go and help yourself to the water."

She thanked him warmly. "How can you be so kind to me?" she asked. "You must know I am a foreigner."

"Yes, I know," Boaz replied, "and I also know about the love and kindness you have shown your mother-in-law. May the Lord God of Israel, under whose wings you have come to take refuge, bless you for it."

"Thank you, sir," she replied. "You are so good to me."

At lunchtime Boaz called to her, "Come and eat with us." So she sat with his reapers and he gave her food. When she went back to work, Boaz told his young men to snap off some heads of barley and drop them on purpose for her to glean. She worked there all day, and in the evening when she had beaten out the barley she had gleaned, it came to a whole bushel! She carried it back into the city and gave it to her mother-in-law.

"So much!" Naomi exclaimed. "Praise the Lord for whoever was so kind to you."

Ruth told her mother-in-law about it and mentioned that the owner of the field was Boaz.

"God has continued his kindness to us," Naomi cried excitedly. "That man is one of our closest relatives! Stay with his girls right through the whole harvest."

So Ruth did, and gleaned with them until the end of the barley harvest, and then the wheat harvest, too.

One day Naomi said to Ruth, "My dear, isn't it time that I try to find a husband for you? The man I'm thinking of is Boaz! I happen to know that he will be winnowing barley tonight on the threshing-floor. Now do what I tell you—bathe and put on some perfume and some nice clothes and go on down to the threshing-floor, but don't let him see you until he has finished his supper. Notice where he lies down to sleep; then go and lift the cover off his feet and lie down there, and he will tell you what to do concerning marriage."

Ruth replied, "All right. I'll do whatever you say."

She went down to the threshing-floor that night. After Boaz lay down beside a heap of grain and went to sleep, Ruth came quietly and lifted the covering off his feet and lay there. Suddenly, around midnight, he wakened and sat up, startled.

"Who are you?" he demanded.

"It's I, sir—Ruth," she replied. "Make me your wife according to God's law, for you are my close relative."

"It's true that I am a close relative, but there is someone else more closely related than I am. Stay here tonight, and in the morning I'll talk to him, and if he will marry you, fine; let him do his duty. But if he won't, then I will."

"Well, what happened, dear?" Naomi asked her when she arrived home. She told Naomi everything.

Naomi said, "Be patient until we hear what happens, for Boaz will settle it today."

Boaz went to the marketplace and found the relative he had mentioned. "I want to talk to you a minute."

They sat down together, then Boaz called for ten of the chief men of the village and asked them to sit as witnesses.

Boaz said to his relative, "You know Naomi, who came back to us from Moab. She is selling our brother Elimelech's property. I felt that I should speak to you about it so you can buy it if you wish. If you want it, let me know right away; for if you don't take it, I will. You have the first right to purchase it and I am next."

The man replied, "All right, I'll buy it."

Then Boaz told him, "Your purchase of the land from Naomi requires your marriage to Ruth so that she can have children to carry on her husband's name and to inherit the land."

"Then I can't do it," the man replied. "For her son would become an heir to my property, too; you buy it."

Boaz said to the witnesses and to the crowd standing around, "You have seen that today I have bought the property of Elimelech, Chilion, and Mahlon from Naomi, and that with it I have purchased Ruth the Moabitess, the widow of Mahlon, to be my wife, so that she can have a son to carry on the family name of her dead husband."

The people replied, "We are witnesses. May the Lord make this woman as fertile as Rachel and Leah, from whom all the nation of Israel descended! And may the descendants the Lord will give you be as numerous and honorable as those of our ancestor Perez, the son of Tamar and Judah."

So Boaz married Ruth, and the Lord gave her a son.

Naomi took care of the baby and the neighbor women said, "Now at last Naomi has a son again!" They named him Obed; he was the father of Jesse and grandfather of King David.[5]

SAMUEL Elkanah, of the tribe of Ephraim, had two wives, Hannah and Peninnah. Each year Elkanah and his families journeyed to the Tabernacle at Shiloh to worship the Lord. On the day he presented his sacrifice, Elkanah would celebrate by giving presents to Peninnah and her children; but although he loved Hannah very much, he could give her only one present, for she had no children. Peninnah made matters worse by taunting Hannah because of her barrenness.

One evening after supper Hannah went over to the Tabernacle. Eli the priest was sitting at his customary place beside the entrance. In deep anguish and crying bitterly, she prayed to the Lord. "O Lord of heaven, if you will look down upon my sorrow and answer my prayer and give me a son, I will give him back to you, and he'll be yours for his entire lifetime."

Eli noticed her mouth moving as she was praying silently and thought she had been drinking. "Must you come here drunk?" he demanded.

"Oh, no, sir!" she replied. "I am very sad and I was pouring out my heart to the Lord."

"In that case," Eli said, "may the Lord of Israel grant you your petition, whatever it is!"

"Oh, thank you," she exclaimed, and went happily back to take her meals again.

The family was up early the next morning and went to the Tabernacle to worship the Lord once more, then they returned home to Ramah. When Elkanah slept with Hannah, the Lord remembered her petition; in the process of time a baby boy was born to her. She named him Samuel, meaning "asked of God."

The next year Elkanah and Peninnah and her children went on the annual trip to the Tabernacle without Hannah, for she told her husband, "Wait until the baby is weaned, and then I will take him to the Tabernacle and leave him there."

"Whatever you think best," Elkanah agreed. "May the Lord's will be done."

She stayed home until the baby was weaned, then they took him to the Tabernacle in Shiloh, along with a three-year-old bull for sacrifice. After the sacrifice, they took the child to Eli.

"Do you remember me?" Hannah asked. "I am the woman who stood here praying to the Lord to give me this child, and now I am giving him to the Lord for as long as he lives." So she left him there at the Tabernacle for the Lord, and the child became the Lord's helper, for he assisted the priest.

The sons of Eli were evil men. They treated the people's offerings to the Lord with contempt.

Samuel, though only a child, wore a little linen robe just like the priest's. Each year his mother made a coat for him and brought it when she came with her husband for the sacrifice. Before they returned home, Eli would bless Elkanah and Hannah and ask God to give them other children to take the place of this one they had given to the

Lord. And the Lord gave Hannah three sons and two daughters. Meanwhile Samuel grew up in the service of the Lord.

Eli, now old, was aware that his sons were seducing young women who assisted at the entrance to the Tabernacle. "I have been hearing terrible reports from the Lord's people about what you are doing," Eli told his sons. "It is an awful thing to make the Lord's people sin." But they wouldn't listen.

One day a prophet came to Eli and gave him this message from the Lord: "Didn't I choose your ancestor Levi to be my priest, and to sacrifice upon my altar? And didn't I assign the sacrificial offerings to you priests? Then why are you so greedy for all the other offerings which are brought to me? Why have you honored your sons more than me? I, the Lord God of Israel, will put an end to your family so that it will no longer serve as priests. Every member will die before his time. To prove that what I have said will come true, I will cause your two sons, Hophni and Phineas, to die on the same day! Then I will raise up a faithful priest who will do whatever I tell him."

Messages from the Lord were very rare in those days, but one night after Eli had gone to bed and Samuel was sleeping in the Tabernacle near the Ark, the Lord called out, "Samuel! Samuel!"

"Yes?" Samuel replied, "what is it?" He jumped up and ran to Eli. "Here I am. What do you want?"

"I didn't call you," Eli said. "Go back to bed."

Then the Lord called again, "Samuel!" And again Samuel jumped up and ran to Eli. "Yes?" he asked. "What do you need?"

"No, I didn't call you, my son," Eli said. "Go on back to bed."

The Lord called the third time, and once more Samuel jumped up and ran to Eli. "Yes?" he asked. "What do you need?"

Then Eli realized it was the Lord who had spoken to the child. "Go and lie down and if he calls again, say, 'Yes, Lord, I'm listening.'" So Samuel went back to bed.

The Lord came and called as before, "Samuel! Samuel!" And Samuel replied, "Yes, I'm listening."

Then the Lord said, "I am going to do the dreadful things I warned Eli about. His sons are blaspheming God, and he doesn't stop them!"

Samuel stayed in bed until morning, then opened the doors of the Tabernacle as usual. He was afraid to tell Eli what the Lord had said.

But Eli called him. "My son," he said, "what did the Lord say to you? Tell me everything."

So Samuel told him what the Lord had said.

"It is the Lord's will," Eli replied; "let him do what he thinks best."

As Samuel grew, the people listened carefully to his advice. And all Israel from Dan to Beer-sheba knew that Samuel was going to be a prophet of the Lord.

At that time Israel was at war with the Philistines, and the Philistines defeated Israel. After the battle, Israel returned to their camp and their leaders discussed why the Lord had let them be defeated.

"Let's bring the Ark here from Shiloh," they said. "If we carry it into battle with us, the Lord will be among us and he will surely save us from our enemies."

So they sent for the Ark. Hophni and Phinehas, the sons of Eli, accompanied it into battle. When the Israelis saw the Ark coming, their shout of joy almost made the ground shake!

"What's going on?" the Philistines asked. When they were told the Ark of the Lord had arrived, they panicked. "God has come into their camp!" they cried out. "Who can save us from these mighty gods of Israel who destroyed the Egyptians with plagues? Fight as never before, Philistines, or we will become their slaves as they have been ours."

So the Philistines fought desperately—and Israel was defeated again. The Ark of God was captured, and Hophni and Phinehas were killed.

A man from the tribe of Benjamin ran from the battle and arrived at Shiloh with his clothes torn. Eli was waiting to hear news of the battle, for his heart trembled for the safety of the Ark. The messenger rushed to Eli and told him what had happened. When the messenger mentioned what had happened to the Ark, Eli fell backward from his seat and his neck was broken. He died, for he was old and fat.

The Philistines took the captured Ark to the temple of their idol Dagon in Ashdod. When the local citizens went to see it the next morning, Dagon had fallen to the ground before the Ark of Jehovah! They set him up again, but the next morning the same thing had happened. Then the Lord began to destroy the people of Ashdod and nearby villages with bubonic plague. The people exclaimed, "We can't keep the Ark of Israel here any longer. We will all perish along with our god Dagon."

They called a conference of the mayors of the cities. The decision was to take it to Gath. But when the Ark arrived at Gath, the Lord began destroying its people with the plague. So they sent the Ark to Ekron, but the people of Ekron summoned the mayors and begged them to send the Ark back to its own country.

The Philistines called their diviners and asked, "What shall we do about the Ark of God?"

They were told, "Don't be stubborn as Pharaoh and the Egyptians were. They wouldn't let Israel go until God had destroyed them with dreadful plagues. Build a new cart and hitch to it two cows that never have been yoked— and shut their calves away from them in the barn. Place the Ark on the cart and let the cows go wherever they want to. If they cross the border of our land into Beth-shemesh, you will know that it was God who brought this great evil upon us; if they return to their calves, we will know the plague was simply a coincidence."

These instructions were carried out and the cows went straight along the road toward Beth-shemesh; the Philistine mayors followed them as far as the border. People of Beth-shemesh were reaping wheat in the valley, and when they saw the Ark they went wild with joy! Many burnt offerings were offered to the Lord that day.

They sent messengers to Kiriath-jearim and told them the Philistines had brought back the Ark. The men of Kiriath-jearim took the Ark to the home of Abinadab and installed his son Eleazar to be in charge. The Ark remained there twenty years; during that time Israel was in sorrow because the Lord had seemingly abandoned them.

At that time Samuel said, "If you are really serious about wanting to return to the Lord, get rid of your foreign gods and your Ashtaroth idols. Obey only the Lord, then he will rescue you from the Philistines."

So they destroyed their idols of Baal and Ashtaroth and worshiped only the Lord.

Then Samuel told them, "Come to Mizpah, and I will pray to the Lord for you."

They gathered there and went without food all day as a sign of sorrow for their sins. At Mizpah, Samuel became Israel's judge.

When the Philistine leaders heard about the crowds at Mizpah, they mobilized their army and advanced. The Israelis were badly frightened. "Plead with God to save us!" they begged Samuel.

Samuel took a lamb and offered it to the Lord and pleaded with him to help Israel. Just as Samuel was sacrificing the offering, the Philistines arrived for battle, but the Lord spoke with a mighty voice of thunder and they were thrown into confusion. The Israelis chased them from Mizpah to Bethcar, killing them all along the way. Samuel took a stone and placed it between Mizpah and Jeshanah and named it Ebenezer, for he said, "The Lord has certainly helped us!" So the Philistines were subdued and didn't invade Israel again throughout the remainder of Samuel's lifetime.

Samuel continued as Israel's judge for the remainder of his life. He rode circuit annually, setting up his court first at Bethel, then Gilgal, and then Mizpah; and cases of dispute were brought to him from all the surrounding territory. Then he would come back to Ramah, his home.

In his old age, Samuel retired and appointed his sons as judges. Joel and Abijah, his oldest sons, held court in Beer-sheba; but they accepted bribes and were very corrupt in the administration of justice. Finally the leaders of Israel met to discuss the matter with Samuel. "Give us a king like all the other nations have," they pleaded.

Samuel was terribly upset and went to the Lord for advice. "Do as they say," the Lord replied, "for I am the one they are rejecting, not you. Ever since I brought them from Egypt, they have continually followed other gods. Do as they ask, but warn them about what it will be like to have a king!"

So Samuel told the people: "If you insist on having a king, he will conscript your sons, while others will be slave laborers forced to plow in the royal fields and harvest crops without pay. He will take your daughters from you and force them to cook and make perfumes for him. He will take away the best of your fields and vineyards and olive groves and give them to his friends. He will demand a tenth of your flocks. You will shed bitter tears because of this king you are demanding."

But the people refused to listen: "Even so, we want to be like the nations around us."[6]

PART
6
KINGDOM
GLORY

TALL, DARK, HANDSOME

Kish was a rich, influential man from the tribe of Benjamin. His son Saul was the most handsome man in Israel and was head and shoulders taller than anyone else in the land.

One day Kish's donkeys strayed away, so he sent Saul and a servant to look for them. They traveled through the hill country of Ephraim and the entire land of Benjamin but couldn't find them. Finally Saul said, "Let's go home; by now my father will be more worried about us than about the donkeys!"

But the servant said, "There is a prophet who lives in this city; let's go find him, and perhaps he can tell us where the donkeys are."

"All right," Saul agreed.

They started into the city where the prophet lived. As they were climbing a hill they saw some young girls going out to draw water and asked them whether the seer was in town.

"Yes," they replied, "stay on this road. He lives just inside the city gates. He just arrived back from a trip to take part in a public sacrifice up on the hill, so hurry."

They went into the city and saw Samuel coming toward them. The Lord had told Samuel the previous day, "About this time tomorrow I will send you a man from the land of Benjamin. You are to anoint him as the leader of my people. He will save them from the Philistines."

When Samuel saw Saul, the Lord said, "That's the man I told you about!"

Saul approached Samuel and asked, "Can you tell me where the seer's house is?"

"I am the seer!" Samuel replied. "Go on up the hill ahead of me and we'll eat together; in the morning I will tell you what you want to know and send you on your way."

Samuel took Saul and his servant into the great hall and placed them at the head of the table, honoring them above thirty special guests. Samuel instructed the chef to bring Saul the choicest cut of meat set aside for the guest of honor. "Go ahead," Samuel said. "I was saving it for you even before I invited these others!" After the feast they returned to the city.

At daybreak Samuel called, "Get up; it's time you were on your way!" Saul got up, and Samuel accompanied him to the edge of the city. Samuel told Saul to send the servant on ahead, then told him, "I have received a special message for you from the Lord."

Samuel took a flask of olive oil and poured it over Saul's head, kissed him on the cheek, and said, "The Lord has appointed you to be the king of Israel! When you leave me, you will see two men beside Rachel's tomb in the land of Benjamin; they will tell you that the donkeys have been found and that your father is worried about you.

"And when you get to the oak of Tabor, you will see three men coming toward you who are on their way to worship God at the altar at Bethel; one will be carrying young goats, another will have loaves of bread, and the third will have a bottle of wine. They will greet you and offer you two of the loaves, which you are to accept. After that you will come to Gibeath-elohim, known as 'God's Hill,' where the garrison of the Philistines is. As you arrive you will meet a band of prophets coming down the hill playing a psaltery, a timbrel, a flute, and a harp, and prophesying as they come.

"At that time the Spirit of the Lord will come mightily upon you, and you will prophesy with them and you will feel and act like a different person. From that time, your decisions should be based on whatever seems best under the circumstances, for the Lord will guide you. Go to Gilgal and wait there seven days for me, for I will be coming to sacrifice offerings. I will give you further instructions when I arrive."

All of Samuel's prophecies came true that day. When Saul and the servant arrived at the Hill of God, they saw the prophets coming toward them, and the Spirit of God came upon him and he too began to prophesy.

Samuel called a convocation of all Israel at Mizpah and gave them this message from the Lord: "I brought you from Egypt and rescued you from the nations that were torturing you. But you have rejected me and have said, 'We want a king instead!' All right, present yourselves before the Lord by tribes and clans."

Samuel called the tribal leaders together and the tribe of Benjamin was chosen by sacred lot. Then he brought each family of Benjamin before the Lord, and the family of the Matrites was chosen. And finally, the sacred lot selected Saul.

Then Samuel said to the people, "This is the man the Lord has chosen as your king. There isn't his equal in all of Israel!"

And the people shouted, "Long live the king!"

Then Samuel told the people the rights and duties of a king; he wrote them in a book and put it in a special place before the Lord. Then Samuel sent the people home.[1]

FLAWED COMMANDER

At this time Nahash led the army of the Ammonites against the Israeli city of Jabesh-gilead. The citizens of Jabesh asked for peace. "Leave us alone, and we will be your servants," they pleaded.

"All right," Nahash said, "but only on one condition: I will gouge out the right eye of every one of you as a disgrace upon all Israel!"

"Give us seven days to see if we can get help!" replied the elders of Jabesh. "If none of our brothers will come, we will agree to your terms."

When a messenger came to Gibe-ah, Saul's home town, and told the people about their plight, everyone broke into tears. Saul was plowing in the field, and when he returned to town he asked, "What's the matter?"

They told him about the message from Jabesh. The Spirit of God came strongly upon Saul and he took two oxen and cut them into pieces and sent messengers to carry them throughout Israel.

"This is what will happen to the oxen of anyone who refuses to follow Saul and Samuel to battle!" he announced. The people came to him as one man: there were three hundred thousand of them in addition to thirty thousand from Judah.

He sent the messengers back to Jabesh-gilead to say, "We will rescue you before tomorrow noon!"

Early the next morning Saul arrived, having divided his army into three detachments, and launched a surprise attack against the Ammonites and slaughtered them all morning. The remnant of their army was badly scattered.

Then Samuel said to the people, "Come, let us go to Gilgal and reconfirm Saul as our king."

They went to Gilgal and in a solemn ceremony crowned him king. Then they offered peace offerings to the Lord.

Saul sent the Israeli army in every direction against Moab, Ammon, Edom, and the Philistines. Wherever he turned, he was successful—he saved Israel from all who had been their conquerors.

Saul had three sons, Jonathan, Ishvi, and Malchishua; and two daughters, Merab and Michal. Saul's wife was Ahino-am. The general of his army was his cousin Abner. The Israelis fought with the Philistines throughout Saul's lifetime, and whenever Saul saw any brave young man he conscripted him into his army.

One day Samuel said to Saul, "I crowned you king of Israel because God told me to. Be sure that you obey him. Here is his commandment to you: 'I have decided to settle accounts with the nation of Amalek for refusing to allow my people to cross their territory when Israel came from Egypt. Now go and completely destroy the Amalek nation—men, women, babies, little children, oxen, sheep, camels, and donkeys.' "

Saul mobilized his army: two hundred thousand troops in addition to ten thousand men from Judah. The Amalekites were camped in the valley below them.

Saul butchered the Amalekites all the way to Shur, east of Egypt. He captured Agag, king of the Amalekites, but killed everyone else. However, Saul and his men kept the best of the sheep and oxen and lambs—they destroyed only what was worthless or of poor quality.

Then the Lord said to Samuel, "I am sorry that I made Saul king, for he has refused to obey me."

Samuel was so moved that he cried to the Lord all night. Early the next morning he went to find Saul. Someone said he had gone to Mount Carmel to erect a monument to himself and then gone to Gilgal. When Samuel finally found him, Saul greeted him cheerfully.

"Well, I have carried out the Lord's command!"

"Then what was all the bleating of sheep and lowing of oxen I heard?" Samuel demanded.

"The army spared the best of the sheep and oxen," Saul admitted, "but they are going to sacrifice them to the Lord, and we have destroyed everything else."

"Stop! Listen to what the Lord told me last night! When you didn't think much of yourself, God made you king of Israel. And he told you, 'Go and destroy the Amalekites until they are all dead.' Why didn't you obey the Lord?"

"I did what he told me to; I brought King Agag but killed everyone else. It was only when my troops demanded it that I let them keep the best of the sheep and oxen to sacrifice to the Lord."

"Has the Lord as much pleasure in your offerings as in your obedience? Rebellion is as bad as the sin of witchcraft, and stubbornness is as bad as worshiping idols. Now, because you have rejected the word of Jehovah, he has rejected you from being king."

"I have sinned," Saul finally admitted. "Yes, I have disobeyed the command of the Lord, for I was afraid of the people."

As Samuel turned to go, Saul grabbed at him to try to hold him back and tore his robe.

Samuel said, "See? The Lord has torn the kingdom from you. Nor will he change his mind, for he is not a man!"

Samuel went home to Ramah and never saw Saul again, but he mourned constantly for him.

Finally the Lord said to Samuel, "You have mourned long enough for Saul; now take a vial of olive oil and go to Bethlehem and find a man named Jesse. I have selected one of his sons to be the new king. Take a heifer with you to make a sacrifice to the Lord. Call Jesse to the sacrifice and I will show you which of his sons to anoint."

When he arrived at Bethlehem, the elders of the city came to meet him. "What is wrong?" they asked. "Why have you come?"

He replied, "All is well. I have come to sacrifice to the Lord. Purify yourselves and come with me to the sacrifice." And he performed the purification rite on Jesse and his sons, and invited them too.

When they arrived, Samuel took one look at Eliab and thought, "Surely this is the man the Lord has chosen!"

But the Lord said, "Don't judge by a man's face or height, for this is not the one. Men judge by outward appearance, but I look at a man's thoughts and intentions."

Then Jesse told his son Abinadab to step forward. But the Lord said, "This is not the right man either." In the same way all seven of his sons presented themselves to Samuel.

"The Lord has not chosen any of them," Samuel told Jesse. "Are these all there are?"

"Well, there is the youngest," Jesse replied. "But he's out in the fields watching the sheep."

"Send for him at once," Samuel said.

So Jesse sent for him. He was fine looking, ruddy-faced, with pleasant eyes. The Lord said, "This is the one; anoint him."

Samuel took the olive oil he had brought and poured it

upon David's head; and the Spirit of Jehovah came upon him and gave him great power from that day onward. Then Samuel returned to Ramah.[2]

TROUBADOUR

The Spirit of the Lord had left Saul, and instead a tormenting spirit filled him with depression and fear. Some of Saul's aides suggested a cure. "We'll find a good harpist to play for you whenever the tormenting spirit is bothering you," they said.

"All right," Saul said.

One of them said he knew a young fellow in Bethlehem, the son of a man named Jesse, who was not only a talented harp player but was handsome, strong, and had good judgment. "What's more," he added, "the Lord is with him."

So Saul sent messengers to Jesse, asking that he send his son David the shepherd. From the instant he saw David, Saul admired him, and David became his bodyguard.

Then Saul wrote to Jesse, "Please let David join my staff, for I am very fond of him." Whenever the tormenting spirit troubled Saul, David would play the harp and Saul would feel better.

"Because the Lord is my Shepherd,
I have everything I need!
He lets me rest in the meadow grass
and leads me beside the quiet streams.
He restores my failing health,
He helps me do what honors him the most.
Even when walking through the dark valley of death
I will not be afraid,
for you are close beside me, guarding, guiding all the way.
You provide delicious food for me
in the presence of my enemies.
You have welcomed me as your guest;
blessings overflow!
Your goodness and unfailing kindness shall be with me
*   all of my life,*

and afterwards I will live with you
forever in your home."

"The heavens are telling the glory of God,
they are.a marvelous display of his craftsmanship.
Day and night they keep on telling about God;
silent in the skies, their message reaches all the world.
God's laws are perfect—
they protect us, make us wise, and give joy and light.
God's laws are pure, eternal, just;
they are more desirable than gold.
For they warn us away from harm
and give success to those who obey them.
But how can I know what sins lurk in my heart?
Cleanse me from these hidden faults.
And keep me from deliberate wrongs,
then can I be innocent of some great crime.
May my spoken words and unspoken thoughts
be pleasing to you, my Rock and my Redeemer."[3]

DAVID AND GOLIATH

The Philistines mustered their army and camped between Judah and Ephes-dammim. Saul countered with a buildup of forces, so the Philistines and Israelis faced each other on opposite hills.

Then Goliath, a Philistine champion, came out of the ranks to face Israel. He was a giant, measuring over nine feet tall! He wore a bronze helmet, a two-hundred-pound coat of mail, bronze leggings, and carried a bronze javelin several inches thick, tipped with a twenty-five-pound iron spearhead. He shouted across to the Israelis, "Do you need a whole army to settle this? I will represent the Philistines, and you choose someone to represent you, and we will settle this in single combat! Send me a man who will fight with me!"

David had seven older brothers—the three oldest, Eliab, Abinadab, and Shammah, had already volunteered for Saul's army. David, on Saul's staff part-time, went back and forth to Bethlehem to help his father with the sheep. One day

Jesse said to David, "Take this roasted grain and these loaves of bread to your brothers. Give this cheese to their captain, and see how the boys are getting along."

David left the sheep with another shepherd and took off early the next morning. He arrived at the outskirts of the camp just as the Israeli army was leaving for the battlefield. David hurried out to the ranks to find his brothers. As he was talking with them, he saw Goliath step out from the Philistine troops and shout his challenge to Israel. The Israeli army began to run away.

"Have you seen the giant?" the soldiers were asking. "He has insulted the entire army of Israel. And have you heard about the reward the king has offered to anyone who kills him? The king will give him one of his daughters for a wife, and his whole family will be exempted from paying taxes!"

David talked to others to verify the report. "What will a man get for killing this Philistine? Who is this heathen that is allowed to defy the armies of the living God?" When it was realized what David meant, someone told King Saul and the king sent for him.

"Don't worry," David told him. "I'll take care of this Philistine!"

"Don't be ridiculous!" Saul replied. "You are only a boy, and he has been in the army since he was a boy!"

David persisted. "When I am taking care of my father's sheep, and a lion or a bear comes and grabs a lamb from the flock, I go after it with a club and take the lamb from its mouth. The Lord who saved me from the claws and teeth of the lion and the bear will save me from this Philistine!"

Saul finally consented. "All right, go ahead; and may the Lord be with you!"

Saul gave David his own armor—a bronze helmet and a coat of mail. David put it on and took a step or two. "I can hardly move!" he exclaimed, and took them off again. He picked up five smooth stones from a stream, put them in his shepherd's bag, and started across to Goliath.

Goliath walked towards David with his shield bearer ahead of him, sneering at this red-cheeked boy! "Am I a dog," he roared at David, "that you come at me with a stick?" And he cursed David by the names of his gods.

David shouted in reply, "You come to me with a sword and a spear, but I come to you in the name of the Lord of the armies of heaven and of Israel—the God whom you have defied. Today the Lord will conquer you and I will kill you, and then I will give the bodies of your men to the birds and the world will know that there is a God in Israel!"

As Goliath approached, David ran to meet him, and reaching into his shepherd's bag took out a stone, hurled it from his sling, and hit the Philistine in the forehead. The man fell on his face to the ground. David had no sword; he pulled Goliath's from its sheath and cut off his head. When the Philistines saw that their champion was dead they turned and ran.

The Israelis gave a great shout of triumph and rushed after the Philistines. Bodies of the dead and wounded Philistines were strewn all along the road. Then the Israeli army returned and plundered the deserted Philistine camp.[4]

JEALOUSY

David met Jonathan, the king's son, and there was an immediate bond of love between them; Jonathan swore to be a blood brother to him. King Saul now kept David at Jerusalem; Saul made him commander of his troops, an appointment applauded by the army and general public alike.

But something had happened when the victorious Israeli army was returning home after David killed Goliath. Women from the towns along the way were singing and dancing for joy. This was their song: "Saul has slain his thousands, and David his ten thousands!"

"What's this?" Saul said to himself. "Next they'll be making him king!" From that time, King Saul kept a jealous watch on David.

One day Saul said to David, "I am ready to give you my oldest daughter Merab as your wife. But first you must prove yourself to be a real soldier." For Saul thought, "I'll send him against the Philistines and let them kill him rather than doing it myself."

"Who am I that I should be the king's son-in-law?" David exclaimed. "My father's family is nothing!" But when the time arrived for the wedding, Saul married her to Adriel instead. In the meantime Saul's daughter Michal had fallen in love with David, and Saul was delighted.

"Here's an opportunity to see him killed by the Philistines!" Saul said to himself. To David he said, "You can be my son-in-law after all, for I will give you my youngest daughter. The only dowry I need is one hundred dead Philistines!"

David was delighted to accept the offer. Before the time limit expired, he and his men killed two hundred Philistines. So Saul gave Michal to him.

When the king realized how much the Lord was with David and how popular he was with the people, he grew to hate him more with every passing day. Whenever the Philistine army attacked, David was more successful against them than the rest of Saul's officers. So David's name became famous throughout the land.

Saul now urged his aides and his son Jonathan to assassinate David, but Jonathan begged him not to be against David. "He's never done anything to harm you," Jonathan pleaded. "He has always helped you in any way he could. Why should you now murder an innocent man?"

Finally Saul agreed, and vowed, "As the Lord lives, he shall not be killed."

Jonathan called David and told him what had happened. Then he took David to Saul, and everything was as it had been before. War broke out shortly after that and David led his troops against the Philistines and put to flight their entire army.

But one day as Saul was listening to David playing the harp, suddenly the tormenting spirit attacked him. He had his spear in his hand, and hurled it at David to kill him. But David dodged out of the way and fled into the night.

David went to Ramah to see Samuel and told him all that Saul had done. So Samuel took David with him to live at Naioth. When the report reached Saul that David was at Naioth, he sent soldiers to capture him. David fled from Naioth and found Jonathan.

"What have I done?" he exclaimed. "Why is your father determined to kill me?"

"Tell me what I can do," Jonathan begged.

David replied, "Tomorrow is the beginning of the celebration of the new moon. Always before, I've been with your father for this occasion, but tomorrow I'll hide in the field. If your father asks where I am, tell him that I asked permission to go home to Bethlehem for a family reunion. If he says, 'Fine!' then I'll know all is well. But if he is angry, then I'll know he is planning to kill me."

Jonathan told David, "I will talk to my father and let you know at once how he feels about you. If he is angry and wants you killed, then you can escape. May the Lord be with you as he used to be with my father. And remember, you must demonstrate the love and kindness of the Lord not only to me during my lifetime but also to my children after the Lord has destroyed all of your enemies."

So Jonathan made a covenant with David, and David swore to it with a curse against himself and his descendants should he be unfaithful to his promise. Jonathan loved him as he loved himself.

The next day Saul asked Jonathan, "Why hasn't David been here for dinner?"

"He asked me if he could go to Bethlehem to a family celebration," Jonathan replied.

Saul boiled with rage. "Do you think I don't know that you want this son of a nobody to be king in your place, shaming yourself and your mother? As long as that fellow is alive you'll never be king. Now go and get him so I can kill him!"

"But what has he done?" Jonathan demanded. "Why should he be put to death?"

Then Saul hurled his spear at Jonathan, intending to kill him. Jonathan left in fierce anger. The next morning, as agreed, Jonathan went out into the field and David came out from where he had been hiding. They sadly shook hands, tears running down their cheeks. Jonathan said, "Cheer up, for we have entrusted each other and each other's children into God's hands forever." So they parted, David going away and Jonathan returning to the city.

David escaped to the cave of Adullam, where his brothers and other relatives soon joined him. Then others began coming—those who were in trouble, such as being in debt, or merely discontented—until David was the leader of about four hundred men.

"Lord, I trust in you alone. Don't let my enemies defeat me. Rescue me because you are the God who always does what is right. Answer quickly when I cry to you; bend low and hear my whispered plea. Be for me a great Rock of safety from my foes. Yes, you are my Rock and my fortress; honor your name by leading me out of this peril. You alone are strong enough. You alone are my God; my times are in your hands.

"Rescue me from those who hunt me relentlessly. Let your favor shine again upon your servant; save me just because you are so kind! Oh, how great is your goodness to those who publicly declare that you will rescue them. You have stored up great blessings for those who trust and reverence you. Hide your loved ones in the shelter of your presence, safe from all conspiring men. Blessed is the Lord, for he has shown me that his never failing love protects me like the walls of a fort!" [5]

HOUNDED

One day news came to David that Philistines were at Keilah robbing the threshing floors. David asked the Lord, "Shall I go and attack them?"

"Yes, go and save Keilah," the Lord told him.

But David's men said, "We're afraid even here in Judah; we certainly don't want to go to Keilah to fight the whole Philistine army!"

David asked the Lord again, and the Lord again replied, "Go down to Keilah, for I will help you conquer the Philistines."

They went to Keilah and slaughtered the Philistines and confiscated their cattle, and so the people of Keilah were saved.

Saul learned that David was at Keilah. "Good!" he exclaimed, "We've got him now! For he has trapped himself in a walled city!"

Saul mobilized his army to march to Keilah and besiege David. But David learned of Saul's plan, and David and his men—about six hundred of them now—left Keilah and began roaming the countryside.

David now lived in the wilderness caves in the hill country of Ziph. One day near Horesh he received news that Saul was on the way to search for him.

Prince Jonathan went to find David; he met him at Horesh. "Don't be afraid," Jonathan reassured him. "My father will never find you! You are going to be the king of Israel, and I will be next to you." So the two renewed their pact of friendship.

"O Lord my God, many and many a time you have done great miracles for us, and we are ever in your thoughts. No one else can be compared with you; there isn't time to tell of all your wonderful deeds. It isn't sacrifices and offerings which you really want from your people; but you have accepted the offer of my lifelong service.

"Then I said, 'See, I have come, just as all the prophets foretold. And I delight to do your will, my God, for your law is written upon my heart!'

"Please, Lord, rescue me! Quick! Come and help me! Confuse them—all these who are trying to destroy me.

"I am poor and needy, yet the Lord is thinking about me right now! O my God, you are my Savior; come quickly, and save me. Please don't delay!"

Shortly afterwards Samuel died, and all Israel gathered for his funeral and buried him in his family plot at Ramah. Meanwhile, David went down to the wilderness.

Saul took his elite corps of three thousand troops and went to hunt him down. Saul camped along the road at the edge of the wilderness, but David knew of Saul's arrival and sent out spies to watch his movements.

David slipped over to Saul's camp one night to look around. "Any volunteers to go down there with me?" David asked.

"I'll go with you," Abishai replied. So David and Abishai went to Saul's camp and found him asleep, with his spear in the ground beside his head.

"God has put your enemy within your power," Abishai whispered. "Let me put that spear through him."

"No," David said. "Surely God will strike him down some day, or he will die in battle or of old age. But may it never be that I should kill the man chosen by God to be the king! We'll take his spear and water jug and get out."

David took the spear and the jug of water and they got away without anyone seeing them. They climbed the mountain slope opposite the camp until they were at a safe distance, then David shouted down to Abner and Saul, "Wake up, Abner!"

"Who is it?" Abner demanded.

"Well, Abner, you're a great fellow," David taunted. "Why haven't you guarded the king when someone came to kill him? You ought to die for your carelessness. Where is the king's spear and the jug of water that was beside his head?"

Saul recognized David's voice and said, "Is that you, David?"

David replied, "Yes. Why are you chasing me? What is my crime? You have driven me out of my home so that I can't be with the Lord's people, and you have sent me away to heathen gods. Must I die on foreign soil?"

Saul confessed, "I have done wrong. Come back home, and I'll no longer try to harm you; for you saved my life today."

"Here is your spear," David replied. "Let one of your young men come and get it. Now may the Lord save my life, even as I have saved yours today."

Saul said, "Blessings on you, David. You shall do heroic deeds and be a great conqueror."

Then David went away, and Saul returned home.

"O Lord, you have examined my heart and know everything about me. You know when I sit or stand. When far away you know my every thought. You chart the path ahead of me, and tell me where to stop and rest.

"This is too wonderful to believe! I can never be lost to your Spirit! I can never get away from my God! If I go up to heaven, you are there; if I go down to the place of the dead, you are there. If I ride the morning winds to the farthest oceans, even there your hand will guide me; your strength will support me. If I try to hide in the darkness, the night shines as bright as day.

"You made all the delicate, inner parts of my body, and knit them together in my mother's womb. Thank you for making me so wonderfully complex! It is amazing to think about. You were there while I was being formed in utter seclusion! You saw me before I was born and scheduled each day of my life before I began to breathe.

"How precious it is, Lord, to realize that you are thinking about me constantly! I can't count how many times a day your thoughts turn towards me.

"Search me, O God, and know my heart; test my thoughts. Point out anything you find in me that makes you sad, and lead me along the path of everlasting life." [6]

CHAOS AND CORONATION

The Philistines mustered their armies for another war with Israel. When Saul saw the vast army, he was frantic and asked the Lord what he should do. But the Lord refused to answer. Saul instructed his aides to try to find a medium so he could ask her what to do, and they found one at Endor.

Saul disguised himself by wearing ordinary clothing. He went to the woman's home at night, accompanied by two of his men. "I've got to talk to a dead man," he pleaded. "Will you bring his spirit up?"

"Are you trying to get me killed?" the woman demanded. "You know that Saul has had mediums and fortunetellers executed. You are spying on me."

But Saul took a solemn oath that he wouldn't betray her. Finally the woman said, "Well, whom do you want me to bring up?"

"Bring me Samuel," Saul replied.

When the woman saw Samuel, she screamed, "You've deceived me! You are Saul!"

"Don't be frightened!" the king told her. "What do you see?"

"I see a specter coming up out of the earth," she said.

"What does he look like?"

"He is an old man wrapped in a robe."

Saul realized it was Samuel and bowed low before him.

"Why have you disturbed me?" Samuel asked Saul.

"Because I am in deep trouble," he replied. "The Philistines are at war with us, and God has left me; so I have called for you to ask you what to do."

Samuel replied, "Why ask me if the Lord has become your enemy? He has taken the kingdom from you and given it to your rival, David. All this has come upon you because you did not obey the Lord. The Israeli army will be routed and destroyed by the Philistines tomorrow, and you and your sons will be here with me."

Saul fell full length upon the ground, paralyzed with fright. He was also faint with hunger, for he had eaten nothing all day. The woman said, "Let me give you something to eat for the trip back." She brought the meal to the king and his men and they ate it, then they went out into the night.

The Philistine army mobilized at Aphek, and the Israelis camped at the springs in Jezreel. The Philistine captains, leading their troops by battalions and companies, went to Jezreel.

The Philistines began the battle and the Israelis fled and were slaughtered wholesale on Mount Gilboa. The Philistines closed in on Saul and killed his sons Jonathan, Abinidab, and Malchishua. Then archers overtook Saul and wounded him badly. He groaned to his armor bearer, "Kill me with your sword before the Philistines capture and torture me." But his armor bearer was afraid to, so Saul took his own sword and fell upon the point of the blade, and it pierced him through. His armor bearer also fell upon his sword and died with him. So Saul, his armor bearer, his three sons, and his troops died together that day.

David and his men, when they heard the news, mourned

and fasted all day for Saul, his son Jonathan, and the men of Israel who had died. David composed a dirge for Saul and Jonathan, and afterwards commanded that it be sung throughout Israel.

David then asked the Lord, "Shall I move back to Judah?"

And the Lord replied, "Yes."

"Which city shall I go to?"

And the Lord replied, "Hebron."

So David and his men and their families all moved to Hebron. The leaders of Judah came to David and crowned him king of the Judean confederacy.

David heard that the men of Jabesh had buried Saul. He sent them this message: "May the Lord bless you for being so loyal to your king. I will be kind to you because of what you have done. Now I ask you to be my loyal subjects. Be like the tribe of Judah who have appointed me as their new king."

But Abner, Saul's commander-in-chief, had gone to Mahanaim to crown Saul's son Ish-bosheth as king. Ish-bosheth, forty years old, reigned in Mahanaim for two years; meanwhile David was reigning in Hebron.

One day General Abner led some of Ish-bosheth's troops to Gibeon, and General Joab led David's troops out to meet them. The two armies began to fight and by the end of the day Abner and the men of Israel had been defeated by the forces of David.

Joab's brothers, Abishai and Asahel, were also in the battle. Asahel could run like a deer, and he began chasing Abner. When Abner saw him, he called out, "Go after someone else!" But Asahel kept on coming.

Again Abner shouted, "Get away from here. I could never face Joab if I have to kill you!" But he refused to turn away, so Abner pierced him through with his spear; he stumbled to the ground and died.

Abner and his men retreated across the Jordan Valley, crossed the river, and traveled to Mahanaim. Joab and his men took Asahel's body to Bethlehem and buried him beside his father, then they traveled all night and reached Hebron at daybreak. That was the beginning of a long war between the troops of Ish-bosheth and of David.

Several sons were born to David while he was at Hebron. The oldest was Amnon, born to his wife Ahino-am. His second son, Chileab, was born to Abigail. The third was Absalom, born to Maacah. The fourth was Adonijah, born to Haggith. Then Shephatiah was born to Abital, and Ithream was born to Eglah.

Abner became a powerful leader among Ish-bosheth's troops. He took advantage of his position by sleeping with one of Saul's concubines. When Ish-bosheth accused Abner of this, Abner was furious.

"After all I have done for you and your father, is this my reward? May God curse me if I don't do everything I can to take away the kingdom from you and give it to David."

Abner consulted with the leaders of Israel and reminded them that for a long time they had wanted David as their king. "Now is the time!" he told them.

Then he went to Hebron and reported to David. Twenty men accompanied him, and David entertained them with a feast.

As Abner left he promised David, "When I get back I will call a convention of all the people of Israel. They will elect you as their king, as you've so long desired."

But just after Abner left, Joab and some troops returned from a raid. When Joab was told that Abner had just been sent away in peace, he rushed to the king. "What do you mean by letting him get away? He came to spy on us and plans to return and attack us!"

Joab sent messengers to catch up with Abner and tell him to come back. He returned with them, but David knew nothing about it. When Abner arrived at Hebron, Joab took him aside at the city gate as if to speak with him privately, then pulled out a dagger and killed him in revenge for the death of his brother.

When David heard about it, he declared, "I vow by the Lord that I and my people are innocent of this crime against Abner." King David accompanied the bier to the cemetery and wept at the graveside. Thus the nation understood that he was in no way responsible for Abner's death.

When King Ish-bosheth heard about Abner's death, he

was badly frightened. The command of the Israeli troops then fell to two brothers, Baanah and Rechab, captains of raiding bands. They arrived at King Ish-bosheth's home one noon as he was taking a nap, sneaked into his bedroom, and cut off his head. Taking his head with them, they fled across the desert and presented the head to David at Hebron.

"Look!" they exclaimed. "Today the Lord has given you revenge upon Saul and his entire family!"

But David replied, "How much more shall I do to wicked men who kill a good man in his own house? Shall I not demand your lives?" So David ordered his young men to kill them, and they did.

Then representatives of all the tribes of Israel came to David. "We are your blood brothers," they said. "Even when Saul was our king, you were our real leader. The Lord has said that you should be the shepherd and leader of his people."

So David made a contract before the Lord with the leaders of Israel at Hebron, and they crowned him king of Israel. He had already been king of Judah for seven years, since the age of thirty.[7]

DAVID'S CITY

David now led his troops to Jerusalem to fight against the Jebusites who lived there.

"You'll never come in here," they told him. "Even the blind and lame could keep you out!"

When the insulting message reached David, he told his troops, "Go up through the water tunnel into the city and destroy those Jebusites. The first man to kill a Jebusite shall be made commander-in-chief!" Joab was the first, so he became the general of David's army.

David lived in the fortress, and that area of Jerusalem is called the City of David. He extended the city out around the fortress while Joab rebuilt the rest of Jerusalem. And David became more and more famous and powerful.

Then King Hiram of Tyre sent cedar lumber, carpenters, and masons to build a palace for David. David now realized God wanted to pour out his kindness on Israel.

*"I will praise the Lord no matter what happens; I will
constantly speak of his glories and grace; I will boast of
all his kindness to me.*

*"Let all who are discouraged take heart. Let us praise
the Lord together, and exalt his name. For I cried to him
and he answered me! He freed me from all my fears.*

*"Others too were radiant at what he did for them; theirs
was no downcast look of rejection! This poor man cried
to the Lord—and the Lord heard him and saved him out
of his troubles. For the Angel of the Lord guards and rescues
all who reverence him.*

*"Oh, put God to the test and see how kind he is! See
for yourself the way his mercies shower down on all who
trust in him!*

*"If you belong to the Lord, reverence him; for everyone
who does this has everything he needs. Even strong young
lions sometimes go hungry, but those of us who reverence
the Lord will never lack any good thing.*

*"Sons and daughters, come and listen and let me teach
you the importance of trusting and fearing the Lord. Turn
from all known sin and spend your time in doing good.
Try to live in peace with everyone.*

*"For the eyes of the Lord are intently watching all who
live good lives, and he gives attention when they cry to
him. But the Lord has made up his mind to wipe out
even the memory of evil men from the earth.*

*"The Lord is close to those whose hearts are breaking;
he rescues those who are humbly sorry for their sins. The
good man does not escape all troubles—he has them too.
But the Lord helps him in each and every one.*

*"Calamity will surely overtake the wicked; but as for
those who serve the Lord, he will redeem them; everyone
who takes refuge in him will be freely pardoned."*[8]

NEW TABERNACLE

When the Philistines heard
that David had been
crowned king of Israel,
they tried to capture him. Philistines arrived and spread
out across the valley of Rephaim.

David asked the Lord, "Shall I fight against them? Will you defeat them for me?"

The Lord replied, "Yes, go ahead; I will give them to you."

So David went out and fought and defeated them. "The Lord did it!" he exclaimed. "He burst through my enemies like a raging flood."

But the Philistines returned and again spread out across the valley. When David asked the Lord what to do, he replied, "Don't make a frontal attack. Go behind them and come out by the balsam trees. When you hear a sound like marching feet in the tops of the balsam trees, attack! It will signify the Lord has prepared the way for you."

David did as the Lord had instructed and destroyed the Philistines. David's fame spread everywhere, and the Lord caused all the nations to fear him.

After David had consulted with his army officers, he addressed the assembled men of Israel:

"Since you think I should be your king and since the Lord has given his approval, let us send messages to our brothers throughout the land of Israel, including the priests and Levites, inviting them to join us. And let us bring back the Ark of our God. We have been neglecting it ever since Saul became king."

There was unanimous consent, so David summoned people from across the nation so they could be present when the Ark of God was brought from Kiriath-jearim.

Then David and all Israel went to bring back the Ark. It was taken from the house of Abinadab on a new cart. Uzzah and Ahio drove the oxen. David and all the people danced before the Lord with great enthusiasm, accompanied by singing and by zithers, harps, tambourines, cymbals, and trumpets.

But when they arrived at the threshing floor of Nacon, the oxen stumbled and Uzzah put out his hand to steady the Ark. Then the anger of the Lord flared out against Uzzah and killed him for doing this. David named the spot, "The Place of Wrath upon Uzzah."

David now asked, "How can I ever bring the Ark home?" So he carried it to the home of Obed-edom. It remained there for three months, and the Lord blessed Obed-edom and all his household.

David built several palaces for himself in Jerusalem; he also built a new Tabernacle to house the Ark of God and issued these instructions: "When we transfer the Ark to its new home, no one except the Levites may carry it, for God has chosen them for this purpose."

Then David summoned all Israel to Jerusalem to celebrate the bringing of the Ark into the new Tabernacle.

The priests and Levites underwent ceremonies of sanctification, then the Levites carried the Ark on their shoulders with its carrying poles, just as the Lord had instructed Moses. King David also ordered the Levite leaders to organize the singers into an orchestra, and they played joyously upon psaltries, harps, and cymbals. So the leaders of Israel took the Ark to Jerusalem with shouts of joy, the blowing of horns and trumpets, crashing of cymbals, and loud playing on the harps and zithers.

The Ark was brought into the Tabernacle David had prepared. He appointed certain Levites to minister before the Ark by giving constant praise and thanks to the Lord and by asking for blessings upon his people. At that time David began the custom of using choirs in the Tabernacle. Asaph was the director. They sang:

"Oh, give thanks to the Lord and pray to him,
Tell the peoples of the world about his mighty doings.
Sing to him; yes, sing his praises and tell of his marvelous works.
Glory in his holy name; let all rejoice who seek the Lord.
Seek the Lord; yes, seek his strength and seek his face untiringly.
Sing to the Lord, O earth; declare each day that he is the one who saves!
Show his glory to the nations! Tell everyone about his miracles.
For the Lord is great, and should be highly praised; he is to be held in awe above all gods.
The other so-called gods are demons, but the Lord made the heavens.

*Majesty and honor march before him, strength and glad-
ness walk beside him.*

*O people of all nations of the earth, ascribe great strength
and glory to his name!*

Yes, ascribe to the Lord the glory due his name!

*Bring an offering and come before him; worship the
Lord when clothed with holiness!*

*Tremble before him, all the earth! The world stands un-
moved.*

*Let the heavens be glad, the earth rejoice; let all the nations
say, 'It is the Lord who reigns.'*

*Let the vast seas roar, let the countryside and everything
in it rejoice!*

*Let the trees in the woods sing for joy before the Lord,
for he comes to judge the earth.*

*Oh, give thanks to the Lord, for he is good; his love
and his kindness go on forever.*

*Cry out to him, 'Oh, save us, God of our salvation;
bring us safely back from among the nations.*

*Then we will thank your holy name, and triumph in
your praise.'*

*Blessed be Jehovah, God of Israel, forever and forever-
more."*

And all the people shouted, "Amen!"[9]

NEW DYNASTY

When the Lord finally sent peace upon the land, David said to Nathan the prophet, "Here I am living in this beautiful cedar palace while the Ark of God is in a tent!"

"Go ahead with what you have in mind," Nathan replied, "for the Lord is with you."

But that night the Lord said to Nathan, "My home has been a tent ever since I brought Israel out of Egypt. And I have never complained to Israel's leaders. Now give this message to David:

" 'I chose you to be the leader of my people when you were tending sheep. I have been with you wherever you have gone, and I will make your name greater so that you will be one of the most famous men in the world! I have selected a homeland for my people where the nations won't bother them as they did when the judges ruled my people. Your descendants shall rule this land for generations to come! When you die, I will put one of your sons upon your throne and I will make his kingdom strong. He is the one who shall build me a temple. I will be his father and he shall be my son. If he sins, I will use other nations to punish him, but my love and kindness shall not leave him as I took it from Saul, your predecessor. Your family shall rule my kingdom forever.' "

So Nathan went back to David and told him everything the Lord had said.

Then David went into the Tabernacle and sat before the Lord and prayed, "O Lord, why have you showered your blessings on such an insignificant person as I? In addition to everything else, you speak of giving me an eternal dynasty! Such generosity is far beyond any human standard! Lord, you are doing these things because you promised to and you want to! How great you are, Lord! We have never heard of any other god like you.

"You revealed, O Lord of heaven, that I am the first of a dynasty which will rule your people forever; your words are truth—so do as you have promised! May our dynasty continue on and on, for you, Lord God, have promised it.

"O Lord our God, the glory of your name fills the earth and overflows the heavens. You have taught little children to praise you perfectly. May their example shame and silence your enemies!

"When I look up into the night skies and see the work of your fingers—the moon and the stars you have made— I cannot understand how you can bother with mere puny man, to pay attention to him! And yet you have made him only a little lower than the angels, and placed a crown of glory and honor upon his head.

"You have put him in charge of everything you made; everything is under his authority: all sheep and oxen, and wild animals too, the birds and fish, and all the life in the sea. O Jehovah, our Lord, the majesty and glory of your name fills the earth.

"What fools the nations are to rage against the Lord!

How strange that men should try to outwit God! A summit conference of the nations has been called to plot against the Lord and his Messiah. 'Come, let us break his chains,' they say, 'and free ourselves from this slavery to God.'

"But God in heaven is amused by their puny plans. And in fury he rebukes them. For the Lord declares, 'This is the King of my choice, and I have enthroned him in Jerusalem, my holy city.'

"His chosen one replies, 'I will reveal the everlasting purposes of God, for the Lord has said to me, "You are my Son. This is your Coronation Day. Today I am giving you your glory. Only ask, and I will give you all the nations of the world. Rule them with an iron rod." '

"O kings and rulers of the earth, listen while there is time. Serve the Lord with reverent fear; rejoice with trembling. Fall down before his Son and kiss his feet before his anger is roused and you perish. I am warning you. But oh, the joys of those who put their trust in him!

"Jehovah said to my Lord the Messiah, 'Rule as my regent—I will subdue your enemies and make them bow low before you.' "

After this David subdued the Philistines by conquering Gath, their largest city. He also devastated the land of Moab. He destroyed the forces of King Hadadezer of Zobah in a battle at the Euphrates River. David placed army garrisons in Damascus, and the Syrians brought him annual tribute money.

When King Toi of Hamath heard about David's victory over Hadadezer, he sent his son Joram to congratulate him. He gave David presents made from silver, gold, and bronze. David dedicated all of these to the Lord, along with the silver and gold he had taken from Syria, Moab, Ammon, the Philistines, Amalek, and King Hadadezer.

David reigned with justice over Israel. The general of his army was Joab, his secretary of state was Jehoshaphat, Zadok and Ahimelech were the High Priests, Seraiah was the king's private secretary, Benaiah was captain of his bodyguard, and David's sons were his assistants.

One day David began wondering if any of Saul's family

was still living, for he wanted to be kind to them as he had promised Prince Jonathan. He heard about a man named Ziba who had been one of Saul's servants, and summoned him. "Is anyone left from Saul's family? If so, I want to fulfill a sacred vow to him."

"Yes," Ziba replied, "Jonathan's lame son is still alive."

So King David sent for Jonathan's son. Mephibosheth arrived in great fear, bowing low before him.

David said, "Don't be afraid! I've asked you to come because of my vow to your father. I will restore to you all the land of your grandfather Saul, and you shall live here at the palace!"

Then the king summoned Ziba. "I have given your master's grandson everything that belonged to Saul and his family," he said. "You and your sons and servants are to farm the land for him, to produce food for his family; but he will live here with me."

From that time on, Mephibosheth ate regularly with King David as though he were one of his own sons. All the household of Ziba became Mephibosheth's servants.[10]

BATH-SHEBA The following spring, the season when wars usually began, Joab led the Israeli army in successful attacks against the cities and villages of Ammon. After destroying them, he laid siege to Rabbah. Meanwhile, David had stayed in Jerusalem.

One night he couldn't sleep and went for a stroll on the roof of the palace. As he looked over the city, he noticed a woman of unusual beauty taking her evening bath. He sent to find out who she was and was told that she was Bath-sheba, the wife of Uriah.

David sent for her and when she came he slept with her; then she returned home.

When she found that he had gotten her pregnant, she sent a message to inform him.

So David dispatched a memo to Joab: "Send me Uriah the Hittite." When he arrived, David asked him how the army was getting along, then told him to go home and relax. But Uriah didn't go there; he stayed that night at the gateway of the palace with the other servants of the king.

When David heard what Uriah had done, he summoned him and asked, "Why didn't you go home to your wife last night after being away so long?"

Uriah replied, "The Ark and the armies and the officers are camping in open fields, and should I go home to dine and sleep with my wife? I will never be guilty of acting like that."

"Well, stay here tonight," David told him, "and tomorrow you may return to the army."

The next morning David wrote a letter to Joab and gave it to Uriah to deliver. The letter instructed Joab to put Uriah at the front of the battle—and then pull back and leave him there to die!

So Joab assigned Uriah to a spot close to the besieged city where the enemy's best men were fighting; Uriah was killed along with several other Israeli soldiers.

Joab sent a report to David of how the battle was going. The messenger arrived at Jerusalem and gave the report. "The enemy came out against us," he said, "and as we chased them back to the city gates, the men on the wall attacked and some of our men were killed; and Uriah the Hittite is dead too."

"Tell Joab the sword kills one as well as another! Fight harder next time, and conquer the city."

When Bath-sheba heard that her husband was dead, she mourned for him. When the period of mourning was over, David brought her to the palace. She became one of his wives, and gave birth to his son.

The Lord, very displeased, sent the prophet Nathan to tell David this story:

"There were two men, one very rich, owning many flocks of sheep and herds of goats, and the other very poor, owning nothing but a little lamb he had managed to buy. It was his children's pet and he fed it from his own plate and let it drink from his own cup; he cuddled it in his arms like a baby daughter. Recently a guest arrived at the home of the rich man. Instead of killing a lamb from his own flocks for food for the traveler, he took the poor man's lamb and roasted it and served it."

David was furious. "Any man who would do a thing like that should be put to death; he shall repay four lambs to the poor man for the one he stole and for having no pity."

Then Nathan said, "You are that rich man! The Lord God says, 'I made you king of Israel and saved you from the power of Saul. I gave you his palace and the kingdoms of Israel and Judah; and if that had not been enough, I would have given you much more. Why, then, have you despised the laws of God and done this horrible deed? You have murdered Uriah and stolen his wife. Therefore murder shall be a constant threat in your family. Because of what you have done, I will cause your own household to rebel against you. You did it secretly, but I will do this to you in the sight of all Israel.'"

"I have sinned against the Lord," David confessed.

Nathan replied, "Yes, but the Lord has forgiven you, and you won't die for this sin. You have given great opportunity to the enemies of the Lord to despise him, so your child shall die."

And the Lord made Bath-sheba's baby deathly sick. David begged him to spare the child, and went without food. Leaders of the nation pleaded with him to eat, but he refused. On the seventh day the baby died. David's aides were afraid to tell him.

When David saw them whispering, he realized what had happened. "Is the baby dead?" he asked.

"Yes," they replied.

David got up, washed, changed his clothes, and went into the Tabernacle and worshiped the Lord. Then he returned to the palace and ate.

His aides were amazed. "We don't understand you. While the baby was still living, you wept and refused to eat; but now that the baby is dead, you have stopped your mourning."

David replied, "I fasted and wept while the child was alive, for I said, 'Perhaps the Lord will be gracious to me and let the child live.' But why should I fast when he is dead? Can I bring him back again? I shall go to him, but he shall not return to me."[11]

"HAVE MERCY"

"O loving and kind God, have mercy. Have pity upon me and take away the awful stain of my transgressions. Oh, wash me; cleanse me from this guilt. Let me be pure again. For I admit my shameful deed— it haunts me day and night. It is against you I sinned, and your sentence against me is just. I was born a sinner; yes, from the moment my mother conceived me. You deserve honesty from the heart; yes, utter sincerity and truthfulness.

"Sprinkle me with the cleansing blood and I shall be clean again. Wash me and I shall be whiter than snow. And after you have punished me, give me back my joy again.

"Create in me a clean heart, O God, filled with right desires. Restore to me again the joy of your salvation, and make me willing to obey you. Then I will teach your ways to other sinners, and they—guilty like me—will repent and return to you.

"O my God, you alone can rescue me. Then I will sing of your forgiveness, for my lips will be unsealed. You aren't interested in offerings burned before you on the altar—it is a broken spirit you want, remorse and penitence. A broken and a contrite heart, O God, you will not ignore. And when my heart is right, you will rejoice in the good that I do."

Then David comforted Bath-sheba. When he slept with her, she conceived, and gave birth to a son and named him Solomon. The Lord loved the baby, and sent blessings through Nathan the prophet. David nicknamed the baby Jedidiah, meaning "Beloved of Jehovah."

Meanwhile Joab and the Israeli army were ending their siege of Rabbah. Joab sent messengers to tell David: "Bring the rest of the army and finish the job." So David led his army to Rabbah and captured it. David took the crown of

Rabbah's king—a treasure made from solid gold set with gems—and placed it on his own head.[12]

HAVOC Prince Absalom, David's son, had a beautiful sister named Tamar. Prince Amnon, her half-brother, fell in love with her. He had no way of talking to her for the girls and young men were kept apart. But Amnon had a crafty friend—his cousin Jonadab. One day Jonadab said to Amnon, "What's the trouble? Why should the son of a king look so haggard morning after morning?"

Amnon told him, "I am in love with Tamar, my half-sister."

"Well," Jonadab said, "go back to bed and pretend you are sick. When your father comes to see you, ask him to let Tamar come and prepare some food for you."

So Amnon did. And the king sent word to Tamar to go to Amnon's quarters and prepare food for him. She did, but when she set the serving tray before him, he refused to eat!

"Everyone get out," he told his servants; so they left.

Then he said to Tamar, "Now bring me the food again in my bedroom and feed it to me." Tamar took it to him, but as she was standing there he grabbed her and demanded, "Come to bed with me."

"Oh, Amnon," she cried. "Don't be foolish! Don't do this to me! You know what a serious crime it is in Israel. Please, speak to the king about it, for he will let you marry me."

But he wouldn't listen, and since he was stronger than she, he forced her. Then suddenly his love turned to hate, and he hated her more than he had loved her.

"Get out of here!" he snarled.

"No, no!" she cried. "To reject me now is a greater crime than the other you did to me."

But he shouted for his valet and demanded, "Throw this woman out and lock the door behind her."

She was wearing a long robe with sleeves, the custom for virgin daughters of the king. She tore the robe, put ashes on her head, and went away crying.

When King David heard what had happened, he was very angry. Absalom said nothing to Amnon; however, he hated him because of what he had done.

Later, when Absalom's sheep were being sheared, Absalom invited his father and brothers to come to a feast.

The king replied, "No, my boy; if we all came, we would be too much of a burden."

Absalom kept urging the matter until the king let all of his sons attend.

Absalom told his men, "Wait until Amnon gets drunk, then at my signal kill him! I give the orders here, and this is a command."

So they murdered Amnon. The other sons of the king fled. As they were on the way to Jerusalem, the report reached David: "Absalom has killed all of your sons!"

The king ripped off his robe and fell prostrate to the ground. Just then Jonadab, the son of David's brother Shime-ah, arrived and said, "No, not all have been killed! It was only Amnon! Absalom has been plotting this ever since Amnon raped Tamar."

Absalom fled to King Talmai of Geshur and stayed there three years. Meanwhile David, reconciled to Amnon's death, longed for fellowship with his son.

When General Joab realized the king was longing to see Absalom, he sent for a woman of Tekoa who had a reputation for great wisdom and told her to ask for an appointment with the king. He told her what to say to him.

When the woman approached the king, she cried out, "O king! Help me!"

"What's the trouble?" he asked.

"I am a widow," she replied, "and my two sons had a fight out in the field, and one of them was killed. The rest of the family is demanding I surrender my other son to them to be executed for murdering his brother. But if I do that, I will have no one left."

"Leave it with me," the king told her; "I'll see to it that no one touches him."

"Please let me ask one more thing of you!" she said. "Why don't you do as much for all the people? You have convicted yourself in making this decision, because you have refused to bring home your own banished son. I know that you can discern good from evil. May God be with you."

"I want to know one thing," the king replied.

"Yes, my lord?" she asked.

"Did Joab send you here?"

"Yes, Joab sent me and told me what to say. He did it in order to place the matter before you in a different light."

So the king sent for Joab and told him, "All right, go and bring back Absalom. He may go to his own quarters, but I refuse to see him."

After Absalom had been in Jerusalem two years and had not yet seen the king, he sent for Joab to ask him to intercede. "I want you to ask the king why he brought me back if he didn't intend to see me. Let me have an interview with the king; then if he finds that I am guilty of murder, let him execute me."

So Joab told the king what Absalom said. At last David summoned Absalom, and he came and bowed low before the king, and David kissed him.[13]

REBELLION

Now no one in Israel was such a handsome specimen of manhood as Absalom, and no one else received such praise. He cut his hair only once a year—and then only because it was too much of a load to carry around! He bought a magnificent chariot and chariot horses, and hired fifty footmen to run ahead of him. He got up early every morning and went to the gate of the city; and when anyone came to bring a case to the king for trial, Absalom expressed interest in his problem.

He would say, "I see that you are right in this matter; it's unfortunate that the king doesn't have anyone to assist him in hearing these cases. I wish I were the judge; then anyone could come to me, and I would give him justice!"

When anyone came to bow to him, Absalom shook his hand instead! In this way Absalom stole the hearts of the people of Israel.

After four years, Absalom said to the king, "Let me go to Hebron to sacrifice to the Lord in fulfillment of a vow I made while I was at Geshur."

"All right," the king told him.

While Absalom was there, he sent spies to every part of Israel to incite rebellion against the king. "As soon as you hear the trumpets," his message read, "you will know that Absalom has been crowned in Hebron." He took two hundred men from Jerusalem with him, but they knew nothing of his intentions. While offering the sacrifice, he sent for Ahithophel, one of David's counselors. Ahithophel declared for Absalom, as did more and more others, so the conspiracy became very strong.

A messenger arrived in Jerusalem to tell King David: "All Israel has joined Absalom in a conspiracy against you!"

"Then we must flee at once," was David's response. "If we get out of the city before he arrives, both we and the city will be saved."

"We are with you," his aides replied.

So the king and his household set out. David paused at the edge of the city to let his troops move past to lead the way—six hundred Gittites who had come with him from Gath, and the Cherethites and Pelethites.

There was deep sadness throughout the city as the king and his retinue passed by, crossed Kidron Brook, and went out into the country. Abiathar and Zadok and the Levites took the Ark of the Covenant of God and set it down beside the road until everyone had passed. "If the Lord sees fit," David said, "he will bring me back to see the Ark and the Tabernacle again."

The king told Zadok, "Return quietly to the city with your son Ahima-az and Abiathar's son Jonathan. I will stop at the ford of the Jordan River and wait there for a message from you. Let me know what happens in Jerusalem."

So Zadok and Abiathar carried the Ark of God back into the city and stayed there.

David walked up the road that led to the Mount of Olives, weeping as he went. His head was covered and his feet were bare as a sign of mourning. The people with him covered their heads and wept as they climbed the mountain.

When someone told David that Ahithophel, his advisor, was backing Absalom, David prayed, "O Lord, please make Ahithophel give Absalom foolish advice!"

As they reached the top of the Mount, David found Hushai waiting for him. David told him, "Return to Jerusalem and tell Absalom, 'I will counsel you as I did your father.' Then you can counter Ahithophel's advice. Zadok and Abiathar are there. Tell them the plans that are being made to capture me, and they will send their sons to tell me what is going on."

"As the deer pants for water, so I long for you, O God. I thirst for God, the living God. Where can I find him to come and stand before him? Day and night I weep for his help, and all the while my enemies taunt me.

"Take courage, my soul! Do you remember those times when you led a great procession to the Temple on festival days, singing with joy, praising the Lord? Why then be downcast? Hope in God! I shall yet praise him again.

"I will meditate upon your kindness to this lovely land where the Jordan River flows and where Mount Hermon and Mount Mizar stand. All your waves and billows have gone over me, and floods of sorrow pour upon me like a thundering cataract. Yet day by day the Lord also pours out his steadfast love upon me, and through the night I sing his songs and pray to God who gives me life. I know that I shall again have reason to praise him for all that he will do. He is my help! He is my God!"

David's friend Hushai returned to the city, getting there just as Absalom arrived. He went immediately to see Absalom. "Long live the king!" he exclaimed.

"Is this the way to treat your friend David?" Absalom asked. "Why aren't you with him?"

"I work for the man who is chosen by the Lord and by Israel," Hushai replied.

Absalom turned to Ahithophel and asked him, "What shall I do next?"

"Give me twelve thousand men to start out after David tonight. I will come upon him while he is weary and discouraged, and he and his troops will be thrown into a panic. I

will kill only the king and let all those who are with him
live and restore them to you."

Absalom and the elders approved the plan, but Absalom
said, "Ask Hushai what he thinks about this."

"Well," Hushai replied, "this time I think Ahithophel has
made a mistake. Your father is an old soldier and isn't
going to be spending the night among the troops; he has
probably already hidden in some cave. And when he comes
out and attacks and a few of your men fall, then even the
bravest will be paralyzed with fear; for all Israel knows
what a mighty man your father is and how courageous
his soldiers are.

"I suggest you mobilize the entire army from as far away
as Dan and Beer-sheba so that you will have a huge force.
And I think you should personally lead the troops. Then
we can destroy his entire army. And if David has escaped
into some city, the army of Israel can take ropes and drag
the walls of the city into the nearest valley."

Absalom and the men said, "Hushai's advice is better
than Ahithophel's."

Then Hushai reported to Zadok and Abiathar what Ahithophel had said and what he himself had suggested instead.
"Find David and urge him not to stay at the Jordan River
tonight. He must go across into the wilderness beyond."

Ahithophel—publicly disgraced when Absalom refused
his advice—went to his home town, set his affairs in order,
and hanged himself.

Meanwhile, Absalom had mobilized the entire army of
Israel and was leading the men across the Jordan River.
Absalom had appointed Amasa as general, replacing Joab.
Amasa was Joab's second cousin.

David appointed regimental colonels and company commanders over his troops. A third were placed under Joab's
brother, Abishai, and a third under Ittai, the Gittite. And
the king commanded Joab, Abishai, and Ittai: "For my sake,
deal gently with young Absalom."

The battle began in the forest of Ephraim, and the Israeli
troops were beaten back. During the battle, Absalom came
upon some of David's men, and as he fled on his mule it
went beneath the thick boughs of a great oak tree, and

his hair caught in the branches. His mule went on, leaving him dangling in the air. One of David's men saw him and told Joab.

"What? You saw him there and didn't kill him?" Joab demanded. "Enough of this nonsense." He took three daggers and plunged them into the heart of Absalom. Then Joab blew the trumpet, and his men returned from chasing the army of Israel. They threw Absalom's body into a deep pit in the forest and piled a great heap of stones over it.

Then Joab said to a man from Cush, "Go tell the king what you have seen."

The man from Cush arrived and said, "I have good news for the king. Today Jehovah has rescued you from all those who rebelled against you."

"What about young Absalom? Is he all right?" the king demanded.

"May all of your enemies be as that young man is!"

The king broke into tears. "O my son Absalom, my son, my son Absalom. If only I could have died for you! O Absalom, my son."

There was much discussion across the nation: "Why aren't we bringing the king back? He saved us from our enemies; and Absalom, whom we made our king, is dead. Let's ask David to return and be our king again."

David sent Zadok and Abiathar the priests to say to the elders of Judah, "Israel is ready, and you are holding out. Yet you are my own tribe."

Then Amasa convinced the leaders of Judah, and they sent word to the king, "Return to us."

So the king started back to Jerusalem. When he arrived at the Jordan River it seemed as if everyone in Judah had come to escort him across the river! They all worked hard ferrying the king's household and troops across, and helped in every way they could. The men of Judah stayed with their king, accompanying him from the Jordan to Jerusalem.

"The Lord is my light and my salvation;
Whom shall I fear?
When evil men come to destroy me,
they will stumble and fall!

Yes, though a mighty army marches against me,
I am confident that God will save me.
The one thing I seek most of all
is the privilege of meditating in his Temple,
living in his presence every day of my life,
delighting in his perfections and glory.
There I will bring him sacrifices
and sing his praises with much joy.
My heart has heard you say,
'Come and talk with me, my people.'
And my heart responds,
'Lord, I am coming.'
You have been my help in all my trials;
don't leave me now.
If my father and mother should abandon me,
you would welcome and comfort me.
I expect the Lord to rescue me again,
so that I see his goodness in the land."[14]

GIANT ENEMIES

Once when the Philistines were at war with Israel, and David and his men were in the thick of the battle, David became exhausted. Ishbi-benob, a giant whose speartip weighed more than twelve pounds, closed in on David and was about to kill him. But Abishai came to his rescue and killed the Philistine. After that David's men declared, "You are not going out to battle again! Why should we risk snuffing out the light of Israel?"

Then Satan brought disaster upon Israel, for he made David decide to take a census.

The king said to Joab, commander-in-chief of his army, "Take a census of the people from one end of the nation to the other."

Joab replied, "God grant that you will live to see a hundred times as many people in your kingdom as there are now! But you have no right to rejoice in their strength."

But the king's command overcame Joab's remonstrance; so Joab and the other army officers went out to count the people of Israel. Having gone through the entire land, they completed their task in nine months and twenty days.

And Joab reported the number of the people to the king—800,000 men of conscription age in Israel, and 500,000 in Judah.

After he had taken the census, David's conscience began to bother him, and he said to the Lord, "What I did was very wrong. Please forgive this wickedness of mine."

The next morning the word of the Lord came to the prophet Gad, who was David's contact with God. "Go and tell David, 'The Lord has offered you three choices. You may have three years of famine, or three months of destruction by the enemies of Israel, or three days of deadly plague as the angel of the Lord brings destruction. Think it over and let me know what answer to return to the one who sent me.' "

"This is a terrible decision to make," David replied, "but let me fall into the hands of the Lord rather than into the power of men, for God's mercies are very great."

So the Lord sent a plague for three days. As the death angel was preparing to destroy Jerusalem, the Lord told him to stop.

When David saw the angel, he said, "I am the one who has sinned! Let your anger be only against me and my family."

Gad came to David and said, "Go and build an altar to the Lord on the threshing floor of Ornan the Jebusite." David went to do what the Lord commanded.

When Ornan saw the king coming, he fell on the ground. "Why have you come?" Ornan asked.

"To buy your threshing floor, so that I can build an altar to the Lord."

"Use anything you like," Ornan told the king. "Here are oxen for the burnt offering, and you can use the threshing instruments and ox yokes for wood on the altar. I will give it all to you."

But the king said, "No, I will buy it, for I don't want to offer to the Lord burnt offerings that have cost me nothing."

So David paid him for the threshing floor and the oxen, and built an altar there and offered burnt offerings and peace offerings. And the plague was stopped.

"I bless the holy name of God with all my heart. Yes, I will bless the Lord and not forget the glorious things he does for me.

"He forgives all my sins. He heals me. He ransoms me from hell.

"He surrounds me with lovingkindness and tender mercies. He fills my life with good things!

"He revealed his will and nature to Moses and the people of Israel.

"He is merciful and tender toward those who don't deserve it; he is slow to get angry and full of kindness and love.

"He has not punished us as we deserve for all our sins, for his mercy toward those who fear and honor him is as great as the height of the heavens above the earth. He has removed our sins as far away from us as the east is from the west.

"He is like a father to us, tender and sympathetic to those who reverence him. For he knows we are but dust and that our days are few and brief, like grass, like flowers, blown by the wind and gone forever.

"The lovingkindness of the Lord is from everlasting to everlasting to those who reverence him; his salvation is to children's children of those who are faithful to his covenant and remember to obey him!"[15]

PEERLESS SOLOMON

In his old age, King David was confined to his bed. About that time, David's son Adonijah decided to crown himself king in place of his aged father. He hired chariots and drivers and recruited fifty men to run before him as royal footmen. A very handsome man and Absalom's younger brother, he took General Joab and Abiathar the priest into his confidence, and they agreed to help him become king.

Adonijah went to En-rogel, where he sacrificed sheep, oxen, and young goats. Then he summoned other sons of King David and royal officials of Judah, requesting that they come to his coronation. But he didn't invite Nathan the prophet, Benaiah, the loyal army officers, or his brother Solomon.

Nathan went to Bath-sheba, Solomon's mother, and asked her, "Do you realize that Haggith's son, Adonijah, is now the king and that David doesn't even know about it? If you want to save your life and the life of your son, go at once to King David and ask him, 'My lord, didn't you promise me that Solomon would be the next king? Then why is Adonijah reigning?' And I'll come and confirm everything you've said."

So Bath-sheba went to the king's bedroom. Bath-sheba bowed low before him.

"What do you want?" he asked.

"My lord, you vowed to me that Solomon would be the next king. But instead, Adonijah is the new king, and he has celebrated his coronation by sacrificing oxen, goats, and many sheep, and has invited your sons and Abiathar the priest and General Joab. But he didn't invite Solomon. And now all Israel is waiting for your decision as to whether Adonijah is the one you have chosen to succeed you."

While she was speaking, the king's aides told him, "Nathan the prophet is here to see you."

Nathan came in and bowed before the king and asked, "My lord, have you appointed Adonijah to be the next king? Today he celebrated his coronation, and they are feasting and drinking and shouting, 'Long live King Adonijah!' Has this been done with your knowledge?"

"Call Bath-sheba," David said. She came back in and stood before the king. The king vowed, "I decree that your son Solomon shall be the next king, just as I swore to you before by the Lord God."

Bath-sheba bowed low and exclaimed, "Thank you, my lord."

"Call Zadok the priest," the king ordered, "and Benaiah."

When they arrived, he said, "Take Solomon and my officers to Gihon. Solomon is to ride on my personal mule, and Zadok the priest and Nathan the prophet are to anoint him there as king of Israel. Then blow the trumpets and shout, 'Long live King Solomon!' When you bring him back here, place him upon my throne as the new king; for I have appointed him king of Israel and Judah."

"Amen! Praise God!" replied Benaiah, and added, "May the Lord be with Solomon as he has been with you, and may God make Solomon's reign even greater than yours!"

Zadok, Nathan, Benaiah, and David's bodyguard took Solomon to Gihon, riding on King David's mule. Zadok took a flask of sacred oil from the Tabernacle and poured it over Solomon; and the trumpets were blown and all the people shouted, "Long live King Solomon!" Then they returned to Jerusalem, making a joyous celebration along the way.

Adonijah and his guests heard the commotion just as they were finishing their banquet. "What's going on?" Joab demanded.

While he was speaking, Jonathan, the son of Abiathar, rushed in. "King David has declared Solomon king!" Jonathan shouted.

Adonijah and his guests jumped up from the banquet table and fled in panic; they were fearful for their lives.

David summoned all his officials to Jerusalem—the political leaders, commanders of the twelve army divisions, other army officers, those in charge of his property and livestock, and all the other men of authority. He stood before them and addressed them as follows:

"My brothers and my people! It was my desire to build a temple in which the Ark of the Covenant of the Lord could rest—a place for our God to live in. I have collected everything that is necessary for the building, but God has told me, 'You are not to build my temple, for you are a warrior and have shed much blood.'

"Nevertheless, the Lord has chosen me to begin a dynasty that will rule Israel forever; he has chosen the tribe of Judah, and from among the families of Judah, my father's family; and from among his sons, the Lord took pleasure in me and has made me king over Israel. And from among my sons—he has chosen Solomon to succeed me on the throne of his kingdom. He has told me, 'I have chosen him as my son and I will be his father. And if he continues to obey my commandments I will make his kingdom last forever.' "

David turned to Solomon and said: "Here before the

leaders of Israel, the people of God, and in the sight of our God, I am instructing you to search out every commandment of the Lord so that you may continue to rule this good land and leave it to your children to rule forever. Solomon, my son, get to know the God of your fathers. Worship and serve him with a clean heart and a willing mind, for the Lord sees every heart and understands and knows every thought."

Then David gave Solomon the blueprint of the Temple and its surroundings. The king also passed on instructions concerning the work of various groups of priests and Levites. "Every part of this blueprint," David told Solomon, "was given to me from the Lord. And these groups of priests and Levites will serve in the Temple. Others with skills of every kind will volunteer, and the army and the entire nation are at your command."

Then King David turned to the assembly and said: "My son Solomon, whom God has chosen to be the next king, is still young, and the work ahead of him is enormous. Using every resource at my command, I have gathered as much as I could for building it—gold, silver, bronze, iron, wood, and great quantities of onyx, other precious stones, costly jewels, and marble. Because of my devotion to the Temple of God, I am giving all of my own treasures to aid in the construction. Now then, who will follow my example?"

Clan leaders, army officers, and administrative officers of the king pledged gold, foreign currency, silver, bronze, and iron. They also contributed great amounts of jewelry. Everyone was happy for this opportunity of service, and King David was moved with joy.

While still in the presence of the assembly, David expressed his praises to the Lord: "O Lord God of our father Israel, praise your name for ever and ever! Yours is the mighty power and glory and victory and majesty. Everything in the heavens and earth is yours, O Lord, and this is your kingdom. We adore you as being in control of everything. Riches and honor come from you alone, and you are the Ruler of all mankind.

"O Lord God of our fathers: Abraham, Isaac, and Israel!

Give my son Solomon a good heart toward God, so that he will want to obey you and will look forward to finishing the building of your temple, for which I have made these preparations."

Then David said to the people, "Give praise to the Lord your God!" And they did, bowing low before the Lord.

The next day they brought a thousand young bulls, a thousand rams, and a thousand lambs as burnt offerings to the Lord. They also offered drink offerings and many other sacrifices on behalf of all Israel. Then they feasted before the Lord with great joy.

As the time of King David's death approached, he gave this charge to his son Solomon:

"I am counting on you to be a strong and worthy successor. Obey the laws of God and follow all his ways; keep each of his commands written in the law of Moses so that you will prosper in everything you do.

"O God, help the king to walk in godliness. Help him to give justice to your people. May the mountains and hills flourish in prosperity because of his good reign. Help him to defend the poor and needy and to crush their oppressors.

"May the reign of this son of mine be as gentle and fruitful as the springtime rains upon the grass. May all good men flourish in his reign, with abundance of peace to the end of time. Let him reign from sea to sea, and from the Euphrates River to the ends of the earth. The kings of Tarshish and the islands—and those from Sheba and from Seba—all will bring their gifts. All will bow before him!

"Blessed be Jehovah God, who only does wonderful things! Blessed be his glorious name forever! Let the whole earth be filled with his glory. Amen."

Then David died, and was buried in Jerusalem. He had reigned over Israel for forty years, seven of them in Hebron and thirty-three in Jerusalem.

Solomon was now the undisputed ruler of Israel. He summoned the army officers and judges to Gibeon as well as the political and religious leaders. He led them up the hill to the old Tabernacle constructed by Moses—the bronze altar made by Bezalel still stood in front. Solomon and those he had invited assembled before it as he sacrificed 1,000 burnt offerings to the Lord.

That night God appeared to Solomon and told him, "Ask me for anything, and I will give it to you!"

Solomon replied, "O God, you have been so kind to my father David, and now you have given me the kingdom—this is all I want! Give me wisdom and knowledge to rule properly, for who is able to govern by himself such a great nation?"

God replied, "Because your greatest desire is to help your people and you haven't asked for personal wealth and honor, I am giving you the wisdom and knowledge you asked, and also such riches, wealth, and honor as no other king has ever had. And there will never again be so great a king in all the world!"

Solomon left the Tabernacle and went back to Jerusalem to rule Israel. He built up a force of 1,400 chariots and recruited 12,000 cavalry to guard the cities where the chariots were garaged. During Solomon's reign, silver and gold were as plentiful in Jerusalem as rocks on the road! And expensive cedar lumber was used like common sycamore!

King Solomon ruled the whole area from the Euphrates River to the land of the Philistines and down to the borders of Egypt. The conquered peoples of those lands sent taxes to Solomon and continued to serve him throughout his lifetime. All of Judah and Israel lived in peace and safety; and each family had its own home and garden.

Solomon's wisdom excelled that of any wise men of the East. He was the author of 3,000 proverbs and wrote 1,005 songs. He was a great naturalist, with interest in animals, birds, snakes, fish, and trees. Kings from many lands sent ambassadors to him for advice.[16]

PROVERBS

These are proverbs of King Solomon, David's son; he wrote them to teach his people how to live.

"How does a man become wise? The first step is to trust and reverence the Lord!

"Wisdom shouts in the streets for a hearing. She calls out to the crowds along Main Street, to the judges in their courts, and to everyone in all the land.

"Every young man who listens to me and obeys my instructions will be given good sense. If you want insight and discernment, and search for them as you would for hidden treasure, wisdom will be given to you, and knowledge of God himself.

"For the Lord grants wisdom! His every word is a treasure of knowledge and understanding. He grants good sense to the godly. He is their shield, protecting them and guarding their pathway. He shows how to distinguish right from wrong, how to find the right decision. Wisdom and truth will enter the very center of your being, filling your life with joy.

"Follow the steps of the godly and stay on the right path, for only good men enjoy life to the full; evil men lose the good things they might have had, and they themselves shall be destroyed.

"If you want favor with both God and man, trust the Lord completely. In everything you do, put God first, and he will direct you and crown your efforts with success.

"The man who knows right from wrong and has common sense is happier than the man who is immensely rich! Such wisdom is far more valuable than precious jewels. Wisdom is a tree of life to those who eat her fruit; happy is the man who keeps on eating it.

"Have two goals: wisdom—that is, knowing and doing right—and common sense. With them on guard you need not be afraid of disaster or the plots of wicked men, for the Lord is with you; he protects you.

"Drink from your own well, my son—be faithful and true to your wife. Rejoice in the wife of your youth. Let her charms and tender embrace satisfy you. Let her love alone fill you with delight.

"Take a lesson from the ants, you lazy fellow. For though they have no king to make them work, they labor hard all summer, gathering food for the winter. But you—all you do is sleep. And as you sleep, poverty creeps upon you like a robber and destroys you.

"Young man, obey your father and your mother. Take to heart their advice. Their counsel will keep you far away from prostitutes with all their flatteries. A prostitute will bring a man to poverty, and an adulteress may cost him his very life. Can a man hold fire against his chest and not be burned? So it is with the man who commits adultery. He shall not go unpunished for this sin; he destroys his own soul.

"The hope of good men is eternal happiness; the hopes of evil men are all in vain.

"The good shall never lose God's blessings, but the wicked shall lose everything. The good man gives wise advice, but the liar's counsel is shunned. The upright speak what is helpful; the wicked speak rebellion. The good influence of godly citizens causes a city to prosper, but the moral decay of the wicked drives it downhill.

"The evil man gets rich for the moment, but the good man's reward lasts forever. The good man finds life; the evil man, death.

"A beautiful woman lacking discretion and modesty is like a gold ring in a pig's snout.

"It is possible to give away and become richer! It is also possible to hold on too tightly and lose everything. Yes, the liberal man shall be rich! By watering others, he waters himself.

"A soft answer turns away wrath. Gentle words cause life and health.

"The man who tries to be good, loving, and kind finds life, righteousness, and honor.

"The rich and the poor are alike before the Lord who made them all.

"Teach a child to choose the right path, and when he is older he will remain upon it.

"Wine gives false courage; hard liquor leads to brawls; what fools men are to let it master them.

"Whose heart is filled with anguish and sorrow? Who is the man with bloodshot eyes and many wounds? It is the one who spends long hours in the taverns, trying out new mixtures. Don't let the sparkle and the smooth taste of strong wine deceive you. For in the end it bites like a poisonous serpent.

"Discipline your son, and he will give you happiness and peace of mind. Sometimes mere words are not enough—discipline is needed.

"Pride ends in a fall, while humility brings honor."[17]

TEMPLE OF JEHOVAH

Solomon decided the time had come to build a temple for the Lord and a palace for himself. This required 70,000 laborers, 80,000 stonecutters in the hills, and 3,600 foremen. Solomon sent an ambassador to King Hiram at Tyre requesting shipments of cedar lumber such as Hiram had supplied to David when he was building his palace.

"I am about to build a temple for the Lord my God," Solomon told Hiram. "It is going to be a wonderful temple because he is a great God. So send me skilled craftsmen—goldsmiths and silversmiths, brass and iron workers; weavers to make purple, crimson, and blue cloth; and skilled engravers to work beside the craftsmen who were selected by my father. Also send cedar trees, fir trees, and algum trees from the forests of Lebanon, for your men are without equal as lumbermen, and I will send my men to help them."

King Hiram replied, "Blessed be the God of Israel who made the heavens and the earth and who has given to David such a wise son to build God's Temple. I am sending you a master craftsman—my famous Huramabi! He is a brilliant man, the son of a Jewish woman from Dan in Israel; his father is from here in Tyre. He is a skillful goldsmith and silversmith, also does exquisite work with brass and iron, and knows all about stonework, carpentry, and weaving. And he is an expert in the dying of purple and blue linen and crimson cloth. He is an engraver besides, and an inventor! We will begin cutting wood from the Lebanon mountains, as much as you need, and bring it to you in log floats across the sea to Joppa, and from there you can take them inland to Jerusalem."

The Temple location was at the top of Mount Moriah, where the Lord had appeared to Solomon's father, and where the threshingfloor of Ornan the Jebusite had been. Construction began on the seventeenth day of April in the fourth year of King Solomon's reign.

The foundation was 90 feet long and 30 feet wide. A covered porch ran along the entire thirty-foot width of the house, with the inner walls and ceiling overlaid with pure gold! The roof was 180 feet high.

The main part of the Temple was paneled with cypress wood, plated with pure gold, and engraved with palm trees and chains. Beautiful jewels were inlaid into the walls. All the walls, beams, doors, and thresholds were plated with gold, with angels engraved on the walls.

Within the Temple at one end was the most sacred room—the Holy of Holies—thirty feet square. This was overlaid with the finest gold. The upper rooms were also plated with gold.

Within the innermost room, Solomon placed two sculptured statues of angels, and plated them with gold. They stood on the floor facing the outer room, with wings stretched wingtip to wingtip across the room. Across the entrance to this room he placed a veil of blue and crimson fine-spun linen, decorated with angels.

At the front of the Temple were two pillars 52½ feet high, topped by a 7½ foot capital flaring out to the roof.

He also made a bronze altar thirty feet long, thirty feet wide, and fifteen feet high. Then he forged a huge, round tank fifteen feet across. This tank was set on the backs of two rows of metal oxen. It held 3,000 barrels of water. Priests used the tank for their washing.

Carefully following God's instructions, he then cast ten gold lampstands and placed them in the Temple, five against each wall. He also built ten tables and placed five against each wall on the right and left. And he molded 100 solid gold bowls. Then he constructed a court for the priests, also the public court, and overlaid the doors of these courts with bronze. But in the Temple only gold was used. So the Temple was finally finished.

Then Solomon brought in the gifts dedicated to the Lord

by his father, King David. They were stored in the Temple treasuries.

Solomon summoned to Jerusalem all of the leaders of Israel for the ceremony of transferring the Ark from the Tabernacle to its new home in the Temple. As the leaders watched, Levites lifted the Ark, and with all the other sacred vessels, carried the Ark into the Holy of Holies—and placed it beneath the angels' wings.

The Levites were praising the Lord as the priests came out. The choir was accompanied by 120 priests who were trumpeters, while others played cymbals, lyres, and harps. The band and chorus united as one to praise and thank the Lord; their selections were interspersed with trumpet obbligatos, the clashing of cymbals, and the loud playing of other musical instruments—all praising and thanking the Lord. Their theme was "He is so good! His lovingkindness lasts forever!"

At that moment the glory of the Lord, coming as a bright cloud, filled the Temple.

Solomon was standing before the people on a platform in the center of the outer court, in front of the altar of the Lord. He knelt down, reached his arms toward heaven, and prayed:

"O Lord God, there is no God like you in all of heaven and earth. You are the God who keeps his kind promises to all who obey you and are anxious to do your will. Look down with favor day and night upon this Temple—this place where you have said that you would put your name. Listen to my prayers and to those of your people when they pray toward this Temple, and when you hear, forgive.

"When the skies are shut and there is no rain because of our sins, and then we pray toward this Temple and claim you as our God, and turn from our sins because you have punished us, then listen from heaven and forgive the sins of your people and send rain upon this land.

"And when foreigners hear of your power and come from distant lands to worship your great name and to pray toward this Temple, hear them from heaven and do what they request of you. Then all the peoples of the earth will reverence you, just as your people Israel do.

"If your people sin against you (and who has never sinned?) and you become angry with them and let their enemies defeat them and take them away as captives to some foreign nation, and if in that land of exile they turn to you again and plead with you with all their hearts to forgive them, then hear from heaven and help them.

"O my God, be attentive to all the prayers made to you in this place. And now, O Lord God, enter this resting place where the Ark of your strength has been placed."

As Solomon finished praying, fire flashed down from heaven and burned up the sacrifices! And the glory of the Lord filled the Temple. All the people fell flat on the pavement and worshiped.

For the next seven days, they celebrated the Tabernacle Festival, with large crowds coming in from all over Israel. A final religious service was held on the eighth day. Then Solomon sent the people home, joyful because the Lord had been so good to David and Solomon and to his people.

One night the Lord appeared to Solomon and told him, "I have heard your prayer. If I shut up the heavens so there is no rain, or if I command the locust swarms to eat up your crops, or if I send an epidemic among you, then if my people will humble themselves and pray, and search for me, and turn from their wicked ways, I will hear them from heaven and forgive their sins and heal their land. I will listen to every prayer made in this place, for I have chosen this Temple and sanctified it to be my home forever.

"As for yourself, if you follow me as your father David did, then I will see to it that you and your descendants will always be the kings of Israel. But if you refuse the laws I have given you, and worship idols, then I will destroy my people from this land which I have given them, and this Temple shall be destroyed, even though I have sanctified it for myself."

Then Solomon built his own palace, which took thirteen years to construct. One of the rooms was called the Hall of the Forest of Lebanon. It was huge—measuring 150 feet long, 75 feet wide, and 45 feet high. There were forty-five windows in three tiers, facing each other from three walls.

Another room was called the Hall of Pillars. It was 75 feet long and 45 feet wide, with a porch covered by a canopy which was supported by pillars. There was also the Throne Room or Judgment Hall, where Solomon sat to hear legal matters.

His cedar-paneled living quarters surrounded a courtyard behind this hall. (He designed similar living quarters, the same size, in the palace which he built for Pharaoh's daughter—one of his wives.) These buildings were constructed from huge stones, cut to measure.[18]

HOUSEKEEPING

"Unless the Lord builds a house, the builders' work is useless. Unless the Lord protects a city, sentries do no good.

"It is senseless to work from early morning until late at night, fearing you will starve to death; for God wants his loved ones to get their proper rest.

"Children are a gift from God; they are his reward. Children born to a young man are like sharp arrows to defend him. Happy is the man who has his quiver full of them."[19]

THE LOVERS

This song of songs was composed by King Solomon:

"Ah, I hear my beloved! Here he comes, leaping upon the mountains and bounding over the hills. My beloved is like a gazelle or young deer. Look, there he is behind the wall, now looking in at the windows.

"My beloved said to me, 'Rise up, my love, my fair one, and come away. For the winter is past, the rain is over and gone. The flowers are springing up and the time of the singing of birds has come. Yes, spring is here. The leaves are coming out and the grape vines are in blossom. How delicious they smell! Arise, my love, my fair one, and come away.'

"My beloved is mine and I am his. Before the dawn comes and the shadows flee away, come to me, my beloved, like a gazelle or a young stag on the mountains of spices."

"How beautiful you are, my love, how beautiful! Your
eyes are those of doves. Your hair falls across your face
like flocks of goats that frisk across the slopes of Gilead.
Your teeth are white as sheep's wool, newly shorn and
washed; perfectly matched. Your lips are like a thread of
scarlet—and how beautiful your mouth. Your cheeks are
matched loveliness behind your locks. Your neck is stately
as the tower of David, jeweled with a thousand heroes'
shields. Your breasts are like twin fawns of a gazelle, feeding
among the lilies. Until the morning dawns and the shadows
flee away, I will go to the mountain of myrrh and to the
hill of frankincense.

"My darling bride is like a private garden, a spring that
no one else can have, a fountain of my own. You are like
a lovely orchard bearing precious fruit, with the rarest of
perfumes: as myrrh and aloes, and every other lovely spice.
You are a well of living water, refreshing as the streams
from the Lebanon mountains."

"My beloved one is tanned and handsome, better than
ten thousand others! His head is purest gold, and he has
wavy, raven hair. His eyes are like doves beside the water
brooks, deep and quiet. His cheeks are like sweetly scented
beds of spices. His lips are perfumed lilies, his breath like
myrrh. His arms are round bars of gold set with topaz;
his body is bright ivory encrusted with jewels. His legs
are as pillars of marble set in sockets of finest gold, like
cedars of Lebanon; none can rival him. Such, O women
of Jerusalem, is my beloved, my friend.

"I adjure you not to awaken him until he please."[20]

SATED KING   It was twenty years since Solomon
had become king and the great build-
ing projects were completed. He
turned his energies to rebuilding the cities which King Hiram
of Tyre had given to him. He built supply centers and
constructed cities where his chariots and horses were kept.
He built to his heart's desire throughout the entire realm.

Then he went to the seaport towns of Ezion-geber and

Eloth to launch a fleet presented to him by King Hiram. These ships, with King Hiram's experienced crews working alongside Solomon's men, went to Ophir and brought back gold.

When the Queen of Sheba heard of Solomon's wisdom, she came to Jerusalem to test him with hard questions. A great retinue of aides and servants accompanied her, including camel-loads of spices, gold, and jewels. And Solomon answered all her problems.

When she discovered how wise he was and how breathtaking the beauty of his palace, she exclaimed, "Everything I heard about you is true! I didn't believe it until I saw it with my own eyes. Blessed be the Lord your God!"

She gave the king a gift of over a million dollars in gold, great quantities of spices of incomparable quality, and many, many jewels.

King Solomon gave the Queen of Sheba gifts of the same value as she had brought, plus everything else she asked for! Then she and her retinue returned to their own land.

Solomon married many girls, many of them from nations where idols were worshiped—even though the Lord had clearly instructed his people not to marry into those nations. He had seven hundred wives and three hundred concubines; and they turned his heart away from the Lord. They encouraged him to worship their gods instead of trusting completely in the Lord as his father had done. He even built a temple on the Mount of Olives, across the valley from Jerusalem, for Chemosh, the depraved god of Moab, and another for Molech, the vile god of the Ammonites. Solomon built temples for these foreign wives to use for burning incense and sacrificing to their gods.

Jehovah was very angry with Solomon about this. So the Lord said to him, "Since you have not kept our agreement, I will tear the kingdom away from you and your family and give it to someone else. However, for the sake of your father David, I won't do this while you are still alive. I will take the kingdom away from your son. And even so I will let him be king of one tribe, for David's sake and for the sake of Jerusalem, my chosen city."

Solomon of Jerusalem, King David's son, wrote:
There is a right time for everything,
a time to be born,
a time to die;
a time to plant,
a time to harvest;
a time to kill,
a time to heal;
a time to destroy,
a time to rebuild;
a time to cry,
a time to laugh;
a time to grieve,
a time to dance;
a time for scattering stones,
a time for gathering stones;
a time to hug,
a time not to hug;
a time to find,
a time to lose;
a time for keeping,
a time for throwing away;
a time to tear,
a time to repair;
a time to be quiet,
a time to speak up;
a time for loving,
a time for hating;
a time for war,
a time for peace.

And I know this, that whatever God does is final—nothing can be added or taken from it; God's purpose in this is that man should fear the all-powerful God.

I found that though God has made men upright, each has turned away to follow his own downward road.

Young man, it's wonderful to be young! Enjoy every minute of it! But realize that you must account to God for everything you do.

Don't let the excitement of being young cause you to forget your Creator. Honor him in your youth before the evil years come—when your limbs will tremble with age, and your teeth will be too few to do their work. And you will waken at dawn with the first note of the birds, but you yourself will be tuneless, with quavering voice. You will be white-haired, dragging along, standing at death's door.

Yes, remember your Creator now before the silver cord of life snaps and the dust returns to the earth as it was, and the spirit returns to God who gave it.

Here is my final conclusion: fear God and obey his commandments; for God will judge us for everything we do, including every hidden thing, good or bad.[21]

PART
7

KINGDOM
CALAMITIES

JEROBOAM A rebel leader, Jeroboam, came from the city of Zeredah in Ephraim. Solomon was rebuilding Fort Millo, repairing the walls of this city his father had built. Jeroboam was very able, and Solomon put him in charge of his labor battalions.

One day as Jeroboam was leaving Jerusalem, the prophet Ahijah met him and called him aside. Ahijah tore his robe into twelve parts and said to Jeroboam, "Take ten of these pieces, for the Lord God says, 'I will tear the kingdom from Solomon and give ten of the tribes to you! For Solomon has forsaken me. I will not take the kingdom from him now, however; I will take away the kingdom from his son. His son shall have the other so descendants of David will continue to reign in Jerusalem, the city I have chosen for my name to be enshrined. I will place you on the throne of Israel, and give you absolute power. If you listen to what I tell you and walk in my path, I will bless you, and your descendants shall rule Israel forever.' "

Jeroboam fled to Egypt and stayed there until the death of Solomon. Solomon reigned for forty years; he was buried in Jerusalem, and his son Rehoboam became the new king.[1]

SECESSION All the leaders of Israel came to She-chem for Rehoboam's coronation. Meanwhile, friends of Jeroboam sent word to him of Solomon's death. He was in Egypt at the time. He quickly returned and was present at the coronation, and led the people's demands on Rehoboam:

"Your father was a hard master," they said. "Be easier on us, and we will let you be our king!"

Rehoboam told them to return in three days for his decision. He discussed their demand with the old men who had counseled his father Solomon. "What shall I tell them?" he asked.

"If you want to be their king," they replied, "you will have to treat them with kindness."

He asked the opinion of the young men who had grown up with him. "What do you fellows think I should do? Shall I be easier on them than my father was?"

"No!" they replied. "Tell them: If you think my father was hard on you, just wait and see what I'll be like! I am going to be tougher."

When Jeroboam and the people returned to hear King Rehoboam's decision, he spoke roughly: "My father gave you heavy burdens, but I will give you heavier!"

When the people realized what the king was saying, they deserted him. "Forget David and his dynasty!" they shouted. "We'll get someone else to be our king. Let Rehoboam rule his own tribe of Judah! Let's go home!" So they did.

When King Rehoboam sent Hadoram to draft forced labor from the other tribes of Israel, the people stoned him to death. When this news reached Rehoboam, he mobilized the armies of Judah and Benjamin, 180,000 strong, and declared war against the rest of Israel in an attempt to reunite the kingdom.

But the Lord told Shemaiah the prophet, "Go and say to King Rehoboam and to the people of Judah and Benjamin, 'The Lord says: Do not fight against your brothers. Go home.'" They obeyed the Lord, and Rehoboam stayed in Jerusalem and fortified the cities of Judah with walls and gates.[2]

IDOLATRY

Jeroboam built the city of Shechem in the hill country of Ephraim, and it became his capital. Jeroboam thought, "Unless I'm careful, the people will want a descendant of David as their king. When they go to Jerusalem to offer sacrifices at the Temple, they will become friendly with King Rehoboam; then they will ask him to be their king."

So on the advice of his counselors the king had two gold calf-idols made, and told the people: "It's too much trouble to go to Jerusalem to worship; from now on these will be your gods."

One of the calf-idols was placed in Bethel and the other in Dan. He also made shrines on the hills and ordained priests from the rank and file of the people—who were not from the priest-tribe of Levi. Jeroboam also announced that the annual Tabernacle Festival would be held at Bethel, similar to the annual festival at Jerusalem; he himself offered sacrifices upon the altar to the calves at Bethel.

As Jeroboam approached the altar to burn incense to the golden calf-idol, a prophet of the Lord from Judah walked up to him. The prophet shouted, "O altar, the Lord says that a child named Josiah shall be born into the family line of David, and he shall sacrifice upon you the priests from the shrines on the hills who come here to burn incense." Then he gave his proof that his message was from the Lord: "This altar will split apart, and the ashes on it will spill to the ground."

The king shouted to his guards, "Arrest that man!" and shook his fist at him. Instantly the king's arm became paralyzed. At the same moment, a wide crack appeared in the altar and the ashes poured out.

"Oh, please," the king cried out, "beg the Lord your God to restore my arm again."

So he prayed to the Lord, and the king's arm became normal again.

Despite the prophet's warning, Jeroboam did not turn away from his evil ways; he made more priests than ever from the common people to offer sacrifices to idols in the shrines on the hills.

Jeroboam's son Abijah now became very sick. Jeroboam told his wife, "Disguise yourself so that no one will recognize you as the queen, and go to Ahijah, the prophet at Shiloh—the man who told me I would become king. Ask him whether the boy will recover."

So his wife went to Ahijah's home at Shiloh. He was old now and could no longer see. But the Lord told him the queen would come and told him what to tell her.

When Ahijah heard her at the door, he called out, "Come in, wife of Jeroboam!" Then he told her, "I have sad news for you. Give your husband this message from the Lord God. 'I promoted you from the ranks of the common people. I ripped the kingdom away from the family of David and gave it to you, but you have not obeyed my commandments as David did. You have made other gods with your gold calves. Since you have refused to acknowledge me, I will bring disaster upon your home and will destroy all of your sons—this boy who is sick and all those who are well.' "

Jeroboam's wife returned to Tirzah, and the child died just as she walked through the door of her home.

Meanwhile, Rehoboam was king in Judah. During his reign the people of Judah built shrines and idols on every high hill. There was homosexuality throughout the land, and the people of Judah became as depraved as the heathen nations.

Rehoboam married his cousin Mahalath. Later he married Maacah, the daughter of Absalom. The children she bore him were Abijah, Attai, Ziza, and Shelomith. Abijah was his favorite, and he intended to make him the next king.

King Shishak of Egypt attacked Jerusalem in the fifth year of Rehoboam's reign, with twelve hundred chariots, sixty thousand cavalrymen, and an unnumbered host of infantrymen. The prophet Shemaiah met with Rehoboam and the Judean leaders from every part of the nation and told them, "The Lord says, "You have forsaken me, so I have abandoned you to Shishak.' "

Then the king and the leaders confessed their sins and exclaimed, "The Lord is right in doing this to us!"

When the Lord saw them humble themselves, he sent Shemaiah to tell them, "I will not completely destroy you but you must pay annual tribute to him. Then you will realize how much better it is to serve me than to serve him!"

King Shishak conquered Jerusalem and took away the treasures of the Temple and of the palace. Even after Shishak's invasion, the economy of Judah remained strong.

King Rehoboam reigned seventeen years. He never did decide to please the Lord. When Rehoboam died, he was buried in Jerusalem, and his son Abijah became the new king.

Early in his reign, war broke out between Judah and Israel. Judah fielded 400,000 warriors against twice as many Israeli troops. When the army of Judah arrived in the hill country of Ephraim, King Abijah shouted to King Jeroboam and the Israeli army:

"Listen! Don't you realize the Lord swore that David's descendants would always be the kings of Israel? Your King Jeroboam is a servant of David's son, and was a traitor to his master. And you have driven away the priests of the Lord and appointed heathen priests instead.

"As for us, the Lord is our God and only the descendants of Aaron are our priests. The golden lampstand is lighted every night, for we are careful to follow the instructions of the Lord. So God is our Leader. His priests, trumpeting as they go, will lead us into battle."

Meanwhile Jeroboam had sent part of his army around behind the men of Judah, so Judah was surrounded. With the enemy before and behind them, they cried out to the Lord for mercy. Priests blew the trumpets, and Judah, depending upon the Lord, defeated Israel.

King Jeroboam never regained his power. Jeroboam reigned twenty-two years, and when he died, his son Nadab took the throne.

During Abijah's reign there was constant war between Israel and Judah. When he died he was buried in Jerusalem, and his son Asa reigned in his place.

Asa pleased the Lord like his ancestor King David. He executed male prostitutes and removed the idols his father had made. However, the shrines on the hills were not removed, for Asa did not realize that these were wrong.

In Israel, Nadab reigned two years. Not a good king, he worshiped many idols. Then Baasha, from the tribe of Issachar, plotted against him and assassinated him. He immediately killed all of the descendants of King Jeroboam.

There was continuous warfare between King Asa and King Baasha. Baasha reigned for twenty-four years, but all that time he followed the evil paths of Jeroboam in worshiping idols.

Elah, Baasha's son, began reigning during the twenty-sixth year of King Asa, but he reigned only two years. Then General Zimri, who had charge of half the royal chariot troops, plotted against him. One day Elah was half drunk at the home of the superintendent of the palace, in the capital city of Tirzah. Zimri walked in and struck him down and killed him. Then Zimri declared himself king.

But Zimri lasted only seven days; for when the army of Israel, which was then attacking the Philistine city of Gibbethon, heard that Zimri had assassinated the king, they decided on General Omri, commander-in-chief of the army, as their new ruler. Omri led the army to besiege Israel's capital. When Zimri saw the city had been taken, he went into the palace and burned it over him and died in the flames.

Omri began his reign in Tirzah, then bought the hill now known as Samaria from Shemer, and built a city on it. But Omri was worse than any of the kings before him. When Omri died, his son Ahab became king. King Asa of Judah had been on the throne thirty-eight years when Ahab became king of Israel.

Asa's Judean army was 300,000 strong, equipped with light shields and spears. His army of Benjaminites numbered 280,000, armed with large shields and bows. But he was attacked by an army of 1,000,000 troops from Ethiopia with 300 chariots.

"O Lord," he cried out to God, "we are powerless against this mighty army. Help us, Lord, for we trust in you alone to rescue us, and in your name we attack."

Asa and the army of Judah triumphed as the Ethiopians fled. The Ethiopian army was wiped out.

The Spirit of God came upon Azariah, son of Oded, and

he went to meet King Asa as he was returning from battle. "Listen to me, Asa! Listen, armies of Judah and Benjamin!" he shouted. "The Lord will stay with you as long as you stay with him! Whenever you look for him, you will find him. But if you forsake him, he will forsake you. In times of rebellion against God there was no peace, crime was on the increase, there were external wars and internal fighting of city against city. But keep up the good work and you will be rewarded."

When King Asa heard this, he destroyed all the idols in Judah and Benjamin and in the cities he had captured in the hill country of Ephraim. Asa even removed his mother Maacah from being the queen mother because she made an Asherah-idol.

In the thirty-ninth year of his reign, Asa became seriously diseased. He died in the forty-first year of his reign, and was buried in his vault hewn for himself in Jerusalem. His people made a great burning of incense for him at his funeral.

His son Jehoshaphat became king and mobilized for war against Israel. He followed in the footsteps of his father's early years, and did not worship idols. So the Lord strengthened his position as king.

In the third year he began a nationwide religious education program. He sent out government officials as teachers in all the cities of Judah. He also used Levites for this purpose. They took copies of the Book of the Law of the Lord to all the cities of Judah to teach the Scriptures to the people.

The fear of the Lord fell on surrounding kingdoms so that none of them declared war on Jehoshaphat. Even some of the Philistines brought him annual tribute, and Jehoshaphat built supply cities throughout Judah. His public works program was also extensive.[3]

THE AWESOME PROPHET

Ahab reigned for twenty-two years; he was more wicked than his father Omri. He married Jezebel, the daughter of King Ethbaal of the Sidonians, and began worshiping Baal. He built a temple and an altar for Baal in Samaria. Then he made other idols and did more to anger the Lord than any of the kings before him.

Elijah, the prophet from Tishbe, told King Ahab, "As surely as the Lord God of Israel lives—there won't be any dew or rain for several years until I say the word!"

Then the Lord said to Elijah, "Go to Cherith Brook east of where it enters the Jordan River. Drink from the brook and eat what the ravens bring you, for I have commanded them to feed you."

He did as the Lord told him and camped beside the brook. Ravens brought him bread and meat each morning and evening, but after awhile the brook dried up.

Then the Lord said, "Go and live in Zarephath, near Sidon. A widow there will feed you. I have given her my instructions."

As he arrived at the gates of the city, he saw a widow gathering sticks and asked her for a cup of water. As she was going to get it, he called, "Bring me a bite of bread, too."

She said, "I swear by the Lord your God that I haven't a single piece of bread in the house. And I have only a handful of flour left and a little cooking oil. I was gathering a few sticks to cook this last meal, then my son and I must die of starvation."

But Elijah said, "Don't be afraid! Cook that 'last meal,' but bake me a little loaf of bread first; and afterwards there will still be enough food for you and your son. For God says there will always be plenty of flour and oil in your containers until the Lord sends rain and the crops grow again!"

She did as Elijah said, and she and Elijah and her son continued to eat from her supply of flour and oil as long as it was needed. No matter how much they used, there was always plenty left in the containers.

It was three years later that the Lord said to Elijah, "Go and tell King Ahab that I will soon send rain again!" So Elijah went to tell him.

The man in charge of Ahab's household was Obadiah, a devoted follower of the Lord. Once when Queen Jezebel had tried to kill all of the Lord's prophets, Obadiah had hidden one hundred of them in two caves—and had fed them with bread and water.

That day, while Elijah was on the way to see King Ahab, the king said to Obadiah, "We must check every stream and brook to see if we can find enough grass to save at least some of my horses and mules. You go one way and I'll go the other."

So they did. Suddenly Obadiah saw Elijah coming toward him! Obadiah fell to the ground. "Is it really you, Elijah?" he asked.

"It is," Elijah replied. "Go and tell the king I am here."

Obadiah went to tell Ahab, and Ahab went out to meet him. "So it's you—the man who brought disaster upon Israel!" Ahab exclaimed.

"You're talking about yourself," Elijah answered. "For you and your family have refused to obey the Lord, and have worshiped Baal instead. Now bring all the people of Israel to Mount Carmel, with all 450 prophets of Baal and the 400 prophets of Asherah who are supported by Jezebel."

So Ahab summoned all the people and the prophets to Mount Carmel.

Then Elijah talked to them. "How long are you going to waver between two opinions? If the Lord is God, follow him! But if Baal is God, then follow him!

"Now bring two young bulls. The prophets of Baal may choose whichever one they wish and cut it into pieces and lay it on the wood of their altar, without putting any fire under the wood. I will prepare the other young bull and lay it on the wood on the Lord's altar, with no fire under it. Then pray to your god, and I will pray to the Lord; the God who answers by sending fire to light the wood is the true God!"

All the people agreed to this test. Then Elijah turned to the prophets of Baal. "Choose one of the bulls and prepare it and call to your god."

They prepared one of the young bulls and placed it on the altar; and they called to Baal all morning, shouting, "O Baal, hear us!" But there was no reply. Then they began to dance around the altar. About noontime, Elijah began mocking them.

"You'll have to shout louder than that to catch the attention of your god! Perhaps he is talking to someone, or maybe away on a trip, or is asleep and needs to be wakened!"

They shouted louder, and cut themselves with knives until blood gushed out. They raved until the time of the evening sacrifice, but there was no reply.

Then Elijah called to the people, "Come over here."

They all crowded around the altar of the Lord which had been torn down. He took twelve stones, one to represent each of the tribes of Israel, and used the stones to build the altar. Then he dug a trench around the altar. He piled wood upon the altar and cut the young bull into pieces and laid the pieces on the wood.

"Fill four barrels with water," he said, "and pour the water over the carcass and the wood."

After they had done this he said, "Do it again." And they did.

"Now, do it once more!" And they did; and the water ran off the altar and filled the trench.

At the customary time for offering the evening sacrifice, Elijah walked up to the altar and prayed, "O Lord God of Abraham, Isaac, and Israel, prove today that you are the God of Israel and that I am your servant; prove that I have done all this at your command. O Lord, answer me!"

Suddenly fire flashed down from heaven and burned up the young bull, the wood, the stones, the dust, and even evaporated all the water in the ditch!

When the people saw it they fell to their faces on the ground shouting, "Jehovah is God! Jehovah is God!"

Then Elijah told them to grab the prophets of Baal. They seized them all, and Elijah took them to Kishon Brook and killed them.

When Ahab told Queen Jezebel what Elijah had done, she sent this message to Elijah: "You killed my prophets, and now I swear that I am going to kill you by this time tomorrow night."

Elijah fled for his life to Beer-sheba, then on into the wilderness, traveling all day, and sat down under a bush and prayed that he might die. "I've had enough," he told the Lord. "Take away my life. I've got to die sometime, and it might as well be now."

Then he lay down and slept beneath the bush. As he was sleeping, an angel touched him and told him to get up and eat! He looked around and saw some bread baking on hot stones, and a jar of water! He ate and drank and lay down again.

Then the angel came again and said, "Get up and eat some more, for there is a long journey ahead of you."

He got up and ate and drank, and the food gave him strength to travel forty days and forty nights to Mount Horeb, the mountain of God, where he lived in a cave.

The Lord said to him, "What are you doing here, Elijah?"

He replied, "I have worked very hard for the Lord, but the people of Israel have broken their covenant with you and killed your prophets, and only I am left; and now they are trying to kill me, too."

"Go out and stand before me on the mountain," the Lord told him. As Elijah stood there, the Lord passed by, and a mighty windstorm hit the mountain; it was such a blast that the rocks were torn loose, but the Lord was not in the wind.

After the wind, there was an earthquake, but the Lord was not in the earthquake.

After the earthquake, there was a fire, but the Lord was not in the fire.

And after the fire, there was the sound of a gentle whisper. And a voice said, "Why are you here, Elijah?"

He replied again, "I have been working hard for the God of heaven, but the people have torn down your altars; they have killed every one of your prophets except me. And now they are trying to kill me, too."

Then the Lord told him, "Go back and anoint Jehu to be king of Israel, and anoint Elisha to replace you as my prophet. And incidentally, there are 7,000 men in Israel who have never bowed to Baal."

Elijah went and found Elisha who was plowing a field. Elijah went over to him and threw his coat across his shoulders and walked away.

Elisha ran after Elijah and said, "First let me go and say good-bye to my father and mother; then I'll go with you!"

Rich, popular King Jehoshaphat of Judah made a marriage alliance for his son with the daughter of King Ahab. Later he went to Samaria to visit Ahab, and King Ahab gave a great party for him and his aides. Then he asked King Jehoshaphat to join forces with him against Ramoth-gilead.

"Of course!" King Jehoshaphat replied. "My troops are at your command! However, let's check with the Lord."

King Ahab summoned his heathen prophets and asked, "Shall we go to war with Ramoth-gilead or not?"

They replied, "Go ahead, for God will give you a great victory!"

But Jehoshaphat wasn't satisfied. "Isn't there some prophet of the Lord around here too? I'd like to ask him the same question."

"Well," Ahab told him, "there is one, but I hate him, for he never prophesies anything but evil! His name is Micaiah."

The king called one of his aides. "Quick! Go and get Micaiah."

When he arrived the king asked, "Micaiah, shall we go to war against Ramoth-gilead or not?"

Micaiah replied, "In my vision I saw Israel scattered upon the mountain as sheep without a shepherd. And the Lord said, 'Their master has been killed. Send them home.'"

"Didn't I tell you?" the king of Israel exclaimed to Jehoshaphat. "He never prophesies anything but evil against me. Arrest this man and take him back to Governor Amon and to my son Joash," the king of Israel ordered. "Tell them to put this fellow in prison and feed him with bread and water until I return safely from the battle!"

Micaiah replied, "If you return safely, the Lord has not spoken through me."

The king of Israel and king of Judah led their armies to Ramoth-gilead. The king of Israel said to Jehoshaphat, "I'll disguise myself so that no one will recognize me, but you put on your royal robes!" That is what they did.

The king of Syria had issued these instructions: "Ignore

everyone but the king of Israel!" So when the Syrian charioteers saw King Jehoshaphat in his royal robes, they went for him, supposing he was the man they were after. But Jehoshaphat cried out to the Lord to save him, and the charioteers saw their mistake and stopped chasing him. But one of the Syrian soldiers shot an arrow haphazardly at the Israeli troops and it struck the king of Israel. The battle grew hotter, and King Ahab, propped up in his chariot, went back to fight the Syrians, but as the sun sank in the skies he died.

Ahaziah, Ahab's son, began to reign over Israel. He was not a good king, for he followed in the footsteps of his father and mother and of Jeroboam, who had led Israel into worshiping idols.

After King Ahaziah had fallen off the upstairs porch of his palace and was seriously injured, he sent messengers to the temple of Baal-zebub to ask whether he would recover.

An angel told Elijah the prophet, "Go meet the messengers and ask them, 'Is it true that there is no God in Israel? Is that why you are going to Baal-zebub, to ask whether the king will get well? Because King Ahaziah has done this, the Lord says he will never leave the bed he is lying on.'"

Ahaziah died as the Lord had predicted, and his brother Joram became the new king—for Ahaziah did not have a son to succeed him.

When Jehoshaphat died, he was buried in the cemetery of the kings in Jerusalem, and his son Jehoram became the new ruler of Judah. When Jehoram had become solidly established, he killed all of his brothers and many other leaders. Thirty-two years old when he began to reign, he was as wicked as the kings over in Israel; yes, as wicked as Ahab, for Jehoram had married one of the daughters of Ahab, and his whole life was one constant binge of evil. Jehoram constructed idol shrines in the mountains of Judah and compelled his people to worship them.

Then Elijah wrote him this letter: "The God of your ancestor David says that because you have not followed in the good ways of your father Jehoshaphat nor of King

Asa, and because you killed your brothers who were better than you, the Lord will destroy your children, your wives, and all that you have. You will be stricken with an intestinal disease."

The Philistines and the Arabs living next to the Ethiopians marched against Judah, broke across the border, and carried away everything of value in the king's palace, including his sons and his wives; only his youngest son escaped. After this Jehovah struck him down with the incurable disease. At the end of two years he died.[4]

A MIGHTY SUCCESSOR

The time came for the Lord to take Elijah to heaven. Elijah said to Elisha, "Please stay here, for the Lord has sent me to the Jordan River."

Elisha replied, "I swear to God that I won't leave you."

So they went on together and stood beside the Jordan River as fifty young prophets watched from a distance. Then Elijah folded his cloak together and struck the water with it, and the river divided and they went across on dry ground!

When they arrived on the other side, Elijah said to Elisha, "What wish shall I grant you before I am taken away?"

And Elisha replied, "Please grant me twice as much prophetic power as you have had."

"You have asked a hard thing," Elijah replied. "If you see me when I am taken from you, then you will get your request. But if not, then you won't."

As they were walking along, talking, suddenly a chariot of fire drawn by horses of fire appeared and drove between them, separating them, and Elijah was carried by a whirlwind into heaven.

Elisha saw it and cried out, "My father! My father! The Chariot of Israel and the charioteers!"

As they disappeared from sight, he tore his robe. Then he picked up Elijah's cloak and returned to the bank of the Jordan River, and struck the water with it.

"Where is the Lord God of Elijah?" he cried out. And the water parted and Elisha went across!

When the young prophets of Jericho saw what happened, they exclaimed, "The spirit of Elijah rests upon Elisha!"

The king of Syria had high admiration for Naaman, commander-in-chief of his army. He was a great hero, but he was a leper. Syrians had invaded Israel and among their captives was a girl who had been given to Naaman's wife as a maid.

One day the girl said, "I wish my master would go to the prophet in Samaria. He would heal him."

Naaman told the king what the girl said. "Go and visit the prophet," the king said. "I will send a letter of introduction for you." The letter said, "The man bringing this letter is my servant Naaman. I want you to heal him of his leprosy."

When the king of Israel read it, he tore his clothes and said, "He is only trying to get an excuse to invade us again."

When Elisha heard about the king of Israel's plight, he sent this message: "Send Naaman to me, and he will learn that there is a true prophet of God in Israel."

So Naaman arrived at the door of Elisha's home. Elisha sent a messenger out to tell him to wash in the Jordan seven times and he would be healed. Naaman, angry, said, "I thought at least he would come out and talk to me! Aren't the Abana River and Pharpar River of Damascus better than all the rivers of Israel?"

But his officers said, "You should certainly obey him when he says simply to go and wash."

So Naaman went down to the Jordan and dipped himself seven times, and his flesh became as healthy as a little child's! Then he went back to the prophet and said, "I know at last that there is no God except in Israel."

When the king of Syria was at war with Israel, he said to his officers, "We will mobilize our forces at ———" (naming the place).

Immediately Elisha warned the king of Israel, "Don't go near ———" (naming the same place) "for the Syrians are planning to mobilize their troops there!"

The king sent a scout to see if Elisha was right, and

sure enough, he had saved him from disaster. This happened several times.

The king of Syria was puzzled. He called together his officers and demanded, "Which of you is the traitor? Who has been informing Israel about my plans?"

"It's not us, sir," one of the officers replied. "Elisha, the prophet, tells the king of Israel even the words you speak in the privacy of your bedroom!"

"Go and find out where he is, and we'll send troops to seize him," the king exclaimed.

And the report came back, "Elisha is at Dothan."

So the king of Syria sent a great army with many chariots and horses to surround the city. When the prophet's servant got up early the next morning and went outside, there were troops, horses, and chariots everywhere.

"Alas, my master, what shall we do now?" he cried out to Elisha.

"Don't be afraid!" Elisha told him. "For our army is bigger than theirs!"

Then Elisha prayed, "Lord, open his eyes and let him see!" And the Lord opened the young man's eyes so that he could see horses of fire and chariots of fire everywhere upon the mountain!

As the Syrian army advanced upon them, Elisha prayed, "Lord, please make them blind." And he did.

Then Elisha went out and told them, "You've come the wrong way! This isn't the right city! Follow me and I will take you to the man you're looking for." And he led them to Samaria!

As soon as they arrived Elisha prayed, "Lord, now open their eyes and let them see." And the Lord did, and they discovered that they were in Samaria, the capital city of Israel!

When the king of Israel saw them, he shouted to Elisha, "Shall I kill them?"

"Of course not!" Elisha told him. "Do we kill prisoners of war? Give them food and drink and send them home again."

So the king made a great feast for them, and then sent

them home to their king. After that the Syrian raiders stayed away from Israel.

The people of Jerusalem chose Ahaziah as their new king. His mother was Athaliah, granddaughter of King Omri of Israel. He was an evil king, as all King Ahab's descendants were. He joined King Joram of Israel, son of Ahab, in war against Hazael, the king of Syria, at Ramoth-gilead. King Joram was wounded in the battle, so he went to Jezreel to rest and recover from his wounds. While he was there, King Ahaziah came to visit him.

Meanwhile Elisha summoned one of the young prophets. "Go to Ramoth-gilead," he told him. "Take this vial of oil with you, and find Jehu. Call him into a private room away from his friends, and pour the oil over his head. Tell him the Lord has anointed him to be king of Israel."

The prophet arrived in Ramoth-gilead and found Jehu sitting with other army officers. "I have a message for you, sir," he said.

Jehu left the others and went into the house, and the young man poured the oil over his head and said, "The Lord God says, 'I anoint you king of Israel. You are to destroy the family of Ahab; you will avenge the murder of my prophets and of all my other people who were killed by Jezebel."

Jehu went back to his friends and told them what the man had said. They quickly carpeted the bare steps with their coats and blew a trumpet, shouting, "Jehu is king!"

Jehu jumped into a chariot and rode to Jezreel to find King Joram. The watchman on the tower saw Jehu and his company approaching and shouted, "Someone is coming. It must be Jehu, for he is driving so furiously."

"Quick! Get my chariot ready!" King Joram commanded. Then he and King Ahaziah rode out to meet Jehu. King Joram demanded, "Do you come as a friend, Jehu?"

"How can there be friendship as long as the evils of your mother Jezebel are all around us?"

King Joram reined the chariot horses around and fled. Then Jehu drew his bow and shot Joram between the shoulders; the arrow pierced his heart and he sank down dead in his chariot.

King Ahaziah had fled along the road to Beth-haggan. Jehu rode after him, shouting, "Shoot him, too."

They shot him; he was able to go on as far as Megiddo, but died there. His officials took him to Jerusalem where they buried him in the royal cemetery.

When Jezebel heard that Jehu had come to Jezreel, she painted her eyelids and fixed her hair and sat at a window. When Jehu entered the gate of the palace, she shouted at him, "You murderer! You son of a Zimri who murdered his master!"

He saw her at the window and shouted, "Who is on my side?"

Two or three eunuchs looked out at him.

"Throw her down!" he yelled.

So they threw her out the window, and her blood spattered against the wall, and she was trampled by the horses' hoofs.

But Jehu didn't follow the Lord with all his heart; he continued to worship Jeroboam's gold calves. When Jehu died, he was buried in Samaria; his son Jehoahaz became the new king.[5]

PLOWSHARES INTO SWORDS

This message came from the Lord to Joel:

Listen, aged men of Israel! In all your lifetime, have you heard of such a thing as I am going to tell you? In years to come, pass the story down from generation to generation.

A vast army of locusts covers the land. They have ruined vines and stripped fig trees, leaving trunks and branches white and bare. Gone are the offerings of grain and wine to bring to the Temple of the Lord; the priests are starving. Sorrow and sadness are everywhere. Seed rots in the ground; barns and granaries are empty; cattle groan with hunger; sheep bleat in misery; creeks are dry and pastures are scorched.

Sound the alarm in Jerusalem! The day of the Lord's judgment approaches. It is a day of darkness and gloom.

A mighty army covers the mountains. The likes have not been seen before; fire goes before them and follows them on every side! They look like tiny horses, and they run as fast. Listen to the noise they make, like the rumbling of chariots, and like a mighty army moving into battle. The earth quakes before them and the heavens tremble. The sun and moon are obscured and the stars are hid.

The day of judgment is a terrible thing—who can endure it? That is why the Lord says, "Turn to me now, while there is time. Give me your hearts." Return to the Lord your God, for he is gracious and merciful. Perhaps yet he will give you a blessing instead of his curse. Perhaps you can offer your grain and wine to the Lord as before!

Sound the trumpet in Zion! Call a fast and gather all the people for a solemn meeting. The priests will stand between the people and the altar, weeping; and they will pray, "Spare your people, O our God; don't let them be disgraced by the taunts, 'Where is this God of theirs? How weak and helpless he must be!'"

Then the Lord will pity his people and reply, "See, I am sending you corn and wine and oil, to fully satisfy your need. No longer will I make you a laughingstock among the nations. I will remove these armies from the north; half shall be driven into the Dead Sea and the rest into the Mediterranean.

"Rejoice, O Jerusalem, for the rains are tokens of forgiveness. Once more the autumn rains will come, as well as those of spring. Threshing floors will pile high again with wheat, and the presses overflow with olive oil and wine. I will give you back the crops the locusts ate—my great destroying army that I sent against you. And you will know that I am here among my people and that I alone am your God.

"After I have poured out my rains again, I will pour out my Spirit upon all of you! Your sons and daughters will prophesy; your old men will dream dreams, and your young men see visions. I will put strange symbols in the earth and sky—blood and fire and pillars of smoke. The sun will be turned into darkness and the moon to blood before the great and terrible Day of the Lord shall come. Everyone who calls upon the name of the Lord will be saved.

"At that time, when I restore the prosperity of Judah and Jerusalem," says the Lord, "I will gather the armies of the world into the 'Valley Where Jehovah Judges' and punish them there for harming my people. I will bring them back from all the places you have sold them to."

Announce this far and wide: Get ready for war! Melt your plowshares into swords and beat your pruning hooks into spears. Come, all nations everywhere.

Multitudes, multitudes waiting in the valley for the verdict of their doom! For the Day of the Lord is near in the Valley of Judgment.

The Lord shouts from his Temple in Jerusalem, and the earth and sky begin to shake. But to his people Israel, the Lord will be very gentle. "Then you shall know at last that I am your God in Zion, my holy mountain. Jerusalem shall be mine forever; the time will come when no foreign armies will pass through her any more."[6]

CAULDRON When Athaliah, the mother of King Ahaziah of Judah, learned that her son was dead, she killed all of his children, except for his year-old son Joash. Joash was rescued by his Aunt Jehosheba, a sister of Ahaziah. She hid him and his nurse in a storeroom of the Temple. They lived there for six years while Athaliah reigned as queen.

In the seventh year, Jehoiada the priest took some of the army officers into his confidence. These men traveled across the nation secretly to tell the Levites and clan leaders about his plans and to summon them to Jerusalem. On arrival they swore allegiance to the young king who was hiding at the Temple.

"At last the time has come for the king's son to reign!" Jehoiada exclaimed. "The Lord's promise—that a descendant of King David shall be our king—will be true again."

Jehoiada issued spears and shields to the army officers—these had once belonged to King David and were stored in the Temple. The officers formed a line in front of the

Temple and around the altar in the outer court. Then they brought out the little prince, placed the crown upon his head, and handed him a copy of the law of God and proclaimed him king.

A great shout went up, "Long live the king!" as Jehoiada and his sons anointed him.

When Queen Athaliah heard the commotion, she rushed over to the Temple to see what was going on. There stood the king by his pillar at the entrance with army officers and trumpeters surrounding him, and people from all over the land rejoicing and singers singing, accompanied by an orchestra leading the people in a great psalm of praise.

Athaliah ripped her clothes and screamed, "Treason! Treason!"

"Take her out and kill her," Jehoiada the priest shouted to the army officers.

The crowd opened up for them to take her out, and they killed her at the palace stables.

Then Jehoiada made a solemn contract that he and the king and the people would be the Lord's. Jehoiada appointed the Levite priests as guards, and to sacrifice the burnt offering to the Lord as prescribed in the law of Moses. He made identical assignments of the Levite clans that King David had.

Army officers, nobles, governors, and all the people escorted the king from the Temple to the palace and seated the king upon his throne. And the city was quiet and peaceful.

The followers of Athaliah had ravaged the Temple, and everything dedicated to the worship of God had been removed to the temple of Baalam. Now the king instructed that a chest be made and set outside the Temple gate, then a proclamation was sent to all of Judah telling the people to bring to the Lord the tax that Moses had assessed on Israel.

The people brought money and placed it in the chest until it was full. Levites carried the chest to the king's accounting office where the representative of the High Priest counted the money, and took the chest back to the Temple. This went on day after day.

The king and Jehoiada gave the money to the building superintendents who hired masons and carpenters to restore the Temple and to foundrymen who made articles of iron and brass. Finally the Temple was in much better condition.

Burnt offerings were sacrificed continually during the lifetime of Jehoiada. He lived to a very old age, finally dying at 130. After his death the leaders of Judah came to King Joash and induced him to abandon the Temple and to worship idols instead! God sent prophets to bring them back to the Lord, but the people wouldn't listen.

Then the Spirit of God came upon Zechariah, Jehoiada's son. He called a meeting of the people. Standing before them, he said, "God wants to know why you are disobeying his commandments. When you do, everything you try fails. You have forsaken the Lord, and now he has forsaken you."

The leaders plotted to kill Zechariah, and King Joash himself ordered him executed in the court of the Temple.

A few months later, the Syrian army arrived and conquered Judah and Jerusalem, killing the leaders of the nation and sending back great quantities of booty to the king of Damascus. When the Syrians left—leaving Joash severely wounded—his own officials decided to kill him for murdering the son of Jehoiada the priest. They assassinated him as he lay in bed; his son Amaziah became the new king.

Amaziah was twenty-five years old when he became king. When he was well established, he executed the men who had assassinated his father.

Amaziah took the advice of his counselors and declared war on King Jehoash of Israel. King Jehoash replied with this parable:

"In the Lebanon mountains a thistle demanded of a cedar tree, 'Give your daughter in marriage to my son.' Just then a wild animal came by and stepped on the thistle, crushing it!

"You are very proud; my advice is to stay home and don't meddle with me, lest you and all Judah get badly hurt."

But Amaziah wouldn't listen. The armies met at Beth-shemesh and Judah was defeated. King Jehoash captured King Amaziah and took him as a prisoner to Jerusalem. Then Jehoash ordered two hundred yards of the walls of Jerusalem dismantled. He carried off the treasures and golden bowls from the Temple as well as treasures from the palace, and he took hostages to Samaria.

When Jehoash died, his son Jeroboam became king. Jeroboam II was as evil as Jeroboam I who had led Israel into worshiping idols. Jeroboam recovered lost territories of Israel between Hamath and the Dead Sea. When Jeroboam II died, his son Zechariah became the new king of Israel.[7]

"SEEK—AND LIVE"

Amos, a herdsman living in the village of Tekoa, sat all day long on the hillsides watching sheep, keeping them from straying. One day in a vision God told him some of the things that were going to happen to his nation, Israel; this vision came while Jeroboam, son of Jehoash, was king of Israel.

The Lord says, "The people of Israel have sinned again and again. This is your doom! It is spoken by the Lord against both Israel and Judah—against the entire family brought from Egypt:

"Of all the peoples of the earth, I have chosen you. That is why I must punish you the more for your sins. For how can we walk together with your sins between us? I, the Lord, am sending disaster into your land. But always, first of all, I warn you through my prophets. This I now have done.

"My people have forgotten what it means to do right. Their beautiful homes are full of the loot from their thefts and banditry. Therefore an enemy is coming! He is surrounding them and will shatter their forts and plunder those beautiful homes. On the same day that I punish Israel for her sins, I will destroy the idol altars at Bethel. And I will destroy the beautiful homes of the wealthy—their winter mansions and their summer houses, too—and demolish their ivory palaces.

"I sent you hunger," says the Lord, "but it did no good; you would not return to me. People would make their weary journey for a drink of water to a city that had rain, but there wasn't ever enough. Yet you wouldn't return to me.

"I sent blight and mildew on your farms and vineyards; locusts ate your figs and olive trees. I destroyed some of your cities, as I did Sodom and Gomorrah; those left are like half-burned firebrands snatched away from fire. And still you won't return to me," says the Lord.

"Therefore prepare to meet your God in judgment, Israel. For you are dealing with the one who formed the mountains and made the winds, and knows your every thought; Jehovah, the Lord, the God of Hosts, is his name."

The Lord says to the people of Israel, "Seek me—and live. Don't seek the idols of Bethel, for the people of Bethel shall surely come to grief."

Seek him who created the Seven Stars and the constellation Orion, who turns darkness into morning, and day into night, who calls forth the water from the ocean and pours it out as rain upon the land. The Lord, Jehovah, is his name. Be good, flee evil—and live! Then the Lord will truly be your Helper, as you have claimed he is. Hate evil and love the good; remodel your courts into true halls of justice. Perhaps even yet the Lord God of Hosts will have mercy on his people who remain.

You lie on ivory beds surrounded with luxury, eating the meat of the tenderest lambs and the choicest calves. You sing idle songs to the sound of the harp, and fancy yourselves to be as great musicians as King David was.

You drink wine by the bucketful and perfume yourselves with sweet ointments, caring nothing at all that your brothers need your help. Therefore you will be the first to be taken as slaves; suddenly your revelry will end.

Jehovah the Lord of Hosts has sworn by his own name, "I despise the pride and false glory of Israel, and hate her beautiful homes. I will turn over this city and everything in it to her enemies. O Israel, I will bring against you a nation that will bitterly oppress you from your northern boundary to your southern tip.

"The eyes of the Lord are watching Israel, and I will root her up and scatter her across the world. Yet this rooting out will not be permanent. For I have commanded that

Israel be sifted in a sieve, yet not one true kernel will be lost. Then I will rebuild the City of David, and return it to its former glory."

So the Lord, who plans it all, has said.[8]

HOLY INDICTMENT

The message from the Lord to Hosea, during the reigns of the kings of Judah: Uzziah, Jotham, Ahaz, and Hezekiah; and of the king of Israel, Jeroboam. Hear the word of the Lord, O people of Israel.

"There is no faithfulness, no kindness, no knowledge of God in your land. You swear and lie and kill and steal and commit adultery. There is violence everywhere. That is why your land is not producing; all living things grow sick and die; the animals, the birds, and even the fish begin to disappear.

"My people are destroyed because they don't know me, and it is your fault, you priests, for you yourselves refuse to know me. Since you have forgotten my laws, I will 'forget' to bless your children. Because the priests are wicked, the people are too. Therefore I will punish both priests and people for all their wicked deeds.

"Wine, women, and song have robbed my people of their brains, for they are asking a piece of wood to tell them what to do. Divine truth comes to them through tea leaves! They sacrifice to idols on the tops of mountains; they go up into the hills to burn incense in the pleasant shade of oaks and poplars and terebinth trees. There your daughters turn to prostitution and your brides commit adultery. You men are doing the same thing, sinning with harlots and temple prostitutes. Fools! Your doom is sealed.

"Israel, you have left me as a prostitute leaves her husband; the spirit of adultery is deep within you, and you cannot know the Lord.

"I don't want your sacrifices—I want your love; I don't want your offerings—I want you to know me. But, like Adam, you broke my covenant; you refused my love. You may no longer stay here in this land; you will be carried off to Assyria, and live there on scraps of food.

"O Israel, return to the Lord. Come and say, 'O Lord, take away our sins; be gracious to us and receive us, and we will offer you the sacrifice of praise. Assyria cannot save us, nor can our strength in battle; never again will we call the idols our gods; for in you alone, O Lord, the fatherless find mercy.'

"Then I will cure you of faithlessness, and my love will know no bounds, for my anger will be forever gone! I will refresh Israel like the dew from heaven; she will blossom as the lily, and root deeply in the soil like cedars in Lebanon. Her people will return from exile far away and rest beneath my shadow. They will be a watered garden and blossom like grapes.

"Whoever is wise, let him understand these things. For the paths of the Lord are true and right, and good men walk along them."[9]

FOREIGN ASSIGNMENT

The Lord sent this message to Jonah.

"Go to the great city of Nineveh, and give them this announcement from the Lord: 'I am going to destroy you, for your wickedness smells to highest heaven.' "

But Jonah was afraid to go and ran away. He went down to the seacoast to the port of Joppa where he found a ship leaving for Tarshish. He bought a ticket, went on board, and climbed down into the dark hold of the ship to hide from the Lord.

But as the ship was sailing along, the Lord flung a terrific wind over the sea, causing a great storm that threatened to send them to the bottom. Fearing for their lives, the sailors shouted to their gods for help and threw the cargo overboard to lighten the ship. All this time Jonah was sound asleep down in the hold.

The captain went down after him. "What do you mean," he roared, "sleeping at a time like this? Get up and cry to your god, and see if he will have mercy and save us!"

Then the crew decided to draw straws to see which of them had offended the gods and caused this terrible storm— and Jonah drew the short one.

"What have you done," they asked, "to bring this awful storm upon us? What is your nationality?"

He said, "I am a Jew; I worship Jehovah, the God of heaven, who made the earth and sea." Then he told them he was running away from the Lord.

The men were frightened. "Why did you do it?" they shouted. "What should we do to stop the storm?"

"Throw me into the sea," he said, "and it will become calm again. For I know this terrible storm has come because of me."

They tried harder to row the boat ashore, but couldn't make it. Then they shouted out a prayer to Jonah's God: "O Jehovah, don't make us die for this man's sin, and don't hold us responsible for his death, for you have sent this storm upon him for your own good reasons."

Then they picked up Jonah and threw him into the raging sea—and the storm stopped!

The men stood in awe before Jehovah, and sacrificed to him and vowed to serve him.

The Lord had arranged for a great fish to swallow Jonah. And Jonah was inside the fish three days and three nights.

Then Jonah prayed to the Lord from inside the fish: "You threw me into the ocean depths; I was covered by wild and stormy waves. You have rejected me; how shall I ever again see your holy Temple? I went down to the bottoms of the mountains that rise from off the ocean floor. I was locked out of life and imprisoned in the land of death. Those who worship false gods have turned their backs on all the mercies waiting for them from the Lord! I will never worship anyone but you! I will surely fulfill my promises."

The Lord ordered the fish to spit up Jonah on the beach, and it did.

Then the Lord spoke to Jonah again: "Go to that great city, Nineveh, and warn them of their doom as I told you before!"

Jonah obeyed and went to Nineveh, a city so large that it would take three days to walk around it.

But the very first day when Jonah entered the city and began to preach, the people repented. Jonah shouted to the crowds that gathered around him, "Forty days from now Nineveh will be destroyed!" They believed him and declared a fast; from the king on down, everyone put on sackcloth—the rough, coarse garments worn at times of mourning.

The king and his nobles sent this message throughout the city: "Everyone must cry mightily to God, and let everyone turn from his evil ways. Who can tell? Perhaps God will decide to let us live and will hold back his fierce anger."

When God saw that they had put a stop to their evil, he abandoned his plan to destroy them.

This change of plans made Jonah very angry. He complained to the Lord about it: "This is exactly what I thought you'd do, for I knew you were a gracious God, merciful, slow to get angry, and full of kindness."

Jonah went out and sat sulking on the east side of the city. The Lord arranged for a vine to grow up quickly and spread its leaves over Jonah's head to shade him. This made him comfortable and very grateful. But God also prepared a worm! The worm ate through the stem of the plant so that it withered away and died.

When the sun was hot, God ordered a scorching east wind to blow on Jonah, and the sun beat down upon his head until he grew faint and wished to die. He said, "Death is better than this!"

And God said to Jonah, "Is it right for you to be angry because the plant died?"

"Yes," Jonah said, "it is right for me to be angry enough to die!"

The Lord said, "You feel sorry for yourself when your shelter is destroyed, though you did no work to put it there, and it is at best short-lived. And why shouldn't I feel sorry for a great city like Nineveh with its 120,000 people in spiritual darkness?"[10]

RESPITE   King Amaziah of Judah lived fifteen years after the death of King Jehoash of Israel. His people conspired against him in Jerusalem, killed him, and buried him in the royal cemetery. Judah crowned sixteen-year-old Uzziah as their new king.

He followed in the steps of Amaziah, and was in general a good king. As long as the king followed the paths of God, he prospered. He built new cities in the Ashdod area and in other parts of the Philistine country. The Ammonites paid annual tribute to him and his fame spread even to Egypt. He built fortified towers in Jerusalem at the Corner Gate and the Valley Gate. He also constructed forts in the Negeb and made many water reservoirs, for he had great herds of cattle in the valleys and on the plains. He loved the soil and had many farms and vineyards on the hillsides and in the fertile valleys.

He organized his army into regiments to which men were drafted under quotas. Uzziah issued to them shields, spears, helmets, coats of mail, bows, and slingstones. And he produced engines of war to shoot arrows and huge stones from the towers and battlements. So he became very famous.

But at that point he became proud and corrupt. He sinned against the Lord by entering the forbidden sanctuary of the Temple and personally burning incense upon the altar. Azariah the High Priest went in after him and demanded that he get out.

"It is not for you, Uzziah, to burn incense," he declared. "That is the work of the sons of Aaron who are consecrated to this work. The Lord is not going to honor you for this!"

Uzziah was furious and refused to set down the incense burner he was holding. But suddenly leprosy appeared in his forehead! When Azariah and the others saw it, they rushed him out; because the Lord had struck him.

King Uzziah was a leper until the day of his death, cut off from his people and from the Temple. His son Jotham became the new king.[11]

HOLY VISION

These messages came to Isaiah in visions he saw during the reign of King Uzziah. Listen to what the Lord is saying:

"The children I raised and cared for so long and tenderly have turned against me. Even the animals—the donkey and the ox—know their owner and appreciate his care for them, but not my people Israel. They walk bent-backed beneath their load of guilt. Oh, my people, must you forever rebel?

"Come, let's talk this over! No matter how deep the stain of your sins, I can take it out and make you as clean as freshly fallen snow. Even if you are stained as red as crimson, I can make you white as wool! But if you keep on turning your backs, you will be killed by your enemies.

"Jerusalem, once my faithful wife! And now a prostitute running after other gods! Your leaders are rebels, companions of thieves; all of them take bribes and won't defend the widows and orphans. How dare you grind my people in the dust like that?"

The year King Uzziah died, I saw the Lord! He was sitting on a lofty throne; hovering about him were mighty, six-winged seraphs. With two of their wings they covered their faces; with two others they covered their feet; and with two they flew. In a great antiphonal chorus they sang, "Holy, holy, holy is the Lord of Hosts; the whole earth is filled with his glory." Such singing shook the Temple to its foundations, and suddenly the entire sanctuary was filled with smoke.

I said, "My doom is sealed, for I am a foul-mouthed sinner, a member of a sinful race; and I have looked upon the King, the Lord of heaven's armies."

Then one of the seraphs flew over to the altar and with a pair of tongs picked out a burning coal. He touched my lips with it and said, "Now you are pronounced 'Not guilty' because this coal has touched your lips. Your sins are all forgiven."

Then I heard the Lord asking, "Whom shall I send as a messenger to my people? Who will go?"

And I said, "Lord, I'll go! Send me."[12]

DISINTEGRATION

Jotham was twenty-five years old at the time he became king in Jerusalem. He built the Upper Gate of the Temple and did extensive rebuilding of the walls on the hill where the Temple was situated. He built cities in the hill country and erected fortresses and towers on the hills. His war against the Ammonites was successful so that for three years he received an annual tribute of silver, wheat, and barley. He reigned sixteen years; when he died, his son Ahaz became king.

Ahaz was twenty years old. Unlike his ancestor David, he worshiped the idols of Baal. He even went to the Valley of Hinnom and sacrificed his own children in the fire, just like the heathen nations that were thrown out of the land by the Lord to make room for Israel. That is why the Lord allowed the king of Syria to defeat him and deport large numbers of his people to Damascus.

Zechariah, an evil king like Jeroboam I, encouraged Israel in worshiping idols. Shallum conspired against him and assassinated him and took the crown.

One month after Shallum became king, Menahem came to Samaria and assassinated him and took the throne. Menahem worshiped idols as King Jeroboam I had done and led the people into grievous sin.

Then King Tiglath-pileser of Assyria invaded the land; but King Menahem bought him off with a gift of $2,000,000. Menahem extorted the money from the rich, assessing each one a special tax. When he died, his son Pekahiah became king.[13]

SIGN AND WONDER

Pekahiah was evil, and he continued the idol-worship begun by Jeroboam I. Then Pekah, the commanding general of his army, conspired against him with fifty men and assassinated him in the palace at Samaria. So Pekah became the new king.

Pekah, too, continued the example of Jeroboam. During his reign, King Tiglath-pileser led an attack against Israel. He captured cities of Gilead, Galilee, and all the land of Naphtali, and took people to Assyria as captives. Then Hoshea assassinated him and took the throne.

During the reign of Ahaz, Jerusalem was attacked by King Rezin of Syria and King Pekah of Israel. The hearts of the king and his people trembled with fear.

Then the Lord said to Isaiah, "Go meet King Ahaz at the end of the aqueduct which leads from Gihon Spring to the upper reservoir. Tell him he needn't be frightened by Rezin and Pekah. This plan will not succeed, for Damascus will remain the capital of Syria alone, and King Pekah's power will not increase. If you want me to protect you, you must believe what I say."

Not long after, the Lord sent this further message to King Ahaz.

"Ask me for a sign to prove that I will crush your enemies as I have said. Ask anything you like, in heaven or on earth."

But the king refused. "No, I'll not bother the Lord with anything like that."

Then Isaiah said, "O House of David, you aren't satisfied to exhaust my patience; you exhaust the Lord's as well! All right, the Lord will choose the sign—a child shall be born to a virgin, and she shall call him Immanuel, meaning, 'God is with us.' By the time this child is weaned, the kings you fear so much will both be dead."

Write down all these things I am going to do, says the Lord, and seal it up for the future. Entrust it to some godly man to pass on down to godly men of future generations.

The people who walk in darkness shall see a great Light— a Light that will shine on all those who live in the land of the shadow of death. For Israel will again be great, filled with joy.

For unto us a Child is born; unto us a Son is given; and the government shall be upon his shoulder. These will be his royal titles: "Wonderful," "Counselor," "The Mighty God," "The Everlasting Father," "The Prince of Peace." His ever-expanding, peaceful government will never end. He will rule with perfect fairness and justice from the throne of his father David. He will bring true justice and peace to all the nations of the world. The Lord of heaven's armies has dedicated himself to do it![14]

SWORDS INTO PLOWSHARES

These are messages from the Lord to Micah, addressed to both Samaria and Judah.

"Attention! Let all the peoples of the world listen. For the Lord leaves his throne in heaven and comes to earth because of the sins of Israel and Judah. What sins? The idolatry and oppression centering in the capital cities, Samaria and Jerusalem!

"The city of Samaria will crumble into a heap of rubble.

"The Lord stands ready at Jerusalem's gates to punish her.

"Listen, you leaders who hate justice and fill Jerusalem with murder and sin of every kind—you leaders who take bribes, you priests and prophets who won't preach and prophesy until you're paid. (And yet you fawn upon the Lord and say, 'All is well—the Lord is here among us. No harm can come to us.') Because of you, Jerusalem will be plowed like a field; the mountaintop where the Temple stands will be overgrown with brush.

"But in the last days, Mount Zion will be the most renowned of all the mountains of the world, praised by all nations; people from all over the world will make pilgrimages there. In those days the whole world will be ruled by the Lord from Jerusalem!

"He will arbitrate among the nations. They will beat their swords into plowshares and their spears into pruning-hooks; nations shall no longer fight each other, for all war will end. Everyone will live in his own home in peace and prosperity, for there will be nothing to fear. The Lord has promised this.

"O Bethlehem, you are but a small Judean village, yet you will be the birthplace of my King who is alive from everlasting ages past! God will abandon his people to their enemies until the time of Israel's spiritual rebirth; then the nation of Israel will refresh the world like welcome showers of rain."[15]

OVERWHELMED

Assyria attacked and defeated King Hoshea, so Israel had to pay heavy taxes. Then Hoshea conspired against Assyria by asking King So of Egypt to help him shake free, but this treachery was discovered. The king of Assyria put him in prison for his rebellion.

Now Israel was filled with Assyrian troops for three years besieging Samaria, the capital. In the ninth year of King Hoshea's reign, Samaria fell, and the people of Israel were exiled to Assyria. They were placed in colonies in the city of Halah and along the banks of the Habor River and among the cities of the Medes.

Assyria transported colonies of people from Babylon, and resettled them in Samaria and the other cities of Israel.

Assyria decreed that one of the exiled priests from Samaria should return to Israel and teach the new residents the laws of the god of the land. So one of them returned to Bethel and taught the colonists from Babylon how to worship the Lord, but these foreigners also worshiped their own gods.

King Ahaz of Judah asked the king of Assyria to be his ally against the armies of Edom, for Edom was invading Judah and capturing many people as slaves. Meanwhile, Philistines had invaded lowland cities and the Negeb and were living there. But when Tiglath-pileser arrived, he caused trouble for King Ahaz instead of helping him. Though Ahaz had given him the Temple gold and the palace treasures, it did no good.

Ahaz collapsed spiritually; he sacrificed to the gods of the people of Damascus who had defeated him, for he felt these gods would help him. Instead, they were his ruin. The king took gold bowls from the Temple and slashed them to pieces, nailed the door of the Temple shut so no one could worship there, and made altars to the heathen gods in every corner of Jerusalem. He did the same in every city of Judah. When Ahaz died, he was buried in Jerusalem but not in the royal tombs. His son Hezekiah became the new king.[16]

RENAISSANCE

Hezekiah was twenty-five years old, and his reign was good, just as his ancestor David's had been.

In the first month of the first year of his reign, he reopened the doors of the Temple and repaired them. He summoned the priests and the Levites to meet him at the open space east of the Temple, and addressed them thus:

"Listen to me, Levites. Sanctify yourselves and sanctify the Temple of the God of your ancestors—clean all the debris from the Holy Place. For our fathers have committed a deep sin. The doors have been shut tight, the perpetual flame has been put out, and the incense and burnt offerings have not been offered. Therefore the wrath of the Lord has been upon Judah and Jerusalem. Our fathers have been killed in war and our sons and daughters and wives are in captivity because of this. Now I want to make a covenant with God so his anger will turn away from us. Don't neglect your duties any longer, for the Lord has chosen you to minister to him."

The Levites went into action. They summoned their fellow Levites, sanctified themselves, and began to clean up the Temple. The priests cleaned up the inner room of the Temple, and brought out all the decay they found there. The Levites carted it to the brook Kidron.

They went back to the palace and reported to King Hezekiah: "We have completed the cleansing of the Temple, the altar of burnt offerings, and its accessories, also the table of the Bread of the Presence and its equipment. We have recovered the utensils thrown away by King Ahaz when he closed the Temple. They are beside the altar of the Lord."

Early the next morning King Hezekiah went to the Temple with city officials, taking bulls, rams, lambs, and goats for a sin offering for the nation and the Temple. He instructed the priests of Aaron to sacrifice them on the altar of the Lord.

He organized Levites into an orchestral group in accordance with the directions of David and the prophets Gad and Nathan. Then Hezekiah ordered the burnt offering placed on the altar, and as the sacrifice began, the instruments began to play the songs of the Lord. Afterwards the king and his aides bowed low in worship. "The consecration ceremony is now ended," Hezekiah said. "Now bring your sacrifices and thank offerings."

Hezekiah sent letters inviting everyone to the Temple for the Passover celebration.

"Come back to the Lord God of Abraham, Isaac, and Israel," the king's letter said, "so that he will return to us who have escaped from the kings of Assyria. For the Lord is full of kindness and mercy and will not continue to turn away from you if you return to him."

Messengers went from city to city throughout Ephraim and Manasseh, and for the most part they were received with laughter and scorn! But in Judah the entire nation felt a strong desire to obey the king. And so a very large crowd assembled at Jerusalem for the Passover.

They destroyed heathen altars and threw them into Kidron Brook. On the first day of May the people killed their Passover lambs.

For seven days the observance continued and the people confessed their sins to the Lord. Enthusiasm continued, so it was decided to continue the observance for another seven days. Jerusalem hadn't seen a celebration like this since the days of King Solomon. And the Lord heard their prayers.

Some time later, King Sennacherib of Assyria invaded Judah and laid siege to the fortified cities, planning to place them under tribute. When it was clear that Sennacherib was intending to attack Jerusalem, Hezekiah summoned his princes and officers for a council of war.

Then Hezekiah strengthened his defenses by repairing the wall wherever it was broken and by adding to the fortifications and constructing a second wall outside it. He also manufactured large numbers of weapons and shields. He recruited an army, appointed officers, and encouraged them with this address:

"Do not be afraid of the king of Assyria or his mighty army, for there is someone with us who is far greater than he is! We have the Lord our God to fight our battles for us!"

Sennacherib, while still besieging the city of Lachish, sent ambassadors with this message to Jerusalem:

"King Sennacherib of Assyria asks, 'Do you think you can survive my siege of Jerusalem? King Hezekiah is trying to persuade you to commit suicide by staying there—to die by famine and thirst. I and the kings of Assyria before me have never failed to conquer a nation we attacked. The gods of those nations weren't able to do a thing to save their lands! What makes you think your God can do any better? Don't let Hezekiah fool you!'"

The messengers shouted threats to the people gathered on the walls of the city, trying to dishearten them.

As soon as Hezekiah read this letter, he went to the Temple and spread it out before the Lord, saying, "O Lord of Hosts, you alone are God of all the kingdoms of earth. You made heaven and earth. Listen as I plead; see me as I pray. King Sennacherib mocked the living God. It is true that the kings of Assyria have destroyed nations, just as the letter says, and thrown their gods into the fire; for they were merely idols. O Lord our God, save us so that kingdoms will know you are God, and you alone."

Then Isaiah sent this message to Hezekiah: "The God of Israel says, 'This is my answer to your prayer against Sennacherib. The Lord says to him: You have sent your messengers to mock the Lord. You boast, "I came with my mighty army against the nations of the west." It was I who gave you this power. I know you well—your comings and goings and all you do—and the way you have raged against me. Because of your anger against the Lord, I have led you back to your own land by the same road you came.'"

Then God said to Hezekiah, "Here is the proof that I am the one who is delivering this city from Assyria: This year he will abandon his siege. Although you will have only volunteer grain this fall, it will give you enough seed for a small harvest next year, and two years from now you will be living in luxury again. You who are left in Judah will flourish and multiply. As for the king of Assyria, his armies shall not enter Jerusalem nor march outside its gates. For my own honor I will defend it, and in memory of my servant David."

That night the Angel of the Lord went to the camp of the Assyrians and killed 185,000 soldiers. Sennacherib returned to Nineveh, and while he was worshiping in the temple of Nisroch his sons killed him with their swords, then escaped to the land of Ararat.

Just before all this, Hezekiah became deathly sick. Isaiah went to visit him and gave him this message from the Lord: "Set your affairs in order, for you are going to die."

Hezekiah turned his face to the wall and prayed: "O Lord, remember how I've always tried to obey you in everything you said?"

So the Lord sent another message to Isaiah: "Go and tell Hezekiah, 'The Lord hears you praying and will let you live fifteen more years. He will deliver you and this city from the king of Assyria. Here is my guarantee: I will send the sun backwards ten degrees as measured on Ahaz's sun dial!'"

So the sun retraced ten degrees that it had gone down!

When King Hezekiah was well again, he wrote this about his experience:

"My life is cut short as when a weaver stops his working at the loom. All night I moaned, 'O Lord, your discipline is good and leads to life and health. Oh, heal me and make me live!'

"Yes, now I see it was good for me to undergo this bitterness, for you have lovingly delivered me from death. One generation makes known your faithfulness to the next. Every day of my life I will sing songs of praise in the Temple."

Soon afterwards the king of Babylon, Merodach-baladan, sent Hezekiah a present and his best wishes, for he had heard that Hezekiah had been very sick. Hezekiah appreciated this and took the envoys from Babylon on a tour of the palace, showing them his treasure house full of silver, gold, spices, and perfumes.

Then Isaiah came to the king and said, "Where are they from?"

"From far away in Babylon," Hezekiah replied.

"How much have they seen?" asked Isaiah.

"I showed them everything I own."

Then Isaiah said, "Listen to this message from the Lord:

"The time is coming when everything you have—all the treasures stored up by your fathers—will be carried off to Babylon. And some of your own sons will become slaves in the palace of the king of Babylon."

Hezekiah had special buildings for his silver, gold, precious stones, spices, and for his shields and gold bowls. He built storehouses for grain, new wine, and olive oil, with many stalls for animals and folds for flocks of sheep and goats he purchased. He dammed up the Upper Spring of Gihon and brought the water down through an aqueduct to the west side of the City of David sector in Jerusalem. He prospered in everything he did.

When Hezekiah died, he was buried in the royal cemetery among the other kings, and all honored him at his death. His son Manasseh became the new king.

Manasseh was only twelve years old when he became king. He rebuilt the heathen altars his father had destroyed—altars of Baal, the shame-images, and the sun, moon, and stars. He even constructed heathen altars in both courts of the Temple of the Lord for worshiping the sun, moon, and stars. And Manasseh sacrificed his own children as burnt offerings in the Valley of Hinnom. He consulted spirit-mediums, fortune-tellers, and sorcerers, and encouraged every sort of evil.[17]

PROPHECIES

This is the vision God showed Isaiah concerning Babylon:

"The armies of Babylon will run until exhausted, for I will stir up the Medes against Babylon, and no amount of silver or gold will buy them off. And Babylon, the most glorious of kingdoms, will be as utterly destroyed as Sodom and Gomorrah were when God sent fire from heaven. O Babylon, come sit in the dust; for your days of pomp and honor are ended. O daughter of Chaldea, never again will you be the lovely princess, tender and delicate. I will take vengeance upon you and will not repent.

"I was angry with my people Israel and began to punish them by letting them fall into your hands, O Babylon. But you showed them no mercy. You thought your reign would never end, Queen Kingdom of the world. O pleasure-mad kingdom, living at ease, bragging as the greatest in the world—you say, 'I alone am God!' That is why disaster shall overtake you.

"Call out the demon hordes you've worshiped all these years. You have astrologers and stargazers who try to tell you what the future holds; they are as useless as dried grass burning in the fire. They cannot even deliver themselves!"

This is Jehovah's message to Cyrus, God's anointed, whom he has chosen to conquer many lands. God shall empower his right hand and he shall crush mighty kings. God shall open the gates of Babylon to him. "I will go before you, Cyrus, and smash down the city gates of brass and iron bars. And I will give you secret riches; you will know that I am doing this—I, the God of Israel, the one who calls you by your name. I called you when you didn't know me. I am Jehovah."

The royal line of David will be cut off, chopped down like a tree; but from the stump will grow a Shoot—yes, a new Branch from the old root. And the Spirit of the Lord shall rest upon him, the Spirit of wisdom, understanding, counsel, and might; the Spirit of knowledge and of the fear of the Lord. His delight will be obedience to the Lord. He will not judge by appearance, false evidence, or hearsay, but will defend the poor and the exploited. He will rule against the wicked who oppress them, for he will be clothed with fairness and with truth.

Listen! I hear the voice of someone shouting, "Make a road for the Lord through the wilderness; make him a straight, smooth road through the desert. The glory of the Lord will be seen by all mankind together."

The voice says, "Shout!"

"What shall I shout?" I asked.

"O Crier of Good News, shout to Jerusalem, 'Your God is coming!' "

Yes, he will carry the lambs in his arms and gently lead the ewes with young.

"See my Servant, my Chosen One, in whom I delight.

I have put my Spirit upon him; he will reveal justice to the nations of the world. He will be gentle—he will not shout nor quarrel in the streets. He will not break the bruised reed, nor quench the dimly burning flame. He won't be satisfied until truth and righteousness prevail throughout the earth, until distant lands beyond the seas have put their trust in him."

The Lord who created the heavens and the earth and everything in it, and gives life and breath and spirit to everyone in all the world, he is the one who says to his Servant: "I have called you to demonstrate my righteousness. I have given you to my people as the personal confirmation of my covenant with them. You shall also be a light to guide the nations to me. You will open the eyes of the blind and release those who sit in prison darkness and despair. I am the Lord! Everything I prophesied came true, and now I will prophesy again. I will tell you the future before it happens."

But, oh, how few believe! In God's eyes he was like a tender green shoot, sprouting from a root in dry and sterile ground; but in our eyes there was no attractiveness at all. We despised him and rejected him—a man of sorrows, acquainted with bitterest grief.

Yet it was our grief he bore, our sorrows that weighed him down. We thought his troubles were a punishment from God, for his own sins! But he was wounded and bruised for our sins. He was chastised that we might have peace; he was lashed—and we were healed! We strayed away like sheep—we left God's paths to follow our own. Yet God laid on him the guilt and sins of every one of us!

He was oppressed and afflicted, yet he never said a word. He was brought as a lamb to the slaughter, and as a sheep before her shearers is dumb so he stood silent before the ones condemning him. From prison and trial they led him away to his death. But who among the people of that day realized it was their sins that he was dying for?

He was buried in a rich man's grave. Yet it was the Lord's plan to bruise him and fill him with grief. But when his soul has been made an offering for sin, he shall have a multitude of children, many heirs. He shall live again and God's program shall prosper in his hands.

And when he sees all that is accomplished by the anguish of his soul, he shall be satisfied; and because of what he has experienced, my righteous Servant shall make many to be counted righteous before God, for he shall bear all their sins. Therefore I will give him the honors of one who is mighty and great, because he has poured out his soul unto death.

The Spirit of the Lord God is upon me, because the Lord has anointed me to bring good news to the suffering and afflicted. He has sent me to comfort the broken-hearted, to announce liberty to captives, and to open the eyes of the blind. He has sent me to tell those who mourn that the time of God's favor to them has come, and the day of his wrath to their enemies. To all who mourn in Israel he will give beauty for ashes, joy instead of mourning, praise instead of heaviness.

They shall rebuild the ancient ruins, repairing cities long ago destroyed, reviving them though they have lain there many generations. You shall be called priests of the Lord; you shall be fed with the treasures of the nations. Instead of shame, you shall have a double portion of prosperity and everlasting joy.

"I, the Lord, love justice; I will reward my people for their suffering and make an everlasting covenant with them. Their descendants shall be honored among the nations."

In that day the wolf and the lamb will lie down together, and the leopard and goats will be at peace. Calves and fat cattle will be safe among lions, and a little child shall lead them. Lions will eat grass like the cows. Babies will crawl safely among poisonous snakes. Nothing will hurt or destroy in all my holy mountain, for as the waters fill the sea, so shall the earth be full of the knowledge of the Lord.

In the last days, Jerusalem and the Temple of the Lord will become the world's greatest attraction, and people from many lands will flow there to worship. "Come," everyone will say, "let us go up the mountain of the Lord to the Temple of the God of Israel; there he will teach us his laws, and we will obey them." For in those days the world will be ruled from Jerusalem. The Lord will settle international disputes; all the nations will convert their weapons of war into implements of peace. Then at the last all wars will stop and all military training will end.

Seek the Lord while you can find him. Call upon him now while he is near. Turn to the Lord that he may have mercy, and to our God for he will abundantly pardon!

"This plan of mine is not what you would work out, neither are my thoughts the same as yours! For as the heavens are higher than the earth, so are my ways higher than yours, and my thoughts than yours.

"As the rain and snow come down from heaven to water the earth, and cause the grain to grow and to produce seed for the farmer and bread for the hungry, so also is my Word. I send it out and it always produces fruit. It shall accomplish all I want it to, and prosper everywhere I send it."[18]

PRODIGAL KING

Warnings from the Lord were ignored by both Manasseh and his people. So God sent Assyrian armies and they seized him and bound him with chains and carted him away.

At last he came to his senses and cried out to God for help. And the Lord answered his plea by returning him to Jerusalem. At that, Manasseh finally realized that the Lord was really God!

After this he rebuilt the outer wall of the City of David and the wall from west of the Spring of Gihon in the Kidron Valley and then to the Fish Gate and around Citadel Hill. He stationed army generals in all the fortified cities of Judah. He removed foreign gods from the hills, took his idol from the Temple, and tore down the altars he had built on the mountain where the Temple stood and dumped them outside the city. Then he rebuilt the altar of the Lord and offered sacrifices on it—and demanded that the people worship the Lord God.

When Manasseh died, his son Amon became the new king. Amon lasted only two years. It was an evil reign like the early years of Manasseh. He didn't change as his father did; instead he sinned more and more. His own officers assassinated him in his palace. Some public-spirited citizens killed those who assassinated him and declared his son Josiah to be the new king.[19]

**JEHOVAH—
JEREMIAH—
JERUSALEM**

God's messages to Jeremiah, the priest who lived in Anathoth in the land of Benjamin: the first message came in the reign of Josiah; others came during the reign of Josiah's son Jehoiakim and at various times until the eleventh year of Josiah's son Zedekiah when Jerusalem was captured and the people were taken away as slaves.

The Lord said to me, "I knew you before you were formed within your mother's womb; before you were born I appointed you as my spokesman to the world."

"O Lord," I said, "I can't do that! I'm far too young!"

"Don't say that," he replied, "for you will go wherever I send you and speak whatever I tell you. And don't be afraid of the people, for I will see you through."

Then he touched my mouth and said, "I have put my words in your mouth! In accord with my words spoken through your mouth, I will tear down some and destroy them, and plant others and make them strong and great."

Then the Lord said, "Look, Jeremiah! What do you see?"

And I replied, "I see a pot of boiling water, tipping southward, spilling over Judah."

"Yes," he said, "for terror from the north will boil out upon this land. I am calling kingdoms of the north to come to Jerusalem and set their thrones at the gates of the city and in all the other cities of Judah. This is the way I will punish my people for deserting me. My people have forsaken me, the Fountain of Life-giving Water, and have built broken cisterns that can't hold water!

"Pray no more for these people, Jeremiah. Watch how the children gather wood and the fathers build fires, and the women knead dough and make cakes to offer to 'The Queen of Heaven' and their other idol-gods!

"Away with offerings and sacrifices I wanted from your

fathers when I led them out of Egypt. I told them: Obey me and I will be your God and you shall be my people. But they kept on doing whatever they wanted to. I kept on sending my prophets, but they wouldn't listen. This is the nation that continues to live a lie."

The Lord says: "Let not the wise bask in wisdom, nor the mighty in might, nor the rich in riches. Let them boast in this alone: that they truly know me, the Lord of justice and righteousness whose love is steadfast.

"A time is coming," says the Lord, "when I will punish all those who are circumcised in body but not in spirit—the Egyptians, Edomites, Ammonites, Moabites, Arabs, and yes, even people of Judah. For all these pagan nations also circumcise themselves; unless you circumcise your hearts by loving me, your circumcision is only a heathen rite like theirs.

"Can the Ethiopian change the color of his skin? or a leopard take away his spots? Nor can you who are so used to doing evil now start being good. Because you have put me out of your mind and put your trust in false gods, I will scatter you as chaff is scattered by the fierce winds off the desert."[20]

JOSIAH'S SEARCH

Josiah was only eight years old when he became king. When he was sixteen, he began to search for the God of his ancestor David. He began to clean up Judah and Jerusalem, destroying the heathen altars and the shame-idols on the hills. He went out to watch as the altars of Baal were knocked apart, the obelisks above the altars chopped down, and the shame-idols ground into dust and scattered over the graves of those who had sacrificed to them.

After he had purged the land and cleaned up the Temple, he appointed Shaphan, Ma-aseiah, and Joah to repair the Temple. They set up a collection system for gifts for the Temple. Gifts were brought from Manasseh, Ephraim, and other parts of the remnant of Israel, as well as from Jerusalem. The money was taken to Hilkiah the High Priest for accounting, then used by the Levites to pay carpenters and stonemasons and to purchase building materials. He rebuilt what earlier kings of Judah had torn down.

One day when the High Priest was at the Temple, he found an old scroll which turned out to be the laws of God as given to Moses.

"Look!" Hilkiah exclaimed to Shaphan, the king's secretary. "These are the laws of God!" Shaphan took it to the king, along with his report that there was good progress in the reconstruction of the Temple.

When the king heard what the laws required of God's people, he ripped his clothing in despair and summoned Hilkiah, Shaphan, and Asaiah, the king's personal aide. "Go to the Temple and plead with the Lord for me!" the king told them. "Pray for all the remnant of Israel and Judah! For this scroll says that the reason the Lord's great anger has been poured on us is that our ancestors have not obeyed the laws written here."

The men went to Huldah the prophetess, wife of Shallum, the king's tailor. When they told her of the king's trouble, she replied, "The God of Israel says, 'Tell the man who sent you: Yes, the Lord will destroy this city and its people; all the curses written in the scroll will come true. But the Lord also says this to the king of Judah: Because you have humbled yourself when you heard my words against this city, I will not send the promised evil upon this city and its people until after your death.' "

They brought back to the king this word, then the king summoned the elders, priests and Levites, and all the people to accompany him to the Temple. There the king read the scroll to them—the covenant of God that was found in the Temple. As the king stood before them, he made a pledge to the Lord to follow his commandments with all his heart and to do what was written in the scroll. And he required everyone in Jerusalem and Benjamin to subscribe to this pact with God, and all of them did.

Josiah announced that the Passover would be celebrated on the first day of April in Jerusalem. He also reestablished the priests in their duties and encouraged them to begin their work at the Temple again. He issued this order to the Levites, the religious teachers:

"Since the Ark is now in Solomon's Temple, spend your time ministering to the Lord and to his people. Form yourselves into the traditional service corps of your ancestors, as first organized by King David and his son Solomon. Each corps will assist particular clans of the people who bring in their offerings to the Temple. Kill the Passover lambs and prepare to assist the people who come. Follow all the instructions of the Lord through Moses."

When everything was organized and the priests were standing in their places and the Levites were formed into service corps, the Levites killed Passover lambs and presented the blood to the priests, who sprinkled it upon the altar. They did the same with the oxen. Then, as directed by the laws of Moses, they roasted the Passover lambs and boiled the holy offerings in pots, kettles, and pans, and hurried them out to the people to eat. Everyone in Jerusalem took part in the Passover observance, and this was followed by the Feast of Unleavened Bread for the next seven days. Never since Samuel the prophet had there been such a Passover. This happened in the eighteenth year of Josiah.

"Shout with joy before the Lord, O earth!
Obey him gladly; come before him, singing with joy.
We are his people, the sheep of his pasture.
Go through his open gates with great thanksgiving; enter his courts with praise.
Give thanks to him and bless his name.
For the Lord is always good.
He is always loving and kind, and his faithfulness goes on and on to each succeeding generation."

Afterwards King Neco of Egypt led his army against the Assyrians at Carchemish on the Euphrates River, and Josiah declared war on him. Neco sent ambassadors to Josiah with this message: "I have come only to fight the king of Assyria! God has told me to hurry!"

But Josiah led his army into the battle at the Valley of Megiddo. Josiah refused to believe that Neco's message was from God. Enemy archers struck Josiah with their arrows and fatally wounded him.

"Take me out of the battle," he exclaimed to his aides. They lifted him out of his chariot and placed him in his second chariot and brought him back to Jerusalem where he died. All Judah, including Jeremiah, mourned for him.

Josiah's son Jehoahaz was selected king, but lasted only three months. He was deposed by the king of Egypt, who demanded an annual tribute of $250,000. Egypt appointed Eliakim, brother of Jehoahaz, as the new king of Judah. (Eliakim's name was changed to Jehoiakim.)

Jehoiakim reigned eleven years, but his reign was evil.[21]

HABAKKUK'S CRY

This message came to the prophet Habakkuk in a vision from God:

"You will be astounded at what I am about to do! I am raising a new force on the world scene, the Chaldeans, a cruel nation who will march across the world and conquer it. But their guilt is deep for they claim their power is from their gods."

"O Lord my God, my Holy One, is your plan in all of this to wipe us out? Surely not! O God our Rock, you have decreed the rise of these Chaldeans to chasten and correct us for our awful sins. We are wicked, but they far more! Will you, who cannot allow sin in any form, stand idly by while they swallow us up?"

And the Lord said, "Write my answer large and clear, so that anyone can read it at a glance. These things won't happen right away; slowly, surely, the time approaches when the vision will be fulfilled.

"Note this: wicked men trust themselves alone, as these Chaldeans do, and fail, but the righteous man trusts in me, and lives! These arrogant Chaldeans are betrayed by all their wine, for it is treacherous. The time is coming when all their captives will taunt them, saying: 'At last justice has caught up with you!'

"Woe to you who build cities with money gained from murdering and robbery! Has not the Lord decreed that godless nations' gains will turn to ashes in their hands? Woe to you for making your neighboring lands stagger like drunkards beneath your blows, and then gloating over their shame. Soon your glory will be replaced by shame.

"What profit was there in worshiping man-made idols? Woe to those who command their lifeless wooden idols to arise and save them, who call out to the speechless stone to tell them what to do. They are overlaid with gold and silver, but there is no breath inside! The Lord is in his holy Temple; let all the earth be silent before him."

This prayer of triumph Habakkuk sang before the Lord:

"O Lord, now I have heard your report and I worship you in awe for the fearful things you are going to do. Show us your power to save us. In your wrath, remember mercy.

"I see God moving across the deserts from Mount Sinai. His splendor fills the earth and sky; his glory fills the heavens, and the earth is full of his praise! From his hands flash rays of brilliant light. He stands still for a moment, gazing at the earth. Then he shakes the nations, scattering the mountains and leveling the hills. His power is the same as always! I tremble when I hear all this; my lips quiver with fear. I will quietly wait for the day of trouble to come upon the people who invade us.

"Though the fig trees are destroyed and there is neither blossom left nor fruit, and though the olive crops fail and the fields lie barren; even if the flocks die in the fields and the cattle barns are empty, yet I will rejoice in the Lord; I will be happy in the God of my salvation."[22]

CONTEMPTUOUS KING

This message came to Jeremiah from the Lord at the beginning of the reign of Jehoiakim:

"Send messages to the kings of Edom, Moab, Ammon, Tyre, and Sidon through their ambassadors in Jerusalem, saying: 'The Lord of Hosts sends you this message: By my great power I have made the earth and all mankind and every animal; and I give these things of mine to anyone I want to. So now I have given all your countries to King Nebuchadnezzar of Babylon. All the nations shall serve him and his son and his grandson until his time is up, and then many nations shall conquer Babylon and make him their slave. Submit to him and serve him—I will punish any nation refusing to be his slave. The people of any nation submitting to the king of Babylon will be permitted to stay in their own country and farm the land as usual.' "

In the fourth year of Jehoiakim, the Lord gave this message to Jeremiah:

"Get a scroll and write down all my messages against Israel, Judah, and the other nations. Begin with the first message back in the days of Josiah. Perhaps when the people of Judah see in writing the terrible things I will do to them, they will repent. And then I can forgive them."

So Jeremiah sent for Baruch, and as Jeremiah dictated Baruch wrote down all the prophecies. When all was finished, Jeremiah said, "Read the scroll in the Temple on the next Day of Fasting, for on that day people will be there from all over Judah."

Baruch did as Jeremiah told him on the Day of Fasting in December of the fifth year of King Jehoiakim. When Micaiah heard the messages, he went to the palace conference room where administrative officials were meeting. The officials sent Jehudi to ask Baruch to come and read the messages to them too, and Baruch did.

They were badly frightened. "We must tell the king," they said. "You and Jeremiah hide." Then the officials hid the scroll in the room of Elishama the scribe and went to tell the king.

The king sent Jehudi to get the scroll. Jehudi brought it and read it to the king as all his officials stood by. Whenever Jehudi finished reading three or four columns, the king would take his knife, slit off the section, and throw it into the fire, until the whole scroll was destroyed.

The Lord said to Jeremiah: "Get another scroll and write everything again just as you did before, and say to the king: 'You burned the scroll because it said the king of Babylon would destroy this country. Now the Lord adds this concerning you, Jehoiakim: He shall have no one to sit upon the throne of David; I will punish him and his family.' "

This message for Judah came during the fourth year of

Jekoiakim, the year Nebuchadnezzar, king of Babylon, began his reign.

"For the past twenty-three years," Jeremiah said, "God has been sending me his messages. I have faithfully passed them on to you, but you haven't listened. And now the Lord says: 'I will gather together the armies of the north under Nebuchadnezzar, king of Babylon, and will bring them against this land and the other nations near you and will destroy you. Israel shall serve the king of Babylon for seventy years. Then after these years of slavery I will punish the king of Babylon and his people for their sins; I will make the land of Chaldea a waste. Many nations and kings shall enslave the Chaldeans, as they enslaved my people; I will punish them in proportion to their treatment of my people.' "23

CAPTIVE PRINCES

Babylon's King Nebuchadnezzar attacked Jerusalem, and the Lord gave him victory over Jehoiakim. When he returned to Babylon, he took some of the sacred cups from the Temple of God and placed them in the treasury of his god. He ordered Ashpenaz, who was in charge of his palace personnel, to select some of the Jewish youths brought back as captives—young men of the royal family and nobility of Judah—and to teach them the Chaldean language and literature.

The king assigned them the best of food and wine from his own kitchen during their three-year training period, planning to make them his counselors when they graduated.

Daniel, Hananiah, Misha-el, and Azariah were four of the young men chosen, all from the tribe of Judah. However, their superintendent gave them Babylonian names as follows: Daniel was called Belteshazzar; Hananiah was Shadrach; Misha-el was Meshach; Azariah was Abednego.

Daniel made up his mind not to eat the food and wine given to them by the king. He asked the superintendent for permission to eat other things instead.

He was alarmed by Daniel's suggestion. "I'm afraid you will become pale and thin," he said, "and then the king will behead me for neglecting my responsibilities."

Daniel talked it over with the steward appointed by the superintendent and suggested a ten-day diet of only vegetables and water; then at the end of this trial period the steward could see how they looked in comparison with the fellows who ate the king's rich food.

The steward agreed. At the end of ten days Daniel and his three friends looked healthier and better nourished than the youths who had been eating the food supplied by the king! So after that the steward fed them only vegetables and water.

God gave these four youths great ability to learn and they soon mastered the literature and science of the time. God gave Daniel special ability in understanding the meanings of dreams and visions.

One night in the second year of his reign, Nebuchadnezzar had a nightmare and awoke trembling with fear. To make matters worse, he couldn't remember his dream! He immediately called in his magicians, incantationists, sorcerers, and astrologers, and demanded that they tell him what his dream had been. "If you won't tell me what it was and what it means, I'll have you torn limb from limb and your houses made into heaps of rubble! But I will give you wonderful gifts and honors if you tell me what the dream was. So, begin!"

They said, "How can we tell you what the dream means unless you tell us what it was?"

The king retorted, "You're trying to stall for time until the calamity befalls me that the dream foretells. If you don't tell me the dream, you certainly can't expect me to believe your interpretation!"

The Chaldeans replied, "There isn't a man alive who can tell others what they have dreamed! And there isn't a king in all the world who would ask such a thing! No one except the gods can tell you your dream, and they are not here to help."

The king was furious, and sent out orders to execute all the wise men of Babylon. Daniel and his companions were rounded up with the others to be killed.

When Ari-och, the chief executioner, came to kill them,

Daniel asked, "Why is the king so angry? What is the matter?"

Ari-och told him all that had happened.

Daniel went to see the king. "Give me a little time," he said, "and I will tell you the dream and what it means."

Then he went home and told Hananiah, Misha-el, and Azariah. They asked God to show his mercy by telling them the secret so they would not die. And that night in a vision God told Daniel what the king had dreamed.

Daniel praised God, saying, "Blessed be the name of God forever, for he alone has all wisdom and all power. World events are under his control. He removes kings and sets others on their thrones. He gives wise men their wisdom and scholars their intelligence. He reveals profound mysteries beyond man's understanding. He knows all hidden things, for he is light. I thank and praise you, O God of my fathers, for you have given me wisdom and health, and now even this vision of the king's dream and the understanding of what it means."

Daniel went to see Ari-och and said, "Take me to the king and I will tell him what he wants to know."

Ari-och hurried Daniel to the king and said, "One of the Jewish captives will tell you your dream!"

The king said, "Is this true?"

Daniel replied, "No wise man, astrologer, magician, or wizard can tell the king such things, but there is a God in heaven who reveals secrets, and he has told you in your dream what will happen in the future. This was your dream:

"You saw a huge and powerful statue of a man, shining brilliantly, frightening and terrible. The head of the statue was made of purest gold, its chest and arms were of silver, its belly and thighs of brass, its legs of iron, its feet part iron and part clay. But as you watched, a Rock was cut from the mountainside by supernatural means. It came hurtling toward the statue and crushed the feet of iron and clay, smashing them to bits. Then the whole statue collapsed into a heap of iron, clay, brass, silver, and gold; its pieces were crushed as small as chaff, and the wind blew them all away. But the Rock that knocked the statue down became a great mountain that covered the whole earth.

"Your Majesty, you are a king over many kings, for the God of heaven has given you your kingdom, power, and glory. You rule the farthest provinces; you are that head of gold.

"But after your kingdom has come to an end, another world power will arise to take your place. This empire will be inferior to yours. And after that kingdom has fallen, yet a third great power—represented by the bronze belly of the statue—will rise to rule the world. Following it, the fourth kingdom will be strong as iron—smashing, bruising, and conquering. The feet and toes you saw—part iron and part clay—show that later on this kingdom will be divided. Some parts of it will be as strong as iron, and some as weak as clay. This mixture shows these kingdoms will try to strengthen themselves by forming alliances with each other but this will not succeed, for iron and clay don't mix.

"During the reigns of those kings, the God of heaven will set up a kingdom that will never be destroyed; no one will ever conquer it. It will shatter all these kingdoms into nothingness, but it shall stand forever, indestructible. That is the meaning of the Rock cut from the mountain without human hands. Thus the great God has shown what will happen in the future, and this interpretation of your dream is as certain as my description of it."

Nebuchadnezzar fell to the ground before Daniel and worshiped him, and commanded his people to offer sacrifices and burn incense before him. "Truly, Daniel," the king said, "your God is the God of gods, Ruler of kings, the Revealer of mysteries, because he has told you this secret."

The king made Daniel very great, gave him expensive gifts, and appointed him to be ruler over the whole province of Babylon as well as chief over all his wise men. Then, at Daniel's request, the king appointed Shadrach, Meshach, and Abednego as Daniel's assistants, to be in charge of the affairs of the province of Babylon.

King Jehoiakim paid tribute for three years but then rebelled, and the Lord sent bands of Chaldeans, Syrians, Moabites, and Ammonites against Judah. Nebuchadnezzar took away the king in chains to Babylon. Nebuchadnezzar also took some of the golden bowls and other items from the Temple, placing them in his own temple.

The Lord of Hosts had said, "The pillars of bronze standing before the Temple, and the great bronze basin in the Temple court, and the metal stands and all the other ceremonial articles left here by Nebuchadnezzar when he exiled important people of Judah and Jerusalem to Babylon, along with Jeconiah [Jehoiachin], will all yet be carried away to Babylon and will stay there until I send for them."

Jehoiachin became the new king, but he lasted only three months. Nebuchadnezzar besieged Jerusalem; Jehoiachin surrendered and was imprisoned in Babylon. Many treasures from the Temple were taken away to Babylon at that time, and Nebuchadnezzar appointed Jehoiachin's brother Zedekiah as the new king.[24]

THE WATCHMAN

Ezekiel, a priest who lived with the Jewish exiles beside the Chebar Canal in Babylon:

One day in June, when I was thirty years old, the heavens were suddenly opened to me and I saw visions from God. I saw a great storm coming toward me from the north, driving before it a huge cloud glowing with fire, with a mass of fire inside that flashed continually; and in the fire there was something that shone like polished brass.

Then from the center of the cloud, four strange forms appeared that looked like men, except that each had four faces and two pairs of wings! Their legs were like those of men, but their feet were cloven like calves' feet and shone like burnished brass. And beneath each of their wings I could see human hands.

The four living beings were joined wing to wing, and they flew without turning. Each had the face of a man in front, with a lion's face on the right side of his head, and the face of an ox on his left side, and the face of an eagle at the back of his head! Each had two pairs of wings spreading out from the middle of his back. One pair stretched out to attach to the wings of the living beings on each side, and the other pair covered his body.

Going up and down among them were other forms that glowed like bright coals of fire or brilliant torches, and it was from these the lightning flashed. The living beings darted to and fro, swift as lightning.

As I stared at all of this, I saw four wheels on the ground beneath them, one wheel belonging to each. The wheels looked as if they were made of polished amber, and each wheel was constructed with a second wheel crosswise inside. They could go in any of the four directions without having to face around. When the living beings flew forward, the wheels moved forward; when they flew upwards, the wheels went up too. For the spirit of the living beings was in the wheels.

The sky spreading out above them looked as though it were made of crystal; it was inexpressibly beautiful.

Each being's wings stretched straight out to touch the other's wings, and as they flew their wings roared like waves against the shore, or like the voice of God, or like the shouting of a mighty army. When they stopped they let down their wings, and every time they stopped there came a voice from the crystal sky above them.

For high in the sky above them was what looked like a throne made of beautiful blue sapphire stones, and upon it sat someone who appeared to be a Man.

From his waist up, he seemed to be all glowing bronze, dazzling like fire; and from his waist down he seemed to be entirely flame, and there was a glowing halo like a rainbow all around him. That was the way the glory of the Lord appeared to me. And when I saw it, I fell face downward on the ground, and heard the voice of someone speaking to me:

"Stand up, son of dust, and I will talk to you."

And the Spirit entered into me as he spoke, and set me on my feet.

Then he added: "Let my words sink deep into your heart, then go to your people in exile and whether or not they will listen, tell them: This is what the Lord God says!"

Then the Spirit lifted me up and the glory of the Lord began to move away, accompanied by the sound of a great earthquake. It was the noise of the wings of the living beings as they touched against each other, and the sound of their wheels beside them.

The Spirit lifted me up and took me away to Tel Abib, another colony of Jewish exiles beside the Chebar River. And I sat among them, overwhelmed, for seven days.

At the end of the seven days, the Lord said to me:

"I have appointed you as a watchman for Israel; whenever I send my people a warning, pass it on to them at once. If you refuse to warn the wicked when I want you to tell them, 'You are under the penalty of death; therefore repent and save your life'—they will die but I will punish you. But if you warn them and they refuse to repent, they will die but you are blameless."

Then, late in August of the sixth year of King Jehoiachin's captivity, as I was talking with the elders of Judah, the power of the Lord God fell upon me. I saw what appeared to be a Man; from his waist down he was made of fire; from his waist up he was all amber-colored brightness. He put out what seemed to be a hand and took me by the hair. And the Spirit lifted me up into the sky and seemed to transport me to Jerusalem, to the entrance of the north gate, where the large idol was that had made the Lord so angry. Suddenly the glory of the God of Israel was there.

He said, "Look toward the north." So I looked and, sure enough, north of the altar gate in the entrance stood the idol. He said: "Do you see what the people are doing here to push me from my Temple? But come, and I will show you greater sins than these!"

He brought me to the door of the Temple court where I made out an opening in the wall.

"Dig into the wall," he said. I did, and uncovered a door to a hidden room. I went in. The walls were covered with pictures of all kinds of snakes, lizards, and hideous creatures, besides various idols worshiped by the people. Seventy elders were standing there worshiping the pictures.

The Lord said, "They say, 'The Lord doesn't see us; he has gone away!'" Then he added, "Come, and I will show you greater sins."

He brought me to the north gate of the Temple, and there sat women weeping for Tammuz, their god.

Then he brought me into the inner court of the Temple, and there at the door between the porch and the bronze altar were about twenty-five men standing with their backs to the Temple, facing east, worshiping the sun!

"Have you seen this?" he asked. "Is it nothing to the people that they commit these sins, arousing my fury against them? Therefore I will deal with them in fury."

Then he thundered, "Call those to whom I have given the city! Tell them to bring their weapons with them!"

Six men appeared at his call, coming from the upper north gate, each one with his sword. One of them wore linen clothing and carried a writer's case strapped to his side. They all went into the Temple and stood beside the bronze altar. And the glory of the God of Israel rose from the cherubim where it had rested and stood above the entrance to the Temple.

The Lord called to the man with the writer's case, "Walk through the streets of Jerusalem and put a mark on the foreheads of the men who weep because of the sins they see around them."

Then I heard the Lord tell the other men: "Follow him through the city and kill everyone whose forehead isn't marked. Spare not nor pity them—and begin here at the Temple."

So they began by killing the seventy elders, and they went out through the city as they were told.

Suddenly a throne of beautiful blue sapphire appeared in the sky above the heads of the cherubim. Then the Lord spoke to the man in linen clothing: "Go in between the whirling wheels beneath the cherubim and take a handful of glowing coals and scatter them over the city."

The man went in and stood beside one of the wheels, and one of the cherubim reached out his hand, for each cherub had beneath his wings what looked like human hands, and took some live coals from the flames and put them into the hands of the man in linen clothes, who took them and went out.

Each of the four cherubim had a wheel beside him— "The Whirl-Wheels," as I heard them called, for each one had a second wheel crosswise within, sparkling like chrysolite, giving off a greenish-yellow glow. Each of the four wheels was covered with eyes, including the rims and spokes. These were the same beings I had seen beside the Chebar Canal.

Then the glory of the Lord moved from the door of the Temple and stood above the cherubim. And as I watched, the cherubim flew with their wheels beside them to the east gate of the Temple. And the glory of the God of Israel was above them.

Then the Spirit lifted me and brought me over to the east gate of the Temple, where I saw twenty-five prominent men of the city. The Spirit said to me, "These are the men who are responsible for the wicked counsel being given in this city. Therefore prophesy against them loudly."

Then the Spirit told me to say: "The Lord says to the people: I will take you from Jerusalem and hand you over to foreigners who will carry out my judgments against you, and you will know I am the Lord—you who have not obeyed me but rather have copied the nations all around you."

Again a message came from the Lord: "Tell the exiles that the Lord says: Although I have scattered you, yet I will be a sanctuary to you for the time that you are there, and I will gather you back and give you the land of Israel again. And when you return you will remove every trace of all this idol worship."

Then the cherubim lifted their wings and rose into the air with their wheels beside them, and the glory of the Lord rose from over the city and stood above the mountain on the east side.

Afterwards the Spirit of God carried me back again to Babylon to the Jews in exile there. So ended the vision of my visit to Jerusalem. And I told the exiles everything the Lord had shown me.

This message came to me from the Lord:

"Prophesy against the shepherds, the leaders of Israel, and say, 'The Lord God says to you: Woe to the shepherds who feed themselves instead of their flocks. You eat the best food and wear the finest clothes, but you let your flocks starve. You haven't taken care of the weak nor tended the sick nor bound up the broken bones nor gone looking for those who have wandered away and are lost. Instead you have ruled them with force and cruelty. So they were scattered, without a shepherd. They have become a prey to every animal that comes along, and there was no one to search for them or care about them.'

"Therefore I am against the shepherds, and I will hold them responsible for what has happened to my flock. I will search and find my sheep. I will rescue them from all the places they were scattered in that dark and cloudy day. And I will bring them back from nations where they were, and I will feed them upon the mountains of Israel and by the rivers where the land is fertile. There they will lie down in peace and feed in luscious pastures.

"And I, the Lord, will be their God, and my Servant David shall be a Prince among my people. I will drive away the dangerous animals so my people can safely camp in the wildest places. And there shall be showers of blessing, for I will not shut off the rains but send them in their seasons. Their fruit trees and fields will yield bumper crops. When I have broken their chains of slavery and delivered them from those who profiteered at their expense, they shall know I am the Lord. And I will raise up a notable Vine in Israel so my people will never again go hungry. They will know that I, the Lord their God, am with them, and that they are my people."

The power of the Lord was upon me, and I was carried away by the Spirit of the Lord to a valley full of old, dry bones scattered everywhere. He led me among them, and then said to me:

"Son of dust, can these bones become people again?"

"Lord, you alone know the answer to that."

Then he told me to speak to the bones and say: "Listen to the words of God, for I am going to make you live again!"

So I spoke these words from God, and suddenly there was a rattling noise all across the valley. The bones of each body came together and attached to each other as they used to be. As I watched, the muscles and flesh formed over the bones, and skin covered them, but the bodies had no breath. Then he told me to call to the wind and say: "The Lord God says: 'Come from the four winds, O Spirit, and breathe upon these slain bodies, that they may live again.'" So I spoke as he commanded and the bodies began breathing; they lived, and stood up.

Then he told me what the vision meant: "These bones represent the people of Israel. They say: 'We have become a heap of dried-out bones—all hope is gone.' But tell them the Lord says: 'My people, I will open your graves of exile and cause you to return to the land of Israel. I will put my Spirit into you, and then you will know that I have done just what I promised you.'"

Here is another message to me from the Lord:

"Son of dust, face northward toward the land of Magog, and prophesy against Gog, king of Meshech and Tubal. Tell him the Lord God says: 'I am against you, Gog. I will mobilize your troops and armored cavalry, and make you a mighty host. Peras, Cush, and Put shall join you with all their weaponry, and so shall Gomer and all his hordes and the armies of Togarmah from the distant north, as well as many others.

"'A long time from now you will be called to action. You will swoop down onto the land of Israel, which will be lying in peace after the return of its people from many lands. You and your allies will roll down like a storm and cover the land. For at that time you will have said: Israel is an unprotected land; I will march against her and destroy the people. I will capture vast booty and many slaves. For the people are rich now, and the earth revolves around them!'

"But Sheba and Dedan and the merchant princes of Tarshish with whom she trades will ask, 'Who are you to rob them and make them poor?'

"The Lord says to Gog: 'This will happen in the latter years of history. I will bring you against my land, and my holiness will be vindicated in your terrible destruction. I will fight you with sword, disease, torrential floods, great hailstones, fire, and brimstone! Thus the nations will hear what I have done and know that I am God!'

"It will take seven months for the people of Israel to bury the bodies. At the end of the seven months, they will appoint men to search the land for any skeletons and bury them, so the land will be cleansed.

"From that time on, Israel will know I am their God. Their time of shame will be in the past; they will be home again in peace and safety. I will bring them home from the lands of their enemies—and my glory shall be evident to all the nations when I do it. I will leave none of them remaining among the nations. And I will pour out my Spirit upon them."

In the twenty-fifth year of our exile, the hand of the Lord was upon me and in a vision he took me to Israel and set me on a high mountain where I saw what appeared to be a city opposite me. Going nearer, I saw a man whose face shone like bronze standing beside the Temple gate, holding in his hand a measuring tape and stick.

He said, "Watch and listen to everything I show you, for you have been brought here so I can show you many things; and then you are to return to the people of Israel to tell them all you have seen."

The man began to measure the wall around the outside of the Temple area with his stick. He told me: "This wall is 10½ feet tall and 10½ feet wide." Then he took me to the passageway that goes through the eastern wall. There were three guardrooms on each side. We passed through the passageway to the court inside. A stone pavement ran around the inside of the walls, and thirty rooms were built against the walls.

He measured across to the wall on the other side of this court, "the outer court" of the Temple, and found the distance was 175 feet. As I followed, he left the eastern passageway and went over to the passage through the northern wall and measured it. All the measurements were the same as for the east passageway—87½ feet long and 43¾ feet from side to side across the top of the guardrooms. There were windows, an entry hall, and palm tree decorations just the same as on the east side.

Then he took me around to the south gate and measured the various sections of its passageway and found they were just the same as in the others. It had windows along the walls as the others did, and an entry hall.

Then he took me over to the inner wall and its south passageway. It had the same measurements as the passageways of the outer wall. He took me along the court to the eastern entrance of the inner wall, and it had the same measurements as the others.

Then he took me around to the north gate of the inner wall, and the measurements there were just like the others. Its entry hall faced toward the outer court, but a door led from its entry hall into a side room where the flesh of sacrifices was washed before being taken to the altar.

In the inner court there were two one-room buildings, one beside the northern entrance, facing south, and one beside the southern entrance, facing north. And he said to me: "The building beside the inner northern gate is for the priests who supervise the maintenance. The building beside the inner southern entrance is for priests in charge of the altar—the descendants of Zadok—for they alone of all the Levites may come near to the Lord to minister to him."

Then he measured the inner court in front of the Temple and found it to be 175 feet square, and there was an altar standing in front of the Temple.

Afterwards he brought me into the nave, the large main room of the Temple. The nave was seventy feet long by thirty-five feet.

Then he went into the inner room at the end of the nave; the inner room was thirty-five feet square. "This," he told me, "is the Most Holy Place."

The nave of the Temple and the Holy of Holies and the entry hall were paneled, and all three had recessed windows. The walls were decorated with carvings of cherubim, each with two faces, and of palm trees alternating with the cherubim.

When he had finished making measurements, he led me out through the east passageway to measure the entire Temple area. It was in the form of a square, 875 feet long on each side, with a wall all around it to separate the restricted area from the public places.

Afterwards, he brought me out again to the passageway through the outer wall leading to the east. And suddenly the glory of the God of Israel appeared from the east. The sound of his coming was like the roar of rushing waters, and the whole landscape lighted up with his glory. It was just as I had seen it in the other visions, first by the Chebar Canal, and then later at Jerusalem when he came to destroy the city. And I fell down before him with my face in the dust. And the glory of the Lord came into the Temple through the eastern passageway.

Then the Spirit took me up and brought me into the inner court; and the glory of the Lord filled the Temple. I heard the Lord speaking to me from within the Temple (the man who had been measuring was still standing beside me).

And the Lord said, "This is the place of my throne, and my footstool, where I shall remain, living among the people of Israel forever. They will not defile my holy name any longer through worship of other gods. Describe the Temple I have shown you to the people of Israel. Explain the details of its constructions—and everything about it. Write out all the directions and the rules for them to keep."

Then the Lord brought me back to the outer wall's eastern passageway, but it was closed. And he said, "This gate shall remain closed; no man shall pass through it; for the Lord entered here and so it shall remain shut. Only the prince may sit inside the passageway to feast there before the Lord. But he shall go and come only through the entry hall of the passage."

He brought me back to the door of the Temple. I saw a stream flowing eastward from beneath the Temple and passing to the right of the altar, that is, on its south side. Then he brought me outside the wall through the north passageway and around to the eastern entrance, where I saw the stream flowing. Measuring as he went, he took me 1,500 feet east along the stream and told me to go across. At that point the water was up to my ankles. He measured off another 1,500 feet and told me to cross again. This time the water was up to my knees. Fifteen hundred feet after that it was up to my waist. Another 1,500 feet and it had become so deep I wouldn't be able to cross unless I were to swim.

He told me to keep in mind what I had seen, then led me back along the bank. And now, to my surprise, many trees were growing on both sides of the river!

He told me: "This river flows east through the desert and the Jordan Valley to the Dead Sea, where it will heal the salty waters and make them fresh and pure. Everything touching the water of this river shall live. Fish will abound in the Dead Sea, for its waters will be healed. Fishermen will fish all the way from En-gedi to Eneglaim. All kinds of fruit trees will grow along the river banks. The leaves will never turn brown and fall, and there will always be fruit. There will be a new crop every month. The fruit will be for food and the leaves for medicine.

"Each city gate will be named in honor of one of the tribes of Israel. On the north side, with its 1½-mile wall, there will be three gates, one named for Reuben, one for Judah, and one for Levi. On the east the gates will be named for Joseph, Benjamin, and Dan. The south wall will have the gates of Simeon, Issachar, and Zebulun; on the 1½ miles of the west side, they will be named for Gad, Asher, and Naphtali. The entire circumference of the city is six miles. And the name of the city will be The City of God."[25]

KINGDOM COLLAPSE

In Jerusalem Zedekiah refused to take the counsel of Jeremiah the prophet who gave him messages from the Lord. He rebelled against King Nebuchadnezzar even though he had taken an oath of loyalty.

The important people of the nation, including the High Priests, worshiped the heathen idols of the surrounding nations, thus polluting the Temple. Then the Lord brought the king of Babylon against them.

This message came to Jeremiah from the Lord when Nebuchadnezzar and his armies fought against Jerusalem and the cities of Judah:

"Tell Zedekiah that the Lord says: 'I will give this city to the king of Babylon and he shall burn it. You shall be captured and taken before the king of Babylon and he shall pronounce sentence against you, and you shall be exiled to Babylon.' "

So Jeremiah delivered the message.

Jeremiah was imprisoned in the dungeon beneath the palace while the Babylonian army was besieging Jerusalem. Zedekiah put him there for continuing to prophesy that the city would be conquered by Babylon. "You can't win! Surrender now!" Jeremiah had told him again and again.

Then this message from the Lord came to Jeremiah: "Your cousin Hanamel will soon arrive to ask you to buy the farm he owns in Anathoth, for by law you have a chance to buy before it is offered to anyone else."

Hanamel came as the Lord had said, and I bought the field, paying seventeen shekels of silver. I signed and sealed the deed of purchase before witnesses, and took the sealed deed and also the unsealed copy and handed the papers to Baruch. I said to him:

"The Lord of Hosts says, 'Take both this sealed deed and the copy and put them into a pottery jar to preserve them, for in the future these papers will be valuable.' Someday people will again own property in this country and will be buying and selling houses and vineyards and fields."

Then this message came to Jeremiah:

"I am the God of all mankind; is anything too hard for me? This city will fall to Babylon through warfare, famine, and disease, but I will bring my people back from all the countries where I will scatter them.

"The day will come," says the Lord, "when I will make a new contract with the people of Israel and Judah. It won't be like the one I made with their fathers when I took them by the hand to bring them out of Egypt—a contract they broke, forcing me to reject them. This is the new contract I will make with them: I will inscribe my laws upon their hearts so they shall want to honor me. Everyone both great and small shall really know me then, and I will forgive and forget their sins. I am as likely to reject my people Israel as I am to do away with the laws of nature! The time is coming when all Jerusalem shall be rebuilt for the Lord. The entire city, including the graveyard and ash dump in the valley, shall be holy to the Lord; it shall never again be captured or destroyed."

Nebuchadnezzar came with his army and built forts and laid siege to the city for two years. Finally, when the famine was very serious, people in the city tore a hole in the wall and all the soldiers fled during the night and made a dash toward Arabah. But the Chaldean soldiers chased them and caught King Zedekiah near Jericho. They brought him to the king of Babylon who was staying in Riblah, and there judgment was passed upon him. He made Zedekiah watch while his sons and all the princes of Judah were killed before his eyes, then his eyes were gouged out and he was taken in chains to Babylon and put in prison for the rest of his life.

On the tenth day of the fifth month during the nineteenth year of the reign of Nebuchadnezzar, Nebuzaradan, captain of the guard, arrived in Jerusalem and burned the Temple and the palace and all the larger homes, and set the Chaldean army to tearing down the walls of the city.

The Babylonians dismantled the two large bronze pillars that stood at the entrance of the Temple, and the bronze laver and the bronze bulls on which it stood, and carted them off to Babylon. They took along all the bronze pots and kettles, ash shovels used at the altar, and the snuffers, spoons, bowls, and all the other items used in the Temple. The two enormous pillars and the laver and twelve bulls had been made in the days of King Solomon. The pillars were each twenty-seven feet high and eighteen feet in circumference.

Nebuzaradan, captain of the guard, sent the remnant of the population and all those who had defected to him to Babylon. But throughout Judah he left a few people, the very poor, and gave them fields and vineyards.

King Nebuchadnezzar had told Nebuzaradan to find Jeremiah. "See that he isn't hurt," he said. "Look after him well and give him anything he wants." So Nebuzaradan sent soldiers to bring Jeremiah out of the prison to take him back to his home. And Jeremiah lived there among his people who were left in the land.

Thus the word of the Lord spoken through Jeremiah came true, that the land must rest for seventy years to make up for the years when the people refused to observe the Sabbath.

Jerusalem's streets, once thronged with people, are silent now. Like a widow broken with grief, she sits alone in her mourning. She, once queen of nations, is now a slave.

The roads to Zion mourn, no longer filled with joyous throngs who come to celebrate the Temple feasts. The city gates are silent, her priests groan, her virgins have been dragged away. Bitterly she weeps.

Her enemies have plundered her, taking everything precious she owns. She has seen foreign nations violate her sacred Temple—foreigners forbidden even to enter. A cloud of anger from the Lord has overcast Jerusalem. In his day of awesome fury he has shown no mercy even to his Temple.

The Lord without mercy has destroyed every home in Israel. In his wrath he has broken every fortress, every wall. Jerusalem's gates are useless; all their locks and bars are broken. Her kings and princes are enslaved in far-off lands, without a temple, without a divine law to govern them.

I have cried until the tears no longer come; my heart is broken. All who pass by scoff and say, "Is this the city called 'Most Beautiful in All the World'?" Enemies hiss, "We have destroyed her at last!" But it is the Lord who did it, just as he warned.

Yet there is one ray of hope: his compassion never ends. It is only the Lord's mercies that have kept us from complete destruction. Great is his faithfulness; his lovingkindness begins afresh each day.

My soul claims the Lord as my inheritance; therefore I will hope in him. The Lord is wonderfully good to those who wait for him, to those who seek for him. It is good both to hope and wait quietly for the salvation of the Lord.

Jerusalem and the Temple of the Lord are desolate, deserted by all but wild animals lurking in the ruins. "O Lord, turn us around and bring us back to you again! That is our only hope! Give us back the joys we used to have!"[26]

PART

EXILED
NATION

EXPATRIATES King Nebuchadnezzar made a golden statue—ninety feet high and nine feet wide—and set it up on the Plain of Dura. Then he sent messages to all the princes, governors, captains, judges, treasurers, counselors, sheriffs, and rulers of all the provinces of his empire to come to the dedication of his statue. When they all arrived and were standing before the monument, a herald shouted, "O people of all nations and languages, this is the king's command:

"When the band strikes up, you are to fall on the ground to worship King Nebuchadnezzar's golden statue. Anyone who refuses to obey will be thrown into a flaming furnace."

When the band began to play, everyone fell to the ground and worshiped the statue. But officials accused some Jews of refusing to worship!

"Your Majesty," they said, "Shadrach, Meshach, and Abednego have defied you, refusing to serve your gods or to worship the golden statue you set up."

Nebuchadnezzar, in a rage, ordered Shadrach, Meshach, and Abednego to be brought before him.

"Is it true," he asked, "that you are refusing to worship the golden statue? If you refuse, you will be thrown into a flaming furnace within the hour. And what god can deliver you out of my hands then?"

Shadrach, Meshach, and Abednego replied, "O Nebuchadnezzar, we are not worried about what will happen to us. If we are thrown into the flaming furnace, our God is able to deliver us; but if he doesn't, we will never under any circumstance serve your gods or worship the golden statue you erected."

Nebuchadnezzar's face became dark with anger. He commanded that the furnace be heated seven times hotter than usual and called for strong men to bind Shadrach, Meshach, and Abednego and throw them into the fire.

They bound them tight with ropes and threw them into the furnace. Because the king demanded such a hot fire, flames leaped out and killed the soldiers as they threw them in!

But as he was watching, Nebuchadnezzar exclaimed to his advisors, "Didn't we throw three men into the furnace?"

"Yes, we did indeed, Your Majesty."

"Well, look!" Nebuchadnezzar shouted. "I see four men, unbound, walking around in the fire. And the fourth looks like a god!"

Nebuchadnezzar came close to the open door of the furnace and yelled: "Shadrach, Meshach, and Abednego, come out!" So they stepped out of the fire.

Princes, governors, captains, and counselors crowded around them and saw that the fire hadn't touched them— they didn't even smell of smoke!

Then Nebuchadnezzar said, "Blessed be the God of Shadrach, Meshach, and Abednego, for he sent his angel to deliver his servants when they were willing to die rather than serve any god except their own. Therefore I make this decree, that any person of any nation, language, or religion who speaks a word against the God of Shadrach, Meshach, and Abednego shall be torn limb from limb and his house knocked into a heap of rubble. For no other God can do what this one does."

Then the king gave promotions to Shadrach, Meshach, and Abednego, so that they prospered greatly in the province of Babylon.[1]

HUMBLED KING

This is the proclamation of Nebuchadnezzar which he sent to people of every language:

"Greetings: I want you all to know about the strange thing that the Most High God did to me. It was incredible— and now I know that his kingdom is everlasting. One night I had a dream that greatly frightened me. I called the wise men of Babylon to tell me the meaning, but the magicians, astrologers, fortune-tellers, and wizards couldn't interpret it. At last Daniel came in—the man I named Belteshazzar— and I told him the dream.

"I saw a very tall tree out in a field, growing higher and higher into the sky until it could be seen by everyone in the world. Its branches were weighted with fruit enough for everyone to eat. Animals rested beneath its shade, birds sheltered in its branches, and all the world was fed from it. Then I saw one of God's angels coming down from heaven.

"He shouted, 'Cut down the tree, lop off its branches, shake off its leaves, and scatter its fruit. But leave its stump and roots in the ground, banded with a chain of iron and brass, surrounded by the tender grass. Let the dews of heaven drench him and let him eat grass with the wild animals! For seven years let him have the mind of an animal instead of a man. The purpose of this decree is that the world may understand that the Most High dominates the kingdoms of the world, and gives them to anyone he wants to.'

"Daniel sat silent for an hour, aghast at the meaning of the dream. Finally Daniel replied: 'Oh, that the events foreshadowed in this dream would happen to your enemies, and not to you! For the tree you saw growing so tall, Your Majesty, is you. For your greatness reaches up to heaven, and your rule to the ends of the earth.

"'Your Majesty, God has decreed that your people will chase you from your palace, and you will live in the fields like an animal, your back wet with dew. For seven years this will be your life, until you learn that the Most High God gives power to anyone he chooses. But the stump and the roots were left in the ground! This means that you will get your kingdom back again, when you have learned that heaven rules.'

"All these things happened to Nebuchadnezzar. Twelve months after this dream, he was strolling on the roof of the royal palace and saying, 'I, by my mighty power, have built this beautiful city as my royal residence and the capital of my empire.'

"That same hour Nebuchadnezzar was chased from his palace and ate grass like the cows, and his body was wet with dew; his hair grew as long as eagles' feathers and his nails were like birds' claws.

"At the end of the seven years I, Nebuchadnezzar, looked up to heaven, and my sanity returned, and I praised the Most High God and honored him who lives forever. He does whatever he thinks best among the hosts of heaven, as well as here among the inhabitants of earth. No one can stop him or challenge him. When my mind returned to me, so did my honor and kingdom. My counselors and officers came back to me and I was reestablished as head of my kingdom.

"Now, I, Nebuchadnezzar, praise and glorify the King of Heaven, the Judge of all, whose every act is right and good."[2]

DANIEL'S DREAMS

During the first year of Belshazzar's reign over the Babylonian empire, Daniel had a dream and wrote it down.

"I saw a great storm on a mighty ocean, then four huge animals came up out of the water. The first was like a lion, but it had eagle's wings! As I watched, its wings were pulled off so that it could no longer fly, and it was left standing on the ground, on two feet, like a man; and a man's mind was given to it. The second animal looked like a bear with its paw raised, ready to strike. It held three ribs between its teeth, and I heard a voice saying to it, 'Get up! Devour many people!' The third of these strange animals looked like a leopard, but on its back it had wings like those of birds, and it had four heads! And great power was given to it over all mankind.

"Then, as I watched in my dream, a fourth animal rose up out of the ocean, too dreadful to describe and incredibly strong. It devoured some of its victims by tearing them apart with its huge iron teeth, and others it crushed beneath its feet. It was far more vicious than any of the other animals, and it had ten horns.

"As I was looking at the horns, suddenly another small horn appeared among them, and three of the first ones were yanked out, roots and all, to give it room; this little horn had a man's eyes and a bragging mouth.

"I watched as thrones were put in place and the Ancient of Days—the Almighty God—sat down to judge. His clothing was as white as snow, his hair like whitest wool. He sat upon a fiery throne brought in on flaming wheels, and a river of fire flowed from before him. Millions of angels ministered to him and hundreds of millions of people stood before him, waiting to be judged. Then the court began its session and The Books were opened.

"As I watched, the brutal fourth animal was killed and its body handed over to be burned because of its arrogance against Almighty God, and the boasting of its little horn. As for the other three animals, their kingdoms were taken from them, but they were allowed to live a short time longer.

"Next I saw the arrival of a Man—or so he seemed to be—brought there on clouds from heaven; he approached the Ancient of Days and was presented to him. He was given the ruling power and glory over all the nations of the world, so that all people of every language must obey him. His power is eternal—it will never end; his government shall never fall.

"I was confused and disturbed by all I had seen, so I approached one of those standing beside the throne and asked him the meaning of these things.

" 'These four huge animals,' he said, 'represent four kings who will someday rule the earth. But in the end the people of the Most High God shall rule the governments of the world forever and forever.'

"I asked about the fourth animal, the one so shocking.

I asked, too, about the ten horns and the little horn that came up afterwards and destroyed three of the others, for I had seen this horn warring against God's people until the Ancient of Days came and vindicated his people, giving them worldwide powers of government.

" 'This fourth animal,' he told me, 'is the fourth world power that will rule the earth. It will devour the whole world. His ten horns are ten kings that will rise out of his empire; then another king will arise, more brutal than the other ten, and will destroy three of them. He will defy the Most High God, and wear down the saints with persecution, and try to change all laws, morals, and customs. God's people will be helpless in his hands for three and a half years.

" 'But then the Ancient of Days will come and take all power from this vicious king, to consume and destroy it. Then every nation under heaven shall be given to the people of God; they shall rule all things forever.' "

"That was the end of the dream. When I awoke, I was pale with fright, but I told no one what I had seen.

"In the third year of King Belshazzar, I had another dream similar to the first. This time I was at Susa, the capital in the province of Elam. As I was looking around, I saw a ram with two long horns standing on the riverbank; and as I watched, one of these horns began to grow. The ram butted everything out of its way and no one could stand against it.

"While I was wondering what this could mean, a buck goat appeared from the west, so swiftly that it didn't even touch the ground. This goat, which had one very large horn between its eyes, rushed at the two-horned ram. He charged into the ram and broke off both his horns. The ram was helpless, and the buck goat knocked him down and trampled him.

"The victor became powerful, but at the height of his power his horn was broken, and in its place grew four good-sized horns pointing in four directions. One of these became very strong and attacked the south and east, and warred against the land of Israel. He even challenged the

Commander of the army of heaven by canceling the daily sacrifices and defiling his Temple.

"Then I heard two angels talking to each other. One of them said, 'How long will it be until the daily sacrifice is restored again? How long until the destruction of the Temple is avenged and God's people triumph?'

"The other replied, 'Twenty-three hundred days must first go by.'

"As I was trying to understand this vision, suddenly a man was standing in front of me—and I heard a man's voice calling from across the river, 'Gabriel, tell Daniel the meaning of his dream.'

"As he approached, I was too frightened to stand, and fell down with my face to the ground. 'Son of man,' he said, 'you must understand that the events you have seen will not take place until the end times.'

"Then I fainted, lying on the ground. But he roused me with a touch and helped me to my feet. 'I am here,' he said, 'to tell you what is going to happen in the last days of the coming time of terror—for what you have seen pertains to that final event in history.

" 'The two horns of the ram you saw are the kings of Media and Persia; the goat is the nation of Greece, and its long horn represents the first great king of that country. When you saw the horn break off, and four smaller horns replace it, this meant that the Grecian Empire will break into four sections with four kings, none of them as great as the first.

" 'Toward the end of their kingdoms, when they have become morally rotten, an angry king shall rise to power with great shrewdness and intelligence. His power shall be mighty, but it will be satanic strength, not his own. Prospering wherever he turns, he will destroy all who oppose him and he will devastate God's people.

" 'He will be a master of deception, defeating many by catching them off guard. So great will he fancy himself to be that he will even take on the Prince of Princes in battle; but in so doing he will seal his own doom, for he shall be broken by the hand of God.

" 'And in your vision you heard about twenty-three hundred days to pass before the rights of worship are restored. This number is literal, but none of these things will happen for a long time.'

"I grew faint and was sick for several days. Afterward I performed my duties for the king, but I was greatly distressed by the dream and did not understand it."[3]

BABYLON'S FATE

Belshazzar the king invited a thousand of his officers to a great feast where the wine flowed freely. While Belshazzar was drinking, he was reminded of the gold and silver cups taken long before from the Temple in Jerusalem during Nebuchadnezzar's reign and brought to Babylon. Belshazzar ordered these sacred cups brought to the feast, and when they arrived he and his princes, wives, and concubines drank toasts from them to their idols.

Suddenly, as they were drinking, they saw the fingers of a man's hand writing on the plaster of the wall opposite the lampstand. The king's face blanched with fear, and such terror gripped him that his knees knocked together.

"Bring the magicians and astrologers!" he screamed. "Whoever reads that writing on the wall will be dressed in purple robes of royal honor and become the third ruler in the kingdom!"

But none of them could understand the writing.

The king grew more hysterical. When the queen-mother heard what was happening, she rushed to the banquet hall and said to Belshazzar, "Calm yourself, Your Majesty; there is a man in your kingdom who has within him the spirit of the holy gods. In the days of your father this man was found to be full of wisdom and understanding. And in the reign of King Nebuchadnezzar he was made chief of all the magicians, astrologers, and soothsayers. Call for this man, Daniel—or Belteshazzar, as the king called him—for he can interpret dreams."

So Daniel was rushed in. The king asked, "Are you the Daniel that King Nebuchadnezzar brought from Israel as a Jewish captive? My astrologers have tried to read that writing on the wall, but they can't. I am told you can solve all kinds of mysteries. If you can tell me the meaning of those words, I will make you the third ruler in the kingdom."

Daniel answered, "Keep your gifts, but I will tell you what they mean, Your Majesty. The Most High God gave Nebuchadnezzar a kingdom and majesty and honor. All nations trembled before him in fear. At his whim they rose or fell. But when his heart and mind were hardened in pride, God removed him from his royal throne and took away his glory, and he was chased out of his palace into the fields. At last he knew that the Most High overrules the kingdoms of men.

"And you, his successor, knew all this yet you have not been humble. You defied the Lord of Heaven, and brought here these cups from his Temple; and you and your officers have been drinking wine from them while praising gods of silver, gold, brass, iron, wood, and stone. And so God sent those fingers to write this message: *'Mene, Mene, Tekel, Parsin.'*

"This is what it means:

"*Mene* means 'numbered'—God has numbered the days of your reign, and they are ended.

"*Tekel* means 'weighed'—you have been weighed in God's balances and have failed the test.

"*Parsin* means 'divided'—your kingdom will be divided and given to the Medes and Persians."

Then, at Belshazzar's command, Daniel was robed in purple, a golden chain was hung around his neck, and he was proclaimed third ruler in the kingdom.

That very night Belshazzar, the Chaldean king, was killed, and Darius the Mede entered the city and began reigning.[4]

DARIUS AND DANIEL

Darius divided the kingdom into 120 provinces, each under a governor. The governors were accountable to three presidents (Daniel was one of them). Daniel soon proved himself more capable than the other presidents, and the king began to think of placing him over the entire empire as his administrative officer.

This made the other presidents and governors jealous, and they began searching for some fault in the way Daniel was handling his affairs. They couldn't find anything to criticize, so they concluded, "Our only chance is his religion!"

They decided to go to the king and say, "King Darius, we presidents, governors, counselors, and deputies have decided that you should make a law, irrevocable under any circumstance, that for the next thirty days anyone who asks a favor of God or man—except from you, Your Majesty—shall be thrown to the lions. Your Majesty, we request your signature on this law; it will be a 'law of the Medes and Persians' that cannot be revoked."

So King Darius signed the law.

Though Daniel knew about it, he went home and knelt down as usual in his bedroom, with its windows open toward Jerusalem, and prayed three times a day just as he always had.

The men thronged to Daniel's house and found him praying, asking favors of his God. They rushed back to the king and reminded him about his law. "That fellow Daniel is paying no attention to your law. He is asking favors of his God three times a day."

The king was angry with himself for signing the law. He spent the rest of the day trying to think of some way to get Daniel out of this predicament.

In the evening the men came again to the king and said, "Your Majesty, you signed the law and it cannot be changed."

So the king gave the order for Daniel's arrest and he was taken to the den of lions. The king said to him, "May your God, whom you worship continually, deliver you." And then they threw him in.

The king returned to his palace and went to bed without dinner. He didn't sleep all night. Very early the next morning he hurried to the lions' den and called, "Daniel, servant of the Living God, was your God able to deliver you from the lions?"

He heard a voice: "Your Majesty, my God has sent his angel to shut the lions' mouths so they can't touch me."

The king ordered that Daniel be lifted from the den, and not a scratch was found on him.

Then the king issued a command to bring the men who had accused Daniel and throw them into the den. The lions leaped upon them and tore them apart.

Afterwards King Darius wrote this message to his empire:

"Greetings! I decree that everyone shall fear before the God of Daniel in every part of my kingdom. His God is the living, unchanging God whose kingdom shall never be destroyed and whose power shall never end. He delivers his people; he does great miracles in heaven and earth; it is he who delivered Daniel from the power of the lions."

So Daniel prospered in the reign of Darius, and in the reign of Cyrus the Persian.[5]

ANOINTED ONE

The first year of the reign of King Darius, I, Daniel, learned from the book of Jeremiah the prophet that Jerusalem must lie desolate for seventy years. So I earnestly pleaded with the Lord to end our captivity and send us back to our own land. As I prayed, I fasted, wore rough sackcloth, sprinkled myself with ashes, and confessed my sins and those of my people.

"O Lord our God, we have disobeyed you; we have flouted the laws you gave us through the prophets. And so the awesome curse of God has crushed us. Never in history has there been a disaster like what happened at Jerusalem to us. Every curse against us written in the law of Moses has come true. O Lord, you brought lasting honor to your name by removing your people from Egypt in a great display of power. Lord, do it again! Because of all your faithful mercies, please turn away your furious anger from Jerusalem. O God, hear your servant's prayer! Let your face shine again with peace and joy upon your desolate sanctuary for your own glory, Lord."

Even while I was praying, Gabriel, whom I had seen in the earlier vision, flew swiftly to me at the time of the evening sacrifice and said, "Daniel, I am here to help you understand God's plans. The moment you began praying, a command was given. I am here to tell you what it was, for God loves you very much. Listen and try to understand.

"The Lord has commanded 490 years of further punishment upon Jerusalem and your people; then the kingdom
of everlasting righteousness will begin and the Most Holy
Place in the Temple will be rededicated, as the prophets
have declared. It will be forty-nine years plus 434 years
from the time the command is given to rebuild Jerusalem
until the Anointed One comes! Jerusalem's streets and walls
will be rebuilt despite the perilous times.

"After this period, the Anointed One will be killed, his
kingdom still unrealized . . . and a king will arise whose
armies will destroy the city and the Temple. And war and
its miseries are decreed from that time to the very end.
This king will make a seven-year treaty with the people,
but after half that time he will break his pledge and stop
the Jews from all their sacrifices and their offerings; then
as a climax to his terrible deeds the Enemy shall utterly
defile the sanctuary of God. But in God's time and plan
his judgment will be poured out upon this Evil One."[6]

THE RETURN

During the first year of the reign
of King Cyrus of Persia, the Lord
fulfilled Jeremiah's prophecy by giv-
ing Cyrus the desire to send this proclamation throughout
his empire:

"Cyrus, king of Persia, hereby announces that Jehovah,
the God of heaven who gave me my vast empire, has now
given me the responsibility of building him a Temple in
Jerusalem in the land of Judah. All Jews throughout the
kingdom may now return to Jerusalem to rebuild this Temple. May his blessings rest upon you. Those Jews who
do not go should contribute toward the expenses of those
who do, and supply them with clothing, transportation, sup-
plies for the journey, and a freewill offering for the Temple."

Then God gave a great desire to the leaders of Judah
and Benjamin and to the priests and Levites to return to
Jerusalem. All the Jewish exiles who chose to remain in
Persia gave whatever assistance they could.

King Cyrus donated the gold bowls and other valuable
items which King Nebuchadnezzar had taken from the Tem-

ple at Jerusalem. He instructed the treasurer of Persia to present these gifts to Shesh-bazzar, the leader of the exiles returning to Judah.

A total of 42,360 persons returned to Judah. They took with them horses, mules, camels, and donkeys.

The priests and Levites and some of the common people settled in Jerusalem and its nearby villages; singers, gate-keepers, Temple workers, and the rest of the people returned to other cities of Judah from which they had come.

During September, everyone came to Jerusalem from their homes in the other towns. Then Joshua with his fellow priests and Zerubbabel and his clan rebuilt the altar of God on its old site. It was used immediately to sacrifice morning and evening burnt offerings to the Lord.

And they celebrated the Feast of Tabernacles as prescribed in the laws of Moses. They also offered the special sacrifices required for Sabbaths, new moon celebrations, and other annual feasts. Voluntary offerings of the people were also sacrificed.

They hired masons and carpenters and bought cedar logs from Tyre and Sidon, paying for them with food, wine, and olive oil. Construction of the Temple began in June of the second year. The work force was made up of all who had returned under the direction of Zerubbabel, Joshua, and their fellow priests and the Levites.[7]

DANIEL AND THE END

In the third year of Cyrus, Daniel had another vision. It concerned events to happen in the future: times of great tribulation—wars and sorrows.

"When this vision came to me," Daniel said later, "I had been in mourning for three weeks. I tasted neither wine nor meat, and I neither washed nor shaved.

"One day early in April, as I was standing beside the great Tigris River, I looked up and there stood a person in linen garments, with a belt of purest gold around his waist, and glowing, lustrous skin! From his face came flashes like lightning, and his eyes were pools of fire; his arms and feet shone like polished brass, and his voice was like the roaring of a multitude of people. My strength left me, and I grew pale with fright.

"Then he spoke to me, and I fell to the ground in a deep faint. But a hand touched me and lifted me to my hands and knees. And I heard, 'O Daniel, greatly beloved of God, stand up and listen carefully to what I have to say to you, for God has sent me to you.'

"I stood up, still trembling with fear. Then he said, 'Don't be frightened, Daniel, for your request has been heard in heaven the day you began to fast before the Lord and pray for understanding. That very day I was sent here to meet you, but for twenty-one days the mighty Evil Spirit who overrules the kingdom of Persia blocked my way. Then Michael of the heavenly army came to help me so I was able to break through these spirit rulers. Now I am here to tell you what will happen to your people, the Jews, at the end times—for the fulfillment of this prophecy is many years away.

" 'I will show you what the future holds. Three more Persian kings will reign, to be succeeded by a fourth far richer than the others. Using his wealth for political advantage, he will plan total war against Greece.

" 'Then a mighty king will rise in Greece who will rule a vast kingdom and accomplish everything he sets out to do. But at the zenith of his power his kingdom will break apart and be divided into four weaker nations. One of them, the king of Egypt, will increase in power but this king's officials will rebel against him and take away his kingdom and make it still more powerful.

" 'The king of Syria will invade Egypt briefly, but will soon return to his own land. However, the sons of this king will assemble a mighty army that will flow across Israel into Egypt. Then the king of Egypt will rally against the forces of Syria and defeat them.

" 'A few years later the Syrian king will return with an army far greater than the one he lost. The Syrian and his allies will lay siege to a fortified city of Egypt and capture it. The Syrian king will also enter The Glorious Land of Israel and pillage it. He will turn homeward again, but will have trouble on the way, and disappear.

" 'His successor, after a very brief reign, will die mysteriously.

" 'Next will be an evil man; from the first, his method will be deceit; with a mere handful of followers he will become strong. He will besiege and capture powerful strongholds throughout his dominions. He will raise a great army against Egypt; and Egypt, too, will raise a mighty army, but to no avail.

" 'The Syrian will return home with great riches, first marching through Israel and destroying it. Then, he will once again turn his armies southward, but now it will be very different. For Roman warships will scare him off, and he will withdraw. Angered by having to retreat, the Syrian king will pillage Jerusalem and pollute the sanctuary, putting a stop to the daily sacrifices, and worshiping idols inside the Temple. He will leave godless Jews in power, but the people who know their God shall be strong and do great things.

" 'The king will do exactly as he pleases, claiming to be greater than every god, even blaspheming the God of gods. He will worship the Fortress god—a god his fathers never knew.

" 'Then at the time of the end, the king of the south will attack again, and the northern king will react with the fury of a whirlwind. He will invade various lands on the way, including Israel, and overthrow the governments of many nations. Then news from the east and north will alarm him, and he will return. He will halt between Jerusalem and the sea and there pitch his tents, but while there his time will run out and there will be no one to help him.

" 'At that time Michael, the angelic prince who stands guard over your nation, will fight for you in heaven against satanic forces, and there will be a time of anguish for the Jews greater than any previous suffering. And yet every one of your people whose names are written in The Book will endure it. Many whose bodies lie dead will rise up, some to everlasting life and some to shame and everlasting contempt. And those who are wise—the people of God— shall shine as the sun and those who turn many to righteousness will glitter like stars forever.

" 'But Daniel, keep this prophecy a secret; seal it up so that it will not be understood until the end times, when travel and education shall be vastly increased!'

"Then I, Daniel, saw two men on each bank of a river. One of them asked the man in linen robes, who was standing now above the river, 'How long will it be until all these terrors end?'

"He replied that they will not end until three and a half years after the power of God's people has been crushed.

"I didn't understand, so I said, 'Sir, how will this all come out?'

"He said, 'Go now, Daniel, for what I have said is not to be understood until the time of the end. Many shall be purified by great trials and persecutions, but the wicked shall continue in their wickedness. Only those who are willing to learn will know what it means. From the time the daily sacrifice is taken away and the Horrible Thing is set up to be worshiped, there will be 1,290 days. And blessed are those who wait and remain until the 1335th day!

" 'But go now to the end of your life and your rest; for you will rise again and have your full share of those last days.' "[8]

PART
9
REBUILDING

TEMPLE FOES When the builders completed the foundation of the Temple, the priests put on their robes and blew their trumpets and the descendants of Asaph crashed their cymbals to praise the Lord in the manner ordained by King David. They sang rounds of praise and thanks to God. Then all the people gave a great shout, praising God because the foundation of the Temple had been laid. The commotion could be heard far away!

When the enemies of Judah and Benjamin heard that the exiles were rebuilding the Temple, they approached Zerubbabel and other leaders and suggested, "Let us work with you, for we are interested in your God; we have sacrificed to him ever since King Esar-haddon of Assyria brought us here."

But Zerubbabel and other leaders replied, "No, the Temple must be built by Israelis, just as King Cyrus commanded."

Then the local residents tried to discourage and frighten them by sending agents to tell lies about them to King Cyrus. This went on during his entire reign.

Afterwards, when King Ahasuerus began to reign, they wrote him a letter of accusation against the people of Jerusalem, and did the same thing during the reign of Ar-ta-xerxes. Participating were Persians, Babylonians, and men from several other nations taken from their own lands and relocated in Jerusalem, Samaria, and throughout the neighboring lands west of the Euphrates River.

The prophets in Jerusalem and Judah at that time, Haggai and Zechariah, brought messages from God to Zerubbabel and Joshua, encouraging them.[1]

GLORIOUS TEMPLE

A message from the Lord to Haggai who delivered it to Zerubbabel, governor of Judah, and to Joshua the High Priest:

"Why is everyone saying it is not the right time for rebuilding my Temple?" asks the Lord.

His reply is: "Is it the right time for you to live in luxurious homes when the Temple lies in ruins? Look at the result: you plant much but harvest little; you have scarcely enough to eat or drink, and not enough clothes to keep you warm. Think it over; consider how you have acted and what has happened as a result! Then go up into the mountains and bring down timber and rebuild my Temple. And I will be pleased with it and appear there in my glory."

Zerubbabel and Joshua and the people obeyed Haggai's message from the Lord. They began to worship him in earnest; they all gathered and volunteered their help.

The Lord sent this message through Haggai:

"Ask this question of the governor and High Priest and everyone left in the land: 'Who among you can remember the Temple as it was before? In comparison, it is nothing now, is it?' But take courage and work, for I am with you.

"The Lord of Hosts says: 'In a little while I will begin to shake the heavens and earth—the oceans and the dry land—I will shake all nations, and the Desire of All Nations shall come to this Temple, and I will fill this place with my glory. The future splendor of this Temple will be greater than the splendor of the first one! And here I will give peace.' "[2]

GLORIOUS KING

These messages from the Lord were given to Zechariah, grandson of Iddo the prophet.

"Listen to me, O Joshua the High Priest, and you other

priests: Joshua represents my servant, The Branch, whom I will send. He will be the Foundation Stone of the Temple that Joshua is standing beside, and I will engrave this inscription on it seven times: 'I will remove the sins of this land in a single day.' And after that, the Lord of Hosts declares, you will all live in peace and prosperity."

Another message that I received from the Lord said:

"Zerubbabel laid the foundation of this Temple, and he will complete it. Do not despise this small beginning, for the eyes of the Lord rejoice to see the work begin."

In another message the Lord said:

"Heldai, Tobijah, and Jedaiah will bring gifts of silver and gold from the Jews exiled in Babylon. Meet them at the home of Josiah, where they will stay. Accept their gifts and make a crown from the silver and gold, then put the crown on the head of Joshua, the High Priest. Tell him the Lord of Hosts says, 'You represent the Man who will come, whose name is The Branch—he will grow up and will build the Temple of the Lord. To him belongs the royal title. He will rule both as King and as Priest, with perfect harmony between the two!'

"Then put the crown in the Temple to honor those who gave it. These three who have come from so far away represent many others who will some day come from distant lands to rebuild the Temple of the Lord."

Again the Lord's message came:

"Jerusalem will have peace and prosperity so long that there will once again be aged men and women, and the streets will be filled with boys and girls at play.

"Rejoice greatly, O my people! Shout with joy! For look— your King is coming! He is the Righteous One, the Victor! Yet he is lowly, riding on a donkey's colt! I will disarm all peoples of the earth, including my people in Israel, and he shall bring peace among the nations. His realm shall stretch from sea to sea, from the river to the ends of the earth."

This is the fate of Israel, as pronounced by the Lord, who stretched out the heavens and laid the foundation of the earth and formed the spirit of man within him:

"I will make Jerusalem and Judah like a cup of poison

to the nearby nations that send their armies to surround Jerusalem. Jerusalem will be a heavy stone burdening the world, and though all the nations of the earth unite in an attempt to move her they will all be crushed.

"Then I will pour out the spirit of grace and prayer on all the people of Jerusalem, and they will look on him they pierced and mourn for him as for an only son. All of Israel will weep in profound sorrow.

"At that time a Fountain will be opened to the people of Israel and Jerusalem, a Fountain to cleanse them from all their sins and uncleanness."

And the Lord of Hosts declares, "In that day I will get rid of every vestige of idol worship throughout the land, so that the names of the idols will be forgotten." ·

Watch, for the day of the Lord is coming. On that day the Lord will gather the nations to fight Jerusalem; the city will be taken, half the population will be taken away as slaves, and half will be left. Then the Lord will go out fully armed for war, to fight against those nations. That day his feet will stand upon the Mount of Olives, to the east of Jerusalem, and the Mount of Olives will split apart, making a very wide valley running from east to west. You will escape through that valley, for it will reach across to the city gate. Yes, you will escape, and the Lord my God shall come, and all his saints and angels with him.

The sun and moon and stars will no longer shine, yet there will be continuous day! Only the Lord knows how! There will be no normal day and night—at evening time it will still be light. Life-giving waters will flow out from Jerusalem, half toward the Dead Sea and half toward the Mediterranean, flowing continuously both in winter and in summer.

. And the Lord shall be King over all the earth. In that day there shall be one Lord—his name alone will be worshiped. And Jerusalem shall be inhabited, safe at last, never again to be cursed or destroyed.[3]

TEMPLE JOY

Tattenai, governor of the lands west of the Euphrates, and Shethar-boze-nai and their companions arrived in Jerusalem and demanded, "Who gave you permission to rebuild this Temple?"

Following is the letter Governor Tattenai and other officials sent to King Darius:

"Greetings!

"We wish to inform you that we went to the construction site of the Temple of the God of Judah. The work is going forward with energy and success. We asked the leaders, 'Who has given you permission to do this?' Their answer was, 'We are servants of the God of heaven and earth, and we are rebuilding the Temple that was constructed here many centuries ago by a great king of Israel. But our ancestors angered God and he let King Nebuchadnezzar destroy this Temple and exile the people to Babylonia.'

"But they insist that King Cyrus issued a decree that the Temple should be rebuilt. We request that you search in the royal library to discover whether King Cyrus ever made such a decree; and then let us know your pleasure in this matter."

So King Darius issued orders that a search be made in the Babylonian archives. Eventually the record was found in the palace at Ecbatana, in the province of Media. So King Darius sent this message to the officials west of the Euphrates:

"Do not disturb the construction of the Temple, and don't molest the governor of Judah and the other leaders in their work. Moreover, I decree that you are to pay the full construction costs without delay from my taxes collected in your territory. Give the priests in Jerusalem young bulls, rams, and lambs for burnt offerings to the God of heaven; and give them wheat, wine, salt, and olive oil each day without fail. Then they will be able to offer acceptable sacrifices and to pray for me and my sons. Anyone who attempts to change this message in any way shall have the beams pulled from his house and built into a gallows on which he will be hanged. The God who has chosen the city of

Jerusalem will destroy any king and any nation that alters this commandment and destroys this Temple. I have issued this decree; let it be obeyed with all diligence."

Governor Tattenai, Shethar-bozenai, and their companions complied at once with the command. So the Jewish leaders continued in their work, and they were greatly encouraged by the preaching of Haggai and Zechariah.

The Temple was finally finished, as had been commanded by God and decreed by Cyrus, in the sixth year of King Darius. The Temple was then dedicated with great joy by the priests, Levites, and all the people. During the dedication celebration 100 young bulls, 200 rams, and 400 lambs were sacrificed; and twelve male goats were presented as a sin offering for the twelve tribes of Israel. Then the priests and Levites were divided into their various service corps to do the work of God as instructed in the laws of Moses.

The Passover was celebrated on the first day of April. Some of the heathen people who had been relocated in Judah turned from their immoral customs and joined the Israelis in worshiping the Lord God.[4]

QUEEN OF PERSIA

The third year of the reign of King Ahasuerus, emperor of Media-Persia with its 127 provinces stretching from India to Ethiopia, was the year of the great celebration at Shushan Palace. The emperor invited all his governors, aides, and army officers from every part of Media-Persia. The celebration lasted six months, a tremendous display of the wealth and glory of his empire.

When it was over, the king gave a party for the palace servants and officials—janitors and cabinet officials alike—for seven days of revelry in the courtyard of the palace garden. Gold and silver benches stood on pavements of black, red, white, and yellow marble. Drinks were served in golden goblets.

Queen Vashti gave a party for the women of the palace at the same time.

On the final day, when the king was half-drunk from wine, he told the seven eunuchs who were his personal aides to bring Queen Vashti to him so all the men could gaze upon her beauty. When they conveyed the emperor's order to Queen Vashti, she refused to come. The king was furious, but first consulted his lawyers—personal friends as well as chief officers of the government.

"What shall we do about this situation?" he asked them. "What penalty does the law provide for a queen who refuses to obey the king's orders?"

Memucan answered for the others: "Queen Vashti has wronged not only the king but every official and citizen of your empire. For women everywhere will begin to disobey their husbands when they learn what Queen Vashti has done. We suggest that you issue a royal edict, a law of the Medes and Persians that can never be changed, that Queen Vashti be forever banished from your presence and that you choose another queen."

The king and his aides thought this made good sense, so he followed Memucan's counsel.

But after King Ahasuerus' anger had cooled, he began brooding over the loss of Vashti. So his aides suggested, "Let us go and find the most beautiful girls in the empire and bring them to the king. We will appoint agents in each province to select young lovelies for the royal harem. Hegai will see that they are given beauty treatments, and after that the girl who pleases you most shall be the queen instead of Vashti."

This suggestion pleased the king and he put the plan into immediate effect.

There was a Jew at the palace named Mordecai, a Benjaminite. He had been captured when Jerusalem was destroyed by King Nebuchadnezzar and exiled to Babylon along with King Jeconiah and many others. This man had a beautiful young cousin, Hadassah, also called Esther, whose father and mother were dead, and whom he had adopted. Now, as a result of the king's decree, Esther was brought to the king's harem at Shushan Palace along with many other girls.

Hegai, who was responsible for the harem, was much impressed with her; he ordered a special menu for her, favored her for beauty treatments, gave her seven girls

from the palace as her maids, and gave her the most luxurious apartment in the harem. Esther hadn't told anyone
she was a Jewess, for Mordecai had said not to. He came
daily to the court of the harem to find out what was happening to her.

As each girl's turn came for spending the night with
King Ahasuerus, she was given her choice of clothing or
jewelry to enhance her beauty. She was taken to the king's
apartment in the evening, and the next morning returned
to the second harem where the king's wives lived. There
she lived the rest of her life, never seeing the king again
unless he called for her by name.

When it was Esther's turn to go to the king, she accepted
the advice of Hegai, dressing according to his instructions.
The king loved Esther more than any of the other girls.
He was so delighted that he set the royal crown on her
head and declared her queen instead of Vashti. To celebrate
the occasion, he threw another big party for all his officials
and servants, giving generous gifts to everyone and making
grants to the provinces in the form of remission of taxes.

One day as Mordecai was on duty at the palace, two
of the king's eunuchs who were guards at the palace gate
became angry at the king and plotted to assassinate him.
Mordecai heard about it and passed on the information to
Queen Esther who told the king, crediting Mordecai with
the information. An investigation was made, the two men
found guilty and impaled alive.

Soon afterwards King Ahasuerus appointed Haman as
prime minister. All the king's officials bowed before him
whenever he passed, for so the king had commanded. But
Mordecai refused to bow.

"Why are you disobeying the king's commandment?"
others demanded day after day, but he still refused. Finally
they spoke to Haman about it, to see whether Mordecai
could get away with it because of his being a Jew, which
was the excuse he had given them. Haman, furious, decided
not to lay hands on Mordecai alone but to move against
all of Mordecai's people throughout the kingdom. The most
propitious time for this action was determined by throwing
dice. This was done in April of the twelfth year of the

reign of Ahasuerus, and February of the following year
was the date indicated.

Haman approached the king about the matter. "There
is a certain race of people scattered through all the provinces
of your kingdom," he began, "and their laws are different
from those of any other nation; they refuse to obey the
king's laws. Therefore, it is not in the king's interest to
let them live. If it please the king, issue a decree that they
be destroyed, and I will pay the royal treasury for the
expenses involved in this purge."

The king agreed, confirming his decision by removing
his ring from his finger and giving it to Haman, telling
him, "Keep the money, but go ahead and do as you like
with these people."

Two weeks later Haman called in the king's secretaries
and dictated letters to the governors and officials throughout
the empire, signed in the name of King Ahasuerus and
sealed with his ring. They were then sent to all the provinces
of the empire, decreeing that the Jews—young and old,
women and children—must all be killed on the 28th day
of February of the following year, and their property given
to those who killed them. "A copy of this edict," the letter
stated, "must be proclaimed as law in every province and
made known to all your people so that they will be ready
to do their duty on the appointed day." The edict went
out, after being first proclaimed in the city of Shushan.
Then the king and Haman sat down for a drinking spree
as the city fell into confusion.

When Mordecai learned what had been done, he tore
his clothes and put on sackcloth and ashes and stood outside
the gate of the palace, for no one was permitted to enter
in mourning clothes. And throughout the provinces there
was great mourning among the Jews.

When Esther's maids told her about Mordecai, she sent
for Hathach, one of the king's eunuchs who had been appointed as her attendant, and told him to find out what
the trouble was. Hathach found Mordecai and heard the
whole story. Mordecai gave Hathach a copy of the king's
decree and told him to show it to Esther and to tell her
she should go to the king to plead for her people.

Hathach returned to Esther with Mordecai's message. Esther told Hathach to go back and say to Mordecai:

"Anyone who goes into the king's inner court without his summons is doomed to die unless the king holds out his golden scepter; and the king has not called for me to come to him in more than a month."

Hathach gave Esther's message to Mordecai. This was Mordecai's reply:

"Do you think you will escape when all other Jews are killed? If you keep quiet at a time like this, God will deliver the Jews from some other source, but you and your relatives will die. What's more, who can say but that God has brought you into the palace for just such a time as this?"

Then Esther said to tell Mordecai: "Go and gather all the Jews of Shushan and fast for me for three days, and I and my maids will do the same. Then, though it is strictly forbidden, I will go to see the king; and if I perish, I perish."

Three days later Esther put on her royal robes and entered the inner court just beyond the royal hall of the palace, where the king was sitting upon his throne. When he saw Queen Esther standing in the inner court, he welcomed her, holding out the golden scepter. So Esther approached and touched its tip.

"What do you wish, Queen Esther? What is your request? I will give it to you, even if it is half the kingdom!"

Esther replied, "If it please Your Majesty, I want you and Haman to come to a banquet today."

The king turned to his aides. "Tell Haman to hurry!" he said. So the king and Haman came to Esther's banquet.

During the wine course, the king said to Esther, "Now tell me what you really want, and I will give it to you."

Esther replied, "My request is that if Your Majesty loves me, you come again with Haman tomorrow to the banquet I shall prepare. And tomorrow I will explain what this is all about."

What a happy man was Haman as he went home and gathered his friends and his wife and boasted how he had become the greatest man in the kingdom next to the king. "Yes, and Esther the queen invited only me and the king to the banquet she prepared, and tomorrow we are invited again! But yet," he added, "all this is nothing when I see Mordecai the Jew sitting in front of the king's gate, refusing to bow to me."

"Well," suggested Zeresh his wife, "get ready a 75-foot-high gallows, and in the morning ask the king to let you hang Mordecai on it; and when this is done you can go on your merry way to the banquet." This pleased Haman immensely and he ordered the gallows built.

That night the king had trouble sleeping and decided to read awhile. He ordered the historical records of his kingdom from the library, and in them he came across the item telling how Mordecai had exposed the plot of the king's eunuchs who plotted to assassinate him.

"What reward did we give Mordecai for this?" the king asked.

His courtiers replied, "Nothing!"

"Who is on duty in the outer court?" the king inquired. As it happened, Haman had just arrived in the outer court to ask the king to hang Mordecai from the gallows he was building.

The courtiers replied, "Haman is out there."

"Bring him in," the king ordered. Haman came in and the king said, "What should I do to honor a man who truly pleases me?"

Haman thought to himself, "Whom would he want to honor more than me?" So he replied, "Bring out some of the royal robes the king himself has worn and the king's own horse and the royal crown, and instruct one of the king's most noble princes to robe the man and lead him through the streets on the king's horse, shouting before him, 'This is the way the king honors those who truly please him!' "

"Excellent!" the king said. "Hurry and take these robes and my horse, and do just as you have said—to Mordecai the Jew who works at the chancellery. Follow every detail you have suggested."

Haman took the robes and put them on Mordecai, mounted him on the king's steed, and led him through the city, shouting, "This is the way the king honors those he delights in." Afterwards Mordecai returned to his job, but Haman, utterly humiliated, told his wife and his friends what had happened. While they were discussing it, the king's messengers arrived to conduct Haman to the banquet Esther had prepared.

Again, during the wine course, the king asked, "What is your petition, Queen Esther? Whatever it is, I will give it to you, even if it is half of my kingdom!"

Esther replied, "If I have won your favor, O king, save my life and the lives of my people. For I and my people are doomed to destruction and slaughter. If we were only to be sold as slaves, perhaps I could remain quiet."

"What are you talking about?" King Ahasuerus demanded. "Who would dare touch you?"

Esther replied, "This wicked Haman is our enemy."

The king jumped to his feet and went out into the palace garden as Haman stood up to plead for his life. In despair he fell upon the couch where Queen Esther was reclining, just as the king returned from the garden.

"Will he rape the queen in the palace before my eyes?" the king roared.

Instantly the death veil was placed over Haman's face. Then one of the king's aides said, "Sir, Haman has just ordered a 75-foot gallows constructed to hang Mordecai, the man who saved the king from assassination! It stands in Haman's courtyard."

"Hang Haman on it," the king ordered.

So they did, and the king's wrath was pacified.

Then Mordecai was brought before the king, for Esther had told the king that he was her cousin and foster father. The king took off his ring—which he had taken back from Haman—and gave it to Mordecai, appointing him Prime Minister.

And now once more Esther came before the king, falling down at his feet. Again the king held out the golden scepter to Esther. She arose and stood before him and said, "If it please Your Majesty, send out a decree reversing Haman's order to destroy the Jews throughout the provinces. For how can I endure to see my people butchered?"

King Ahasuerus said, "Go ahead and send a message to the Jews, telling them whatever you want to in the king's name, and seal it with the king's ring."

The king's secretaries were called—and they wrote as Mordecai dictated—a decree to the Jews and to the officials, governors, and princes of all the provinces from India to Ethiopia. This decree gave the Jews permission to unite in the defense of their lives and their families, to destroy all the forces opposed to them, and to take their property. The day chosen for this was the 28th day of February.

In every city and province as the king's decree arrived, the Jews were filled with joy and declared a holiday. And many people pretended to be Jews, for they feared what the Jews might do to them.

On the 28th day of February, Jews gathered in their cities to defend themselves against any who might try to harm them. Jews on that day slaughtered their enemies; they even killed 500 men in Shushan. They also killed the ten sons of Haman, the Jews' enemy, but they did not try to take Haman's property.

Mordecai wrote a history of these events and sent letters to the Jews near and far, encouraging them to declare an annual holiday on the last days of the month to celebrate with feasting, gladness, and the giving of gifts this historic day when Jews were saved from their enemies. The Jews adopted Mordecai's suggestion and began this annual custom as a reminder of the time when Haman plotted to destroy them at the time determined by a throw of the dice. This celebration is called "Purim," because the word for "throwing dice" in Persian is "pur."

Meanwhile Queen Esther had written a letter throwing her support behind Mordecai's letter inaugurating his Feast of Purim. Indeed, the Jews themselves decided upon this tradition as a remembrance of the time of their national fasting and prayer.[5]

**JERUSALEM
RESTORED**

The autobiography of Nehemiah: In December of the twentieth year of King Ar-ta-xerxes of Persia when I was at the palace at Shushan, one of my fellow Jews named Hanani came to visit me with some men who had arrived from Judah. I took the opportunity to inquire how things were going in Jerusalem.

They replied, "Things are not good; the wall of Jerusalem is still torn down, and the gates are burned."

When I heard this I cried. In fact, I refused to eat for several days for I spent the time in prayer.

"O Lord," I cried out, "hear my prayer! I confess that we have sinned against you; yes, I and my people have not obeyed the commandments you gave us through Moses. Oh, please remember what you told Moses! You said,

" 'If you sin, I will scatter you among the nations; but if you obey my laws, even though you are exiled to the farthest corners of the universe, I will bring you back to Jerusalem. For Jerusalem is the place in which I have chosen to live.'

"O Lord, heed the prayers of us who delight to honor you. Help me as I ask the king for a great favor—put it into his heart to be kind to me."

Later, as I was serving the king his wine, he asked me, "Why so sad? You aren't sick, are you?"

Until then I had always been cheerful when with him. I replied, "Sir, why shouldn't I be sad? For the city where my ancestors are buried is in ruins and the gates have been burned down."

"Well, what should be done?" the king asked.

With a quick prayer to God, I replied, "If it please Your Majesty, send me to Judah to rebuild the city of my fathers!"

The king replied, "How long will you be gone? When will you return?"

So it was agreed! And I set a time for my departure!

Then I added to my request: "If it please the king, give me letters to the governors west of the Euphrates River instructing them to let me travel through their countries on my way to Judah; also a letter to Asaph, the manager of the king's forest, instructing him to give me timber for the beams and for the gates of the fortress near the Temple, for the city walls, and for a house for myself."

The king granted these requests.

When I arrived in the provinces west of the Euphrates, I delivered the king's letters to the governors there. But when Sanballat the Horonite and Tobiah, an Ammonite who was a government official, heard of my arrival they were angry that anyone was interested in helping Israel.

Three days after my arrival at Jerusalem I stole out during the night, taking a few men with me, for I hadn't told a soul about the plans for Jerusalem which God put into my heart. I was mounted on my donkey and the others were on foot, and we went out through the Valley Gate toward the Jackal's Well and over to the Dung Gate to see the broken walls and burned gates. Then we went to the Fountain Gate and to the King's Pool, but my donkey couldn't get through the rubble. So we circled the city, and I followed the brook, inspecting the wall, and entered again at the Valley Gate.

The city officials did not know I had been out there, or why, but now I told them, "You know the tragedy of our city; it lies in ruins and its gates are burned. Let us rebuild the wall of Jerusalem and rid ourselves of this disgrace!" Then I told them about the desire God had put into my heart, my conversation with the king, and the plan to which he had agreed.

They replied at once, "Good! Let's rebuild the wall!" And so the work began.

When Sanballat and Tobiah and Geshem the Arab heard of our plan, they scoffed. But I replied, "The God of heaven will help us, and we his servants will rebuild this wall."

When Sanballat and Tobiah and the Arabians, Ammonites, and Ashdodites heard that the work was going ahead and the breaks in the wall were being repaired, they plotted to lead an army against Jerusalem, but we prayed to God and guarded the city day and night to protect ourselves.

Then some of the leaders began complaining that the workmen were becoming tired; and there was so much rubble to be removed that we could never get it done by ourselves. I called together the leaders and the people and said to them, "Don't be afraid! Remember the Lord who is great and glorious; fight for your friends, your families, and your homes!"

We all returned to our work on the wall, but from then on only half worked while the other half stood guard behind them. The trumpeter stayed with me to sound the alarm.

We worked from sunrise to sunset; and I told everyone living outside the walls to move into Jerusalem so their servants could go on guard duty as well as work during the day. During this period none of us ever took off our clothes. And we carried our weapons with us at all times.

Sanballat, Tobiah, Geshem the Arab, and the rest of our enemies found out that we had almost completed the rebuilding of the wall—though we had not yet hung all the doors of the gates. They sent me a message asking me to meet them in one of the villages in the Plain of Ono. But I realized they were plotting to kill me, so I replied, "I am doing a great work! Why should I stop to come and visit with you?"

The wall was finally finished in early September—just fifty-two days after we had begun! When our enemies and the surrounding nations heard about it, they were humiliated and they realized that the work had been done with the help of our God.

After the wall was finished and we had hung the doors in the gates and had appointed gatekeepers, singers, and Levites, I gave the responsibility of governing Jerusalem to my brother Hanani and to Hananiah, the commander of the fortress—a very faithful man who revered God. I issued instructions not to open the Jerusalem gates until well after sunrise, and to close and lock them while the guards were still on duty. I also directed that the guards be residents of Jerusalem, that they must be on duty at regular times, and that each homeowner who lived near the wall must guard the section of wall next to his home. For the city was large, but the population was small; and only a few houses were scattered throughout the city.

The Lord told me to call together all the leaders of the city along with the ordinary citizens for registration, for I had found the record of the genealogies of those who had returned to Judah.

The priests, Levites, gatekeepers, choir members, Temple attendants, and the rest of the people now returned to their own towns and villages throughout Judah, but during the month of September they came back to Jerusalem.

In mid-September, all the people assembled at the plaza in front of the Water Gate and requested Ezra, their religious leader, to read to them the law of God which he had given to Moses.

So Ezra brought out the scroll of Moses' laws. He stood on a stand so that everyone could see him, faced the square in front of the Water Gate, and read from early morning until noon. Everyone stood up as he opened the scroll, and all who were old enough to understand paid close attention.

Ezra blessed the Lord, the great God, and all the people said, "Amen," and lifted their hands toward heaven. Then they bowed and worshiped the Lord with their faces toward the ground.

As Ezra read from the scroll, Levites went among the people and explained the meaning of the passage. People began sobbing when they heard the commands of the law.

Then Ezra and I and the Levites who were assisting said to them, "Don't cry on such a day as this! Today is a sacred day before the Lord—it is a time to celebrate with a hearty meal and to send presents to those in need, for the joy of the Lord is your strength."

So the people went to eat a festive meal and to send presents; it was a great and joyful celebration because they could hear and understand God's words.

The next day clan leaders and priests and Levites met with Ezra to go over the law in greater detail. As they studied, they noted that Jehovah had told Moses the people of Israel should live in tents during the Festival of Tabernacles to be held that month. He said also a proclamation should be made telling the people to go to the hills to get branches from olive, myrtle, palm, and fig trees and to make huts in which to live for the duration of the feast.

So the people went out and cut branches and used them to build huts on the roofs of their houses, in their courtyards, in the court of the Temple, on the plaza beside the Water Gate, or at the Ephraim Gate Plaza. This procedure had not been carried out since the days of Joshua. Ezra read from the scroll on each of the seven days of the feast, and on the eighth day there was a solemn closing service.

On October 10 the people returned for another observance. The laws of God were read aloud for two or three hours and for several more hours they took turns confessing their sins and those of their ancestors. And everyone worshiped the Lord.

Then Ezra prayed, "You alone are God. You made the skies and the heavens, the earth and the seas, and everything in them. You preserve it all; and all the angels of heaven worship you.

"You are the Lord who chose Abram and brought him from Ur of the Chaldeans and renamed him Abraham. When he was faithful to you, you made a contract with him to forever give him and his descendants the land of the Canaanites.

"O awesome God, great trouble has come upon us from the days when the kings of Assyria triumphed over us. Because of all this, we promise to serve the Lord! And we and our princes and Levites and priests put our names to this covenant."

I, Nehemiah the governor, signed the covenant. Others signed on behalf of the entire nation—for the common people, the priests, the Levites, the gatekeepers, the choir members, the Temple servants, and all the rest who with their wives and sons and daughters were old enough to understand. For we all vowed to accept the curse of God unless we obeyed God's laws as issued by his servant Moses.

We further agreed not to do any work every seventh year and to forgive and cancel the debts of our brother Jews. We also agreed to charge ourselves annually with a Temple tax so there would be enough money to care for the Temple of our God.

We agreed to give to God our oldest sons and the firstborn of all our cattle, herds, and flocks just as the law requires; we presented them to the priests who minister in the Temple of our God. And we promised to bring to the Levites a tenth of everything our land produced. A priest—a descendant of Aaron—would be with the Levites as they received these tithes, and a tenth of all that was collected as tithes was delivered to the Temple and placed in the storage areas.

During the dedication of the new Jerusalem wall, Levites throughout the land came to Jerusalem to assist in the ceremonies with their cymbals, psalteries, and harps. Choir members also came from surrounding villages, for the singers had built their own villages as suburbs of Jerusalem. The priests and Levites first dedicated themselves, then the people, the gates, and the wall.

I led the Judean leaders to the top of the wall and divided them into two long lines to walk in opposite directions along the top of the wall, giving thanks as they went. The group which went to the right consisted of half of the leaders of Judah. The priests who played the trumpets used the original instruments of King David. Ezra the priest led this procession.

The other group, of which I was a member, went around the other way to meet them. Both choirs then proceeded to the Temple. They sang loudly and clearly under the direction of the choirmaster. Women and children rejoiced too, and the joy of the people of Jerusalem was heard far away!

"Hallelujah! Yes, praise the Lord! How good it is to sing his praises! How delightful, and how right!

"He is rebuilding Jerusalem and bringing back the exiles. He heals the brokenhearted, binding up their wounds.

"He counts the stars and calls them all by name. How great he is! His power is absolute! His understanding is unlimited.

"The Lord supports the humble, but brings the wicked into the dust. Sing out your thanks to him; sing praises to our God, accompanied by harps.

"Praise him, O Jerusalem! Praise your God, O Zion!

For he has fortified your gates against all enemies, and blessed your children. He sends peace across your nation, and fills your barns with plenty of the finest wheat.

"He sends his orders to the world. How swiftly his word flies. He sends the snow in all its lovely whiteness, scatters the frost upon the ground, and hurls the hail upon the earth. Who can stand before this freezing cold? But then he calls for warmer weather, and the spring winds blow and all the river ice is broken.

"Praise the Lord, O heavens! Praise him, all his angels, all the armies of heaven. Praise him, sun and moon, and all you twinkling stars. Praise him, vapors high above the clouds.

"Let everything he has made give praise to him. Let everything alive give praises to the Lord! You praise him! "Hallelujah!" [6]

PORTENTS

Here is the Lord's message to Israel through the prophet Malachi:

"I have loved you deeply," says the Lord. You retort, "Really? When was this?"

And the Lord replies, "I showed my love for you by loving your father, Jacob. A son honors his father, a servant honors his master. I am your Father and Master, yet you don't honor me. But my name will be honored by Gentiles around the world; my name shall be great among the nations.

"Listen: I will send my messenger before me to prepare the way. And then the one you are looking for will come to his Temple—the Messenger of God's promises, to bring you great joy. Yes, he is surely coming.

"But who can endure his coming? For he is like a blazing fire refining precious metal. Like a refiner of silver he will purify the Levites, the ministers of God, refining them like gold or silver, so they will do their work for God with pure hearts. At that time my punishments will be quick and certain; I will move swiftly against wicked men who trick the innocent, against adulterers and liars, against all those who cheat their hired hands or oppress widows and orphans or defraud strangers and do not fear me.

"Though you have scorned my laws from earliest time,

yet you may still return to me," says the Lord of Hosts. "Come, and I will forgive you.

"But you say, 'We have never even gone away!'

"Will a man rob God? Surely not! And yet you have robbed me.

" 'What do you mean? When did we ever rob you?'

"You have robbed me of the tithes and offerings due to me. Bring all the tithes into the storehouse so that there will be food enough in my Temple; if you do, I will open up the windows of heaven for you and pour out a blessing so great you won't have room enough to take it in! Try it! Let me prove it to you!

"Your attitude toward me has been arrogant. But you say, 'What do you mean? What have we said that we shouldn't?'

"You have said, 'It is foolish to worship God and obey him. From now on, as far as we're concerned, blessed are the arrogant. For those who do evil shall prosper.' "

Then those who feared and loved the Lord spoke often of him to each other. And he had a Book of Remembrance drawn up in which he recorded the names of those who feared him. "They shall be mine," says the Lord of Hosts, "in that day when I make up my jewels. Then you will see the difference between God's treatment of good men and bad, between those who serve him and those who don't.

"Watch," the Lord of Hosts declares; "the day of judgment is coming, burning like a furnace. The proud and wicked will be consumed. But for you who fear my name, the Sun of Righteousness will rise with healing in his wings. And you will go free.

"See, I will send you the prophet Elijah before the coming of the judgment day of God. His preaching will bring fathers and children together again, to be of one mind and heart, for they will know that if they do not repent I will utterly destroy their land."[7]

PART
10
THE NEW
KINGDOM

ELIJAH'S MESSIAH A Jewish priest who lived when Herod was king of Judea, Zacharias was a member of the Temple service corps. His wife Elizabeth, like himself, was a descendant of Aaron. Zacharias and Elizabeth were careful to obey God's laws in spirit as well as in letter. They had no children, for Elizabeth was barren; and now they were both very old.

One day as Zacharias was going about his work in the Temple, the honor fell to him by lot to enter the inner sanctuary and burn incense before the Lord. In the sanctuary, an angel suddenly appeared to the right of the altar of incense! Zacharias was terrified.

But the angel said, "Don't be afraid, Zacharias! I have come to tell you that God has heard your prayer and your wife will bear you a son! You are to name him John. He will be one of the Lord's great men. He must never touch wine or hard liquor—he will be filled with the Holy Spirit from before his birth and will persuade many a Jew to turn to the Lord. He will be a man of rugged spirit like Elijah, the prophet of old, and he will precede the coming of the Messiah. He will soften adult hearts to become like little children's, and will change disobedient minds to the wisdom of faith."

Zacharias said, "This is impossible! I'm an old man and my wife is also well along in years."

The angel said, "I am Gabriel! I stand in the very presence of God—he sent me to you with this good news! Because you haven't believed me, you are to be stricken silent until the child is born. My words will come true at the proper time."

The crowds outside, waiting for Zacharias to appear, wondered why he was taking so long. When he finally came out, he couldn't speak and they realized from his gestures that he must have seen a vision. He stayed at the Temple for the remaining days of his duties and then returned home. Soon afterwards his wife became pregnant and went into seclusion for five months.

"How kind the Lord is," she exclaimed, "to take away my disgrace of having no children!"[1]

VIRGIN MOTHER

The following month God sent the angel Gabriel to Nazareth, a village in Galilee, to a virgin, Mary, engaged to be married to Joseph, a descendant of King David. Gabriel appeared to her and said, "Congratulations, favored lady! The Lord is with you!"

Confused and disturbed, Mary tried to think what the angel could mean.

"Don't be frightened, Mary," the angel told her, "for God has decided to wonderfully bless you! Soon you will become pregnant and have a baby boy, and you are to name him Jesus. He shall be called the Son of God. And the Lord God shall give him the throne of his ancestor David and he shall reign over Israel forever!"

Mary asked, "How can I have a baby? I am a virgin."

The angel replied, "The Holy Spirit shall come upon you, so the baby born to you will be utterly holy—the Son of God. Furthermore, six months ago your Aunt Elizabeth—'the barren one,' they called her—became pregnant in her old age! For every promise from God shall surely come true."

Mary said, "I am the Lord's servant, and I am willing to do whatever he wants. May everything you said come true." Then the angel disappeared.

A few days later Mary hurried to the highlands of Judea where Zacharias lived, to visit Elizabeth.

At the sound of Mary's greeting, Elizabeth's child leaped within her, and she was filled with the Holy Spirit. She exclaimed to Mary, "You are favored by God above all other women, and your child is destined for God's mightiest praise. What an honor this is, that the mother of my Lord should visit me! When you greeted me, my baby moved in me for joy! You believed God would do what he said; that is why he has given you this wonderful blessing."

"Oh, how I praise the Lord," Mary responded. "I rejoice in God my Savior! For he took notice of his lowly servant, and now generation after generation shall call me blest of God. The mighty Holy One has done great things to me. His mercy goes on from generation to generation, to all who reverence him. How powerful is his arm! He scatters the proud and haughty. He has torn princes from their thrones, and exalted the lowly. He has satisfied the hungry hearts, and sent the rich away with empty hands. And how he has helped Israel! He has not forgotten his promise to be merciful, for he promised our fathers—Abraham and his children—to be merciful to them forever."

Mary stayed with Elizabeth three months, and then went back to her own home.

By now Elizabeth's waiting was over; the time had come for the baby to be born—and it was a boy. Word spread quickly to her neighbors and relatives, and everyone rejoiced.

When the baby was eight days old, relatives and friends came for the circumcision ceremony. They assumed the baby's name would be Zacharias, but Elizabeth said, "No! He must be named John!" Instantly Zacharias could speak again, and he began praising God.

Wonder fell upon the neighborhood, and everyone asked, "What will this child turn out to be? The hand of the Lord is upon him in some special way."

Zacharias, filled with the Holy Spirit, gave this prophecy:

"The God of Israel has come to visit his people. He is sending us a Mighty Savior from the royal line of his servant

David, just as he promised through his holy prophets long ago. He has been merciful to our ancestors; yes, to Abraham, by remembering his promise to him, and by making us acceptable to stand in his presence forever.

"And you, my little son, shall be the prophet of the glorious God, for you will prepare the way for the Messiah. You will tell his people how to find salvation through forgiveness of their sins. The mercy of our God is tender, and heaven's dawn is about to break upon us to give light to those who sit in darkness and death's shadow, and to guide us to the path of peace."[2]

ROYAL SON

About this time Caesar Augustus, the Roman Emperor, decreed that a census should be taken throughout the nation. Everyone was required to return to his ancestral home for this registration.

These are the facts concerning the birth of Jesus: his mother, Mary, was engaged to be married to Joseph, but while still a virgin she became pregnant. Joseph, her fiancé, being a man of principle, decided to break the engagement but to do it quietly as he didn't want to disgrace her.

As he lay awake considering this, he fell into a dream and saw an angel standing beside him. "Joseph, son of David," the angel said, "don't hesitate to take Mary as your wife! For the child within her has been conceived by the Holy Spirit. She will have a Son, and you shall name him Jesus, meaning 'Savior,' for he will save his people from their sins. This will fulfill God's message through his prophets—'Listen! The virgin shall conceive a child! She shall give birth to a Son, and he shall be called Emmanuel (meaning "God is with us").' " When Joseph awoke, he did as the angel commanded and brought Mary home to be his wife, but she remained a virgin until her Son was born.

Joseph, a member of the royal line, had to go to Bethlehem in Judea, King David's ancient home—journeying from Nazareth. He took Mary with him, who was obviously pregnant by this time. While they were there, she gave birth to a son. She wrapped him in a blanket and laid him in a manger, because there was no room for them in the village inn.

That night some shepherds were outside the village guarding their flocks of sheep. Suddenly an angel appeared among them, and the landscape shone with the glory of the Lord. They were badly frightened, but the angel reassured them.

"Don't be afraid! I bring you the most joyful news ever announced: the Savior—yes, the Messiah, the Lord—has been born tonight in Bethlehem! How will you recognize him? You will find a baby wrapped in a blanket lying in a manger!"

Suddenly the angel was joined by a host of others— praising God: "Glory to God in the highest heaven, and peace on earth for all those pleasing him."

When this army of angels had returned to heaven, the shepherds said, "Come on! Let's go see this wonderful thing the Lord has told us about."

They ran to the village and found their way to Mary and Joseph—and there was the baby, lying in the manger. The shepherds told everyone what the angel had said to them; all who heard the story expressed astonishment. Then the shepherds went back to their fields and flocks, praising God for the visit of the angels and because they had seen the child just as the angel told them.

Eight days later, at the baby's circumcision ceremony, he was named Jesus, the name given him by the angel before he was conceived.

When the time came for Mary's purification offering at the Temple, as required by the laws of Moses after the birth of a child, his parents took him to Jerusalem to present him to the Lord; for in these laws God had said, "If a woman's first child is a boy, he shall be dedicated to the Lord."

That day a Jerusalem resident named Simeon was in the Temple. He was a good man, filled with the Holy Spirit, and constantly expecting the Messiah to come. For the Holy Spirit had revealed that he would not die until he had seen God's anointed King. When Mary and Joseph arrived to present the baby Jesus to the Lord, Simeon was there and took the child in his arms. "Lord," he said, "now I can die content! For I have seen him as you promised I would. He is the Light that will shine upon the nations, and he will be the glory of your people Israel!"

Joseph and Mary stood there marveling at what was said about Jesus.

Simeon blessed them, but then said to Mary: "A sword shall pierce your soul, for this child shall be rejected by many in Israel, and this to their undoing. But he will be the greatest joy of many others. And the deepest thoughts of many hearts shall be revealed."

Anna, a prophetess, was also there that day. Very old, she had been a widow for eighty-four years following seven years of marriage. She never left the Temple, but stayed there worshiping God by praying and often fasting. She came along as Simeon was talking with Mary and Joseph, and she also began thanking God and telling everyone that the Messiah had finally arrived!

These are the ancestors of Jesus Christ:

Abraham was the father of Isaac, the father of Jacob, the father of Judah, the father of Perez (Tamar was the mother). Perez was the father of Hezron, the father of Aram, the father of Amminadab, the father of Nahshon, the father of Salmon, the father of Boaz (Rahab was his mother).

Boaz was the father of Obed (Ruth was his mother); Obed was the father of Jesse, the father of King David, the father of Solomon (his mother was the widow of Uriah).

Solomon was the father of Rehoboam, the father of Abijah, the father of Asa, the father of Jehoshaphat, the father of Joram, the father of Uzziah, the father of Jotham, the father of Ahaz, the father of Hezekiah, the father of Manasseh, the father of Amos, the father of Josiah, the father of Jeconiah, the father of Shealtiel, the father of Zerubbabel, the father of Abiud, the father of Eliakim, the father of Azor, the father of Zadok, the father of Matthan, the father of Jacob, the father of Joseph.

Jesus was born in Bethlehem in Judea during the reign

of King Herod. About that time some astrologers from eastern lands arrived in Jerusalem, asking, "Where is the newborn King of the Jews? We have seen his star in eastern lands and have come to worship him."

King Herod was deeply disturbed by their question. He called the religious leaders. "Did the prophets tell us where the Messiah would be born?" he asked.

"Yes, in Bethlehem," they said, "for Micah wrote: 'O little town of Bethlehem, you are not an unimportant Judean village, for a Governor shall rise from you to rule my people Israel.' "

Then Herod sent a message to the astrologers, asking them to come to see him. At this meeting he found out the exact time when they first saw the star. He told them, "Go to Bethlehem and search for the child. When you find him, come back and·tell me so that I can go and worship him too!"

The astrologers started out again. And the star appeared to them again, standing over Bethlehem.

Entering the house where the baby and Mary were, they threw themselves down before him, worshiping. Then they opened presents and gave him gold, frankincense, and myrrh. When they returned to their own land, they didn't go through Jerusalem to report to Herod, for God had warned them in a dream to go home another way.

After they were gone, an angel appeared to Joseph: "Get up and flee to Egypt with the baby and his mother; stay there until I tell you to return, for King Herod is going to try to kill the child." That same night he left for Egypt with Mary and the baby.

Herod was furious when he learned the astrologers had disobeyed him. Sending soldiers to Bethlehem, he ordered them to kill every baby boy two years old and under, for the astrologers had told him the star first appeared to them two years before.[3]

PRODIGY

When Herod died, an angel appeared in a dream to Joseph and told him, "Take the baby and his mother back to Israel, for those trying to kill the child are dead."

He returned to Israel and lived in Nazareth. There the child became a robust lad and was known for wisdom beyond his years; and God poured out blessings on him.

When Jesus was twelve years old, he accompanied his parents to Jerusalem for the annual Passover Festival. After the celebration they started home, but Jesus stayed behind. His parents didn't miss him for they assumed he was with friends among the other travelers. But when he didn't show up that evening, they started to look for him among their relatives and friends. When they couldn't find him, they went back to Jerusalem to search for him.

Three days later they finally discovered him: he was in the Temple among the teachers of the Law, discussing deep questions with them and amazing everyone with his understanding. "Son!" his mother said, "why have you done this? Your father and I have been frantic, searching for you everywhere."

"But why did you need to search?" he asked. "Didn't you realize I would be here in my Father's house?"

They didn't understand what he meant. He returned to Nazareth and was obedient to them, and his mother stored away these things in her heart. So Jesus grew both tall and wise, and was loved by God and man.[4]

JOHN AND JESUS

In the fifteenth year of Emperor Tiberius Caesar, a message came from God to John, the son of Zacharias, as he was living in the deserts. Then John went from place to place on both sides of the Jordan River, preaching that people should be baptized to show they had turned to God and away from their sins in order to be forgiven.

In the words of Isaiah the prophet, John was "a voice shouting from the wilderness: 'Prepare a road for the Lord to travel on! Level the mountains! Fill up the valleys! Straighten the curves! Smooth out the ruts! And then all mankind shall see the Savior sent from God.' "

John's clothing was woven from camel's hair and he wore a leather belt; his food was locusts and wild honey. People from Jerusalem, all over the Jordan Valley, and, in fact, from every section of Judea went to the wilderness to hear him preach. When they confessed their sins he baptized them in the Jordan River.

But when he saw many Pharisees and Sadducees coming to be baptized, he denounced them. "You sons of snakes! Who said you could escape the wrath of God? Before being baptized, prove that you have turned from sin by doing worthy deeds. Don't try to get by as you are, thinking, 'We are safe, for we are descendants of Abraham.' The axe of God's judgment is poised to chop down every unproductive tree."

The crowd replied, "What do you want us to do?"

"If you have two coats, give one to the poor. If you have extra food, give it to those who are hungry."

Even tax collectors—notorious for their corruption—came to be baptized and asked, "How shall we prove to you that we have abandoned our sins?"

"By your honesty," he replied. "Make sure you collect no more taxes than the Roman government requires."

"And us," asked some soldiers, "what about us?"

"Don't extort money by threats and violence; don't accuse anyone of what you know he didn't do; and be content with your pay! With water I baptize those who repent of their sins; but someone else is coming, far greater than I am. He shall baptize you with the Holy Spirit. He will separate the chaff from the grain, burning the chaff and storing away the grain."

Then Jesus went from Galilee to the Jordan River to be baptized by John. John didn't want to do it; he said, "I am the one who needs to be baptized by you."

But Jesus said, "Please do it, for I must do all that is right." So John baptized him.

As soon as Jesus came up out of the water, the heavens were opened to him and he saw the Spirit of God coming down in the form of a dove. And a voice from heaven said, "This is my beloved Son, and I am wonderfully pleased with him."[5]

THE LIGHT

Before anything else existed, there was Christ, with God. He has always been alive and is himself God. He created everything there is—nothing exists that he didn't make. Eternal life is in him, and this life gives light to all mankind. His life is the light that shines through the darkness—and the darkness can never extinguish it.

God sent John the Baptist as a witness that Jesus Christ is the true Light. Later the true Light arrived to shine on everyone coming into the world. Christ became a human being among us, full of loving forgiveness and truth. And some of us have seen his glory—the glory of the only Son of the heavenly Father.

John pointed him out, telling the crowds, "This is the one I was talking about when I said, 'Someone is coming who is greater by far than I am—he existed long before I did!'" Moses gave us the Law with its rigid justice, while Jesus Christ brought us loving forgiveness as well.[6]

PRECIPICE

Jesus, full of the Holy Spirit, left the Jordan River, being urged by the Spirit into the wastelands of Judea where Satan tempted him for forty days. He ate nothing all that time.

Then Satan tempted him to get food by changing stones into loaves of bread. "It will prove you are the Son of God," he said.

But Jesus told him, "No! The Scriptures tell us that bread won't feed men's souls; obedience to every word of God is what we need."

Then Satan took him to Jerusalem to the roof of the Temple. "Jump off," he said, "and prove you are the Son of God; for the Scriptures declare, 'God will send his angels to keep you from harm'—they will prevent you from smashing on the rocks below."

Jesus retorted, "It also says not to put the Lord your God to a foolish test!"

Next Satan took him to the peak of a high mountain and showed him the nations of the world and their glory.

"I'll give it all to you," he said, "if you will kneel and worship me."

"Get out of here, Satan," Jesus told him. "The Scriptures say, 'Worship only the Lord God. Obey only him.'"

Then Satan went away, and angels came and cared for Jesus.[7]

MIRACLE MAN

Jewish leaders sent priests from Jerusalem to ask John whether he claimed to be the Messiah.

"I am not the Christ," he said.

"Who are you? Elijah?"

"No," he replied.

"Are you the Prophet?"

"No."

"Then who are you? Tell us so we can give an answer to those who sent us."

"I am a voice from the wilderness, shouting as Isaiah prophesied, 'Get ready for the coming of the Lord!'"

This took place at Bethany, a village on the other side of the Jordan River. The next day John saw Jesus coming toward him and said, "Look! There is the Lamb of God who takes away the world's sin! I am here baptizing in order to point him out to Israel."

Then John told about seeing the Holy Spirit in the form of a dove descending from heaven and resting upon Jesus. "At the time God sent me to baptize he told me, 'When you see the Holy Spirit descending and resting upon someone—he is the one you are looking for. He is the one who baptizes with the Holy Spirit.' I saw it happen to this man, and I therefore testify that he is the Son of God."

The following day as John was standing with two of his disciples, Jesus walked by. John looked at him intently and declared, "See—there is the Lamb of God!"

John's two disciples turned and followed Jesus.

Jesus saw them following. "What do you want?" he asked.

"Sir," they replied, "where do you live?"

"Come and see," he said. So they went with him to

the place where he was staying and were with him until the evening.

One of these men was Andrew. Andrew went to find his brother and told him, "We have found the Messiah!" And he brought Simon to meet Jesus.

Jesus looked intently at Simon and said, "You are Simon, John's son—but you shall be called Peter, the rock!"

The next day Jesus decided to go to Galilee. He found Philip and told him, "Come with me." Philip was from Bethsaida, Andrew and Peter's hometown.

Philip went off to look for Nathanael and told him, "We have found the Messiah—the very person Moses and the prophets told about! His name is Jesus, the son of Joseph from Nazareth!"

"Nazareth!" exclaimed Nathanael. "Can anything good come from there?"

"Come and see for yourself," Philip declared.

As they approached, Jesus said, "Here comes an honest man—a true son of Israel."

"How do you know what I am like?" Nathanael demanded.

Jesus replied, "I could see you under the fig tree before Philip found you."

Nathanael replied, "Sir, you are the Son of God—the King of Israel!"

Jesus asked him, "Do you believe this just because I told you I had seen you under the fig tree? You will see greater proofs than this."

Jesus was about thirty years old when he began his public ministry. He became known throughout that region for his sermons in the synagogues.

Jesus' mother was a guest at a wedding in the village of Cana, and Jesus and his disciples were invited too. The wine supply ran out during the festivities, and Jesus' mother came to him with the problem.

"I can't help you now," he said. "It isn't yet my time."

His mother told the servants, "Do whatever he tells you to."

Six stone waterpots were standing there; they held perhaps twenty to thirty gallons each. Jesus told the servants to fill them with water. When this was done, he said,

"Dip some out and take it to the master of ceremonies."

When the master of ceremonies tasted the water that was now wine, he called the bridegroom over. "This is wonderful," he said. "Usually a host uses the best wine first, but you have kept the best for the last!"

This miracle at Cana was Jesus' first public demonstration of his heaven-sent power. And his disciples believed he really was the Messiah.

It was time for the annual Jewish Passover, and Jesus went to Jerusalem. In the Temple area he saw merchants selling cattle, sheep, and doves for sacrifices, and money changers behind their counters. Jesus made a whip from ropes and chased them all out, and drove out the sheep and oxen, scattering the money changers' coins over the floor and turning over their tables! Going to the men selling doves, he told them, "Get these things out of here—don't turn my Father's House into a market!"

Then his disciples remembered this prophecy from the Scriptures: "Concern for God's House will be my undoing."

"What right have you to order them out?" the Jewish leaders demanded. "If you have this authority from God, show us a miracle to prove it."

"All right," Jesus replied, "this is the miracle I will do: destroy this sanctuary and in three days I will raise it up!"

"What!" they exclaimed. "It took forty-six years to build this Temple, and you can do it in three days?"

But by "this sanctuary" he meant his body. Because of miracles he did at the Passover celebration, many people were convinced that he was the Messiah.[8]

MYSTERY MAN

After dark one night, Nicodemus, a Pharisee, came for an interview with Jesus. "Sir," he said, "we know God has sent you to teach us. Your miracles are proof of this."

Jesus replied, "With all the earnestness I possess, I tell you this: unless you are born again, you can never get into the Kingdom of God."

"Born again!" exclaimed Nicodemus. "How can an old man go back into his mother's womb and be born again?"

Jesus replied, "What I am telling you is: unless one is born of water and the Spirit, he cannot enter the Kingdom of God. Men can only reproduce human life, but the Holy Spirit gives new life from heaven; so don't be surprised at my statement that you must be born again! You can hear the wind but can't tell where it comes from or where it will go next; so it is with the Spirit."

"What do you mean?" Nicodemus asked.

Jesus replied, "You, a respected Jewish teacher, don't understand these things? I am telling you what I know and have seen—and yet you won't believe me. If you don't believe me when I tell you about things that happen among men, how can you possibly believe if I tell you what is going on in heaven? Only I, the Messiah, have come to earth and will return to heaven again. For God loved the world so much that he gave his only Son so that anyone who believes in him shall not perish but have eternal life. God did not send his Son into the world to condemn it, but to save it. Those who don't trust him have been condemned for not believing in the only Son of God. The Light from heaven came into the world, but they loved darkness more than the Light, for their deeds were evil. Those doing right come gladly to the Light to let everyone see they are doing what God wants them to."

Afterwards Jesus and his disciples left Jerusalem and stayed for a while in Judea and baptized there. At this time John the Baptist was baptizing at Aenon. Someone began an argument with John's disciples, telling them that Jesus' baptism was best. So they came to John and said, "Master, the man you met on the other side of the Jordan River— the one you said was the Messiah—he is baptizing too, and everybody is going over there instead of coming here."

John replied, "God appoints each man's work. My work is to prepare the way for that man. The bride will go where the bridegroom is! I am the Bridegroom's friend, and I am filled with joy at his success. He must become greater and greater, and I must become less and less.

"He has come from heaven and is greater than anyone else. I am of the earth, and my understanding is limited to the things of earth. He tells what he has seen and heard, but how few believe what he tells them! Those who believe him discover that God is a fountain of truth. For this one— sent by God—speaks God's words. The Father loves this man because he is his Son, and God has given him everything there is. All who trust him—God's Son—have eternal life; those who don't believe and obey him shall never see heaven."[9]

THIRSTY WOMAN

When the Lord knew that the Pharisees heard about great crowds coming to him to be his disciples, he left Judea and returned to Galilee. He had to go through Samaria on the way, and around noon as he approached Sychar he came to Jacob's Well on the parcel of ground Jacob gave to his son Joseph. Jesus was tired from the long walk in the hot sun and sat wearily beside the well.

Soon a Samaritan woman came to draw water, and Jesus asked her for a drink. He was alone as his disciples had gone into the village to buy food. The woman was surprised that a Jew would ask a "despised Samaritan" for anything, and she remarked about this to Jesus.

He replied, "If you only knew what a wonderful gift God has for you, and who I am, you would ask me for some living water!"

"But you don't have a rope or a bucket," she said. "Where would you get living water?"

Jesus replied that people soon became thirsty after drinking this water. "But the water I give them," he said, "becomes a perpetual spring within them, watering them forever with eternal life."

"Please, sir," the woman said, "give me some of that water! Then I won't have to make this long trip out here every day."

"Go and get your husband," Jesus told her.

"But I'm not married," the woman replied.

"All too true!" Jesus said. "For you have had five husbands, and you aren't married to the man you're living with now."

"Sir," the woman said, "you must be a prophet. Tell

me, why is it that you Jews insist Jerusalem is the only place of worship, while we Samaritans claim it is here at Mount Gerazim where our ancestors worshiped?"

Jesus replied, "The time is coming when we will no longer be concerned about whether to worship here or in Jerusalem. For it's not where we worship that counts, but how we worship—is our worship spiritual and real? Do we have the Holy Spirit's help? For God is Spirit, and we must have his help to worship as we should. The Father wants this kind of worship from us. But you Samaritans know little about him, worshiping blindly, while we Jews know all about him, for salvation comes to the world through the Jews."

The woman said, "Well, at least I know that the Messiah will come—the one they call Christ—and when he does he will explain everything to us."

Then Jesus told her: "I am the Messiah!"

Just then his disciples arrived. They were surprised to find him talking to a woman, but none of them asked him why.

The woman left her waterpot beside the well and went back to the village and told everyone: "Come and meet a man who told me everything I ever did! Can this be the Messiah?" The people came streaming from the village to see him.

Meanwhile the disciples were urging Jesus to eat. "No," he said, "I have food you don't know about."

"Who brought it to him?" the disciples asked each other.

Jesus explained: "My nourishment comes from doing the will of God and finishing his work. Do you think the work of harvesting will not begin until the summer ends four months from now? Look around you! Vast fields of human souls are ripening all around us and are ready now for reaping. What joys await the sower and the reaper, both together! For it is true that one sows and someone else reaps."

Many from the Samaritan village believed he was the Messiah because of the woman's report. When they came out to see him at the well, they begged him to stay at their village and he did for two days. They said to the

woman, "Now we believe because we have heard him ourselves, not just because of what you told us. He is indeed
the Savior of the world."[10]

REJECTION One day as Jesus was walking along
the shore of the Sea of Galilee, he
saw Simon and his brother Andrew
fishing with nets, for they were commercial fishermen. Jesus
called out, "Come, follow me! And I will make you fishermen
for the souls of men!" At once they left their nets and
went with him.

A little farther up the beach, he saw James and John in
a boat mending their nets. He called them too, and immediately they left their father Zebedee in the boat with the
hired men and went with him.

Jesus and his companions arrived at Capernaum, and
on Saturday morning went into the Jewish place of worship,
where he preached. A man possessed by a demon was
present and began shouting, "Why are you bothering us,
Jesus of Nazareth—have you come to destroy us demons?
I know who you are—the holy Son of God!"

Jesus commanded the demon to say no more and to
come out of the man. At that, the evil spirit screamed and
convulsed the man violently and left him. Amazement
gripped the audience. "What sort of new religion is this?"
they asked. "Even evil spirits obey his orders!"

Leaving the synagogue, he and his disciples went to Simon and Andrew's home where they found Simon's mother-
in-law sick with a high fever. He went to her bedside and
as he took her by the hand and helped her to sit up the
fever suddenly left. She got up and prepared dinner for
them!

By sunset the courtyard was filled with the sick and
demon-possessed brought to him for healing; and a huge
crowd from all over Capernaum gathered outside the
door. So Jesus healed great numbers of sick folk that
evening and ordered many demons to come out of their
victims.

The next morning he was up long before daybreak and
went out alone into the wilderness to pray. Later, Simon

and the others went out to find him and told him, "Everyone is asking for you."

But he replied, "We must go on to other towns as well, and give my message to them, for that is why I came."

So he traveled throughout the province of Galilee, preaching in the synagogues and releasing many from the power of demons. When he came to Nazareth, his boyhood home, he went as usual to the synagogue on Saturday, and stood up to read the Scriptures. The book of Isaiah the prophet was handed to him, and he opened it to the place where it says:

"The Spirit of the Lord is upon me: he has appointed me to preach Good News to the poor; he has sent me to heal the brokenhearted and to announce that captives shall be released and the blind shall see, that the downtrodden shall be freed from their oppressors, and that God is ready to give blessings to all who come to him."

He closed the book and handed it back to the attendant while everyone in the synagogue gazed at him intently. Then he added, "These Scriptures came true today!"

All were amazed by the beautiful words. "How can this be?" they asked. "Isn't this Joseph's son?"

Then he said, "Probably you will quote me that proverb, 'Physician, heal yourself'—meaning, 'Why don't you do miracles here in your home town like those you did in Capernaum?' But I solemnly declare that no prophet is accepted in his hometown! Remember how Elijah used a miracle to help the widow of Zarephath—a foreigner from the land of Sidon. There were many Jewish widows needing help in those days for there had been no rain for three and one-half years and hunger stalked the land; yet Elijah was not sent to them."

These remarks stung them to fury; jumping up, they mobbed him and took him to the edge of the hill on which the city was built to push him over the cliff. But he walked away through the crowd and left them!

He returned to Capernaum and preached there in the synagogue every Saturday. People were amazed at the things he said, for he spoke as one who knew the truth instead of quoting others as his authority.

Report of his miracles spread far beyond Galilee so that sick folk were soon coming from as far away as Syria. Whatever their illness and pain, or if they were possessed by demons or were insane or paralyzed—he healed them all. Enormous crowds followed him from Galilee, the Ten Cities, Jerusalem, all over Judea, and even from across the Jordan River.

One day as he was preaching on the shore of Lake Gennesaret, great crowds pressed in on him to listen. He noticed two empty boats at the water's edge while the fishermen washed their nets. Stepping into one of the boats, Jesus asked Simon, its owner, to push out a little into the water so he could sit in the boat and speak to the crowds from there.

When he had finished, he said to Simon, "Now go out where it is deeper and let down your nets and you will catch a lot of fish!"

"Sir," Simon replied, "we worked hard all last night and didn't catch a thing. But if you say so, we'll try again."

This time their nets were so full that they began to tear! A shout for help brought their partners in the other boat and soon both boats were filled with fish and on the verge of sinking.

When Simon Peter realized what had happened, he fell to his knees before Jesus and said, "Please leave us—I'm too much of a sinner for you to have around." He was awestruck by the size of their catch, as were his partners James and John.

Jesus replied, "Don't be afraid! From now on you'll be fishing for men!"

As soon as they landed, they left everything and went with him.

One day while he was teaching, some religious leaders and teachers of the Law were sitting nearby. It seemed that these men showed up from every village in Galilee and Judea as well as from Jerusalem. Then some men came carrying a paralyzed man on a sleeping mat. They tried to push through the crowd to Jesus but couldn't reach him. So they went up on the roof above him, took off some tiles, and lowered the sick man, still on his sleeping mat, in front of Jesus.

Seeing their faith, Jesus said to the man, "My friend, your sins are forgiven!"

"Who does this fellow think he is?" the Pharisees and teachers exclaimed. "This is blasphemy! Who but God can forgive sins?"

Jesus replied, "Why is it blasphemy? I, the Messiah, have the authority on earth to forgive sins. But talk is cheap—anybody could say that. So I'll prove it to you by healing this man." Then, turning to the paralyzed man, he commanded, "Pick up your stretcher and go on home, for you are healed!"

Immediately the man jumped to his feet, picked up his mat, and went home praising God! Everyone was gripped with awe, and they praised God.

Later as Jesus left the town he saw a tax collector—with the usual reputation for cheating—sitting at a tax collection booth. The man's name was Levi. Jesus said to him, "Come and be one of my disciples!" So Levi left everything and went with him.

Soon Levi held a reception in his home with Jesus as the guest of honor. Many of Levi's fellow tax collectors and other guests were there. The Pharisees and teachers of the Law complained bitterly to Jesus' disciples about his eating with such notorious sinners.

Jesus answered, "It is the sick who need a doctor; my purpose is to invite sinners to turn from their sins, not to spend my time with those who think themselves already good enough."

Their next complaint was that Jesus' disciples were feasting instead of fasting. "John the Baptist's disciples are constantly going without food and praying," they declared, "and so do the disciples of the Pharisees. Why are yours wining and dining?"

Jesus asked, "Do happy men fast? Do wedding guests go hungry while celebrating with the groom? But the time will come when the bridegroom will be killed; then they won't want to eat."

On a Sabbath he was in the synagogue teaching, and a

man was present whose right hand was deformed. The Pharisees watched closely to see whether he would heal the man since it was the Sabbath.

He knew their thoughts, but he said to the man with the deformed hand, "Come and stand here where everyone can see." Then Jesus said, "I have a question: Is it right to do good on the Sabbath day, or to do harm? To save life, or to destroy it?"

He looked around and then said to the man, "Reach out your hand." As he did, it became completely normal.

At this, the enemies of Jesus were wild with rage and began to plot his murder.[11]

KINGDOM WAYS

Soon afterwards he went into the mountains to pray and prayed all night. At daybreak he called together his followers and chose twelve of them to be the inner circle of his disciples. They were appointed "apostles," or "missionaries." Their names: Simon (he also called him Peter), Andrew (Simon's brother), James, John, Philip, Bartholomew, Matthew, Thomas, James—the son of Alphaeus, Simon—a member of the Zealots, a subversive political party, Judas—son of James, Judas Iscariot.

When they came down the slopes of the mountain, they stood with Jesus on a large, level area surrounded by many of his followers who, in turn, were surrounded by crowds. People from as far as the seacoasts of Tyre and Sidon had come to hear him or to be healed. Everyone was trying to touch him, for when they did, healing power went out from him and they were cured.

As the crowds were gathering, Jesus went up the hillside with his disciples and sat down and taught them.

"Humble men are very fortunate," he told them, "for the Kingdom of Heaven is given to them. Those who mourn are fortunate, for they shall be comforted. The meek and lowly are fortunate, for the whole world belongs to them.

"Happy are those who long to be just and good, for they shall be completely satisfied. Happy are the kind and merciful, for they shall be shown mercy. Happy are those whose hearts are pure, for they shall see God. Happy are those who strive for peace—they shall be called the sons of God. Happy are those who are persecuted because they are good, for the Kingdom of Heaven is theirs.

"When you are reviled and persecuted and lied about because you are my followers—wonderful! Be very glad! For a tremendous reward awaits you in heaven. And remember, the ancient prophets were persecuted, too.

"You are the world's seasoning, to make it tolerable. If you lose your flavor, what will happen to the world? You are the world's light—a city on a hill, glowing in the night for all to see. Don't hide your light! Let your good deeds glow for all to see, so that they will praise your heavenly Father.

"Don't misunderstand why I have come—it isn't to cancel the laws of Moses and the warnings of the prophets. I came to fulfill them, to make them all come true. With all the earnestness I have I say: Every law in the Book will continue until its purpose is achieved. Those who teach God's laws and obey them shall be great in the Kingdom of Heaven.

"But I warn you—unless your goodness is greater than that of the Pharisees and other Jewish leaders, you can't get into the Kingdom of Heaven!

"The laws of Moses said, 'You shall not commit adultery.' But I say: Anyone who looks at a woman with lust in his eye has already committed adultery with her in his heart.

"The law of Moses says, 'If anyone wants to be rid of his wife, he can divorce her by giving her a letter of dismissal.' But I say that a man who divorces his wife, except for fornication, causes her to commit adultery if she marries again.

"The law of Moses says, 'If a man gouges out another's eye, he must pay with his own eye. If a tooth gets knocked out, knock out the tooth of the one who did it.' But I say: Don't resist violence! If you are slapped on one cheek, turn the other. If the military demand that you carry their gear for a mile, carry it two. Give to those who ask, and don't turn away from those who want to borrow.

"There is a saying, 'Love your friends and hate your enemies.' But I say: Love your enemies! Pray for those who persecute you! In that way you will be acting as true sons of your Father in heaven. For he gives his sunlight to both the evil and the good, and sends rain on the just and on the unjust too. If you are friendly only to your friends, how are you different from anyone else? You are to be perfect, even as your Father in heaven is perfect.

"Don't do your good deeds publicly, to be admired, for then you will lose the reward from your Father in heaven. Do it secretly, and your Father who knows all secrets will reward you.

"When you pray, don't be like the hypocrites who pretend piety by praying where everyone can see them. Go away by yourself and pray to your Father secretly, and your Father, who knows your secrets, will reward you. Don't recite the same prayer over and over; remember, your Father knows exactly what you need even before you ask him!

"Pray along these lines: 'Our Father in heaven, we honor your holy Name. We ask that your kingdom will come now. May your will be done here on earth, just as it is in heaven. Give us our food again today; and forgive our sins just as we have forgiven those who have sinned against us. Don't bring us into temptation, but deliver us from the Evil One. Amen.'

"When you fast, declining your food for a spiritual purpose, don't do it publicly as the hypocrites do. But put on festive clothing so no one will suspect you are hungry—except your Father who knows every secret, and he will reward you.

"Don't store up treasures on earth where they can erode away or be stolen. Store them in heaven where they will never lose their value, and are safe from thieves. If your profits are in heaven, your heart will be there, too.

"If your eye is pure, there will be sunshine in your soul. But if your eye is clouded with evil thoughts and desires, you are in deep spiritual darkness. And oh, how deep that darkness can be!

"You cannot serve two masters—God and money. For you will hate one and love the other, or else the other way around.

"So don't worry about things—food, drink, and clothes. For you have life and a body—and they are far more important than what to eat and wear. Look at the birds! They don't worry about what to eat—they don't need to sow or reap or store up food—for your heavenly Father feeds them. And you are far more valuable to him than they are.

"And why worry about your clothes? Look at the field lilies! They don't worry about theirs. Yet King Solomon in all his glory was not clothed as beautifully as they. And if God cares so wonderfully for flowers that are here today and gone tomorrow, won't he more surely care for you?

"So don't worry at all about food and clothing. Your heavenly Father knows perfectly well that you need them, and he will give them to you if you give him first place in your life and live as he wants you to.

"Don't be anxious about tomorrow. God will take care of your tomorrow, too. Live one day at a time.

"Do for others what you want them to do for you. This is the teaching of the laws of Moses in a nutshell.

"Heaven can be entered only through the narrow gate! The highway to hell is broad, and its gate is wide enough for all the multitudes who choose its easy way. But the gateway to life is small, and the road is narrow, and only a few ever find it.

"Not all who sound religious are really godly people. They may refer to me as 'Lord,' but still won't get to heaven. For the decisive question is whether they obey my Father in heaven. At the judgment many will tell me, 'Lord, Lord, we told others about you and used your name to cast out demons and to do many other great miracles.' But I will reply, 'You have never been mine. Go away, for your deeds are evil.'

"All who listen to my instructions and follow them are wise, like a man who builds his house on solid rock. Though the rain comes in torrents and the floods rise and the winds beat against his house, it won't collapse for it is built on rock.

"But those who hear my instructions and ignore them are foolish, like a man who builds his house on sand. For when the rains and floods come and winds beat against his house, it will fall with a mighty crash."[12]

KINGDOM SIGNS

The crowds were amazed at Jesus' sermon. When Jesus finished, he went back to the city of Capernaum. Just at that time the highly prized slave of a Roman army captain was sick and near death. The captain heard about Jesus; he sent some respected Jewish elders to ask Jesus to come and heal his slave. They began pleading with Jesus: "If anyone deserves your help, it is he, for he loves the Jews and paid to build us a synagogue!"

Jesus went with them, but the captain sent some friends to say, "Sir, don't inconvenience yourself by coming to my home, for I am not worthy of any such honor. Just speak a word from where you are, and my servant will be healed! I know, because I am under the authority of superior officers and I have authority over my men. So just say, 'Be healed!' and my servant will be well again!"

Jesus, turning to the crowd, said, "Never among the Jews have I met a man with faith like this!"

And when the captain's friends returned to his house, they found the slave healed.

Not long afterwards Jesus went with his disciples to the village of Nain, with the usual crowd at his heels. A funeral procession was coming out as he approached the village gate. The boy who had died was the only son of his widowed mother, and many mourners were with her.

When the Lord saw her, his heart overflowed with sympathy. "Don't cry!" he said. Then he walked over to the coffin and touched it, and the bearers stopped. "Laddie," he said, "come back to life again."

The boy sat up and began to talk to those around him, and Jesus gave him back to his mother!

A great fear swept the crowd, and they exclaimed, "A mighty prophet has risen among us. We have seen the hand of God at work today!"

The report of what he did that day raced from end to end of Judea and across the borders.

Disciples of John the Baptist heard all that Jesus was

doing. When they told John about it, he sent two of his disciples to Jesus to ask him, "Are you really the Messiah?" (After John had publicly criticized Herod, governor of Galilee, for many wrongs he had done, Herod put John in prison.)

The two disciples found Jesus while he was curing sick people of various diseases—healing the lame and the blind and casting out evil spirits. When they asked him John's question, this was his reply: "Go back to John and tell him all you have seen and heard here today: how those who were blind can see; the lame are walking without a limp; lepers are completely healed; the deaf can hear again; the dead come back to life; the poor are hearing the Good News. And tell him, 'Blessed is the one who does not lose his faith in me.'"

After they left, Jesus talked to the crowd about John. "He is the one to whom the Scriptures refer when they say, 'Look! I am sending my messenger ahead of you, to prepare the way before you.' In all humanity there is no one greater than John. And yet the least citizen of the Kingdom of God is greater than he."

Not long afterwards he began a tour of the cities and villages of Galilee to announce the coming of the Kingdom of God, and took his twelve disciples with him. Some women went along; among them were Mary Magdalene, Joanna, Chuza's wife (Chuza was King Herod's business manager), Susanna, and others who were contributing from their private means to the support of Jesus and his disciples.

One day he gave this illustration to a crowd that was gathering to hear him.

"A farmer went out to his field to sow grain. As he scattered the seed on the ground, some of it fell on a footpath and was trampled on; and the birds came and ate it as it lay exposed. Other seed fell on shallow soil with rock beneath. This seed began to grow, but soon withered and died for lack of moisture. Other seed landed in thistle patches, and the young grain stalks were soon choked out. Still other fell on fertile soil; this seed grew and produced a crop one hundred times as large as he had planted. If anyone has listening ears, use them now!"

His apostles asked him what the story meant.

He replied, "Parables tell a great deal about the Kingdom of God. The seed is God's message to men. The hard path where some seed fell represents hard hearts of those who hear the words of God, but then the devil comes and steals the words away and prevents people from believing. The stony ground represents those who enjoy listening to sermons, but somehow the message doesn't take root and grow. They believe for awhile, but when the hot winds of persecution blow they lose interest. The seed among the thorns represents those who listen and believe God's words but whose faith afterwards is choked out by worry, riches, and the responsibilities and pleasures of life.

"But the good soil represents hearts of those who truly accept God's message and produce a plentiful harvest for God—thirty, sixty, or even a hundred times as much as was planted in their hearts."

Once when his mother and brothers came to see him, they couldn't get into the house where he was teaching because of the crowds. When Jesus heard they were outside and wanted to see him, he remarked, "My mother and my brothers are all those who hear the message of God and obey it."

As evening fell, Jesus said to his disciples, "Let's cross to the other side of the lake." So they started out, leaving the crowds behind. Soon a terrible storm arose. High waves began to break into the boat until it was nearly full of water and about to sink. Jesus was asleep at the back of the boat. Frantically they wakened him, shouting, "Teacher, don't you care that we are about to drown?"

Then he rebuked the wind and said to the sea, "Quiet down!" The wind fell, and there was a great calm! He asked them, "Why were you so fearful? Don't you yet have confidence in me?"

They were filled with awe and said among themselves, "Who is this, that even the winds and seas obey him?"

When they arrived at the other side of the lake, a demon-possessed man ran out from a graveyard just as Jesus was climbing from the boat. This man had such strength that whenever he was put into handcuffs and shackles he snapped the handcuffs from his wrists and smashed the shackles and walked away. All day long and through the night he would wander among the tombs and in the hills, screaming and cutting himself with sharp pieces of stone. When Jesus was still far out on the water, the man had seen him and had run to meet him. He fell down before him.

Jesus spoke to the demon in the man: "Come out, you evil spirit."

It gave a terrible scream, shrieking, "What are you going to do to me, Jesus, Son of the Most High God? Don't torture me!"

"What is your name?" Jesus asked. The demon replied, "Legion, for there are many of us in this man." Then the demons begged him not to send them to some distant land. There was a huge herd of hogs rooting around on the hill above the lake. "Send us into those hogs," the demons begged.

And Jesus gave them permission.

The evil spirits came out of the man and entered the hogs, and the entire herd plunged down the steep hillside into the lake and drowned. The herdsmen fled to nearby towns, spreading the news as they ran.

A large crowd soon gathered, but as they saw the man sitting there fully clothed and perfectly sane, they were frightened. The crowd began pleading with Jesus to go away, so he got back into the boat. The man who had been possessed by demons begged Jesus to let him go along, but Jesus said, "Go home to your friends and tell them what wonderful things God has done for you."

So the man started off to the Ten Towns of that region and began to tell about the things Jesus had done. They were awestruck by his story.

When Jesus had gone to the other side of the lake, a crowd gathered around him on the shore. In the crowd was a woman who had been sick for twelve years with a hemorrhage. She had heard about the miracles Jesus did and she came up behind him through the crowd and touched his clothes. As soon as she touched him, she knew she was well!

Jesus realized at once that healing power had gone out from him, so he turned and asked, "Who touched my clothes?"

His disciples said, "All this crowd pressing around you, and you ask who touched you?"

But he kept looking around to see who it was. The frightened woman, trembling at the realization of what had happened to her, came and fell at his feet and told him what she had done. He said to her, "Daughter, your faith has made you well; go in peace."

Soon afterwards he returned with his disciples to Nazareth. The next Sabbath he went to the synagogue to teach, and the people were astonished at his wisdom and miracles because he was a local man like themselves. "He's no better than we are," they said. "He's just a carpenter, Mary's boy, and a brother of James and Joseph, Judas and Simon. And his sisters live right here among us."

Jesus told them, "A prophet is honored everywhere except in his hometown and by his own family." Because of their unbelief, he couldn't do any mighty miracles among them.

Then he went out among the villages, teaching. And he called his twelve disciples together and sent them out two by two. He told them to take nothing except walking sticks.

"Stay at one home in each village," he said. "Whenever a village won't listen to you, shake off the dust from your feet as a sign that you have abandoned it to its fate.

"Don't be afraid of those who can kill only your bodies— but can't touch your souls! Fear only God who can destroy both soul and body in hell. Not one sparrow can fall to the ground without your Father knowing it. And the very hairs of your head are all numbered. So don't worry!

"If anyone publicly acknowledges me as his friend, I will openly acknowledge him as my friend before my Father in heaven. But if anyone publicly denies me, I will openly deny him before my Father in heaven."

So the disciples went out, telling everyone they met to turn from sin. And they cast out many demons and healed many sick people.

King Herod heard about Jesus, for his miracles were

talked about everywhere. The king thought Jesus was John the Baptist come back to life—for Herod had sent soldiers to arrest John because he kept saying it was wrong for the king to marry Herodias, his brother Philip's wife. Herodias wanted John killed in revenge, but Herod respected John. Herodias' chance finally came. It was Herod's birthday and he gave a stag party for his palace aides, army officers, and the leading citizens of Galilee. Then Herodias' daughter came in and danced and greatly pleased them.

"Ask me for anything you like," the king vowed, "even half of my kingdom, and I will give it to you!"

She consulted her mother, who told her, "Ask for John the Baptist's head!"

She hurried back to the king and told him, "I want the head of John the Baptist—right now—on a tray!"

The king was sorry, but he was embarrassed to break his oath so he sent one of his bodyguards to the prison to cut off John's head. The soldier killed John in the prison and brought back his head on a tray and gave it to the girl. She took it to her mother.

When John's disciples heard what had happened, they came for his body and buried it. As soon as Jesus heard the news, he went off by himself in a boat to a remote area to be alone. But the crowds saw where he was headed, and followed by land.

When Jesus came out of the wilderness, a crowd was waiting and he healed their sick. Pilgrims on their way to Jerusalem for the annual Passover celebration were following wherever he went. When Jesus went up into the hills and sat down with his disciples, he soon saw a multitude climbing the hill, looking for him.

Turning to Philip, he asked, "Where can we buy bread to feed all these people?" (He was testing Philip, for he already knew what he was going to do.)

Philip replied, "It would take a fortune to do it!"

Andrew spoke up. "There's a youngster here with five barley loaves and a couple of fish! But what good is that with all this mob?"

"Tell everyone to sit down," Jesus ordered. All of them—the approximate count of only the men was 5,000—sat down on the grassy slopes. Then Jesus took the loaves, gave thanks to God, and passed them out to the people. Afterwards he did the same with the fish. And everyone ate until full!

"Now gather the scraps," Jesus told his disciples, "so that nothing is wasted." And twelve baskets were filled with the leftovers!

When the people realized what a great miracle had happened, they exclaimed, "Surely he is the Prophet we have been expecting!"

Jesus saw that they were ready to take him by force and make him their king, so he went higher into the mountains alone.

That evening his disciples went down to the shore to wait for him. But as darkness fell and Jesus still hadn't come back, they got into the boat and headed across the lake toward Capernaum. Soon a gale swept down upon them and the sea grew very rough. They were three or four miles out when suddenly they saw Jesus walking toward the boat! They screamed in terror, for they thought he was a ghost.

But Jesus immediately spoke. "Don't be afraid!" he said.

Then Peter called to him: "Sir, if it is really you, tell me to come over to you, walking on the water."

"All right," the Lord said, "come along!"

Peter went over the side of the boat and walked on the water toward Jesus. But when he looked around at the high waves he was terrified and began to sink. "Save me, Lord!" he shouted.

Instantly Jesus reached out his hand and rescued him. "O man of little faith," Jesus said, "why did you doubt me?" And when they had climbed into the boat, the wind stopped.

The others sat there, awestruck. "You really are the Son of God!" they exclaimed.[13]

KINGDOM FAITH

They landed at Gennesaret. The news of their arrival spread quickly and soon people were telling everyone to bring their sick to be healed.

Back across the lake, crowds began gathering on the shore waiting to see Jesus. Several small boats from Tiberias were nearby, so when the people saw that Jesus wasn't there, nor his disciples, they got into boats and went across to Capernaum to look for him.

When they arrived and found him, they said, "Sir, how did you get here?" Jesus replied, "The truth of the matter is that you want to be with me because I fed you, not because you believe in me. You shouldn't be so concerned about perishable things like food; spend your energy seeking the eternal life that I can give you. For God the Father sent me for this purpose."

They replied, "What should we do to satisfy God?"

"This is the will of God, that you believe in the one he has sent."

They replied, "You must show us more miracles if you want us to believe you are the Messiah. Give us free bread every day like our fathers had while they journeyed through the wilderness! As the Scriptures say, 'Moses gave them bread from heaven.' "

Jesus said, "Moses didn't give it to them. My Father did. And now he offers you true Bread from heaven. The true Bread is a Person—the one sent by God from heaven, and he gives life to the world."

"Sir," they said, "give us that bread every day of our lives!"

Jesus replied, "I am the Bread of Life. No one coming to me will ever be hungry again. Those believing in me will never thirst. I have come here from heaven to do the will of God who sent me. And this is the will of God, that I should not lose even one of all those he has given me but that I should raise them to eternal life at the Last Day. For it is my Father's will that everyone who sees his Son and believes on him should have eternal life.

"When your fathers in the wilderness ate bread from the skies, they all died. But the Bread from heaven gives eternal life to everyone who eats it. I am that Living Bread that came down out of heaven. Anyone eating this Bread shall live forever; this Bread is my flesh given to redeem humanity."

The Jews began arguing with each other about what he meant. "How can this man give us his flesh to eat?"

Jesus said again, "With all the earnestness I possess, I tell you this: unless you eat the flesh of the Messiah and drink his blood, you cannot have eternal life. My flesh is the true food, and my blood is the true drink. Everyone who eats my flesh and drinks my blood is in me, and I in him."

Even his disciples said, "This is very hard to understand. Who can tell what he means?"

Jesus knew that his disciples were complaining and said to them, "Does this offend you? Then what will you think if you see me, the Messiah, return to heaven again? Those born only once, with physical birth, will never receive this gift. Now I have told you how to get true spiritual life. But some of you don't believe me."

At this point many disciples turned away and deserted him.

Jesus turned to the Twelve and asked, "Are you going, too?"

Peter replied, "To whom shall we go? You alone have the words that give eternal life, and we believe them and know you are the holy Son of God."

Pharisees and other leaders arrived from Jerusalem to interview Jesus. "Why do your disciples disobey the ancient Jewish traditions? They ignore our ritual of ceremonial handwashing before they eat."

He replied, "And why do your traditions violate the direct commandments of God? For instance, God's law is, 'Honor your father and mother'; but you say, 'Even if your parents are in need, you may give their support money to the church instead.' And so by your man-made rule you nullify the direct command of God. You hypocrites! Well did Isaiah prophesy of you, 'These people say they honor me, but their hearts are far away. Their worship is worthless, for they teach their man-made laws instead of those from God.' "

Then Jesus called to the crowds and said, "Listen to what I say and try to understand: you aren't made unholy by eating nonkosher food! It is what you say and think that makes you unclean."

One day Pharisees and Sadducees came to test Jesus' claim of being the Messiah by asking him to show some great demonstrations in the skies.

He replied, "You are good at reading the weather signs of the skies—red sky tonight means fair weather tomorrow; red sky in the morning means foul weather all day—but you can't read the obvious signs of the times!

"Only an evil, faithless nation would ask for further proof; and none will be given except what happened to Jonah the prophet! For as Jonah was in the great fish for three days and three nights, so I, the Messiah, shall be in the heart of the earth three days and three nights. The men of Nineveh shall arise against this nation at the judgment and condemn you. For when Jonah preached to them, they repented and turned to God from their evil ways. And now a greater than Jonah is here—and you refuse to believe him." Then Jesus walked out on them.

When Jesus came to Caesarea Philippi, he asked his disciples, "Who are the people saying I am?"

They replied, "Some say John the Baptist; some, Elijah; some, Jeremiah or one of the other prophets."

"Who do you think I am?"

Simon Peter answered, "The Christ, the Messiah, the Son of the living God."

"God has blessed you, Simon, son of Jonah," Jesus said, "for my Father in heaven has personally revealed this to you—this is not from any human source. You are Peter, a stone; and upon this rock I will build my church; and all the powers of hell shall not prevail against it. And I will give you the keys of the Kingdom of Heaven; whatever doors you lock on earth shall be locked in heaven; and whatever doors you open on earth shall be open in heaven!"

From then on Jesus began to speak plainly to his disciples about going to Jerusalem and what would happen to him there—that he would suffer at the hands of the Jewish leaders, that he would be killed, and that three days later he would be raised to life again.

But they didn't understand and were afraid to ask what he meant.

Then Jesus said, "If anyone wants to be a follower of mine, let him deny himself and take up his cross and follow me. For anyone who keeps his life for himself shall lose it; and anyone who loses his life for me shall find it again. What profit is there if you gain the whole world—and lose eternal life? For I shall come with my angels in the glory of my Father and judge each person according to his deeds."

Six days later Jesus took Peter, James, and his brother John to the top of a high and lonely hill to pray. And as he was praying, his face began to shine and his clothes became dazzling white and blazed with light. Then two men appeared and began talking with him—Moses and Elijah! They were splendid in appearance, glorious to see; and they were speaking of his death at Jerusalem, to be carried out in accordance with God's plan.

Peter and the others, very drowsy, had fallen asleep. Now they woke up and saw Jesus covered with brightness and glory, and the two men standing with him. As Moses and Elijah were starting to leave, Peter, confused, blurted out, "Master, this is wonderful! We'll put up three shelters—one for you and one for Moses and one for Elijah!"

But even as he was saying this a bright cloud formed above them, and terror gripped them as it covered them. A voice from the cloud said, "This is my Son, my Chosen One; listen to him."

At this the disciples fell face downward to the ground, terribly frightened. Jesus came over and touched them. "Get up," he said; "don't be afraid."

And when they looked, only Jesus was with them.

As they were going down the mountain, Jesus commanded them not to tell anyone what they had seen until after he had risen from the dead.

His disciples asked, "Why do the Jewish leaders insist Elijah must return before the Messiah comes?"

Jesus replied, "They are right. Elijah must come and set everything in order. And, in fact, he has already come, but he wasn't recognized, and was badly mistreated by many. And I, the Messiah, shall also suffer at their hands."

Then the disciples realized he was speaking of John the Baptist.

On their arrival in Capernaum, Temple tax collectors came to Peter and asked him, "Doesn't your master pay taxes?"

"Of course he does," Peter replied. He went into the house to talk to Jesus about it, but before he had a chance to speak Jesus asked him, "What do you think, Peter? Do kings levy assessments against their own people, or against conquered foreigners?"

"Against the foreigners," Peter replied.

"Well, then," Jesus said, "the citizens are free! However, we don't want to offend them, so go down to the shore and throw in a line, and open the mouth of the first fish you catch. You will find a coin to cover the taxes for both of us; take it and pay them!"

The disciples came to Jesus to ask which of them would be greatest in the Kingdom of Heaven!

Jesus called a small child over to him, set the little fellow down among them, and said, "Unless you turn to God from your sins and become as little children, you will never get into the Kingdom of Heaven. Therefore anyone who humbles himself as this little child is the greatest in the Kingdom of Heaven. And any of you who welcomes a little child like this because you are mine is welcoming me and caring for me. Beware that you don't look down upon a single one of these little children. For in heaven their angels have constant access to my Father.

"If a man has a hundred sheep, and one wanders away and is lost, won't he leave the ninety-nine others and go out to search for the lost one? It is not my Father's will that even one of these little ones should perish."[14]

DEITY OR DEVIL

Soon it was time for the Tabernacle Ceremonies, one of the annual Jewish holidays, and Jesus' brothers urged him to go for the celebration. "Go where more people can see your miracles!" they scoffed. "If you're so great, prove it to the world!" For his brothers didn't believe in him.

Jesus replied, "It is not the right time for me; you go on, and I'll come when it is the right time."

After his brothers left he went secretly, staying out of the public eye. Jewish leaders tried to find him and kept asking if anyone had seen him. There was a lot of discussion about him among the crowds. Some said, "He's a wonderful man," while others said, "No, he's duping the public."

Midway through the festival Jesus went to the Temple and preached openly. The Jewish leaders were surprised: "How can he know so much when he's never been to our schools?"

Jesus told them, "I'm not teaching my own thoughts, but those of God who sent me. If any of you really determines to do God's will, then you will certainly know whether my teaching is from God or is merely my own."

Some of the people who lived in Jerusalem said among themselves, "Isn't this the man they are trying to kill? Here he is preaching in public and they say nothing to him. Can it be that our leaders have learned that he really is the Messiah?"

Many among the crowds believed on him: "After all," they said, "what miracles do you expect the Messiah to do that this man hasn't done?"

When the Pharisees heard the crowds were in this mood, they and the chief priests sent officers to arrest Jesus. But Jesus told them, "Not yet. I am to be here a little longer, then I shall return to the one who sent me. You will search for me but not find me. And you won't be able to come where I am!"

The leaders were puzzled by this statement. "Where is he planning to go?" they asked. "What does he mean about our looking for him and not being able to find him?"

On the climax of the holidays, Jesus shouted to the crowds, "If anyone is thirsty, let him come to me and drink. For the Scriptures declare that rivers of living water shall flow from the inmost being of anyone who believes in me." He was speaking of the Holy Spirit, who would be given to everyone believing in him; but the Spirit had not yet been given, because Jesus had not yet returned to his glory in heaven.

When the crowds heard this, some declared, "This man is the prophet who will come just before the Messiah."

Others said, "He is the Messiah." Still others: "He can't be! Will the Messiah come from Galilee? The Scriptures clearly state that the Messiah will be born of the royal line of David in Bethlehem." So the crowd was divided about him. And some wanted him arrested, but no one touched him.

Temple police who had been sent to arrest him returned to the chief priests and Pharisees.

"Why didn't you bring him in?" they demanded.

"He says such wonderful things!" they mumbled. "We've never heard anything like it."

The Pharisees mocked, "Is there a single one of us who believes he is the Messiah? These stupid crowds do, yes; but what do they know?"

Then Nicodemus spoke up. "Is it legal to convict a man before he is tried?"

They replied, "Are you a wretched Galilean too? Search the Scriptures and see for yourself—no prophets will come from Galilee!" Then the meeting broke up.

Jesus returned to the Mount of Olives, but early the next morning he was back again at the Temple. A crowd soon gathered, and he sat down and talked to them. As he was speaking, the Jewish leaders brought a woman caught in adultery and placed her in front of the staring crowd.

"Teacher," they said, "this woman was caught in the act of adultery. Moses' law says to kill her. What about it?"

They were trying to trap him into saying something they could use against him, but Jesus stooped and wrote in the dust with his finger. They kept demanding an answer, so he stood up and said, "All right, hurl stones at her until she dies but only he who never sinned may throw the first!"

The leaders slipped away one by one, beginning with the eldest, until only Jesus was left in the front of the crowd with the woman. Then Jesus said, "Where are your accusers? Didn't even one of them condemn you?"

"No, sir," she said.

"Neither do I. Go and sin no more."

Later in one of his talks Jesus said to the people, "I am the Light of the world. If you follow me, you won't stumble through the dark, for living light will flood your path."

The Pharisees replied, "You are boasting—and lying!"

Jesus told them, "These claims are true though I make them concerning myself. You pass judgment on me without knowing the facts. You don't know who I am, so you don't know who my Father is. If you knew me, then you would know him too."

Later he said, "You are from below; I am from above. Unless you believe that I am the Messiah, the Son of God, you will die in your sins."

"Tell us who you are," they demanded.

"I am the one I have always claimed to be. When you have killed the Messiah, then you will realize that I am he and that I have spoken what the Father taught me. For I always do those things that are pleasing to him."

Then many of the Jewish leaders began believing him to be the Messiah.

Jesus said to them, "You are truly my disciples if you live as I tell you to, and you will know the truth and the truth will set you free."

"But we descendants of Abraham have never been slaves to any man! What do you mean, 'set free'?"

Jesus replied, "You are slaves of sin, every one of you. If the Son sets you free, you will indeed be free. I realize you are descendants of Abraham, and yet some of you are trying to kill me because my message does not find a home in your hearts. I tell you what I saw when I was with my Father, but you are following the advice of your father."

"Our father is Abraham," they declared.

"No!" Jesus replied, "for if he were, you would follow his good example. No, you are obeying your real father."

"Our true Father is God himself!"

"If that were so, you would love me, for I have come to you from God. You are the children of your father the devil, and you love the evil things he does. He was a murderer from the beginning and a hater of truth, so when I tell the truth you just naturally don't believe it! Anyone whose Father is God listens gladly to the words of God. Since you don't, it proves you aren't his children."

"You foreigner! Devil!" the Jewish leaders snarled. "Didn't we say all along you were possessed by a demon?"

"I have no demon in me. For I honor my Father—and my God judges those who reject me. With all the earnestness I have, I tell you—no one who obeys me shall ever die!"

The leaders said, "Now we know you are possessed by a demon. Abraham and the mightiest prophets died, and yet you say that obeying you will keep a man from dying! So you are greater than Abraham, who died, and greater than the prophets, who died?"

Jesus told them, "Abraham rejoiced to see my day. He knew I was coming and was glad."

"You aren't even fifty years old—sure, you've seen Abraham!"

"The absolute truth is that I was in existence before Abraham was born!"

At that point the leaders picked up stones to kill him, but Jesus walked past them and left the Temple.

"I am the Good Shepherd. The Good Shepherd lays down his life for the sheep. A hired man will run when he sees a wolf coming, for he has no real concern for the sheep. The Father loves me because I lay down my life that I may have it back again. No one can kill me without my consent—I lay down my life voluntarily. For I have the right and power to lay it down and also the right and power to take it again."

When he said these things, the leaders were again divided. Some said, "He has a demon." Others said, "This doesn't sound like a man possessed by a demon!" Leaders surrounded him and asked, "How long are you going to keep us in suspense? If you are the Messiah, tell us plainly."

"I have already told you, and you don't believe me," Jesus replied. "The proof is in the miracles I do in the name of my Father. But you don't believe me because you are not part of my flock. My sheep recognize my voice, and I know them, and they follow me. I give them eternal life and they shall never perish. My Father has given them to me, and he is more powerful than anyone else. I and the Father are one."

Again the leaders picked up stones to kill him.

Jesus said, "At God's direction I have done many a miracle to help the people. For which one are you killing me?"

"For blasphemy; you, a mere man, have declared yourself to be God!"

Once again they started to arrest him. But he left them and went beyond the Jordan River to the place where John was first baptizing. And many followed him. "John didn't do miracles," they remarked to one another, "but all his predictions concerning this man have come true." And many came to the decision that he was the Messiah.

Someone came to Jesus with this question: "Good master, what must I do to have eternal life?"

"You know the commandments: don't kill, don't commit adultery, don't steal, don't lie, don't cheat, respect your father and mother."

"Teacher," the man replied, "I've never broken one of those laws."

Jesus felt genuine love for this man. "You lack one thing; go and sell all you have and give the money to the poor— and you shall have treasure in heaven—and come, follow me."

The man went sadly away, for he was very rich.

Jesus watched him go, then turned to his disciples. "It's almost impossible for the rich to get into the Kingdom of God! It is easier for a camel to go through the eye of a needle than for a rich man to enter the Kingdom of God."

The disciples were incredulous! "Then who can be saved, if not a rich man?"

Jesus said, "Without God, it is utterly impossible. But with God everything is possible."[15]

ROAD TO JERUSALEM

The Lord now chose seventy other disciples and sent them ahead in pairs to towns and villages he planned to visit. These were his instructions: "Plead with the Lord of the harvest to send out more laborers to help you. If a town welcomes you, heal the sick; and as you heal them, say, 'The Kingdom of God is very near you now.' Those who welcome you are welcoming me, and those who reject you are rejecting me. Those who reject me are rejecting God who sent me."

When the seventy disciples returned, they joyfully reported to him, "Even the demons obey us when we use your name."

"Yes," he told them, "I have given you authority over the power of the Enemy. However, the important thing is that your names are registered as citizens of heaven."

Filled with the joy of the Holy Spirit, he said, "I praise you, Father, for hiding these things from the worldly-wise and revealing them to those who are as trusting as little children. No one really knows the Father except the Son and those to whom the Son chooses to reveal him."

Turning to the twelve disciples, he said quietly, "How privileged you are to see what you have seen. Many a prophet and king of old has longed to see and hear what you have seen and heard!"

One day an expert on Moses' laws came to test Jesus' orthodoxy. "Teacher, what does a man do to live forever in heaven?"

Jesus replied, "What does Moses' law say about it?"

"It says that you must love the Lord God with all your heart and soul and strength and mind. And you must love your neighbor as you love yourself."

"Right!" Jesus told him. "Do this and you shall live!"

The man asked, "Which neighbors?"

Jesus replied with an illustration: "A Jew going from Jerusalem to Jericho was attacked by bandits. They stripped him of his clothes and money and beat him up and left him lying half-dead beside the road. By chance a Jewish priest came along, and when he saw the man lying there he crossed to the other side of the road and passed by. A Jewish Temple-assistant walked over and looked at him lying there, but then went on.

"But a despised Samaritan came along and felt deep pity.

Kneeling beside him, the Samaritan soothed his wounds with medicine and bandaged them. Then he put the man on his donkey and walked beside him till they came to an inn where he nursed him through the night. The next day he handed the innkeeper two twenty-dollar bills and told him to take care of the man. 'If his bill runs higher than that,' he said, 'I'll pay the difference the next time I am here.' Now which of these three would you say was a neighbor to the bandits' victim?"

"The one who showed him some pity."

"Yes, now go and do the same."

Teaching them about prayer, he used this illustration: "Suppose you went to a friend's house at midnight, wanting to borrow bread. You would shout, 'A friend of mine has just arrived and I've nothing to give him to eat.' If you keep knocking long enough, he will get up and give you everything you want—because of your persistence. And so it is with prayer—keep on asking and you will keep on getting; keep on looking and you will keep on finding; knock and the door will be opened. Everyone who asks, receives; all who seek, find; and the door is opened to everyone who knocks.

"You men who are fathers—if your boy asks for bread, do you give him a stone? If sinful persons like yourselves give children what they need, don't you realize that your heavenly Father will give the Holy Spirit to those who ask for him?"

He went from city to city and village to village, teaching as he went, always pressing onward toward Jerusalem.

Some Pharisees said to him, "Get out of here if you want to live, for King Herod is after you!"

Jesus replied, "Go tell that fox that I will keep on casting out demons and doing miracles of healing today and tomorrow; and the third day I will reach my destination. For it wouldn't do for a prophet of God to be killed except in Jerusalem!

"O Jerusalem, Jerusalem! The city that murders the prophets. How often I have wanted to gather your children together even as a hen protects her brood under her wings, but you wouldn't let me. And now your house is left desolate. And you will never again see me until you say, 'Welcome to him who comes in the name of the Lord.' "

Notorious sinners often came to listen to Jesus. This caused complaints from the experts on law because he was associating with such people. So Jesus used this illustration:

"A man had two sons. When the younger told his father, 'I want my share of your estate now, instead of waiting until you die!' his father agreed to divide his wealth between his sons.

"A few days later this younger son packed his belongings and took a trip to a distant land, and there wasted all his money on parties and prostitutes. About the time his money was gone, a famine swept over the land and he began to starve. He persuaded a local farmer to hire him to feed his pigs. The boy became so hungry that even the pods he was feeding the swine looked good. And no one gave him anything.

"When he finally came to his senses, he said to himself, 'At home even the hired men have food enough and to spare, and here I am dying of hunger! I will go home and say: "Father, I have sinned against both heaven and you, and am no longer worthy of being called your son. Please take me on as a hired man." '

"So he returned home to his father. And while he was still a long distance away, his father saw him coming and was filled with loving pity and ran and embraced him and kissed him.

"His son said, 'Father, I have sinned against heaven and you, and am not worthy of being called your son—'

"But his father said, 'Quick! Bring the finest robe in the house and put it on him. And a jeweled ring for his finger; and shoes! And kill the calf we have in the fattening pen. We must celebrate with a feast, for this son of mine was dead and has returned to life.'

"Meanwhile, the older son was in the fields working; when he returned home, he asked one of the servants what was going on. 'Your brother is back,' he was told, 'and your father has prepared a great feast to celebrate his coming home.'

"The older brother was angry and wouldn't go in. His father came out and begged him, but he replied, 'All these years I've worked hard for you, and you never gave me even one goat for a feast with my friends.'

" 'Look, dear son,' his father said to him, 'you and I are very close, and everything I have is yours. But it is right to celebrate, for he was lost and is found!' "

"There was a certain rich man," Jesus said, "who was splendidly clothed and lived each day in mirth and luxury. One day Lazarus, a diseased beggar, was laid at his door. As he lay there longing for scraps from the rich man's table, the dogs would come and lick his open sores. Finally the beggar died and was carried by the angels to be with Abraham in the place of the righteous dead. The rich man also died and was buried, and his soul went into hell. There, in torment, he saw Lazarus in the far distance with Abraham.

" 'Father Abraham,' he shouted, 'have pity! Send Lazarus over here if only to dip the tip of his finger in water and cool my tongue, for I am in anguish.'

"But Abraham said, 'Remember that during your lifetime you had everything you wanted, and Lazarus had nothing. So now he is here being comforted and you are in anguish. And besides, there is a great chasm separating us, and no one can cross.'

" 'O Father Abraham, then please send him to my father's home—to warn them about this place of torment lest they come here when they die.'

"But Abraham said, 'The Scriptures have warned them again and again. Your brothers can read them any time they want to.'

" 'No, Father Abraham, they won't bother to read them. But if someone is sent to them from the dead, then they will turn from their sins.'

"Abraham said, 'If they won't listen to Moses and the prophets, they won't listen even though someone rises from the dead.' "

Then he told this story to some who boasted of their virtue.

"Two men went to the Temple to pray. One was a proud, self-righteous Pharisee, and the other a cheating tax collector. The Pharisee 'prayed' this prayer: 'Thank God, I am not a sinner like everyone else, especially like that tax collector over there! For I never cheat, I don't commit adultery, I go without food twice a week, and I give to God a tenth of everything I earn.'

"But the corrupt tax collector stood at a distance and dared not even lift his eyes to heaven as he prayed, but beat upon his chest in sorrow, exclaiming, 'God, be merciful to me, a sinner.' I tell you, this sinner, not the Pharisee, returned home forgiven! For the proud shall be humbled, but the humble shall be honored."

Gathering the Twelve around him, he told them, "As you know, we are going to Jerusalem. And when we get there, all the predictions of the ancient prophets concerning me will come true. I will be handed over to the Gentiles to be mocked and treated shamefully and spat upon and lashed and killed. And the third day I will rise again."

But they didn't understand; he seemed to be talking in riddles.

As Jesus was passing through Jericho, a man named Zacchaeus, one of the most influential Jews in the Roman tax-collecting business, tried to get a look at Jesus but he was too short to see over the crowds. He climbed a sycamore tree beside the road to watch from there.

When Jesus came by, he looked up at Zacchaeus and called, "Zacchaeus! Quick! Come down! I am going to be a guest in your home today!"

Zacchaeus climbed down and took Jesus to his house in great excitement, but the crowds were displeased. "He has gone to be the guest of a notorious sinner," they grumbled.

Meanwhile, Zacchaeus stood before the Lord and said, "Sir, from now on I will give half my wealth to the poor, and if I find I have overcharged anyone on his taxes, I will penalize myself by giving him back four times as much!"

Jesus told him, "This shows that salvation has come to this home today. This man was one of the lost sons of Abraham, and I, the Messiah, have come to search for and save such souls as his."

On the way to Jerusalem, the mother of James and John

brought them to Jesus and respectfully asked a favor. "In your Kingdom, will you let my two sons sit on thrones next to yours?"

Jesus told her, "You don't know what you are asking!" He turned to James and John: "Are you able to drink from the terrible cup I am about to drink from?"

"Yes," they replied, "we are able!"

"You shall indeed drink from it," he told them, "but I have no right to say who will sit on the thrones next to mine. Those places are reserved for the persons my Father selects."

The other ten disciples were indignant when they heard what James and John had asked for. Jesus called them together and said, "Among the heathen, kings are tyrants and each minor official lords it over those beneath him. But among you it is quite different. Anyone wanting to be a leader among you must be your servant. And if you want to be right at the top, you must serve. Your attitude must be like my own, for I, the Messiah, did not come to be served but to serve, and to give my life as a ransom for many."

Lazarus, who lived in Bethany with his sisters Mary and Martha, was sick. The two sisters sent a message to Jesus: "Sir, your good friend is very sick."

When Jesus heard about it he said, "The purpose of his illness is not death, but for the glory of God."

Although Jesus was very fond of Martha, Mary, and Lazarus, he stayed where he was for the next two days. Finally he said to his disciples, "Let's go to Judea."

His disciples objected. "The Jewish leaders were trying to kill you; are you going there again?"

Jesus replied, "There are twelve hours of daylight every day, and during every hour a man can walk safely and not stumble; only at night is there danger of a wrong step because of the dark." Then he said, "Our friend Lazarus has gone to sleep, but now I will go and waken him! Come, let's go."

Thomas said to his fellow disciples, "Let's go—and die with him."

When they arrived in Bethany, they were told Lazarus

had already been in his tomb four days. Bethany was only a couple of miles from Jerusalem, and many Jewish leaders had come to pay their last respects.

When Martha got word that Jesus was coming, she went to meet him. "Sir, if you had been here, my brother wouldn't have died."

Jesus told her, "Your brother will come back to life again."

"Yes," Martha said, "when everyone else does on Resurrection Day."

Jesus told her, "I am the one who raises the dead and gives them life again. Anyone who believes in me, even though he dies like anyone else, shall live again. He is given eternal life for believing in me and shall never perish. Do you believe this, Martha?"

"Yes, Master," she told him. "I believe you are the Messiah, the Son of God, the one we have so long awaited."

She left and returned to Mary and, calling her aside from the mourners, told her, "He is here and wants to see you." Mary went at once.

Jesus had stayed outside the village where Martha met him. When the Jewish leaders trying to console Mary saw her leave, they assumed she was going to Lazarus' tomb so they followed her.

When Mary arrived where Jesus was, she fell down at his feet, saying, "Sir, if you had been here my brother would still be alive."

Jesus saw her weeping and was deeply troubled. "Where is he buried?" he asked. Tears came to Jesus' eyes.

"They were close friends," the Jewish leaders said. "See how much he loved him."

They came to the tomb, a cave with a heavy stone rolled across its door.

"Roll the stone aside," Jesus told them.

But Martha said, "By now the smell will be terrible, for he has been dead four days."

"Didn't I tell you that you will see a wonderful miracle from God if you believe?" Jesus asked her.

So they rolled the stone aside. Then Jesus looked up to heaven and said, "Father, thank you for hearing me. You always hear me, of course, but I said it because of

all these people here, so they will believe you sent me."
Then he shouted, "Lazarus, come out!"

And Lazarus came—bound up in the gravecloth, his face muffled in a head swath. Jesus told them, "Unwrap him and let him go!"

And many who saw it happen believed on him. But some went to the Pharisees and reported it to them. The chief priests and Pharisees convened a council to discuss the situation. "What are we going to do? If we let him alone, the whole nation will follow him—and then the Roman army will come and kill us and take over the Jewish government."

Caiaphas, who was High Priest that year, said, "You idiots—let this one man die for the people—why should the whole nation perish?"

From that time on, the leaders began plotting Jesus' death.[16]

THE PEOPLE'S KING

The Passover was near, and many country people arrived in Jerusalem several days early so they could go through the cleansing ceremony before Passover began. They wanted to see Jesus, and as they gossiped in the Temple they asked each other, "What do you think? Will he come for the Passover?" Meanwhile the chief priests had announced that anyone seeing Jesus must report him immediately so that they could arrest him.

Jesus and the disciples approached Jerusalem, near Bethphage on the Mount of Olives. Jesus sent two of them into the village ahead. "Just as you enter," he said, "you will see a donkey tied there with its colt beside it. Untie them and bring them here. If anyone asks you what you are doing, just say, 'The Master needs them,' and there will be no trouble."

The disciples did as Jesus said and brought the animals to him and threw their garments over the colt for him to ride on.

News that Jesus was on the way to Jerusalem swept through the city, and a huge crowd took palm branches and went down the road to meet him, shouting, "The Savior! God bless the King of Israel! Hail to God's Ambassador!"

Jesus rode along on a young donkey, fulfilling the prophecy that said: "Don't be afraid of your King, people of Israel, for he will come to you meekly, sitting on a donkey's colt!"

(His disciples didn't realize at the time that this was a fulfillment of prophecy; but after Jesus returned to heaven they noticed how many prophecies of Scripture had come true before their eyes.)

Those who had seen Jesus call Lazarus back to life were telling all about it. That was the main reason so many went out to meet him.

The Pharisees said to each other, "We've lost. Look—the whole world has gone after him!"

Crowds surged ahead and pressed along behind, shouting, "God bless King David's Son!" . . . "God's Man is here!" . . . "Bless him, Lord!" . . . "Praise God in highest heaven!"

Some of the Pharisees said, "Sir, rebuke your followers for saying things like that!"

He replied, "If they keep quiet, the stones along the road will burst into cheers!"

As they came closer to Jerusalem and he saw the city, he began to cry. "Eternal peace was within your reach and you turned it down; now it is too late. Enemies will encircle you and close in on you and crush you to the ground; your enemies will not leave one stone upon another—for you have rejected the opportunity God offered you."

The entire city was stirred as he entered. "Who is this?" they asked.

The crowds replied, "It's Jesus, the prophet from Nazareth in Galilee."

He went into the Temple, looked around carefully at everything, and then left—for it was late in the afternoon—and went out to Bethany with the twelve disciples.

The next morning he went to the Temple and began to drive out the merchants and their customers, knocked over the tables of the moneychangers and the stalls of those selling doves, and stopped everyone from bringing in loads of merchandise.

The blind and crippled came to him and he healed them. When the chief priests saw these miracles and heard even little children in the Temple shouting, "God bless the Son of David," they were indignant and asked him, "Do you hear what these children are saying?"

"Yes," Jesus replied. "Didn't you ever read the Scriptures? They say, 'Even little babies shall praise him!' "[17]

THE VIPERS' FOE

The priests and other leaders began planning how best to get rid of him: the problem was their fear of riots because the people were so enthusiastic about Jesus.

When he had returned to the Temple and was teaching, the leaders came to him and demanded by whose authority he had thrown out the merchants.

"I'll tell you if you answer one question first: Was John the Baptist sent from God, or not?"

They talked it over among themselves. "If we say, 'From God,' then he will ask why we didn't believe what John said. And if we deny that God sent him we'll be mobbed, for the crowd all think he was a prophet." So they finally replied, "We don't know!"

Jesus said, "Then I won't answer your question either. Now listen to this story: A certain landowner planted a vineyard with a hedge around it and built a platform for the watchman, then leased the vineyard to some farmers on a share-crop basis and went away to live in another country.

"At the time of the grape harvest he sent his agents to the farmers to collect his share. But the farmers attacked his men—beat one, killed one, and stoned another. Then he sent a larger group of his men to collect for him, but the results were the same. Finally the owner sent his son, thinking they would surely respect him.

"But when these farmers saw the son coming they said among themselves, 'Here comes the heir; let's kill him and get it for ourselves!' So they dragged him out of the vineyard and killed him. When the owner returns, what do you think he will do to those farmers?"

The leaders replied, "He will put the wicked men to a horrible death, and lease the vineyard to others who will pay him promptly."

Jesus asked, "Didn't you ever read the Scriptures: 'The stone rejected by the builders has been made the honored cornerstone; how remarkable! what an amazing thing the Lord has done'? The Kingdom of God shall be taken away from you, and given to a nation that will give God his share of the crop."

The Pharisees met to think of some way to trap Jesus into saying something for which they could arrest him. They decided to ask him this question: "We know you are very honest and teach the truth regardless of the consequences; now tell us, is it right to pay taxes to the Roman government, or not?"

Jesus saw what they were after. "You hypocrites!" he exclaimed. "Here, show me a coin." And they handed him a penny.

"Whose picture is stamped on it?" he asked. "And whose name is this beneath the picture?"

"Caesar's," they replied.

"Well, then, give it to Caesar if it is his, and give God everything that belongs to God."

His reply surprised them, and they went away.

That same day some Sadducees, who say there is no resurrection after death, came to him and asked, "Sir, Moses said that if a man died without children his brother should marry the widow, and their children would get all the dead man's property. Well, we had among us a family of seven brothers. The first of these men married and then died without children, so his widow became the second brother's wife. This brother also died without children, and the wife was passed to the next brother, and so on until she had been the wife of each of them. And then she also died. So whose wife will she be in the resurrection?"

Jesus said, "Your error is caused by your ignorance of the Scriptures and of God's power! For in the resurrection there is no marriage; everyone is as the angels in heaven.

But as to whether there is a resurrection of the dead—don't you read the Scriptures? Don't you realize that God was speaking directly to you when he said, 'I am the God of Abraham, Isaac, and Jacob'? So God is not the God of the dead, but of the living."

A lawyer spoke up: "Sir, which is the most important command in the laws of Moses?"

Jesus replied, "The one that says, 'Hear, O Israel! The Lord our God is the one and only God. And you must love him with all your heart and soul and mind and strength.' The second is: 'You must love others as yourself.' "

The teacher of religion replied, "Sir, you have spoken a true word; I know it is far more important to love him with all my heart and understanding and strength, and to love others as myself, than to offer all kinds of sacrifices on the altar of the Temple."

Jesus said, "You are not far from the Kingdom of God."

Then, surrounded by Pharisees, he asked, "What about the Messiah? Whose son is he?"

"The son of David," they replied.

"Then why does David, speaking under the inspiration of the Holy Spirit, call him 'Lord'?" Jesus asked. "For David said, 'God said to my Lord: Sit at my right hand until I put your enemies beneath your feet.' Since David called him 'Lord,' how can he be merely his son?"

They had no answer. After that, no one dared ask him any more questions.

"Woe to you, Pharisees, and you other religious leaders. For you won't let others enter the Kingdom of Heaven, and won't go in yourselves. You pretend to be holy with your long, public prayers in the streets, while you are evicting widows from their homes. You go to all lengths to make one convert and then turn him into twice the son of hell you are yourselves. Blind guides!

"You tithe down to the last mint leaf in your garden, but ignore the important things—justice and mercy and faith. You should tithe, but you shouldn't leave the more important things undone. You strain out a gnat and swallow a camel.

"Woe to you, Pharisees, and you religious leaders—hypocrites! You are so careful to polish the outside of the cup, but the inside is foul with extortion and greed. You are like beautiful mausoleums—full of dead men's bones. You try to look like saintly men, but underneath those pious robes are hearts besmirched with every sort of hypocrisy and sin. Snakes! Sons of vipers! How shall you escape the judgment of hell?

"I send you prophets and wise men and inspired writers, and you kill some by crucifixion and rip open the backs of others with whips in your synagogues and hound them from city to city so that you become guilty of all the blood of murdered godly men from righteous Abel to Zechariah, slain by you in the Temple. Yes, all the accumulated judgment of the centuries shall break upon the heads of this very generation!"[18]

KINGDOM DAY

As Jesus was leaving the Temple grounds, his disciples wanted to take him on a tour of the various Temple buildings. But he told them, "All these buildings will be knocked down, with not one stone left on top of another!"

"When will this happen?" the disciples asked later as he sat on the slope of the Mount of Olives. "What events will signal your return, and the end of the world?"

Jesus told them, "Don't let anyone fool you. For many will come claiming to be the Messiah, and will lead many astray. When you hear of wars beginning, this does not signal my return; these must come, but the end is not yet. The nations and kingdoms of the earth will rise against each other and there will be famines and earthquakes in many places. But this will be only the beginning of the horrors to come.

"You will be tortured and killed and hated all over the world because you are mine, and many of you shall fall back into sin and betray each other. False prophets will appear and lead many astray. Sin will be rampant and will cool the love of many. But those enduring to the end shall be saved. And the Good News about the Kingdom will be preached throughout the whole world so that all nations will hear it, and then, finally, the end will come.

"So, when you see the horrible thing told about by Daniel the prophet standing in a holy place, those in Judea must flee into the hills. For there will be persecution such as the world has never before seen and will never see again. In fact, unless those days are shortened all mankind will perish. But they will be shortened for the sake of God's chosen people.

"Then if anyone tells you, 'The Messiah has arrived at such and such a place,' don't believe it. For as the lightning flashes across the sky from east to west, so shall my coming be when I return.

"Immediately after the persecution of those days, the sun will be darkened, the moon will not give light, the stars will seem to fall from the heavens, and the powers overshadowing the earth will be convulsed.

"And then the signal of my coming will appear in the heavens, and there will be deep mourning around the earth. The nations of the world will see me arrive in the clouds of heaven, with power and great glory. And I shall send forth my angels with the sound of a mighty trumpet blast, and they shall gather my chosen ones from the farthest ends of the earth and heaven.

"When you see all these things beginning to happen, you can know that my return is near. Then at last this age will come to its close. Heaven and earth will disappear, but my words remain forever.

"But no one knows the date and hour when the end will be—not even the angels. Nor even God's Son. Only the Father knows.

"The world will be at ease—banquets and parties and weddings—just as it was in Noah's time before the sudden coming of the flood; people wouldn't believe what was going to happen until the flood actually arrived and took them all away. So shall my coming be. Be prepared, for you don't know what day your Lord is coming.

"When I, the Messiah, come in my glory and all the angels with me, then I shall sit upon my throne. And nations shall be gathered before me. And I will separate the people as a shepherd separates sheep from goats—the sheep at my right hand, the goats at my left.

"Then I shall say to those at my right, 'Come, blessed of my Father, into the Kingdom prepared for you. For I was hungry and you fed me; I was thirsty and you gave me water; I was a stranger and you invited me into your homes; naked and you clothed me; sick and in prison, and you visited me.'

"These righteous ones will reply, 'Sir, when did we ever see you hungry and feed you? Or thirsty and give you drink? Or a stranger, and help you? Or naked, and clothe you? When did we ever see you sick or in prison, and visit you?'

"And I will tell them, 'When you did it to these my brothers, you were doing it to me!' Then I will turn to those on my left and say, 'Away with you, cursed ones, into the eternal fire prepared for the devil and his demons. When you refused to help my brothers, you were refusing help to me.' And they shall go away into eternal punishment; but the righteous into everlasting life."[19]

PASSOVER LAMB When Jesus finished this talk with his disciples, he told them, "The Passover celebration begins in two days, and I shall be betrayed."

At that very moment the chief priests and other officials were meeting at the residence of the High Priest to discuss ways of capturing Jesus quietly. "Not during the Passover celebration," they agreed, "for there would be a riot."

Jesus proceeded to Bethany to the home of Simon the leper. While he was eating, a woman came in with a bottle of expensive perfume and poured it over his head.

The disciples were indignant. "What a waste of money," they said. "She could have sold it for a fortune and given it to the poor."

Jesus knew what they were thinking, and said, "Why are you criticizing her? She has poured this perfume on me to prepare my body for burial. And she will always be remembered for this deed."

Then Satan entered into Judas Iscariot, one of the twelve disciples, and he went to the chief priests and captains of the Temple guards to discuss the best way to betray Jesus to them. They were delighted to know that he was ready to help them.

"How much will you pay me to get Jesus into your hands?" And they gave him thirty silver coins. From that time on, Judas watched for an opportunity to betray Jesus.

Some Greeks who had come to Jerusalem to attend the Passover paid a visit to Philip and said, "We want to meet Jesus." Philip went to ask Jesus.

Jesus replied that the time had come for him to return to his glory in heaven. "I must fall and die like a kernel of wheat into the furrows of the earth. Unless I die I will be alone—but my death will produce many new kernels— a plentiful harvest of new lives. If you love your life down here—you will lose it. If you despise your life down here— you will exchange it for eternal glory.

"If these Greeks want to be my disciples, tell them to come and follow me, for my servants must be where I am. And if they follow me, the Father will honor them. Now my soul is deeply troubled. Shall I pray, 'Father, save me from what lies ahead'? But that is the very reason why I came! Father, bring glory and honor to your name."

Then a voice spoke from heaven: "I have already done this, and I will do it again."

Some thought it was thunder, while others declared an angel had spoken to him.

Jesus told them, "The voice was for your benefit, not mine. The time of judgment has come—and the time when Satan, the prince of this world, shall be cast out. And when I am lifted up on the cross, I will draw everyone to me."

"Die?" asked the crowd. "We understood that the Messiah would live forever. What Messiah are you talking about?"

Jesus replied, "My light will shine out for you just a little while longer. Make use of the Light while there is still time; then you will become light bearers."

Even many of the Jewish leaders believed him to be the Messiah but wouldn't admit it because of fear that the

Pharisees would excommunicate them from the synagogue.

Jesus shouted to the crowds, "If you trust me, you are really trusting God. When you see me, you are seeing the one who sent me. I have come as a Light to shine in this dark world, so that all who put their trust in me will no longer wander in the darkness. But all who reject me and my message will be judged at the Day of Judgment by the truths I have spoken—for I have told you what the Father said to tell you."

The day of the Passover celebration arrived, when the Passover lamb was killed and eaten with the unleavened bread. Jesus sent Peter and John to find a place to prepare their Passover meal.

"As soon as you enter Jerusalem, you will see a man carrying a pitcher of water. Follow him into the house he enters and say to the man who lives there, 'Our Teacher says for you to show us the guest room where he can eat the Passover meal with his disciples.' He will take you upstairs to a large room all ready for us. Go and prepare the meal there."

They went to the city and found everything as Jesus had said, and prepared the Passover supper.

In the evening, Jesus arrived with the other disciples and all sat down at the table. He said, "I have looked forward to this hour with deep longing, anxious to eat this Passover meal with you before my suffering begins."

Then he took a glass of wine, and when he had given thanks for it, he said, "Take this and share it among yourselves. For I will not drink wine again until the Kingdom of God has come."

Then he took a loaf of bread; and when he had thanked God for it, he broke it apart and gave it to them, saying, "This is my body, given for you. Eat it in remembrance of me."

After supper he gave them another glass of wine, saying, "This wine is the token of God's new agreement to save you—an agreement sealed with the blood I shall pour out to purchase back your souls."

He got up from the table, took off his robe, wrapped a

towel around his loins, poured water into a basin, and began to wash the disciples' feet.

When he came to Simon Peter, Peter said, "Master, you shouldn't be washing our feet like this!"

Jesus replied, "You don't understand now why I am doing it; some day you will."

"No," Peter protested, "you shall never wash my feet!"

"But if I don't, you can't be my partner," Jesus replied.

"Then wash my hands and head as well—not just my feet!"

Jesus replied, "One who has bathed all over needs only to have his feet washed to be entirely clean. Now you are clean—but that isn't true of everyone here." For Jesus knew who would betray him.

After washing their feet, he put on his robe and sat down and asked, "Do you understand what I was doing? I have given you an example to follow: do as I have done to you. A servant is not greater than his master. Nor is the messenger more important than the one who sends him. You know these things—now do them! That is the path of blessing.

"I am not saying these things to all of you; I know well each one of you I chose. The Scripture declares, 'One who eats supper with me will betray me,' and this will soon come true."

Jesus, in great anguish of spirit, exclaimed, "Yes, it is true—one of you will betray me."

The disciples looked at each other, wondering whom he could mean. John, next to Jesus at the table, being his close friend, asked him, "Lord, who is it?"

"It is the one I honor by giving the bread dipped in the sauce." When he had dipped it, he gave it to Judas Iscariot. As soon as Judas had eaten it, Jesus told him, "Hurry—do it now."

None of the others knew what Jesus meant. Some thought that since Judas was their treasurer, Jesus was telling him to go and pay for the food or to give some money to the poor. Judas left at once, going out into the night.[20]

FATHER, SON, SPIRIT

As soon as Judas left, Jesus said, "My time has come; God shall receive great praise because of all that happens to me. And God shall give me his own glory very soon. Dear children, how brief are these moments before I must leave you! I am giving you a new commandment now—love each other just as I love you. Your strong love for each other will prove to the world that you are my disciples.

"Because you have stood true to me in these terrible days and because my Father has granted me a Kingdom, I here and now grant you the right to eat and drink at my table in that Kingdom; and you will sit on thrones judging the twelve tribes of Israel.

"Simon, Simon, Satan has asked to have you, to sift you like wheat, but I have pleaded in prayer that your faith should not completely fail. So when you have repented and turned to me again, strengthen and build up the faith of your brothers.

"Tonight you will all desert me. For it is written in the Scriptures that God will smite the Shepherd and the sheep of the flock will be scattered. But after I have been brought back to life again I will go to Galilee and meet you there."

Peter declared, "If everyone else deserts you, I won't."

Jesus told him, "The truth is that this very night, before the cock crows at dawn, you will deny me three times!"

"I would die first!" Peter insisted. And all the other disciples said the same thing.

"Let not your heart be troubled. You are trusting God; now trust in me. There are many homes up there where my Father lives, and I am going to prepare them for your coming. When everything is ready, then I will come and get you so you can always be with me where I am. And you know where I am going and how to get there."

"No, we don't," Thomas said. "We haven't any idea where you are going, so how can we know the way?"

Jesus told him, "I am the Way—yes, and the Truth and the Life. No one can get to the Father except by means of me."

Philip said, "Show us the Father, and we will be satisfied."

Jesus replied, "Don't you yet know who I am, Philip, after all this time I have been with you? Anyone who has seen me has seen the Father!

"I will ask the Father and he will give you another Comforter, and he will never leave you. He is the Holy Spirit, who leads into all truth. The world cannot receive him, for it isn't looking for him and doesn't recognize him. But you do, for he lives with you now and some day shall be in you. The one who obeys me is the one who loves me, and I will love him and reveal myself to him."

Judas (not Iscariot, but his other disciple with that name) said, "Why are you going to reveal yourself to us and not to the world at large?"

Jesus replied, "Because I will only reveal myself to those who love me and obey me. The Father will love them too, and we will come to them and live with them. I am telling you these things while I am still with you, but when the Father sends the Comforter, the Holy Spirit, he will teach you much, as well as remind you of everything I have told you.

"I don't have much more time to talk to you, for the evil prince of this world approaches. He has no power over me, but I will freely do what the Father requires of me so that the world will know that I love the Father. Come, let's be going.

"I am the true Vine, and my Father is the Gardener. He lops off every branch that doesn't produce. And he prunes those branches that bear fruit for even larger crops. Take care to live in me, and let me live in you. For a branch can't produce fruit when severed from the vine, nor can you be fruitful apart from me. My true disciples produce bountiful harvests. This brings great glory to my Father.

"I have loved you even as the Father has loved me. Live in my love. When you obey me, you are living in my love. Love each other as I love you—the greatest love is shown when a person lays down his life for his friends; and you are my friends if you obey me.

"Do you remember I told you a slave isn't greater than his master! So since they persecuted me, they will persecute you. The people of the world will persecute you because you belong to me, for they don't know God. Anyone hating me is also hating my Father. This has fulfilled what the prophets said concerning the Messiah, 'They hated me without reason.'

"I have told you these things so that you won't be staggered by all that lies ahead. The time is coming when those who kill you will think they are doing God a service.

"Now I am going away to the One who sent me. It is best for you that I go away, for if I don't, the Comforter won't come. And when he has come, he will convince the world of its sin, of the availability of God's goodness, and of deliverance from judgment. There is so much more I want to tell you, but you can't understand it now. The Holy Spirit, who is Truth, shall guide you into all truth. He shall bring me great honor by showing you my glory. All the Father's glory is mine; this is what I mean when I say that he will show you my glory. The Father loves you dearly because you love me. I came from the Father into the world, and will leave the world and return to the Father."

His disciples said, "Now we understand that you know everything; from this we believe that you came from God."

"Do you finally believe this?" Jesus asked. "But the time is coming—in fact, it is here—when you will be scattered, leaving me alone. Yet the Father is with me. I have told you all this so that you will have peace of heart and mind. On earth you will have many trials and sorrows; but cheer up, for I have overcome the world."

When Jesus finished saying these things, he looked up to heaven and said, "Father, the time has come. Reveal the glory of your Son so he can give the glory back to you. For you have given him authority over every man and woman in all the earth. He gives eternal life to each one you have given him. And this is the way to have eternal life—by knowing you, the only true God, and Jesus Christ, the one you sent to earth! I brought glory to you here by doing everything you told me to; now, Father, reveal the glory we shared before the world began.

"I have told these men all about you. I have passed on to them the commands you gave me; and they accepted them and know that I came down to earth from you. Now I am leaving the world and coming to you. Holy Father, keep them in your own care so they will be united just as we are. Make them pure through teaching them your words of truth. As you sent me into the world, I am sending them into the world, and I consecrate myself to meet their need for growth in truth and holiness.

"I am not praying for these alone but also for the future believers who will come to me because of the testimony of these. My prayer for them is that they will be of one heart and mind, just as you and I are, Father—so that the world will know you sent me and will understand that you love them as you love me. O righteous Father, these disciples know you sent me. I have revealed you to them, and will keep on revealing you so that the mighty love you have for me may be in them."[21]

ABANDONED

After these things, Jesus crossed the Kidron ravine with his disciples and entered a grove of olive trees. Judas, the betrayer, knew this place, for Jesus had gone there many times with his disciples.

They came to a grove called the Garden of Gethsemane, and he instructed his disciples, "Sit here while I go and pray."

He took Peter, James, and John with him, and began to be filled with horror and deepest distress. He said, "My soul is crushed by sorrow to the point of death; stay here and watch with me."

He went on a little farther and fell to the ground and prayed that if it were possible the awful hour awaiting him might never come. "Father, Father," he said, "everything is possible for you. Take away this cup from me; yet I want your will, not mine."

Then he returned to the three disciples and found them asleep.

"Simon!" he said. "Asleep? Couldn't you watch with me

even one hour? Watch with me and pray lest the Tempter overpower you. For though the spirit is willing enough, the body is weak."

And he went away again and prayed, repeating his pleadings. Again he returned to them and found them sleeping, for they were very tired.

He went back to prayer the third time, saying the same things again. Then an angel from heaven appeared and strengthened him, for he was in such agony of spirit that he broke into a sweat of blood, with great drops falling to the ground. At last he stood up and returned to the disciples—only to find them asleep, exhausted from grief.

He said, "Sleep on now and rest . . . but no! The time has come! I am betrayed into the hands of evil men! Look! Here comes the man who is betraying me!"

At that moment Judas arrived with a crowd armed with swords and clubs, sent by the Jewish leaders. Judas had told them to arrest the man he greeted, so Judas came straight to Jesus and kissed him on the cheek.

Jesus said, "Judas, how can you betray the Messiah with a kiss?"

When the disciples saw what was about to happen, they exclaimed, "Master, shall we fight?" And one of them slashed at the High Priest's servant and cut off his right ear.

But Jesus said, "Don't resist any more." And he touched the place where the man's ear had been and restored it.

"Don't you realize that I could ask my Father for thousands of angels to protect us, and he would send them instantly? But if I did, how would the Scriptures be fulfilled that describe what is happening now?"

Then Jesus spoke to the crowd. "Am I some dangerous criminal that you arm yourselves with swords and clubs before you could arrest me? But this is happening to fulfill the Scriptures."

At that point, all the disciples deserted him and fled.[22]

CONDEMNED The police with soldiers and their lieutenant arrested Jesus and tied him. First they took him to Annas, the father-in-law of Caiaphas, the High Priest that year. Peter followed along behind, as did another of the disciples who was acquainted with the High Priest. That disciple was permitted into the courtyard along with Jesus, while Peter stood outside the gate. Then the other disciple spoke to the girl watching at the gate, and she let Peter in. The girl asked Peter, "Aren't you one of Jesus' disciples?"

"No," he said, "I am not!"

The police and household servants were standing around a fire they had made, for it was cold. And Peter stood there with them, warming himself.

Inside, the High Priest began asking Jesus about his followers and what he had been teaching them.

Jesus replied, "I have preached in the synagogue and Temple, and teach nothing in private that I have not said in public. Ask those who heard me; you have some of them here."

One of the soldiers struck Jesus. "Is that the way to answer the High Priest?" he demanded.

Jesus replied, "Should you hit a man for telling the truth?"

Then Annas sent Jesus, bound, to Caiaphas.

The chief priests and entire Jewish Court assembled there and looked for witnesses to build a case against him that would result in a death sentence. But though they found many who agreed to be witnesses, these always contradicted each other.

Finally two men were found who declared, "This man said, 'I am able to destroy the Temple of God and rebuild it in three days.'"

The High Priest said to Jesus, "Did you say that, or didn't you?"

Jesus remained silent.

The High Priest said, "I demand in the name of the living God that you tell us whether you claim to be the Messiah, the Son of God."

"Yes," Jesus said, "I am. And in the future you will

see me, the Messiah, sitting at the right hand of God and returning on the clouds of heaven."

The High Priest tore at his clothing, shouting, "Blasphemy! What need have we for other witnesses? You have all heard him say it! What is your verdict?"

"Death!—Death!—Death!" they shouted.

The guards in charge of Jesus began mocking him. They blindfolded him and hit him with their fists and asked, "Who hit you that time, prophet?"

Meanwhile, as Peter was sitting in the courtyard a girl came over and said to him, "You were with Jesus, for both of you are from Galilee."

Peter denied it loudly. "I don't know what you are talking about."

Later another girl said, "This man was with Jesus—from Nazareth."

Again Peter denied it. "I don't even know the man."

After a while men who had been standing there came over and said, "We know you are one of his disciples, for we can tell by your Galilean accent."

Peter began to curse. "I don't even know the man," he said. And immediately the cock crowed. Then Peter remembered what Jesus had said; "Before the cock crows, you will deny me three times." And he went away, crying bitterly.

It was morning; the chief priest and leaders met to discuss how to induce the Roman government to sentence Jesus to death. They sent him in chains to Pilate, the Roman governor and began accusing him: "This fellow has been leading our people to ruin by telling them not to pay their taxes to the Roman government and by claiming he is our Messiah—a King."

Pilate asked him, "Are you their Messiah—their King?"

Jesus answered, "I am not an earthly king. If I were, my followers would have fought when I was arrested by the Jewish leaders. But my Kingdom is not of the world."

Pilate replied, "But you are a king, then?"

"Yes," Jesus said, "I was born for that purpose. And I came to bring truth to the world. All who love the truth are my followers."

"What is the truth?" Pilate exclaimed. Then he went out to the people and told them, "He is not guilty of any crime."

They became desperate. "But he is causing riots against the government everywhere he goes; all over Judea, from Galilee to Jerusalem!"

"Is he then a Galilean?" Pilate asked.

When they told him yes, Pilate said to take him to King Herod, for Galilee was under Herod's jurisdiction. Herod happened to be in Jerusalem at the time. Herod was delighted at the opportunity to see Jesus, for he had heard a lot about him and had been hoping to see him perform a miracle.

He asked Jesus question after question, but there was no reply. Meanwhile, the priests and other religious leaders stood shouting their accusations. Herod and his soldiers began mocking Jesus; putting a kingly robe on him, they sent him back to Pilate.

Pilate called together the chief priests and other Jewish leaders, along with the people, and announced his verdict:

"You brought this man to me, accusing him of leading a revolt against the Roman government. I have examined him on this point and find him innocent. Herod came to the same conclusion and sent him back to us—nothing this man has done calls for the death penalty. I will therefore have him scourged with leaded thongs, and release him."

It was Pilate's custom to release one Jewish prisoner each year at Passover time—any prisoner the people requested. One of the prisoners was Barabbas, convicted along with others for murder during an insurrection.

Now a mob began to crowd in toward Pilate, asking him to release a prisoner as usual.

"How about giving you the 'King of Jews'?" Pilate asked.

At this point the priests whipped up the mob to demand the release of Barabbas instead of Jesus.

"But if I release Barabbas," Pilate asked them, "what shall I do with this man you call your king?"

"Crucify him!"

As he was presiding over the court, Pilate's wife sent

him this message: "Leave that good man alone; for I had a terrible nightmare concerning him last night."

A mighty roar rose from the crowd as with one voice they shouted, "Kill him, and release Barabbas to us!"

Then Pilate, afraid of a riot and anxious to please the people, released Barabbas to them. And he ordered Jesus flogged with a leaded whip, and handed him over to be crucified.

Roman soldiers took him into the barracks of the palace, called out the entire palace guard, dressed him in a purple robe, and made a crown of long, sharp thorns and put it on his head. Then they saluted, yelling, "Yea! King of the Jews!" And they beat him on the head with a cane, spat on him, and went down on their knees to "worship" him.

Pilate went outside again and said to the Jews, "I am going to bring him out to you now, but understand clearly that I find him not guilty."

Jesus came out wearing the crown of thorns, and Pilate said, "Behold the man!"

At sight of him, the priests and officials began yelling, "Crucify! Crucify!"

"You crucify him," Pilate said. "I find him not guilty."

They replied, "By our laws he ought to die because he called himself the Son of God."

When Pilate heard this, he was frightened. He took Jesus back into the palace and asked, "Where are you from?" But Jesus gave no answer.

Pilate demanded, "Don't you realize that I have the power to release you or to crucify you?"

"You would have no power over me unless it were given to you from above," Jesus said. "So those who brought me to you have the greater sin."

Then Pilate tried to release him, but the Jewish leaders told him, "If you release this man, you are no friend of Caesar's. Anyone who declares himself a king is a rebel against Caesar."

At these words Pilate brought Jesus out to them again and sat down at the judgment bench on the stone-paved platform. It was about noon of the day before Passover. Pilate said, "Here is your king!"

"Away with him," they yelled. "Away with him."

"What? Crucify your king?" Pilate asked.

"We have no king but Caesar," the chief priests shouted. Then Pilate gave Jesus to them to be crucified.

Judas, when he saw that Jesus had been condemned to die, changed his mind and brought back the money to the chief priests. "I have sinned," he declared, "for I have betrayed an innocent man."

"That's your problem," they retorted.

He threw the money onto the floor of the Temple, and went out and hanged himself.[23]

THE KING IS DEAD!

As the crowd led Jesus away to his death, Simon of Cyrene, who was just coming into Jerusalem from the country, was forced to follow carrying Jesus' cross. Great crowds trailed along behind, and many grief-stricken women.

Jesus turned and said, "Daughters of Jerusalem, don't weep for me, but for yourselves and your children. For the days are coming when the women who have no children will be counted fortunate indeed. Mankind will beg the mountains to fall on them and the hills to bury them. For if such things as this are done to me, what will they do to you?"

Two others, criminals, were led out to be executed with him. There all three were crucified—Jesus on the center cross, and the two criminals on either side.

"Father, forgive these people," Jesus said, "for they don't know what they are doing."

Pilate posted a sign over him reading, "Jesus of Nazareth, the King of the Jews." The sign was written in Hebrew, Latin, and Greek so that many people read it.

The chief priests said to Pilate, "Change it from 'The King of the Jews' to 'He said, I am King of the Jews.'"

Pilate replied, "What I have written, I have written. It stays exactly as it is."

When the soldiers had crucified Jesus, they put his garments into four piles, one for each of them. But they said, "Let's not tear up his robe," for it was seamless. "Let's throw dice to see who gets it." This fulfilled the Scripture that says, "They divided my clothes among them, and cast lots for my robe."

People passing by hurled abuse, saying, "So! You can destroy the Temple and build it again in three days, can you? Well, then, come down from the cross if you are the Son of God!"

And the priests mocked him: "He saved others, but he can't save himself!"

One of the criminals scoffed, "So you're the Messiah, are you? Prove it by saving yourself—and us, too, while you're at it!"

But the other criminal protested, "Don't you even fear God when you are dying? We deserve to die for our evil deeds, but this man hasn't done one thing wrong." Then he said, "Jesus, remember me when you come into your Kingdom."

Jesus replied, "Today you will be with me in Paradise; this is a solemn promise."

Standing near the cross were Jesus' mother, his aunt, Mary the wife of Cleopas, and Mary Magdalene. When Jesus saw his mother beside his close friend, he said, "He is your son"; and, "She is your mother!"

Darkness fell across the whole land for three hours. About three o'clock, Jesus shouted, "Eli, Eli, lama sabachthani," which means, "My God, my God, why have you forsaken me?"

Some of the bystanders thought he was calling for Elijah. One of them ran and filled a sponge with sour wine and put it on a stick and held it up to him to drink. But the rest said, "Leave him alone. Let's see whether Elijah will come and save him."

Jesus knew that everything was now finished. Then Jesus shouted, "Father, I commit my spirit to you," and with those words he died.

The curtain secluding the Holiest Place in the Temple was split apart from top to bottom! The earth shook and rocks broke! Tombs opened and many godly men and women who had died came back to life!

When the captain of the Roman military unit saw what had happened, he was stricken with awe: "Surely this man was innocent!"

The crowd that came to see the crucifixion went home in deep sorrow. Jesus' friends, including the women who had followed him from Galilee, stood in the distance watching—Mary Magdalene, Mary the mother of James the Younger and of Joses, Salome, and others.

Jewish leaders didn't want the victims hanging there the next day, which was a very special Sabbath, the Passover, so they asked Pilate to order the legs of the men broken to hasten death. Soldiers came and broke the legs of the two men crucified with Jesus, but when they came to him they saw that he was dead already so they didn't break his. However, one of the soldiers pierced his side with a spear, and blood and water flowed out. The soldiers did this in fulfillment of the Scripture that says, "Not one of his bones shall be broken," and, "They shall look on him whom they pierced."

Late that afternoon Joseph from Arimathea, an honored member of the Jewish Supreme Court who was eagerly expecting the arrival of God's Kingdom, went to Pilate and asked for Jesus' body.

Pilate couldn't believe that Jesus was already dead, so he called for the Roman officer in charge and asked him. The officer confirmed the fact, and Pilate told Joseph he could have the body.

Nicodemus, the man who had come to Jesus at night, came too, bringing a hundred pounds of embalming ointment made from myrrh and aloes. Together they wrapped Jesus' body in a long linen cloth saturated with the spices. The crucifixion was near a grove of trees where there was a new tomb, and they laid him there and rolled a great stone across the entrance. Mary Magdalene and Mary the mother of Joses were watching as Jesus was laid away.

The next day—at the close of the first day of the Passover ceremonies—the chief priests and Pharisees went to Pilate and told him, "Sir, that liar once said, 'After three days I will come back to life again.' So we request an order from you sealing the tomb until the third day, to prevent his disciples from coming and stealing his body and then telling everyone he came back to life!"

"Use your own Temple police," Pilate told them. "They can guard it safely enough."

So they sealed the stone and posted guards to protect it from intrusion.[24]

LONG LIVE THE KING!

There was a great earthquake—an angel of the Lord came down from heaven and rolled aside the stone; his face shone like lightning and his clothing was a brilliant white. The guards shook with fear when they saw him, and fell into a dead faint.

The women from Galilee, very early on Sunday morning, took ointments to the tomb and found that the huge stone covering the entrance had been rolled aside. They went in—but the Lord Jesus' body was gone. They stood there puzzled, trying to think what could have happened to it.

Suddenly two men appeared before them, clothed in shining robes so bright their eyes were dazzled. The women were terrified.

Then the men asked, "Why are you looking in a tomb for someone who is alive? He isn't here! He has come back to life again! Don't you remember what he told you back in Galilee—that the Messiah must be betrayed into the power of evil men and be crucified and that he would rise from the dead the third day?"

Then they remembered, and rushed back to tell the eleven disciples.

As the women were on the way into the city, some of the Temple police who had been guarding the tomb went to the chief priests and told them what had happened. A meeting of the Jewish leaders was called and it was decided to bribe the police to say they had all been asleep when Jesus' disciples came during the night and stole his body. The story spread widely and is still believed.

When Jesus came back to life, the first person who saw him was Mary Magdalene—the woman from whom he had cast out seven demons. Mary found the stone rolled aside, ran and found Peter and the beloved disciple, and said, "They have taken the Lord's body out of the tomb and I don't know where they have put him!"

Peter and the other disciple ran to the tomb to see. John outran Peter and looked in and saw the linen cloth lying there, but didn't go in. Peter arrived and went inside. He also noticed the cloth lying there, while the swath that had covered Jesus' head was rolled up in a bundle and lying at the side. Then John went in too, and saw and believed that he had risen. The disciples went on home.

Mary returned to the tomb and was standing outside crying. As she wept, she glanced over her shoulder and saw someone standing behind her.

"Why are you crying?" he asked. "Whom are you looking for?"

She thought he was the gardener. "Sir," she said, "if you have taken him away, tell me where you have put him and I will go and get him."

"Mary!" Jesus said.

She turned toward him—"Master!" she exclaimed.

"Go find my brothers and tell them that I ascend to my Father and your Father, my God and your God!"

The women from the tomb, frightened but filled with joy, rushed to find the disciples to give them the angels' message. Suddenly Jesus was there in front of them!

"Good morning!" he said. And they fell to the ground before him, holding his feet and worshiping him.

Jesus said, "Go tell my brothers to leave for Galilee, to meet me there."

That same day, two of Jesus' followers were walking to the village of Emmaus, seven miles out of Jerusalem. They were talking of Jesus' death when suddenly Jesus joined them and began walking beside them, but they didn't recognize him.

"You seem in a deep discussion," he said. "What are you so concerned about?"

They stopped short, sadness across their faces. One of them, Cleopas, replied, "You must be the only person in Jerusalem who hasn't heard about the terrible things that happened there last week."

"What things?" Jesus asked.

"The things that happened to Jesus, the Man from Nazareth," they said. "He was a Prophet who did incredible miracles and was a mighty teacher, highly regarded by both God and man. But the chief priests and our religious leaders arrested him and handed him over to the Roman government to be condemned to death, and they crucified him. We had thought he was the glorious Messiah and that he had come to rescue Israel.

"And now besides all this some women from our group were at his tomb early this morning and came back with an amazing report that his body was missing, and that they had seen some angels there who told them Jesus is alive! Some of our men ran to see, and sure enough, Jesus' body was gone."

Then Jesus said, "You are foolish people—you find it so hard to believe all that the prophets wrote in the Scriptures! Wasn't it clearly predicted by the prophets that the Messiah would have to suffer all these things before entering his time of glory?"

Then Jesus quoted passage after passage beginning with the book of Genesis and on through the Scriptures, explaining what the passages meant about himself.

By this time they were nearing Emmaus; Jesus would have gone on, but they begged him to stay the night with them. As they sat down to eat, he asked God's blessing on the food and took a small loaf of bread and broke it, when suddenly—it was as though their eyes were opened—they recognized him! At that moment he disappeared!

They began telling each other how their hearts had felt strangely warm as he talked with them and explained the Scriptures. Within the hour they were on their way back to Jerusalem where the eleven disciples and other followers of Jesus greeted them with the words, "The Lord has really risen! He appeared to Peter!"

Then the two from Emmaus told how Jesus had appeared to them along the road and how they had recognized him as he was breaking the bread. And just as they were telling about it, Jesus himself was suddenly standing there among them! The group was terribly frightened, thinking they were seeing a ghost!

"Why are you frightened?" he asked. "Look at my hands! Look at my feet! Touch me and make sure that I am not a ghost! For ghosts don't have bodies, as you see that I do!" He held out his hands for them to see the marks of the nails, and showed the wounds in his feet.

Still they stood there undecided, filled with joy and doubt. Then he asked them, "Do you have anything here to eat?"

They gave him a piece of broiled fish, and he ate it as they watched! Then he said, "When I was with you before, don't you remember my telling you that everything written about me by Moses and the prophets and in the Psalms must all come true?" Then he opened their minds to understand these many Scriptures! And he said, "Yes, it was written long ago that the Messiah must suffer and die and rise again from the dead on the third day; and that this message of salvation should be taken from Jerusalem to all the nations: There is forgiveness of sins for all who turn to me. You have seen these prophecies come true."

He spoke again: "As the Father has sent me, even so I am sending you." Then he breathed on them and told them, "Receive the Holy Spirit."

One of the disciples, Thomas "The Twin," was not there at the time. When they kept telling him, "We have seen the Lord," he replied, "I won't believe it unless I see the nail wounds in his hands—and put my fingers into them—and place my hand into his side."

Eight days later the disciples were together again, and this time Thomas was with them. The doors were locked; but suddenly, as before, Jesus was standing among them and greeting them!

He said to Thomas, "Put your finger into my hands. Put your hand into my side. Don't be faithless any longer. Believe!"

"My Lord and my God!" Thomas said.

Jesus told him, "You believe because you have seen me; blessed are those who haven't seen me and believe anyway."

And then he told them, "You are to go into all the world and preach the Good News to everyone, everywhere. Those who believe and are baptized will be saved. But those who refuse to believe will be condemned."

Later Jesus appeared again to the disciples beside the Lake of Galilee. A group of us were there—Simon Peter, Thomas "The Twin," Nathanael from Cana, the sons of Zebedee, and two other disciples. Peter said, "I'm going fishing." "We'll come too," all said, but caught nothing all night. At dawn we saw a man standing on the beach.

He called, "Any fish, boys?"

"No," we replied.

Then he said, "Throw out your net on the right-hand side of the boat, and you'll get plenty of them!" So we did, and couldn't draw in the net because of the weight.

The beloved disciple said to Peter, "It is the Lord!" At that, Peter put on his tunic and jumped into the water and swam ashore. The rest of us stayed in the boat and pulled the loaded net to the beach, about 300 feet away. When we got there, we saw that a fire was kindled and fish were frying over it, and there was bread.

"Bring some of the fish you've just caught," Jesus said. Peter went and dragged the net ashore. By his count there were 153 large fish.

"Now come and have some breakfast!" Jesus said; then Jesus went around serving us the bread and fish. This was the third time Jesus had appeared to us since his return from the dead.

After breakfast Jesus said to Peter, "Simon, son of John, do you love me more than others?"

"Yes," Peter replied, "you know I am your friend."

"Then feed my lambs," Jesus told him.

Jesus repeated the question: "Simon, do you really love me?"

"Yes, Lord," Peter said.

"Then take care of my sheep," Jesus said.

Once more he asked him, "Simon, son of John, are you even my friend?"

Peter was grieved at the way Jesus asked the third time. "Lord, you know my heart; you know I am," he said.

Jesus said, "Then feed my little sheep. When you were young, you were able to do as you liked and go wherever you wanted to; but when you are old, you will stretch out your hands and others will direct you and take you where you don't want to go." Jesus said this to let him know what kind of death he would die to glorify God. Then Jesus told him, "Follow me."

Peter turned and saw the disciple Jesus loved, the one who had leaned around at supper that time to ask Jesus, "Master, which of us will betray you?" Peter asked Jesus, "What about him, Lord? What sort of death will he die?"

Jesus replied, "If I want him to live until I return, what is that to you? You follow me."

So the rumor spread among the brotherhood that that disciple wouldn't die! But that isn't what Jesus said. He only said, "If I want him to live until I come, what is that to you?"

I am that disciple! I saw these events and have recorded them here. And we all know that my account of these things is accurate. And I suppose that if all the other events in Jesus' life were written, the whole world could hardly contain the books![25]

KINGDOM PROMISE

During the forty days after his crucifixion, he proved in many ways that it was really he they were seeing. On these occasions he talked about the Kingdom of God. In one of these meetings he told them not to leave Jerusalem until the Holy Spirit came upon them in fulfillment of the Father's promise. "John baptized you with water," he reminded them, "but you shall be baptized with the Holy Spirit in just a few days."

Another time when he appeared to them they asked, "Lord, are you going to free Israel from Rome now and restore us as an independent nation?"

"The Father sets those dates," he replied, "and they are not for you to know. But when the Holy Spirit has come upon you, you will receive power to testify about me to the people in Jerusalem, throughout Judea, in Samaria, and to the ends of the earth about my death and resurrection.

"I have been given all authority in heaven and earth. Therefore go and make disciples in all nations, baptizing them in the name of the Father and of the Son and of the Holy Spirit. Teach the new disciples to obey all the commands I have given you. And be sure of this—that I am with you always, even to the end of the world."

It was not long afterwards that he led them to Bethany, and lifting his hands to heaven he blessed them, and then began rising into the sky and went on to heaven.

As they were straining their eyes for another glimpse, suddenly two white-robed men were standing among them and said, "Men of Galilee, why are you standing here staring at the sky? Jesus has gone away to heaven, and some day, just as he went, he will return!"

They worshiped him, and returned to Jerusalem filled with mighty joy, and were continually in the Temple praising God.[26]

PART
11
THE NEW
PEOPLE

SPIRIT POWER

Seven weeks had gone by since Jesus' death and resurrection—and the Day of Pentecost had arrived. As the believers met that day, suddenly there was a sound like a mighty windstorm in the skies above and it filled the house where they were meeting. Then tongues of fire appeared and settled on their heads, and everyone present was filled with the Holy Spirit and began speaking in languages they didn't know.

Godly Jews were in Jerusalem that day for the religious celebrations, having arrived from many nations. When they heard the roaring in the sky above the house, crowds came running to see what it was all about and were stunned to hear their own languages being spoken by the disciples.

"How can this be?" they exclaimed. "These men are from Galilee and we hear them speaking the languages of the lands where we were born! We Parthians, Medes, Elamites, men from Mesopotamia, Judea, Capadocia, Pontus, Ausia, Phrygia, Pamphylia, Egypt, the Cyrene language areas of Libya, visitors from Rome—both Jews and Jewish converts—Cretans and Arabians all hear these men telling about the mighty miracles of God!"

Others in the crowd were mocking: "They're drunk, that's all!"

Peter stepped forward and shouted to the crowd, "Listen,

you visitors and residents of Jerusalem alike! People don't get drunk by 9:00 A.M.! What you see this morning was predicted centuries ago by the prophet Joel—'In the last days,' God said, 'I will pour out my Holy Spirit upon all mankind and your sons and daughters shall prophesy, your young men shall see visions, and your old men dream dreams. Yes, the Holy Spirit shall come upon all my servants, men and women alike, and they shall prophesy. And I will cause demonstrations in the heavens and on the earth—blood and fire and clouds of smoke; the sun shall turn black and the moon blood-red before that awesome Day of the Lord arrives. But anyone who asks for mercy from the Lord shall have it and be saved.'

"O men of Israel, listen! God publicly endorsed Jesus of Nazareth by doing tremendous miracles through him. But God, following his prearranged plan, let you use the Roman government to nail him to the cross and murder him. Then God released him from the horrors of death and brought him back to life again, for death could not keep this man within its grip.

"King David quoted Jesus as saying: 'I know the Lord is always with me. I know all will be well with me in death— you will not leave my soul in hell or let the body of your Holy Son decay. You will give me back my life and give me wonderful joy in your presence.'

"Dear brothers, David wasn't referring to himself when he spoke these words I have quoted, for he died and was buried and his tomb is still here. But he knew God had promised that one of David's descendants would be the Messiah and sit on David's throne. David was predicting the Messiah's resurrection, and we all are witnesses that Jesus rose from the dead. Now he sits on the throne of highest honor in heaven, next to God. And the Father gave him the authority to send the Holy Spirit—with the results you are seeing and hearing today!"

These words moved them deeply and they said, "What should we do?"

Peter replied, "Each one of you must turn from sin, return to God, and be baptized in the name of Jesus Christ for the forgiveness of your sins; then you also shall receive this gift, the Holy Spirit. For Christ promised him to each one of you who has been called by the Lord our God, and to your children and even to those in distant lands!"

Those who believed Peter were baptized—about three thousand in all! They joined with the other believers in regular attendance at the apostles' teaching sessions and at the Communion services and prayer meetings. A deep sense of awe was on them all, and the apostles did many miracles.

The believers met constantly and shared everything with each other, selling their possessions and dividing with those in need. They worshiped together at the Temple each day, met in small groups in homes for Communion, and shared their meals with great joy and thankfulness, praising God. The whole city was favorable to them, and each day God added to them all who were being saved.[1]

MIRACLE MESSAGE

Peter and John went to the Temple one afternoon to take part in the three o'clock prayer meeting. As they approached the Temple they saw a man lame from birth carried along the street and laid beside the Temple gate. As Peter and John were passing by he asked them for some money.

They looked at him intently, and then Peter said, "Look here!"

The lame man looked eagerly, expecting a gift.

Peter said, "We don't have any money for you, but I'll give you something else. I command you in the name of Jesus Christ the Nazarene—walk!"

Then Peter took the lame man by the hand and pulled him to his feet. As he did, the man's feet and anklebones were healed so that he came up with a leap, stood there a moment, and began walking! Then, walking, leaping, and praising God, he went into the Temple with them.

When the people inside heard him praising God and realized he was the lame beggar they had seen so often at The Beautiful Gate, they rushed out to Solomon's Hall where he was holding tightly to Peter and John! Everyone stood there awed by the wonderful thing that had happened.

Peter addressed the crowd: "Men of Israel, what is so surprising about this? The God of Abraham, Isaac, Jacob, and all of our ancestors has brought glory to his servant Jesus by doing this. I refer to the Jesus whom you rejected before Pilate. You killed the Author of Life, but God brought him back to life again. And John and I are witnesses of this fact, for after you killed him we saw him alive!

"Dear brothers, I realize that what you did to Jesus was done in ignorance; and the same can be said of your leaders. But God was fulfilling the prophecies that the Messiah must suffer these things. Now change your attitude to God and turn to him so he can cleanse away your sins and send refreshment from the presence of the Lord. Jesus your Messiah must remain in heaven until the final recovery of all things from sin, as prophesied from ancient times. Moses said long ago, 'The Lord God will raise up a Prophet among you who will resemble me! Listen carefully to everything he tells you.' Samuel and every prophet since have spoken about what is going on today. You are the children of those prophets; and you are included in God's promise to your ancestors to bless the entire world through the Jewish race—that is the promise God gave to Abraham. God brought his Servant to life again to bless you by turning you back from your sins."

While they were talking, the chief priests, the captain of the Temple police, and some of the Sadducees came over, very disturbed that Peter and John were claiming Jesus had risen from the dead. They arrested and jailed them. But many of the people who heard their message believed it, so that the number of believers now reached about five thousand men!

The next day the Council of Jewish leaders was in session—Annas the High Priest, Caiaphas, John, Alexander, and others of the High Priest's relatives. The two disciples were brought before them. "By what power or by whose authority have you done this?" the Council demanded.

Peter, filled with the Holy Spirit, said, "Honorable leaders of our nation, if you mean the good deed done to the cripple and how he was healed, let me clearly state that it was done in the name and power of Jesus from Nazareth, the

Messiah—the man you crucified but God raised to life again! By his authority this man stands healed."

When the Council saw the boldness of Peter and John and that they were obviously uneducated, they were amazed and realized what being with Jesus had done for them. They sent them out of the Council chamber and conferred among themselves. "What shall we do with these men? We can't deny that they have done a miracle; everybody in Jerusalem knows about it. But perhaps we can stop them from spreading their propaganda." They called them back and told them never again to speak about Jesus.

Peter and John replied, "You decide whether God wants us to obey you instead of him! We cannot stop telling about the wonderful things we saw Jesus do and heard him say."

The Council threatened them further and finally let them go, because they didn't know how to punish them without starting a riot.

As soon as they were freed, Peter and John found the other disciples and told them what the Council had said. Then all the believers united in this prayer:

"O Lord, Creator of heaven and earth and sea and everything in them—you spoke long ago by the Holy Spirit through our ancestor King David, saying, 'Why do the heathen rage against the Lord, and the foolish nations plan their little plots against Almighty God? The kings of the earth unite against him and against the anointed Son of God!' That is what is happening today! For Herod the king, Pontius Pilate the governor, and all the Romans—as well as the people of Israel—are united against Jesus, your anointed Son. O Lord, hear their threats, grant your servants great boldness in preaching, send your healing power, and may miracles and wonders be done by the name of Jesus."

The building where they were meeting shook, and they were all filled with the Holy Spirit and boldly preached God's message.

All the believers were of one heart and mind, and everyone was sharing. For instance, there was Joseph, nicknamed "Barny the Preacher," from the island of Cyprus. He sold a field he owned and brought the money to the apostles for distribution to those in need.

Meanwhile, the apostles were meeting regularly at the Temple and did remarkable miracles among the people. More and more believers were added to the Lord, crowds of both men and women. Sick people were brought into the streets on mats so at least Peter's shadow would fall across them as he went by! Crowds came in from the Jerusalem suburbs, bringing their sick folk and those possessed by demons; and every one of them was healed.

The High Priest and his relatives and friends among the Sadducees reacted with violent jealousy and arrested the apostles and put them in jail.

But an angel of the Lord came at night, opened the gates of the jail, and brought them out. Then he told them, "Go over to the Temple and preach about this Life!" They arrived at the Temple about daybreak and immediately began preaching!

Later that morning the High Priest and his courtiers arrived at the Temple, and convening the Jewish Council and entire Senate they sent for the apostles to be brought for trial. But when the police arrived at the jail the men weren't there, so they returned to the Council and reported, "The jail doors were locked and the guards were standing outside, but when we opened the gates no one was there!"

When the police captain and chief priests heard this, they were frantic, wondering what would happen next. Then someone arrived with the news that the men they had jailed were in the Temple preaching to the people!

The police captain went with his officers and arrested them and brought them before the Council. "Didn't we tell you never again to preach about Jesus?" the High Priest demanded. "And instead you have filled Jerusalem with your teaching and intend to bring the blame for this man's death on us!"

Peter and the apostles replied, "We must obey God rather than men. God brought Jesus back to life, then with mighty power exalted him so the people of Israel would have an opportunity for repentance and for their sins to be forgiven.

We are witnesses of these things and so is the Holy Spirit, who is given by God to all who obey him."

At this the Council was furious, and decided to kill them. But one member, a Pharisee named Gamaliel, requested that the apostles be sent outside the Council chamber while he addressed his colleagues. "Men of Israel, take care what you are planning to do; my advice is, leave these men alone. If what they teach and do is merely on their own it will soon be overthrown; but if it is of God you will not be able to stop them—lest you find yourselves fighting against God."

The Council accepted his advice and called in the apostles, had them beaten, told them never again to speak in the name of Jesus, and let them go. They left the Council rejoicing that God had counted them worthy to suffer for his name. And every day, in the Temple and in their home Bible classes, they continued to teach and preach that Jesus is the Messiah.[2]

MARTYRED; MASTERED

With believers multiplying rapidly, there were rumblings of discontent. Those who spoke only Greek complained that their widows were not being given as much food as the widows who spoke Hebrew. So the Twelve called a meeting of all the believers. "We should spend our time preaching, not administering a feeding program," they said. "Look among yourselves and select seven men, wise and full of the Holy Spirit, and we will put them in charge of this business."

This sounded reasonable to the assembly, and they elected Stephen, Philip, Prochorus, Nicanor, Timon, Parmenas, Nicolaus of Antioch.

God's message was preached in ever-widening circles and the number of disciples increased vastly in Jerusalem. Many Jewish priests were converted too.

Stephen, full of faith and the Holy Spirit, did spectacular miracles among the people. But one day some men from the Jewish cult "The Freedmen" started an argument with him, and they were soon joined by Jews from Cyrene, Alexandria, the Turkish provinces of Cilicia, and Ausia. They brought in some men to lie about him, claiming they had heard Stephen curse Moses and even God.

This accusation roused the crowds to fury, and the Jewish leaders arrested him and brought him before the Council. Witnesses testified that Stephen was constantly speaking against the Temple and the laws of Moses.

The High Priest asked, "Are these accusations true?"

This was Stephen's reply: "God appeared to our ancestor Abraham in Iraq before he moved to Syria, and told him to leave his native land and start out for a country that God would direct him to. So he left the land of the Chaldeans and lived in Haran in Syria until his father died. Then God brought him here to the land of Israel, but gave him no property.

"However, God promised that eventually the whole country would belong to him and his descendants. God also told him that these descendants would live in a foreign country and there become slaves for 400 years.

"Isaac, Abraham's son, became the father of Jacob, and Jacob was the father of the twelve patriarchs of the Jewish nation. These men were jealous of Joseph and sold him to be a slave in Egypt. But God gave him favor before Pharaoh. Joseph sent for his father Jacob and all his brothers' families to come to Egypt, seventy-five persons in all.

"The Jewish people greatly multiplied in Egypt; but then a king was crowned who had no respect for Joseph's memory, forcing parents to abandon their children.

"About that time Moses was born. His parents hid him for three months, and when they could no longer keep him hidden and had to abandon him, Pharaoh's daughter found him, adopted him as her own son, and taught him all the wisdom of the Egyptians.

"One day as he was nearing his fortieth birthday, he saw an Egyptian mistreating a man of Israel, so Moses killed the Egyptian. At this, Moses fled the country and lived in the land of Midian.

"Forty years later, in the desert near Mount Sinai, an

Angel appeared to him in a flame of fire in a bush. The voice of the Lord called to him, 'I am the God of your ancestors—of Abraham, Isaac, and Jacob. I have seen the anguish of my people and have come to deliver them. Come, I will send you to Egypt.' And by many remarkable miracles he led them out of Egypt and through the wilderness for forty years.

"Moses told the people, 'God will raise up a Prophet much like me from among your brothers.' For in the wilderness Moses was the mediator between the people of Israel and the Angel who gave them the Law of God on Mount Sinai. But our fathers rejected Moses and wanted to return to Egypt.

"Then God turned away from them and let them serve the sun, moon, and stars as their gods! In the book of Amos' prophecies the Lord asks, 'Was it to me you were sacrificing during those forty years in the desert, Israel? No, your real interest was in your heathen gods—Sakkuth, the star god Kaiway, and in all the images you made. So I will send you into captivity far away beyond Babylon.'

"You stiff-necked heathen! Must you forever resist the Holy Spirit? Your fathers did, and so do you! Name one prophet your ancestors didn't persecute! They even killed the ones who predicted the coming of the Righteous One— the Messiah whom you betrayed and murdered."

The leaders were stung to fury by Stephen's accusation.

Stephen, full of the Holy Spirit, gazed steadily upward and told them, "Look, I see the heavens opened and Jesus the Messiah standing beside God."

Then they mobbed him, drowning out his voice with their shouts, and dragged him out of the city to stone him. The executioners took off their coats and laid them at the feet of a young man named Paul.

As stones came hurtling at him, Stephen prayed, "Lord Jesus, receive my spirit." He fell to his knees, shouting, "Lord, don't charge them with this sin!" and with that he died.

Paul was in complete agreement with the killing of Stephen, and a wave of persecution began that day, sweeping over the church in Jerusalem. Everyone except the apostles fled into Judea and Samaria. Paul was like a wild man, going everywhere to devastate the believers, entering private homes and dragging out men and women alike and jailing them.

The believers who fled Jerusalem went everywhere preaching the Good News about Jesus! Philip went to Samaria. Crowds listened intently because of the miracles he did. Many evil spirits were cast out, and many who were paralyzed or lame were healed.

When the apostles in Jerusalem heard that the people of Samaria had accepted God's message, they sent Peter and John. As soon as they arrived, they began praying for the new Christians to receive the Holy Spirit, for they had only been baptized in the name of Jesus. Peter and John laid their hands upon these believers, and they received the Holy Spirit. After testifying in Samaria, Peter and John returned to Jerusalem, stopping at several Samaritan villages along the way.

As for Philip, an angel said to him, "Go over to the road that runs from Jerusalem through the Gaza Desert, arriving around noon." He did, and who should be coming down the road but the Treasurer of Ethiopia, a eunuch of great authority under Candace the queen. He had gone to Jerusalem to worship at the Temple, and was now returning in his chariot, reading aloud from the book of the prophet Isaiah.

The Holy Spirit said to Philip, "Go over and walk along beside the chariot."

Philip ran over and heard what he was reading and asked, "Do you understand it?"

"Of course not!" the man replied. "How can I when there is no one to instruct me?" And he begged Philip to come up into the chariot and sit with him.

The passage of Scripture he had been reading was this:

"He was led as a sheep to the slaughter, and as a lamb is silent before the shearers, so he opened not his mouth; in his humiliation, justice was denied him; and who can express the wickedness of the people of his generation? For his life is taken from the earth."

The eunuch asked Philip, "Was Isaiah talking about himself or someone else?"

Philip began with this same Scripture and then used many others to tell him about Jesus. As they rode along, they came to a small body of water, and the eunuch said, "Look! Why can't I be baptized?"

"You can," Philip answered, "if you believe with all your heart."

The eunuch replied, "I believe that Jesus Christ is the Son of God." He stopped the chariot, and they went down into the water and Philip baptized him. And the eunuch went on his way rejoicing.

Paul, eager to destroy every Christian, went to the High Priest in Jerusalem. He requested a letter addressed to synagogues in Damascus, requiring their cooperation in the persecution of any believers he found there, so he could bring them in chains to Jerusalem.

As he was nearing Damascus on this mission, suddenly a brilliant light from heaven spotted down upon him! He fell to the ground and heard a voice saying to him, "Paul! Paul! Why are you persecuting me?"

"Who is speaking?" Paul asked.

"I am Jesus, the one you are persecuting! Now get up and go into the city and await my further instructions."

The men with Paul stood speechless with surprise, for they heard someone's voice but saw no one! As Paul picked himself up, he found that he was blind. He had to be led into Damascus and was there three days, blind, going without food and water.

There was in Damascus a believer named Ananias. The Lord spoke to him in a vision: "Go over to Straight Street and find the house of a man named Judas and ask there for Paul of Tarsus. He is praying to me right now, for I have shown him a vision of a man named Ananias coming in and laying his hands on him so that he can see again!"

"But Lord," exclaimed Ananias, "I have heard about the terrible things this man has done to the believers in Jerusalem! And we hear that he has warrants authorizing him to arrest every believer in Damascus!"

But the Lord said, "Go and do what I say, for Paul is

my chosen instrument to take my message to the nations as well as to Israel. I will show him how much he must suffer for me."

So Ananias went and found Paul and laid his hands on him and said, "Brother Paul, the Lord Jesus, who appeared to you on the road, has sent me so that you may be filled with the Holy Spirit and get your sight back."

Instantly Paul could see, and was immediately baptized. He stayed with the believers in Damascus for a few days and went to the synagogue to tell everyone there the Good News about Jesus—that he is indeed the Son of God!

All who heard him were amazed. "Isn't this the same man who persecuted Jesus' followers so bitterly in Jerusalem?" they asked.

Paul became more and more fervent in his preaching, and the Damascus Jews couldn't withstand his proofs that Jesus was indeed the Christ.

After a while the Jewish leaders determined to kill him. But Paul was told they were watching the gates of the city day and night, prepared to murder him. So during the night some of his converts let him down in a basket through an opening in the city wall!

Upon arrival in Jerusalem, he tried to meet with the believers but they were all afraid of him. Then Barnabas brought him to the apostles and told how Paul had seen the Lord on the way to Damascus, and about his powerful preaching. Then they accepted him, and he was constantly with the believers. But some Jews with whom he had argued plotted to murder him. When the believers heard about his danger, they took him to Caesarea and then sent him to his home in Tarsus.[3]

CHURCH UNIVERSAL

The church had peace throughout Judea, Galilee, and Samaria, and grew. Believers learned how to walk in the fear of the Lord and in the comfort of the Holy Spirit.

Peter traveled from place to place to visit them, and in his travels came to the town of Lydda. There he met a man named Aeneas, paralyzed and bedridden for eight years.

Peter said to him, "Aeneas! Jesus Christ has healed you! Get up and make your bed." And he was healed instantly. The whole population of Lydda and Sharon turned to the Lord when they saw Aeneas walking around.

In the city of Joppa was a woman named Dorcas, a believer who was always doing kind things for others, especially for the poor. She became ill and died. Her friends prepared her for burial, but when they learned that Peter was nearby at Lydda, they sent two men to beg him to return with them to Joppa.

As soon as he arrived, they took him upstairs where Dorcas lay. Peter asked all to leave the room; then he knelt and prayed. Turning to the body, he said, "Get up, Dorcas," and she opened her eyes! When she saw Peter, she sat up! He called in the believers, presenting her to them. The news raced through the town and many believed in the Lord. Peter stayed a long time in Joppa, living with Simon the tanner.

In Caesarea lived a Roman army officer, Cornelius. He was a godly man, as was his entire household. While wide awake one afternoon, he had a vision—and saw an angel of God coming toward him.

"Cornelius!" the angel said.

Cornelius stared in terror. "What do you want?" he asked.

The angel replied, "Your prayers and charities have not gone unnoticed by God! Now send some men to Joppa to find a man named Simon Peter, who is staying with Simon the tanner down by the shore, and ask him to come and visit you."

As soon as the angel was gone, Cornelius called two of his servants and one of his personal bodyguard, told them what had happened, and sent them off to Joppa.

The next day Peter went up on the flat roof of his house to pray. He fell into a trance, saw the sky open and a great canvas sheet settle to the ground. In the sheet were all sorts of animals. Then a voice said, "Go kill and eat any of them you wish."

"Never, Lord," Peter declared. "I have never eaten such creatures, for they are forbidden by our laws."

The voice spoke again, "Don't contradict God! If he says

something is kosher, it is." The vision was repeated three times.

Just then the men sent by Cornelius found the house and were standing at the gate, inquiring whether this was where Simon Peter lived!

As Peter was puzzling over the vision, the Holy Spirit said, "Go with them; I have sent them." Peter invited them in and lodged them overnight. The next day he went with them, accompanied by other believers from Joppa.

They arrived in Caesarea the following day, and Cornelius was waiting for him. They talked for a while and then went in where others were assembled.

Peter told them, "It is against Jewish laws for me to come into a Gentile home like this, but God has shown me that I should never think of anyone as inferior. Now tell me what you want."

Cornelius replied, "Four days ago I was praying when suddenly a man was standing before me clothed in a radiant robe! He told me, 'Cornelius, your prayers are heard and your charities have been noticed by God! Now send some men to Joppa and summon Simon Peter.' So I sent for you at once, and now we are anxious to hear what he has told you to tell us!"

Peter replied, "I see very clearly that the Jews are not God's only favorites! In every nation he has those who worship him and do good deeds and are acceptable to him. I'm sure you have heard about the Good News for the people of Israel—that there is peace with God through Jesus, the Messiah, who is Lord of all creation. This message has spread through Judea, beginning with John the Baptist in Galilee. Jesus of Nazareth was anointed by God with the Holy Spirit and with power, and he went around doing good and healing all who were possessed by demons.

"We apostles are witnesses of all he did throughout Israel and in Jerusalem, where he was murdered on a cross. But God brought him back to life three days later and showed him to us who ate and drank with him after he rose from the dead. And he sent us to preach the Good News everywhere and to testify that Jesus is ordained of God to be the Judge of all—living and dead. The prophets have written about him, saying that everyone who believes in him will have their sins forgiven through his name."

As Peter was saying these things, the Holy Spirit fell upon those listening! The Jews who came with Peter were amazed that the gift of the Holy Spirit would be given to Gentiles too!

Peter asked, "Can anyone object to my baptizing them, now that they have received the Holy Spirit just as we did?" So he did, baptizing them in the name of Jesus.

Meanwhile, believers who fled from Jerusalem during the persecution after Stephen's death traveled as far as Phoenicia, Cyprus, and Antioch scattering the Good News. When the church at Jerusalem heard what happened, they sent Barnabas to Antioch to help the new converts. He saw the wonderful things God was doing and encouraged the believers to stay close to the Lord, whatever the cost. Barnabas was full of the Holy Spirit and strong in faith; as a result large numbers of people were added to the Lord.

Then Barnabas went on to Tarsus to hunt for Paul. When he found him, he brought him back to Antioch. Both stayed there for a year, teaching the many converts. There at Antioch the believers were first called "Christians."[4]

PETER AND PAUL

About that time King Herod moved against some of the believers and killed the apostle James, John's brother. When Herod saw how this pleased the Jewish leaders, he arrested Peter during the Passover celebration. Herod's intention was to deliver Peter for execution after the Passover. But earnest prayer was going up from the church for his safety.

The night before he was to be executed, he was asleep, double-chained between two soldiers with others standing guard before the prison gate. Suddenly there was a light in the cell and an angel stood beside Peter! The angel slapped him on the side to awaken him and said, "Quick! Get up!" And the chains fell off his wrists! Then the angel told him, "Get dressed, put on your coat, and follow me!"

Peter left the cell, following the angel. But all the time

he thought it was a dream. They passed the first and second cell blocks and came to the iron gate to the street, and this opened to them of its own accord! They passed through and walked along together for a block, and then the angel left him.

Peter finally realized what had happened! "It's really true! The Lord has sent his angel and saved me from Herod."

He went to the home of Mary, mother of John Mark, where many were gathered for prayer. He knocked at the gate and a girl named Rhoda came to open it. When she recognized Peter's voice, she was so overjoyed that she ran back inside to tell everyone that Peter was standing outside. They didn't believe her. When she insisted, they decided, "It must be his angel."

Peter continued knocking. When they finally went out and opened the door, their surprise knew no bounds. He told them how the Lord had brought him out of jail. "Tell the others what happened," he said—and left for safer quarters.

At dawn, the jail was in great commotion. What had happened to Peter? When Herod found he wasn't there, he had the sixteen guards arrested and sentenced to death.

Barnabas and Paul visited Jerusalem, and as soon as they had finished their business returned to Antioch, taking John Mark with them.

Among the prophets and teachers of the church at Antioch were Barnabas, Symeon, Lucius, Manaen (the foster-brother of King Herod), and Paul. One day as these men were worshiping and fasting, the Holy Spirit said, "Dedicate Barnabas and Paul for a special job I have for them." After more fasting and prayer, the men laid their hands on them— and sent them on their way.

Directed by the Holy Spirit, they sailed for Cyprus. John Mark went as their assistant. They preached from town to town across the entire island.

Paul and those with him left by ship for Turkey, landing at Perga. There John deserted them and returned to Jerusalem, but Barnabas and Paul went on to Antioch in the province of Pisidia.

On the Sabbath they went into the synagogue for services. After readings from the Books of Moses and the prophets, those in charge of the service sent them this message: "Brothers, if you have any word of instruction for us, come and give it!"

So Paul began. "Men of Israel, and all others here who reverence God, let me begin with a bit of history. The God of Israel chose our ancestors and gloriously led them out of their slavery. He nursed them through forty years of wandering in the wilderness, then he destroyed seven nations in Canaan and gave Israel their land. Judges ruled for about 450 years, followed by Samuel the prophet.

"Then the people begged for a king, and God gave them Saul. But God replaced him with David, a man about whom God said, 'David is a man after my heart, for he will obey me.' And it is one of King David's descendants who is God's promised Savior!

"You sons of Abraham, and also you Gentiles here who reverence God—this salvation is for all of us! The Jews fulfilled prophecy by killing Jesus; for they didn't realize he is the one the prophets had written about. He was taken from the cross and placed in a tomb. But God brought him back to life and he was seen many times during the next few days by the men who had accompanied him to Jerusalem from Galilee.

"And now Barnabas and I bring you this Good News— that God's promise to our ancestors has come true in our own time, in that God brought Jesus back to life. This is what the second Psalm is talking about when it says concerning Jesus, 'Today I have honored you as my Son.'

"Brothers! In this man Jesus there is forgiveness for your sins! Everyone who trusts in him is freed from all guilt and declared righteous—something the Jewish law could never do."

As the people left the synagogue, they asked Paul to return and speak again the next week. The following week almost the entire city turned out to hear them preach.

But Jewish leaders saw the crowds, were jealous, and argued against whatever Paul said. Then Paul and Barnabas boldly declared, "It was necessary that this Good News from God should be given first to you Jews. But since you have rejected it, we will offer it to Gentiles. For this the Lord commanded: 'I have made you a light to the Gentiles, to lead them from the farthest corners of the earth to my salvation.' "

When the Gentiles heard this, they rejoiced in Paul's message and many believed.

Then the Jewish leaders incited a mob against Paul and Barnabas and ran them out of town. They went on to the city of Iconium.

At Iconium, Paul and Barnabas went to the synagogue and preached with such power that many—both Jews and Gentiles—believed. Paul and Barnabas stayed there a long time, preaching boldly, and the Lord proved their message by giving them power to do great miracles.

The people were divided in their opinion about them. When Paul and Barnabas learned of a plot to incite a mob of Gentiles, Jews, and leaders to attack and stone them, they fled for their lives, going to Lycaonia, Lystra, Derbe, and the surrounding area.

At Lystra they came upon a man with crippled feet who had never walked. Paul noticed him and realized he had faith to be healed. So Paul called, "Stand up!" and the man leaped to his feet and started walking!

When the crowd saw what Paul had done, they shouted, "These men are gods in human bodies!" They decided Barnabas was the Greek god Jupiter, and Paul, because he was the chief speaker, was Mercury! The local priest of Jupiter brought cartloads of flowers and prepared to sacrifice oxen to them at the city gates.

When Barnabas and Paul saw what was happening, they ran among the people, shouting, "We are merely human beings like yourselves! We bring you the Good News that you are invited to turn from the worship of foolish things and to pray instead to the living God who made heaven and earth and sea and everything in them. In bygone days he permitted the nations to go their own ways, but he never left himself without a witness; there were always the kind things he did such as sending rain and crops and gladness."

But Paul and Barnabas could scarcely restrain the people from sacrificing to them!

Only a few days later, some Jews arrived from Antioch and Iconium and turned the crowds into a murderous mob that stoned Paul and dragged him out of the city, apparently dead. But as the believers stood around him, he got up and went back into the city!

The next day he left with Barnabas for Derbe. After preaching there and making many disciples, they returned again to Lystra, Iconium, and Antioch, where they helped the believers, reminding them they must enter into the Kingdom of God through many tribulations. Paul and Barnabas also appointed elders in every church and prayed for them, turning them over to the care of the Lord.

They traveled back through Pisidia to Pamphylia, preached again in Perga, and went on to Attalia. Finally they returned by ship to Antioch, where their journey had begun. Upon arrival they called together the believers and reported on their trip, telling how God had opened the door of faith to Gentiles too. They stayed with the believers at Antioch for a long while.

While Paul and Barnabas were at Antioch, some men from Judea arrived and began to teach the believers that unless they adhered to the ancient Jewish custom of circumcision they could not be saved. Paul and Barnabas argued and discussed this with them at length, and finally the believers sent them to Jerusalem, accompanied by some local men, to talk to the apostles and elders there.

In Jerusalem they met with the church leaders, and Paul and Barnabas reported what God had been doing through their ministry. Some of the men who had been Pharisees before their conversion declared that all Gentile converts must be circumcised and required to follow the Jewish customs. The apostles and elders set a further meeting to decide this question.

At the meeting, after long discussion, Peter addressed them as follows: "Brothers, you all know that God chose me from among you to preach the Good News to the Gentiles, so that they also could believe. God, who knows men's hearts, confirmed the fact that he accepts Gentiles by giving them the Holy Spirit, just as he gave him to us. He cleansed their lives through faith, just as he did ours. And now are you going to correct God by burdening the Gentiles with a yoke that neither we nor our fathers were able to bear? Don't you believe that all are saved the same way, by the free gift of the Lord Jesus?"

There was no further discussion, and everyone listened as Barnabas and Paul told about the miracles God had done through them among the Gentiles.

When they finished, James took the floor. "Brothers, listen to me. Peter has told you about the time God first visited the Gentiles to take from them a people to bring honor to his name. And this fact of Gentile conversion agrees with what the prophets predicted. For instance, the prophet Amos: 'Afterwards, says the Lord, I will return and renew the broken contract with David so that Gentiles, too, will find the Lord.'

"And so my judgment is we should not insist that Gentiles who turn to God must obey our Jewish laws, except that we should write to them to refrain from eating meat sacrificed to idols, from all fornication, and also from eating unbled meat of strangled animals. For these things have been preached against in Jewish synagogues for many generations."

Then the apostles, elders, and congregation voted to send delegates to Antioch with Paul and Barnabas to report on this decision. The men chosen were two of the church leaders—Judas, also called Barsabbas, and Silas.

The four messengers went to Antioch where they called a general meeting of the Christians and gave them the letter. There was great joy as they read it. Then Judas and Silas, both gifted speakers, preached to the believers, strengthening their faith. They stayed several days, and then Judas and Silas returned to Jerusalem. Paul and Barnabas stayed on at Antioch to assist several others who were preaching and teaching there.[5]

**WARNING:
ONE WAY**

From: Paul the missionary and all the other Christians here.

To: The churches of Galatia.

I was not called to be a missionary by any group; my call is from Jesus Christ and from God the Father who raised him from the dead.

I am amazed that you are turning away so soon from God who, in his love and mercy, invited you to share the eternal life he gives through Christ; you are already following a different "way to heaven," which really doesn't go to heaven. For there is no other way than the one we showed you. You are being fooled by those who twist the truth concerning Christ.

Let God's curses fall on anyone, including myself, who preaches any other way to be saved than the one we told you; yes, if an angel comes from heaven and preaches any other message, let him be cursed.

Dear friends, I solemnly swear that the way to heaven I preach is not based on some mere human whim or dream. My message comes from Jesus Christ himself who told me what to say.

I didn't go to Jerusalem to consult with those who were apostles before I was. No, I went into the deserts of Arabia, and then came back to Damascus. It was not until three years later that I went to Jerusalem for a visit with Peter, and stayed there for fifteen days. The only other apostle I met at that time was James, our Lord's brother. After this visit I went to Syria and Cilicia.

Fourteen years later I went back to Jerusalem with Barnabas. I went with orders from God to confer with the brothers about the message I was preaching. The leaders of the church did agree; they had nothing to add to what I was preaching. When Peter, James, and John, known as the pillars of the church, saw how God had used me in winning the Gentiles—just as Peter had been blessed so greatly in his preaching to the Jews—they shook hands with Barnabas and me and encouraged us to keep on with our preaching to the Gentiles.

We are sinners if we start rebuilding the old systems

of trying to be saved by keeping Jewish laws. It was through reading the Scripture that I came to realize I could never find God's favor by trying—and failing—to obey the laws. Acceptance with God comes by believing in Christ.

I have been crucified with Christ: and I myself no longer live, but Christ lives in me. And the real life I now have within this body is a result of my trusting in the Son of God, who loved me and gave himself for me. If we could be saved by keeping laws, then there was no need for Christ to die.

O Galatians! You used to see the meaning of Christ's death clearly. Let me ask you: did you receive the Holy Spirit by trying to keep laws? Of course not, for the Holy Spirit came upon you only after you heard about Christ and trusted him to save you. If trying to obey the Jewish laws never gave you spiritual life in the first place, why do you think that trying to obey them now will make you stronger Christians?

Abraham had the same experience—God declared him fit for heaven only because he believed God's promises. You can see from this that the real children of Abraham are of faith who truly trust in God.

The Scriptures looked forward to this time when God would save Gentiles also through faith. God told Abraham, "I will bless those in every nation who trust in me as you do." As the prophet Habakkuk says, "The man who finds life will find it through trusting God." Now God can bless the Gentiles, too, with this same blessing he promised to Abraham.

God's promise to save through faith—and God wrote this promise down and signed it—could not be canceled or changed four hundred and thirty years later when God gave the Ten Commandments. Then, why were the laws given? They were added after the promise to show men how guilty they are of breaking God's laws. But this system of law was to last only until the coming of Christ.

Let me put it another way: the Jewish laws were our teacher and guide until Christ came to give us right standing with God through our faith. Now we are children of God through faith in Jesus Christ, and we who have been baptized into union with Christ are enveloped by him. We are no longer Jews or Greeks or slaves or free men or even merely men or women, but we are all one in Christ Jesus. And we are the true descendants of Abraham, and all of God's promises to him belong to us.

If a father dies and leaves great wealth for his little son, that child is not much better off than a slave until he grows up, even though he actually owns everything his father had. And that is the way it was with us before Christ came. We were slaves to laws and rituals, for we thought they could save us. But when the right time came, God sent his Son, born of a woman, a Jew, to buy freedom for us who were slaves to the law, so he could adopt us as his very own sons. And because we are his sons, God has sent the Spirit of his Son into our hearts so now we can rightly speak of God as our dear Father. And since we are his sons, everything he has belongs to us.

Before you Gentiles knew God, you were slaves to so-called gods that did not even exist. And now that you have found God (or I should say, now that God has found you) how can you want to go back and become slaves once more to a religion of trying to get to heaven by obeying God's laws? You are trying to find favor with God by what you do or don't do; I fear for you.

You friends who think you have to obey the Jewish laws to be saved: why don't you find out what those laws really mean? For Abraham had two sons, one from his slave-wife and one from his free-born wife. There was nothing unusual about the birth of the slave-wife's baby. But the baby of the free-born wife was born only after God had especially promised he would come.

This true story is an illustration of God's two ways of helping people. One way was by giving his laws on Mount Sinai to Moses. Mount Sinai is called "Mount Hagar" by the Arabs—and in my illustration Abraham's slave-wife Hagar represents Jerusalem, the mother-city of the Jews, the center of that system of trying to please God by trying to obey the Commandments; and Jews who try to follow that system are her children.

But our mother-city is the heavenly Jerusalem, and is

not a slave to Jewish laws. That is what Isaiah meant when he prophesied, "Now you can rejoice, O childless woman; you can shout with joy though you never had a child, for I am going to give you many children—more children than the slave-wife has." You and I, dear brothers, are the children that God promised, just as Isaac was.

The Scriptures say God told Abraham to send away the slave-wife and her son, for the slave-wife's son could not inherit Abraham's home and lands along with the free woman's son. Dear brothers, we are children of the free woman, acceptable to God because of our faith.

I am trusting the Lord to bring you back to believing as I do about these things. God will deal with that person who has been troubling and confusing you.

Dear brothers, you have been given freedom: not freedom to do wrong but freedom to love and serve each other. For the whole Law can be summed up in this one command: "Love others as you love yourself."

I advise you to obey only the Holy Spirit's instructions, then you won't be doing the wrong things your evil nature wants you to. We naturally love evil things that are opposite from the things the Holy Spirit tells us to do; and the good things we do when the Spirit has his way with us are the opposite of our natural desires—these two forces within us are constantly fighting each other.

When you follow your own wrong inclinations, your lives will produce these evil results: impure thoughts, eagerness for lustful pleasure, idolatry, spiritism (that is, encouraging the activity of demons), hatred and fighting, jealousy and anger, constant effort to get the best for yourself, complaints and criticisms, the feeling that everyone else is wrong except your own group—and there will be wrong doctrine, envy, murder, drunkenness, wild parties, and all that sort of thing. Anyone living that sort of life will not inherit the Kingdom of God.

But when the Holy Spirit controls our lives, he will produce this kind of fruit in us: love, joy, peace, patience, kindness, goodness, faithfulness, gentleness, and self-control; and here there is no conflict with Jewish laws. If we are living now by the Holy Spirit's power, let us follow the Holy Spirit's leading in every part of our lives.

Remember that man will always reap the kind of crop he sows! If he sows to please his wrong desires, he will be planting seeds of evil and will surely reap spiritual decay and death; but if he plants the good things of the Spirit, he will reap the everlasting life which the Holy Spirit gives.

Dear brothers, may the grace of our Lord Jesus Christ be with you.

Sincerely, Paul.[6]

BROTHER TO BROTHERS

From: James, a servant of God and of the Lord Jesus Christ.

To: Jewish Christians scattered everywhere, greetings!

Dear brothers, is your life full of difficulties? Be happy, for when the way is rough your patience has a chance to grow. When your patience is in full bloom you will be ready for anything!

If you want to know what God wants you to do, ask him and he will gladly tell you. But when you ask be sure you expect him to tell you, for a doubtful mind will be as unsettled as a wave driven by the wind and every decision you then make will be uncertain.

Happy is the man who doesn't do wrong when he is tempted, for he will get as his reward the crown of life that God has promised to those who love him. And remember, it is never God who tempts anyone; temptation is the pull of man's own evil thoughts and wishes. Evil thoughts lead to evil actions and afterwards to the death penalty from God. But whatever is good and perfect comes from God, the Creator of all light, and he shines forever without change or shadow.

Anyone who says he is a Christian but doesn't control his sharp tongue is fooling himself, and his religion isn't worth much. The Christian who is pure is the one who takes care of orphans and widows and who remains true to the Lord—not soiled by his contacts with the world.

Dear brothers, how can you claim you belong to the Lord Jesus Christ, the Lord of glory, if you show favoritism to rich people and look down on poor people? Judging a man by his wealth shows you are guided by wrong motives. God has chosen poor people to be rich in faith, and the Kingdom of Heaven is the gift God promised to all those who love him. It is usually the rich men who laugh at Jesus Christ whose noble name you bear. It is good when you obey our Lord's command, "You must love your neighbors as you take care of yourself." But you are breaking this law when you favor the rich; it is sin.

Brothers, what's the use of saying you have faith if you aren't proving it by helping others? If you have a friend who is in need of food and clothing and you say, "Well, good-bye and God bless you; stay warm and eat hearty," what good does that do? Faith that doesn't show itself by good works is no faith at all—it is dead.

Someone may argue, "The way to God is by faith alone, plus nothing." Well, I say that good works prove whether you have faith or not; faith that does not result in good deeds is not real faith.

Our father Abraham was declared good because of what he did when he was willing to obey God, even if it meant offering his son Isaac to die on the altar; his faith was made complete by his actions. And so the Scriptures say Abraham trusted God and the Lord declared him good in God's sight. Just as the body is dead when there is no spirit in it, so faith is dead if it is not the kind that results in good deeds.

Dear brothers, don't be eager to tell others their faults, for we all make many mistakes. The tongue is a small thing but what enormous damage it can do! A great forest can be set on fire by one tiny spark. And the tongue is a flame of fire, and is set on fire by hell itself. This is not right! ·

If you are wise, live so that only good deeds pour forth. Jealousy and selfishness are not God's kind of wisdom; such things are earthly, unspiritual, inspired by the devil. But the wisdom that comes from heaven is first of all pure and full of quiet gentleness. Then it is peace-loving and courteous. It is willing to yield to others; it is full of mercy and good deeds. It is wholehearted and straightforward and sincere. Those who are peacemakers will plant seeds of peace and reap a harvest of goodness.

What is causing quarrels and fights among you? Isn't it because there is a whole army of evil desires within you? You long for what others have, and can't afford it, so you start a fight to take it. And yet the reason you don't have what you want is that you don't ask God for it. And when you do ask your aim is wrong—you want only what will give you pleasure.

If your aim is to enjoy the evil pleasure of the world, you cannot be a friend of God. The Holy Spirit, whom God has placed within us, gives us strength to stand against such evil longings. As the Scripture says, God gives strength to the humble but sets himself against the proud and haughty. So give yourselves humbly to God.

Resist the devil and he will flee from you. And when you draw close to God, God will draw close to you. Let your hearts be filled with God alone to make them pure and true to him.

You people who say, "Today or tomorrow we are going to town and open up a profitable business"—how do you know what is going to happen tomorrow? The length of your lives is as uncertain as the morning fog—now you see it; soon it is gone. What you ought to say is, "If the Lord wants us to, we shall do this or that."

Remember, too, that knowing what is right to do and then not doing it is sin.

Dear brothers who are waiting for the Lord's return— be patient, like a farmer who waits until the autumn for his precious harvest to ripen. The great Judge is coming.

For examples of patience in suffering, look at the Lord's prophets. We know how happy they are now because they stayed true to him then, even though they suffered greatly for it. Job is an example of a man who continued to trust the Lord in sorrow; from his experiences we can see how the Lord's plan ended in good, for he is full of tenderness and mercy.

Is anyone among you suffering? He should keep on praying about it. Is anyone sick? He should call for the elders of the church and they should pray over him and pour a little oil upon him, calling on the Lord to heal him. And their prayer, if offered in faith, will heal him, for the Lord will make him well; and if his sickness was caused by some sin, the Lord will forgive him. Admit your faults to one another and pray for each other so that you may be healed.

The earnest prayer of a righteous man has great power and wonderful results. Elijah was as human as we are, and yet when he prayed that no rain would fall, none fell for three and one-half years! Then he prayed that it would rain, and down it poured!

Brothers, if anyone has slipped away from God and someone helps him understand the Truth again, that person who brings him back will bring about the forgiveness of many sins.

Sincerely, James[7]

CRUSADE: EUROPE

Paul suggested to Barnabas that they return to Turkey and visit each city where they had preached before to see how the new converts were getting along. Barnabas agreed and wanted to take along John Mark, but Paul didn't like that idea since John had deserted them in Pamphylia. Their disagreement was so sharp that they separated: Barnabas took Mark with him and sailed for Cyprus, while Paul chose Silas and left for Syria and Cilicia.

Paul and Silas went first to Derbe and then on to Lystra where they met Timothy, a believer whose mother was a Christian Jewess but his father a Greek. Paul asked him to join them, then they went from city to city; so the church grew daily in faith and numbers.

Next they traveled through Phrygia and Galatia, then on through Mysia province to the city of Troas. That night Paul had a vision. He saw a man over in Macedonia, Greece, pleading with him: "Come over here and help us."

We could only conclude that God was sending us to preach the Good News there. We sailed across to Samothrace, the next day on to Neapolis, and finally reached Philippi, a Roman colony just inside the Macedonian border, and stayed there several days.

On the Sabbath we went a little way outside the city to a riverbank where we understood some people met for prayer; and we taught the Scriptures to some women who came. One of them was Lydia from Thyatira, a merchant of purple cloth. She was already a worshiper of God, and as she listened the Lord opened her heart and she accepted all that Paul was saying. She was baptized along with her household and asked us to be her guests.

One day as we were going to the place of prayer beside the river, we met a demon-possessed slave girl who was a fortune-teller and earned much money for her masters. She followed along behind us shouting, "These men are servants of God and have come to tell you how to have your sins forgiven."

This went on day after day until Paul, in great distress, turned and spoke to the demon within her: "I command you in the name of Jesus Christ to come out of her." Instantly it left her.

Her masters' hopes of wealth were now shattered. They grabbed Paul and Silas and dragged them before the judges at the marketplace. "These Jews are corrupting our city," they shouted. "They are teaching the people to do things that are against the Roman laws."

A mob quickly formed, and the judges ordered them stripped and beaten. Again and again the rods slashed across their bared backs, and afterwards they were thrown into prison. The jailer was threatened with death if they escaped, so he put them in the inner dungeon and clamped their feet into stocks.

Around midnight, as Paul and Silas were praying and singing hymns to the Lord, suddenly there was a great earthquake; the doors flew open—and the chains of every prisoner fell off! The jailer wakened to see the prison doors wide open, and assuming the prisoners had escaped he drew his sword to kill himself.

But Paul yelled, "Don't do it! We are all here!"

Trembling, the jailer called for lights and ran to the dungeon and fell down before Paul and Silas. He begged, "Sirs, what must I do to be saved?"

They replied, "Believe on the Lord Jesus, and you will be saved." Then they told him and his household the Good News from the Lord.

That hour he washed their stripes, and he and all his family were baptized. Then he brought them into his house and set a meal before them. How he and his household rejoiced!

The next morning the judges sent officers to tell the jailer, "Let those men go!" So the jailer told Paul they were free to leave.

Paul replied, "Oh, no they don't! They have beaten us without trial and jailed us—and we are Roman citizens! Now they want us to leave secretly? Never!"

The police reported to the judges, who feared for their lives when they heard Paul and Silas were Roman citizens. So they came to the jail and pled with them to leave the city. Paul and Silas then returned to the home of Lydia where they met with the believers and preached once more before leaving town.

They traveled through the cities of Amphipolis and Apollonia and came to Thessalonica, where there was a Jewish synagogue. As was Paul's custom, he went there to preach for three Sabbaths in a row, explaining the prophecies about the sufferings of the Messiah and his coming back to life, and proving that Jesus is the Messiah. Some were persuaded and became converts—including a large number of godly Greek men and also many important women of the city.

But the Jewish leaders incited some fellows from the streets to form a mob and start a riot. They attacked the home of Jason, planning to take Paul and Silas to the City Council for punishment. Not finding them there, they dragged out Jason and some of the other believers and took them before the Council.

"Paul and Silas have turned the rest of the world upside down, and now they are disturbing our city," they shouted, "and Jason has let them into his home. They are all guilty of treason, for they claim another king, Jesus, instead of Caesar."

The people of the city as well as the judges were concerned, and let them go only after they had posted bail.

That night the Christians hurried Paul and Silas to Beroea, and they went to the synagogue to preach. The people of Beroea were more open minded than those in Thessalonica, and gladly listened. They searched the Scriptures to check up on Paul and Silas' statements. As a result, many of them believed, including several prominent Greek women and many men also.

When the Jews in Thessalonica learned that Paul was preaching in Beroea, they went over and stirred up trouble. The believers sent Paul on to the coast, while Silas and Timothy remained behind. Those accompanying Paul went on with him to Athens, and then returned to Beroea with a message for Silas and Timothy to join him.

While Paul was waiting in Athens, he was deeply troubled by all the idols he saw throughout the city. He went to the synagogue for discussions with Jews and devout Gentiles, and spoke daily in the public square to all there.

He also had an encounter with some Epicurean and Stoic philosophers. Their reaction, when he told them about Jesus and his resurrection, was, "He's a dreamer," or, "He's pushing some foreign religion." But they invited him to the forum at Mars Hill: "Come and tell us more about this new religion."

So Paul, standing before them at the Mars Hill forum, addressed them as follows:

"Men of Athens, I notice that you are very religious, for I saw your many altars and one of them had this inscription—'To the Unknown God.' Now I wish to tell you about him.

"He made the world and everything in it, and since he is Lord of heaven and earth he doesn't live in man-made temples. He gives life to everything, and satisfies every need there is. He created all the people of the world from one man, Adam, and scattered the nations across the face of the earth. He decided beforehand which should rise and fall, and when.

"His purpose is that they should seek after God and perhaps find him—though he is not far from any one of us. For in him we live and move and are! God tolerated man's past ignorance about these things, but now he commands everyone to put away idols and worship only him. For he has set a day for justly judging the world by the man he has appointed, and has pointed him out by bringing him back to life again."

When they heard Paul speak of the resurrection of a person who had been dead, some laughed but others said, "We want to hear more about this later." That ended Paul's discussion, but a few joined him and became believers. Among them were Dionysius, a member of the City Council, a woman named Damaris, and others.

Paul left Athens and went to Corinth. There he became acquainted with a Jew named Aquila who had recently arrived from Italy with his wife, Priscilla. They had been expelled from Italy as a result of Claudius Caesar's order to deport all Jews from Rome. Paul lived and worked with them, for they were tentmakers just as he was.

Each Sabbath found Paul at the synagogue, trying to convince Jews and Greeks alike. After the arrival of Silas and Timothy from Macedonia, Paul spent his full time preaching to the Jews that Jesus is the Messiah. But when the Jews blasphemed Jesus, Paul said, "From now on I will preach to the Gentiles."

He stayed with Titus Justus, a Gentile who worshiped God and lived next door to the synagogue. Crispus, the leader of the synagogue, and all his household believed in the Lord and were baptized—as were many others in Corinth.

One night the Lord spoke to Paul in a vision and told him, "Don't be afraid! Speak out! Don't quit! For I am with you and no one can harm you. Many people in this city belong to me." So Paul stayed there the next year and a half, teaching the truths of God.[8]

RESURRECTION DAY

From: Paul, Silas, and Timothy.

To: The church at Thessalonica—to you who belong to God the Father and the Lord Jesus Christ.

We always thank God for you and pray for you constantly. We never forget your strong faith and steady looking forward to the return of our Lord Jesus Christ.

We know that God has chosen you, for when we brought you the Good News it produced a powerful effect upon you. The Holy Spirit gave you assurance that what we said was true; and our lives were further proof of the truth of our message. You became our followers and the Lord's, for you received our message with joy in spite of the trials it brought you.

Then you became an example to the other Christians in Greece. And now the Word of the Lord has spread from you to others far beyond your boundaries, for wherever we go we find people telling us about your remarkable faith in God. They tell us how you turned away from idols so that now the living and true God is your only Master. And they speak of how you are looking forward to the return of God's Son from heaven—Jesus, whom God brought back to life.

We thank God that you didn't think of the words we spoke as being just our own but the very Word of God—which, of course, it was—and it changed your lives when you believed it.

And then you suffered what the churches in Judea did—persecution from your countrymen. Now I want you to know what happens to a Christian when he dies so that you will not be full of sorrow as those are who have no hope. For since we believe that Jesus died and then came back to life, we can also believe that when Jesus returns, God will bring back with him all the Christians who have died.

I tell you this directly from the Lord: we who are still living when the Lord returns will not rise to meet him ahead of those who are in their graves. For the Lord will come down from heaven with a mighty shout and with the soul-stirring cry of the archangel and the great trumpet-call of God. Believers who are dead will be the first to rise to meet the Lord. Then we who are still alive on the earth will be caught up with them in the clouds to meet the Lord in the air and remain with him forever. So encourage each other with this news.

That day of the Lord will come unexpectedly like a thief in the night: when people are saying, "All is well; everything is quiet and peaceful"—then disaster will fall upon them as suddenly as a woman's birth pains begin. And these people will not be able to get away—there will be no place to hide.

But you are not in the dark about these things and won't be surprised as by a thief when that day of the Lord comes. For you are children of the light, and God has not chosen to pour out his anger upon us but to save us through our Lord Jesus Christ. He died for us so that we can live with him forever, whether we are dead or alive at the time of his return.

Be joyful, keep on praying, always be thankful; for this is God's will for you who belong to Christ Jesus. May your spirit and soul and body be kept strong and blameless until that day when our Lord Jesus Christ comes back. In the name of the Lord, read this letter to all the Christians.

Sincerely, Paul[9]

SATAN'S MESSIAH

From: Paul, Silas, and Timothy.

To: The church of Thessalonica—kept safe in God our Father and in the Lord Jesus Christ.

Dear brothers, we are happy to tell other churches about your patience and complete faith in God in spite of the crushing hardships you are going through. God is using your sufferings to make you ready for his Kingdom, while at the same time he is preparing punishment for those who are hurting you.

And so I say to you: God will give you rest when the Lord Jesus appears from heaven in flaming fire with his mighty angels, bringing judgment on those who do not wish to know God and who refuse to accept his plan to save them through our Lord Jesus Christ. They will be forever separated from the Lord when he comes to receive praise because of all he has done for his saints. And you will be among those praising him.

Don't be upset and excited, brothers, by the rumor that this day of the Lord has already begun. For that day will not come until two things happen: first, there will be a time of great rebellion against God, and then the man of rebellion will come—the son of hell. He will defy every god there is and tear down every other object of worship. He will go in and sit as God in the temple of God, claiming that he himself is God. I told you this when I was with you.

The work this man of rebellion will do is already going on, but he himself will not come until the one who is holding him back steps out of the way. Then this wicked one will appear, whom the Lord Jesus will burn up with the breath of his mouth when he returns. This man of sin will come as Satan's tool, full of satanic power, and he will trick with strange demonstrations and great miracles. He will completely fool those who are on their way to hell because they have said "no" to the Truth; so God will allow them to believe lies and all of them will be justly judged for believing falsehood, refusing the Truth, and enjoying their sins.

May our Lord Jesus Christ himself, and God our Father who has given us everlasting hope, comfort your hearts and help you in every good thing you say and do.

Finally, I ask you to pray for us that the Lord's message will spread rapidly and triumph wherever it goes. Pray too that we will be saved out of the clutches of evil men.

Stay away from any Christian who spends his days in laziness and does not follow the ideal of hard work we set up for you. While we were there we gave you this rule: "He who does not work shall not eat."

Here is my greeting which I am writing with my own hand for proof that it is from me. May the blessing of our Lord Jesus be upon you all.

Sincerely, Paul[10]

POWERFUL PREACHER

When Gallio became governor of Achaia, the Jews rose in concerted action against Paul and brought him before the governor for judgment. They accused Paul of "persuading men to worship God in ways that are contrary to Roman law." Just as Paul started to make his defense, Gallio turned to his accusers and said, "If this were a case involving crime I would be obliged to listen, but since it is merely a question of semantics and personalities and silly laws, I'm not interested." And he drove them out of the courtroom.

Paul stayed in the city several days after that and then sailed for Syria. At the port of Ephesus, he went to the synagogue for a discussion with the Jews. They asked him to stay for a few days. "I must be at Jerusalem for the holiday," he said. He promised to return later if God permitted, and we set sail again.

The next stop was at Caesarea, from where he visited the church at Jerusalem, and then sailed on to Antioch. After spending some time there, he left for Turkey again, going through Galatia and Phrygia visiting all the believers.

As it happened, a Jew named Apollos—a wonderful preacher—had arrived in Ephesus from Alexandria. While he was in Egypt, someone told him about John the Baptist and what John had said about Jesus, but he had never heard the rest of the story! So he was preaching enthusiastically in the synagogue: "The Messiah is coming! Get ready to receive him!" Priscilla and Aquila were there and heard him—it was a powerful sermon. Afterwards they met with him and explained what had happened to Jesus since the time of John and all that it meant!

Apollos had been thinking about going to Greece, and the believers encouraged him in this. They wrote to their fellow-believers there, telling them to welcome him. Upon his arrival he was greatly used to strengthen the church, for he powerfully refuted the Jewish arguments in public debate, showing by the Scriptures that Jesus is indeed the Messiah.

While Apollos was in Corinth, Paul traveled through Turkey and arrived in Ephesus where he found several disciples.

"Did you receive the Holy Spirit when you believed?" he asked them.

They replied, "We don't know what you mean. What is the Holy Spirit?"

"What belief did you acknowledge at your baptism?" he asked.

"What John the Baptist taught."

Then Paul pointed out that John's baptism was to demonstrate a desire to turn from sin to God and that those receiving his baptism must then go on to believe in Jesus, the one John said would come.

As soon as they heard this, they were baptized in the name of the Lord Jesus. Then when Paul laid his hands upon their heads, the Holy Spirit came on them and they spoke in other languages and prophesied.

Paul went to the synagogue and preached boldly each Sabbath day for three months, telling what he believed and persuading many to believe in Jesus. But some rejected his message and spoke against Christ, so he left. He began a separate meeting at the lecture hall of Tyrannus and preached there daily. This went on for the next two years, so that everyone in the Turkish province of Asia—both Jews and Greeks—heard the Lord's message.[11]

CORINTH: BODY LIFE

From: Paul, chosen by God to be Jesus Christ's missionary, and from Sosthenes.

To: The Christians in Corinth, and all Christians everywhere.

I can never stop thanking God for the wonderful gifts he has given you; he has enriched your whole life. You have every grace and blessing; every spiritual gift and power for doing his will are yours during this time of waiting for the return of our Lord Jesus Christ.

But, dear brothers, I beg you in the name of the Lord Jesus to be of one mind, united in thought and purpose. For some at Chloe's house have told me of your quarrels: some are saying, "I am a follower of Paul," and others say they are for Apollos or for Peter, and some that they alone are the true followers of Christ. In effect, you have broken Christ into many pieces.

But did I, Paul, die for your sins? Were any of you baptized in my name? I am so thankful now that I didn't baptize any of you except Crispus and Gaius. Oh, yes, and I baptized the family of Stephanas. Christ didn't send me to baptize, but to preach the Gospel; and my preaching sounds poor for I do not fill sermons with profound words and high-sounding ideas, for fear of diluting the power in the simple message of the cross.

I know how foolish it sounds to those who are lost: Jews want a sign from heaven as proof that what is preached is true; and Gentiles believe only what agrees with their philosophy. So the Jews are offended and the Gentiles say it's nonsense. But God has opened the eyes of those called to salvation, both Jews and Gentiles, to see that Christ is the mighty power of God to save them. God in his weakness—Christ dying on the cross—is far stronger than any man.

Our words are wise because they are from God, telling of God's wise plan to bring us into the glories of heaven. This plan was hidden in former times, though it was made for our benefit before the world began. But the great men of the world have not understood it; if they had, they never would have crucified the Lord of Glory.

That is what is meant by the Scriptures which say no mere man has ever seen, heard, or imagined what wonderful things God has ready for those who love the Lord; but we know about these things because God has sent his Spirit to tell us. In telling you about these gifts, we have used the very words given to us by the Holy Spirit, not words that we as men might choose.

Who am I, and who is Apollos, that we should be the cause of a quarrel? We're just God's servants, and with our help you believed. My work was to plant the seed in your hearts, and Apollos' work was to water it, but it was God who made the garden grow. We are only God's co-workers. You are God's garden, not ours; you are God's building, not ours.

I have laid the foundation and Apollos has built on it.

But he who builds on the foundation must be very careful. And no one can lay any other real foundation than Jesus Christ. But there are various kinds of materials that can be used to build on that foundation. Some use gold and silver and jewels; and some build with sticks and hay or even straw! There is going to come a testing at Judgment Day to see what kind of material each has used. Everyone's work will be put through the fire so all can see what was really accomplished.

You are not to keep company with anyone who claims to be a Christian but indulges in sexual sins, or is greedy, or is a swindler, or worships idols, or is a drunkard, or abusive. It isn't our job to judge outsiders, but it certainly is our job to deal strongly with those who are members of the church and are sinning in these ways.

How is it that when you have something against another Christian you "go to law" to decide the matter instead of taking it to other Christians? Some day we Christians are going to govern the world, so why can't you decide these things among yourselves? To have such lawsuits is a real defeat for you as Christians. It would be far more honoring to the Lord to let yourselves be cheated.

I can do anything I want to if Christ has not said "No," but some of these things aren't good for me. Even if I am allowed to do them, I'll refuse to if I think they might get such a grip on me that I can't easily stop when I want to.

But sexual sin is never right: our bodies were made for the Lord. Your bodies are actually members of Christ. If a man joins himself to a prostitute, she becomes a part of him and he a part of her. No other sin affects the body as this one does; this sin is against your own body. Your body does not belong to you, for God has bought you with a great price. So use every part of your body to give glory back to God.

Now about those questions you asked in your last letter. If you do not marry, it is good; but usually it is best to be married, because otherwise you might fall into sin.

The man should give his wife all that is her right as a married woman, and the wife should do the same for her husband: for a girl who marries no longer has full right to her own body, for her husband then has his rights to it, too; and in the same way the husband no longer has full right to his own body, for it belongs also to his wife.

I wish everyone could get along without marrying, just as I do. But God gives some the gift of a husband or wife, and others he gives the gift of being able to stay happily unmarried.

For those who are married, I have a command: the Lord himself said: "A wife must not leave her husband. But if she is separated from him, let her remain single or else go back to him. And the husband must not divorce his wife."

Here I want to add some suggestions, not direct commands from the Lord. If a Christian has a wife who is not a Christian but she wants to stay with him, he must not leave her or divorce her. And if a Christian woman has a husband who isn't a Christian and he wants her to stay with him, she must not leave him. For perhaps the husband who isn't a Christian may become a Christian; and the wife who isn't a Christian may become a Christian.

Be sure in these matters that you are living as God intended, marrying or not marrying in accordance with God's direction and help, and accepting whatever situation God has put you into.

Next on my list of items: it sounds as if more harm than good is done when you meet together for your communion services. Everyone keeps telling me about the arguing that goes on in these meetings, and the divisions developing among you.

This is what the Lord himself said about his Table: On the night when Judas betrayed him, the Lord Jesus took bread, and when he had given thanks to God for it, he broke it and gave it to his disciples and said, "Take this, and eat it; this is my body, which is given for you. Do this to remember me." In the same way, he took the cup of wine after supper, saying, "This cup is the new agreement between God and you that has been established by my blood. Do this in remembrance of me whenever you drink it." Every time you eat this bread and drink this cup, you are retelling the message that he has died for you. Do this until he comes again.

If anyone eats this bread and drinks this cup of the Lord in an unworthy manner, he is guilty of sin against the body and the blood of the Lord. That is why a man should examine himself carefully before eating the bread and drinking from the cup.

And now I want to write about the special abilities the Holy Spirit gives to each of you. Before you became Christians, you went from one idol to another, not one of which could speak a single word. But now you are meeting people who claim to speak messages from the Spirit of God. How can you know whether they are really inspired by God? Here is the test: no one speaking by the power of the Spirit of God can curse Jesus; and no one can say, "Jesus is Lord" and really mean it unless the Holy Spirit is helping him.

God gives many kinds of special abilities, but it is the same Holy Spirit who is the source. There are different kinds of service to God, but it is the same Lord we are serving. There are many ways in which God works in our lives, but it is the same God who does the work in and through us who are his. The Holy Spirit displays God's power through each of us as a means of helping the entire church.

To one person the Spirit gives the ability to give wise advice; someone else may be especially good at studying and teaching. He gives special faith to another, and to someone else the power to heal the sick. He gives power for doing miracles to some, and to others power to prophesy and preach. He gives someone else the power to know whether evil spirits are speaking through those who claim to be giving God's messages—or whether it is really the Spirit of God. Still another person is able to speak in languages he never learned; and others who do not know the language either are given power to understand what he is saying. It is the same Holy Spirit who gives all these gifts and powers, deciding which each one of us should have.

Our bodies have many parts, but the many parts make

up only one body. So it is with the "body" of Christ. Each of us is a part of the one body of Christ: some of us are Jews, some are Gentiles, some are slaves, and some are free; but the Holy Spirit has fitted us all together into one body. We have been baptized into Christ's body by the one Spirit, and have all been given that same Holy Spirit.

Is everyone an apostle? Of course not. Is everyone a preacher? No. Are all teachers? Does everyone have the power to do miracles? Can everyone heal the sick? Of course not. Does God give all of us the ability to speak in languages we've never learned? Can just anyone understand and translate what those are saying? No, but try your best to have the more important of these gifts.

First, however, let me tell you about something else that is better than any of them!

If I had the gift of being able to speak in other languages but didn't love others, I would only be making noise. If I had the gift of prophecy and knew everything about everything but didn't love others, what good would it do? Even if I had the gift of faith so that I could speak to a mountain and make it move, I would still be worth nothing at all without love. If I gave everything I have to poor people and if I were burned alive for preaching the Gospel but didn't love others, it would be of no value whatever.

Love is very patient and kind, never jealous or envious, never boastful or proud, never haughty or selfish or rude. Love does not demand its own way. It is not irritable or touchy. It does not hold grudges and will hardly even notice when others do it wrong. It is never glad about injustice, but rejoices whenever truth wins out. If you love someone, you will be loyal to him no matter what the cost; you will always believe in him, always expect the best of him, and always stand your ground in defending him.

All the special gifts and powers from God will someday come to an end, but love goes on forever. Someday prophecy and speaking in unknown languages and special knowledge—these gifts will disappear. Now we know so little even with our special gifts, and the preaching of those most gifted is still so poor. But when we have been made perfect and complete, then the need for these inadequate special gifts will come to an end and they will disappear.

It's like this: when I was a child I spoke and thought and reasoned as a child does. But when I became a man my thoughts grew far beyond those of my childhood, and now I have put away the childish things. In the same way, we can see and understand only a little about God now—as if we were peering at his reflection ɪ a poor mirror; but someday we are going to see him in his completeness, face to face. Now all that I know is hazy and blurred, but then I will see everything clearly, just as clearly as God sees into my heart right now.

There are three things that remain—faith, hope, and love—and the greatest of these is love. Let love be your greatest aim; nevertheless, ask also for the special abilities the Holy Spirit gives.

You who claim to have the gift of prophecy or any other special ability from the Holy Spirit should be the first to realize that what I am saying is a commandment from the Lord himself.

Let me remind you what the Gospel really is, for it has not changed—it is the same Good News I preached to you before.

I passed on to you what had been told to me, that Christ died for our sins just as the Scriptures said he would, and that he was buried, and that three days afterwards he arose from the grave just as the prophets foretold. He was seen by Peter and later by the rest of "the Twelve." After that he was seen by more than five hundred Christian brothers at one time, most of whom are still alive. Then James saw him. Last of all I saw him too, as though I had been born almost too late for this. I am the least worthy of all the apostles after the way I treated the church of God. But I worked harder than all the other apostles, yet actually I wasn't doing it, but God working in me.

Since you believe what we preach—that Christ rose from the dead—why are some of you saying that dead people will never come back to life? If there is no resurrection of the dead, then Christ must still be dead. And if he is still dead, all our preaching is useless, your trust in God is empty, and we apostles are liars because we have said that God raised Christ from the grave. If being a Christian is of value only in this life, we are the most miserable of creatures.

But the fact is that Christ did actually rise from the dead and has become the first of millions who will come back to life again some day.

Death came into the world because of what one man—Adam—did, and it is because of what this other man—Christ—has done that now there is the resurrection from the dead. Everyone dies because all of us are related to Adam, being members of his sinful race. But all who are related to Christ will rise again, each in his own turn: Christ rose first; then when Christ comes back all his people will become alive again. After that, the end will come when he will turn the kingdom over to God the Father.

If the dead will not come back to life, why should we be continually risking our lives, facing death hour by hour? What value was there in fighting wild beasts if it was only for what I gain in this life? If we will never live again, let us eat, drink, and be merry for tomorrow we die.

But someone may ask, "How will the dead be brought back to life? What kind of bodies will they have?" You will find the answer in your own garden! When you put a seed into the ground it doesn't grow into a plant unless it "dies" first. And when the green shoot comes up out of the seed, it is very different from the seed you first planted. God gives it a beautiful, new body—just the kind he wants it to have. And just as there are different kinds of seeds and plants, so also there are different kinds of flesh: humans, animals, fish, and birds.

The angels have bodies far different from ours, and the beauty and the glory of their bodies is different from the beauty and glory of ours. The sun has one kind of glory while the moon and stars have another kind. And the stars differ from each other in their beauty and brightness.

In the same way, our earthly bodies which die and decay are different from the bodies we shall have when we come back to life. The bodies we have now become sick and die, but they will be full of glory when we come back to life. They are just human bodies at death, but when they come back to life they will be superhuman bodies. For just as there are natural, human bodies, there are also supernatural, spiritual bodies.

The Scriptures tell us that the first man, Adam, was given a natural, human body; but Christ is more than that for he was life-giving Spirit. Adam was made from the dust of the earth; Christ came from heaven above. Every human being has a body just like Adam's, made of dust; but all who become Christ's will have the same kind of body as his—a body from heaven.

A body made of flesh and blood cannot get into God's Kingdom, but I tell you this wonderful secret: we shall not all die but we shall all be given new bodies! It will happen in a moment, in the twinkling of an eye, when the last trumpet is blown. For all the Christians who have died will suddenly become alive, with new bodies that will never die; and then we who are still alive shall suddenly have new bodies too.

When this happens, at last this Scripture will come true—"Death is swallowed up in victory." O death, where then your victory? Where then your sting? For sin—the sting that causes death—will all be gone; and the law, which reveals our sins, will no longer be our judge. How we thank God for all this! It is he who makes us victorious through Jesus Christ our Lord!

So, my dear brothers, since future victory is sure, be strong and steady, always abounding in the Lord's work, for you know that nothing you do for the Lord is ever wasted as it would be if there were no resurrection.

The churches here send their loving greetings; Aquila and Priscilla send their love, and so do all the others who meet in their home for the church service. May the favor of the Lord Jesus Christ rest upon you.

Sincerely, Paul[12]

Dear friends,

PAUL: PERILOUS LIFE

This letter is from Paul and from Timothy. We are writing to all Christians in Corinth and throughout Greece. May God our Father and the Lord Jesus Christ mightily bless each one of you and give you peace.

I think you ought to know, brothers, about the hard time we went through in Asia. We were overwhelmed and feared we would never live through it. We saw how powerless we were to help ourselves, but then we put everything into the hands of God. He did help us and saved us from a terrible death, and we expect him to do it again. You must help us, too, by praying for us.

Thanks be to God! Through what Christ has done he has triumphed so that now wherever we go he uses us to spread the Gospel like a sweet perfume. It is the fragrance of Christ—an aroma to both the saved and the unsaved. To those who are not being saved, we seem a fearful smell of death and doom; while to those who know Christ we are a life-giving perfume.

If the Good News we preach is hidden to anyone, it is hidden from the one who is on the road to eternal death. Satan, the god of this world, has made him blind, unable to see the glorious light of the Gospel or to understand the amazing message we preach about the glory of Christ, who is God. For God who said, "Let there be light in the darkness," has made us understand it is the brightness of his glory that is seen in the face of Jesus Christ.

But this precious treasure—this light and power that now shine within us—is held in a perishable container, that is, our weak bodies. We are pressed on every side by troubles, but not crushed and broken. We are perplexed because we don't know why things happen as they do, but we don't give up. We are hunted down, but God never abandons us. We get knocked down, but we get up again and keep going. These bodies of our are constantly facing death just as Jesus did; so it is clear to all that it is only the living Christ within who keeps us safe.

Though our bodies are dying, our inner strength in the Lord is growing every day. These sufferings, after all, won't last very long. This short time of distress will result in God's richest blessing upon us forever! So we do not look at what we can see now, but we look forward to the joys in heaven which we have not yet seen. The troubles will soon be over, but the joys to come will last forever.

For we know that when this tent we live in now is taken down—when we die and leave these bodies—we will have homes in heaven made by God himself. These dying bodies will, as it were, be swallowed up by everlasting life. This is what God has prepared for us, and as a guarantee he has given us his Holy Spirit.

Every moment we spend in these earthly bodies is time spent away from our eternal home in heaven. We know these things are true by believing, not by seeing. And we are not afraid but are quite content to die. So our aim is to please him always—whether we are here in this body or away from this body and with him in heaven. For we must all stand before Christ to be judged; each of us will receive whatever he deserves for the good or bad things he has done in his earthly body.

Since we believe that Christ died for us, we should also believe that we have died to the old life we used to live. When someone becomes a Christian, he becomes a brand new person inside; he is not the same any more.

All these new things are from God who brought us back to himself through what Christ Jesus did. And God has given us the privilege of urging everyone to be reconciled to him. For God was in Christ, restoring the world to himself, no longer counting men's sins against them but blotting them out. We are Christ's ambassadors: we beg you, as though Christ himself were here pleading with you, receive the love he offers you—be reconciled to God. For God took the sinless Christ and poured into him our sins, then in exchange he poured God's goodness into us!

We try to live in such a way that no one will be kept back from finding the Lord by the way we act. We patiently endure suffering and hardship and trouble of every kind. We have been beaten, put in jail, faced angry mobs, worked to exhaustion, stayed awake through sleepless nights of watching, and gone without food. We have proved ourselves to be what we claim by our wholesome lives and our understanding of the Gospel. We have been kind and loving and filled with the Holy Spirit. We stand true to the Lord whether others honor us or despise us.

The world ignores us, but we are known to God; we live close to death, but we are still very much alive. Our hearts ache, but at the same time we have the joy of the Lord. We are poor, but we give rich spiritual gifts to others. We own nothing, and yet we enjoy everything.

O my dear Corinthian friends! I have told you all my feelings; I love you with all my heart. Any coldness between us is because your love does not reach out and draw me in. I am talking to you as if you truly were my own children.

Don't be teamed with those who do not love the Lord, for what do the people of God have in common with the people of sin? What harmony can there be between God's temple and idols? For you are God's temple, the home of the living God, and God has said of you, "I will live in them and walk among them, and I will be their God and they shall be my people." That is why the Lord has said, "Leave them; separate yourselves from them; and I will welcome you and be a Father to you, and you will be my sons and daughters."

I am anxious that your love should be for Christ alone, just as a pure maiden saves her love for one man only. But I am frightened that you will be led away from your simple devotion to our Lord, just as Eve was deceived by Satan in the Garden of Eden. You seem so gullible: you believe whatever anyone tells you even if he is preaching about another Jesus or a different spirit than the Holy Spirit you received.

Yet I am not surprised! Satan can change himself into an angel of light, so it is no wonder his servants can do it too and seem like godly ministers. They will get every bit of punishment their wicked deeds deserve.

They brag that they are Hebrews, do they? Well, so am I. They say they serve Christ? But I have served him far more! I have worked harder, been put in jail oftener, been whipped times without number, and faced death again and again. Five different times the Jews gave me their terri-

ble thirty-nine lashes. Three times I was beaten with rods.
Once I was stoned. Three times I was shipwrecked. Once
I was in the open sea all night and the whole next day. I
have traveled many weary miles and have been often in
danger from flooded rivers and robbers and my own people
as well as the Gentiles. I have faced mobs in the cities,
death in the deserts, and men who claim to be brothers
in Christ but are not. Often I have been hungry and thirsty
and have gone without food.

Besides all this, I have the worry of how the churches
are getting along: who makes a mistake and I do not feel
his sadness? who falls without my longing to help him?
who is spiritually hurt without my fury rising against the
one who hurt him?

This boasting is foolish, but let me tell about the visions
I've had and revelations from the Lord.

Fourteen years ago I was taken up to heaven for a visit.
Don't ask me whether my body was there or just my spirit,
for I don't know; but there I was in paradise and heard
things so astounding that they are beyond a man's power
to describe (and anyway I am not allowed to tell them to
others).

Because these experiences were so tremendous, God
was afraid I might be puffed up by them; so I was given
a physical condition which has been a thorn in my flesh,
a messenger from Satan to hurt me and prick my pride.
Three different times I begged God to make me well again.
Each time he said, "No. But I am with you; that is all
you need. My power shows up best in weak people."

Now I am glad to boast about how weak I am; I am
glad to be a living demonstration of Christ's power. Since
I know it is for Christ's good, I am quite happy about
"the thorn" and about insults and hardships, persecutions
and difficulties; for when I am weak, then I am strong—
the less I have, the more I depend on him.

Check up on yourselves. Are you really Christians? Do
you feel Christ's presence and power more and more within
you? Or are you just pretending to be Christians? Our greatest wish and prayer is that you will become mature Christians.

I close my letter with these words: be happy; grow in Christ; pay attention to what I have said; live in harmony and peace.

May the grace of our Lord Jesus Christ be with you all; may God's love and the Holy Spirit's friendship be yours.

Paul[13]

TWO WORLDS

God gave Paul the power to do unusual miracles: even when his handkerchiefs or parts of his clothing were placed upon sick people they were healed.

A team of itinerant Jews traveling from town to town casting out demons planned to experiment by using the name of the Lord Jesus. The incantation they decided on was this: "I adjure you by Jesus, whom Paul preaches, to come out!" Seven sons of Sceva, a Jewish priest, were doing this.

When they tried it on a man possessed by a demon, the demon replied, "I know Jesus and I know Paul, but who are you?" And he leaped on two of them and beat them up so they fled out of his house naked and badly injured!

The story of what happened spread all through Ephesus to Jews and Greeks alike, and a solemn fear descended on the city. Many believers who had been practicing black magic confessed their deeds and brought their incantation books and charms and burned them at a public bonfire. (Someone estimated the value of the books at $10,000.) This indicates how deeply the whole area was stirred by God's message.[14]

SLAVERY; LIBERATION

Dear friends in Rome:

This letter is from Paul, Jesus Christ's slave, sent out to preach God's Good News. This Good News was promised long ago by God's prophets in the Old Testament. It is the Good News about his Son, Jesus Christ our Lord, who came as a human baby, born into King David's royal family line; and by being raised from the dead he was proved to be the mighty Son of God with the holy nature of God himself.

Through Christ, all the kindness of God has been poured upon us, and he is sending us around the world to tell people everywhere the great things God has done for them.

And you, dear friends in Rome, are among those he dearly loves. Wherever I go I hear you being talked about! For your faith in God is becoming known around the world. How I thank God through Jesus Christ for each one of you. Day and night I bring you and your needs in prayer to the one I serve.

And one of the things I keep praying for is the opportunity to see you. I planned to come many times before (but was prevented) so I could work among you.

This Good News about Christ was preached first to the Jews, but now everyone is invited to come to God in this way. As the Scripture says, "The man who finds life will find it through trusting God."

But God shows his anger against evil men who push away the truth, for the truth about God is known to them instinctively. Since earliest times men have seen the earth and sky and all God made, and have known of his existence and eternal power. So they will have no excuse when they stand before God at Judgment Day.

They knew about him but they wouldn't admit it or worship him or thank him for his daily care. Instead of worshiping the glorious, ever-living God, they took wood and stone and made idols for themselves: birds and animals and snakes and puny men. They prayed to the things God made, but wouldn't obey the blessed God who made these things.

That is why God let go of them and let them do evil things, so that women turned against God's natural plan for them and indulged in sex sin with each other. And men, instead of having a normal sex relationship with women, burned with lust for each other, doing shameful things and getting paid in their souls with the penalty they deserved.

So when they gave God up, God gave them up to doing everything their evil minds could think of. Their lives became full of wickedness and sin, greed and hate, envy, murder, fighting, lying, bitterness, and gossip. They were haters of God, insolent, braggarts, and disobedient to parents. They broke their promises and were without pity. They were fully aware of God's death penalty for these crimes, yet they did them anyway and encouraged others to do them.

There is going to come a day when God will be the just Judge of all the world. He will give each one whatever his deeds deserve: eternal life to those who do the will of God, seeking for the eternal life he offers; but he will terribly punish those who fight against the truth and walk in evil ways.

He will punish the heathen when they sin even though they never had God's written laws, for in their hearts God's laws are written. Their conscience accuses them, or sometimes excuses them. And God will punish the Jews for sinning because they have his written laws but don't obey them.

Are we Jews better than others? No, not at all, for all are sinners, whether Jews or Gentiles. As the Scriptures say, "No one is good—no one in all the world is innocent." Every one has gone wrong. No one has kept on doing what is right. All the world stands hushed and guilty before Almighty God.

Now do you see no one can be made right in God's sight by doing what the law commands? For the more we know of God's laws, the clearer it becomes that we aren't obeying them; his laws serve to make us see that we are sinners.

But now God has shown us a different way to heaven—not by "being good enough" but by a new way (though not new, really, for the Scriptures told about it long ago). Now God says he will accept and acquit us—declare us "not guilty"—if we trust Jesus Christ to take away our sins. And we can be saved no matter who we are or what we have been like. Yes, all have sinned; all fall short of God's glorious ideal; yet now God declares us "not guilty" of offending him if we trust in Jesus Christ, who takes away our sins.

For God sent Christ Jesus to take the punishment for

our sins and to end God's anger against us. He used Christ's blood and our faith as the means of saving us from his wrath. Our acquittal is based on what Christ has done and our faith in him.

Does this mean we no longer need obey God's laws? Just the opposite! In fact, only when we trust Jesus can we truly obey him.

Abraham is the father of us all when it comes to the matter of faith. That is what the Scriptures mean when they say God made Abraham the father of many nations. God will accept all people in every nation who trust God as Abraham did.

When Adam sinned, his sin spread death throughout the world so everything began to grow old and die, for all sinned. What a contrast between Adam and Christ who was yet to come! The sin of Adam caused death to be king over all, but all who take God's gift of forgiveness are kings of life because of Jesus Christ. Before, sin ruled over all; now God's kindness rules.

Shall we keep on sinning so God can keep on showing more kindness and forgiveness?

Of course not! Sin's power over us was broken when we became Christians. Do not let any part of your bodies become tools of wickedness, but give yourselves completely to God—for you are back from death and you want to be tools in the hands of God. Thank God that though you once chose to be slaves of sin, now you have obeyed with all your heart the teaching to which God has committed you. The wages of sin is death, but the free gift of God is eternal life through Jesus Christ our Lord.

Understand, dear Jewish brothers in Christ, that when a person dies the law no longer holds him in its power. When a woman marries, the law binds her to her husband as long as he is alive. But if he dies, she can marry someone else if she wants to. Your "husband," your master, used to be the Jewish law; but you "died," as it were, with Christ on the cross; and since you are "dead," you are no longer "married to the law." Then you came back to life again when Christ did, and are a new person. Now you are "married," so to speak, to the one who rose from the dead, so that you can produce good fruit, that is, good deeds for God.

I am rotten so far as my old sinful nature is concerned. I love to do God's will so far as my new nature is concerned. There is something in my lower nature that is at war with my mind, so my new life tells me to do right but the old nature loves to sin. Oh, what a terrible predicament I'm in! Who will free me from slavery to this deadly lower nature? Thank God! It has been done by Jesus Christ our Lord. He has set me free.

So there is now no condemnation awaiting those who belong to Christ Jesus. The power of the life-giving Spirit has freed me from the vicious circle of sin and death; now we can obey God's laws if we follow after the Holy Spirit.

All who are led by the Spirit of God are sons of God. And since we are his children, we will share his treasures— for all God gives to his Son Jesus is now ours too.

But if we are to share his glory, we must also share his suffering. Yet what we suffer now is nothing compared to the glory he will give us later. For all creation is waiting patiently for that future day when God will resurrect his children. On that day thorns and thistles, sin, death, and decay—the things that overcame the world at God's command—will all disappear, and the world around us will share the glorious freedom from sin which God's children enjoy.

For we know that even the things of nature, like animals and plants, suffer in sickness and death as they await this great event. Even we Christians, though we have the Holy Spirit within us as a foretaste of future glory, also groan to be released from pain and suffering. We, too, wait anxiously for that day when God will give us our full rights as his children, including the new bodies he has promised us—bodies that will never be sick again and will never die.

The Holy Spirit helps us with our daily problems and in our praying. For we don't know what we should pray for, nor how to pray as we should; but the Holy Spirit prays for us with such feeling that it cannot be expressed in words. And we know that all that happens to us is working for our good if we love God and are fitting into his plans.

For from the very beginning God decided that those who came to him should become like his Son, so that his Son would be the First, with many brothers. Having chosen us, he called us to come; and when we came he declared us "not guilty," filled us with Christ's goodness, gave us right standing with himself, and promised us his glory.

What can we say to such wonderful things as these? If God is on our side, who can be against us? Since he did not spare even his own Son for us, won't he also give us everything else?

Who then can keep Christ's love from us? When we have trouble or calamity, when we are hunted down or destroyed, is it because he doesn't love us anymore? And if we are hungry, or penniless, or in danger, or threatened with death, has God deserted us?

No, for the Scriptures tell us that for his sake we must be ready to face death at every moment—we are like sheep awaiting slaughter; but despite all this, overwhelming victory is ours through Christ. For I am convinced that nothing can ever separate us from his love. Death can't, and life can't. The angels won't, and all the powers of hell cannot keep God's love away. Our fears for today, our worries about tomorrow, or where we are—high above the sky or in the deepest ocean—nothing will ever be able to separate us from the love of God demonstrated by our Lord Jesus Christ when he died for us.

O Israel, my people, how I long for you to come to Christ! I grieve bitterly day and night because of you. Christ knows I would be willing to be forever damned if that would save you. God took you as his own special people and led you with a bright cloud of glory; he gave you mighty promises; great men of God were your fathers, and Christ himself was one of you—a Jew so far as his human nature is concerned.

Has God failed to fulfill his promises to the Jews? No! For the Scriptures say the promises apply only to Abraham's son Isaac and Isaac's descendants, though Abraham had other children too. For God had promised, "Next year I will give you and Sarah a son." And when Isaac married and Rebecca was about to bear him twin children, God told her Esau, the child born first, would be a servant to Jacob, his twin brother. In the words of Scripture, "I chose to bless Jacob." That proves God was doing what he had decided from the beginning; it was not because of what the children did.

Was God being unfair? Of course not. For God had said to Moses, "If I want to be kind to someone, I will." Pharaoh, king of Egypt, was an example of this. For God told him he had given him the kingdom of Egypt for the purpose of displaying the awesome power of God against him. So God is kind to some because he wants to be.

When a man makes a jar of clay, doesn't he have a right to use the same lump of clay to make one jar beautiful to hold flowers, and another to throw garbage into? Does not God have a perfect right to show his fury against those who are fit for destruction—those he has been patient with for all this time? And he has a right to take others who have been made for pouring the riches of his glory into, whether Jews or Gentiles, and to be kind so everyone can see his glory.

What shall we say about these things? God has given Gentiles the opportunity to be acquitted by faith, even though they had not been really seeking God. But Jews, who tried so hard to get right with God by keeping his laws, never succeeded. Instead of depending on faith they have stumbled over the great stumbling stone; God warned them, "I have put a Rock in the path of the Jews, and many will stumble over him (Jesus)."

I know what enthusiasm they have for the honor of God but it is misdirected zeal. They don't understand that Christ gives to those who trust in him everything they are trying to get by keeping his laws.

Salvation from Christ is as near as our own hearts and mouths. For if you tell others that Jesus Christ is your Lord and believe in your heart that God has raised him from the dead, you will be saved. Anyone who calls upon the name of the Lord will be saved.

But how shall they ask him to save them unless they believe in him? And how can they believe in him if they have never heard about him? And how can they hear unless someone tells them? That is what the Scriptures are talking about when they say, "How beautiful are the feet of those who preach the Gospel of peace with God."

But not everyone who hears the Good News has welcomed it, for Isaiah said, "Lord, who has believed me when I told them?"

Then has God rejected the Jews? Oh no; remember that I am a descendant of Abraham and a member of Benjamin's family. Elijah the prophet claimed that he was the only one left who still loved God, and God said, "No, I have seven thousand others who have not bowed down to idols!"

It is the same today. Not all the Jews have turned away from God. When God turned away from them, he turned to the rest of the world to offer his salvation; and now it is even more wonderful when the Jews come to Christ. Notice how God is both kind and severe: he is very hard on those who disobey, but very good to you if you love and trust him.

Some Jews have set themselves against the Gospel now, but this will last only until you Gentiles have come to Christ—those of you who will—and then all Israel will be saved.

Do you remember what the prophets said about this? "There shall come out of Zion a Deliverer and he shall turn the Jews from all ungodliness. At that time I will take away their sins, just as I promised." The Jews are still beloved of God because of his promises to Abraham, Isaac, and Jacob. For God's gifts and his call can never be withdrawn; he will never go back on his promises. Once you were rebels against God—now the Jews are rebels; God has given all up to sin so he could have mercy upon all.

Oh, how great are his wisdom and knowledge and riches! How impossible it is for us to understand his decisions, for who among us can know the mind of the Lord? Everything comes from God, everything lives by his power, and everything is for his glory.

And so, dear brothers, I plead with you to give your bodies to God—let them be a living sacrifice. Don't copy

the behavior of this world but be a new person in all you
do and think. Then you will learn from experience how
his ways really satisfy you.

Obey the government, for God put it there. The police-
man does not frighten people who are doing right, but
those doing evil. Keep the laws and you will get along
well.

Pay your taxes too, for government workers need to
be paid so they can keep on serving you. Pay all your
debts except the debt of love for others—never finish paying
that!

If you love your neighbor as you love yourself, you will
not want to harm or cheat him or do anything else the
Ten Commandments say is wrong.

I know you know these things so well that you are able
to teach others about them. But I have been bold enough
to emphasize some of these points for I am by God's grace
a special messenger from Jesus Christ to you Gentiles. I
have preached the Gospel of Christ from Jerusalem over
into Illyricum. But my ambition has been to go still farther.
I have been following the plan in the Scriptures where
Isaiah says that those who have never heard the name of
Christ will see and understand. That is the reason I have
been so long in coming to visit you.

Now at last I am through with my work here and I
am planning to take a trip to Spain, and when I do I will
stop off in Rome. Before I come, I must go to Jerusalem
to take a gift to the Jewish Christians there. For the Christians in Macedonia and Achaia have taken up an offering
for those in Jerusalem who are going through hard times.
As soon as I have delivered this money I will come to
see you on my way to Spain.

Will you be my prayer partners? Pray with me for my
work. Pray that I will be protected in Jerusalem. Then I
will come to you with a happy heart and we can refresh
each other.

I commit you to God who is able to make you strong
in the Lord. To God, who alone is wise, be glory forever
through Jesus Christ our Lord. Amen.

                                        Sincerely, Paul[15]

FINAL TREK

Paul felt impelled to go across to Greece before returning to Jerusalem. "And after that," he said, "I must go on to Rome!" He sent his two assistants, Timothy and Erastus, on ahead to Greece while he stayed awhile longer in Turkey.

About that time a big blowup developed in Ephesus concerning the Christians. It began with Demetrius, a silversmith who employed many craftsmen to manufacture silver shrines of the Greek goddess Diana. He called a meeting of his men together with others employed in related trades and addressed them as follows:

"Gentlemen, this business is our income. As you know, this man Paul has persuaded many people that handmade gods aren't gods at all. As a result, our sales volume is going down! This trend is evident not only here in Ephesus but throughout the entire province! I am talking not only about our loss of income, but also of the possibility that the temple of the great goddess Diana will lose its influence, and that Diana—this magnificent goddess worshiped not only throughout Turkey but all around the world—will be forgotten!"

At this their anger boiled; they began shouting, "Great is Diana of the Ephesians!" A crowd began to gather and soon the city was filled with confusion. Everyone rushed to the amphitheater, dragging along Gaius and Aristarchus, Paul's companions, for trial. Paul wanted to go in, but the disciples wouldn't let him. Some Roman officers of the province, friends of Paul, also sent a message to him, begging him not to risk his life by entering.

Inside, the people were all shouting; everything was in confusion. At last the mayor was able to quiet them enough to speak. "Men of Ephesus," he said, "everyone knows that Ephesus is the center of the religion of the great Diana, whose image fell down to us from heaven. Since this is an indisputable fact, you shouldn't be disturbed no matter what is said, and should do nothing rash. You have brought these men here who have stolen nothing from her temple and have not defamed her. If Demetrius and the craftsmen have a case against them, the judges can take the case at once. Go through legal channels. And if there are complaints about other matters, they can be settled at the regular City Council meetings; for we are in danger of being called to account by the Roman government for today's riot. And if Rome demands an explanation, I won't know what to say." Then he dismissed them, and they dispersed.

When it was over, Paul sent for the disciples, preached a farewell message to them, and left for Greece. He was in Greece three months and was preparing to sail for Syria when he discovered a plot by Jews against his life, so he decided to go north to Macedonia first. Several men were traveling with him as far as Turkey.

We boarded ship at Philippi in northern Greece and arrived five days later in Troas, Turkey, where we stayed a week. On Sunday we gathered for a communion service, with Paul preaching. Since he was leaving the next day, he talked until midnight! The upstairs room where we met was lighted with many flickering lamps, and as Paul spoke on and on a young man named Eutychus, sitting on the windowsill, went fast asleep and fell three stories to his death below.

Paul went down and took him into his arms. "Don't worry," he said, "he's all right!" And he was! A wave of awesome joy swept through the crowd! They all went back upstairs and ate the Lord's Supper together; then Paul preached another long sermon—so it was dawn when he finally left them!

Paul had decided against stopping at Ephesus this time as he was hurrying to get to Jerusalem for the celebration of Pentecost. But when we landed at Miletus he sent a message to the elders of the church at Ephesus to come to the boat to meet him.

When they arrived he told them, "You men know that from the day I set foot in Turkey until now I have done the Lord's work and faced danger from plots against my life. Yet I never shrank from telling you the truth either publicly or in your homes. I have one message for Jews and Gentiles alike—the necessity of turning from sin to God through faith in our Lord Jesus Christ.

"Now I am going to Jerusalem, drawn there irresistibly

by the Holy Spirit, not knowing what awaits me except the Spirit has told me that jail and suffering lie ahead. But life is worth nothing unless I do the work assigned me by the Lord.

"And now I know that none of you will ever see me again. Beware! Be sure that you shepherd God's flock—his church—for the Holy Spirit is holding you responsible as overseers. I know that after I leave you, false teachers, like vicious wolves, will appear among you. Some of you will distort the truth in order to draw a following. Watch out!

"Now I entrust you to God and to his wonderful words which are able to build your faith and give you the inheritance of those set apart for himself."

When he finished speaking, he knelt and prayed with them. They wept as they embraced him in farewell, sorrowing most of all because he said he would never see them again. Then they accompanied him down to the ship.

After parting, we sailed straight to Cos. The next day we reached Rhodes and then went to Patara. There we boarded a ship sailing for the Syrian province of Phoenicia. We sighted the island of Cyprus, passed it on our left, and landed at the harbor of Tyre, where the ship unloaded. We went ashore, found the local believers, and stayed with them a week.

The next stop was Ptolemais where we greeted the believers, but stayed only one day. Then we went on to Caesarea and stayed at the home of Philip the Evangelist, one of the first seven deacons. He had four unmarried daughters who had the gift of prophecy.

During our stay a man named Agabus, who also had the gift of prophecy, visited us. He took Paul's belt, bound his own feet and hands with it, and said, "The Holy Spirit declares, 'So shall the owner of this belt be bound by the Jews in Jerusalem and turned over to the Romans.'" Hearing this, all of us begged Paul not to go on.

But he said, "Why all this weeping? I am ready not only to be jailed at Jerusalem, but also to die for the sake of the Lord Jesus." When it was clear he wouldn't be dissuaded, we gave up.[16]

JERUSALEM ORDEAL

Shortly afterwards we packed our things and left for Jerusalem. On arrival we were guests at the home of Mnason, one of the early believers from Cyprus. All the believers at Jerusalem welcomed us cordially.

The second day, Paul took us with him to meet with James and the elders of the Jerusalem church. After greetings were exchanged, Paul recounted the many things God had accomplished among the Gentiles through his work.

They praised God but then said, "You know, dear brother, how many thousands of Jews have also believed, and they are all very insistent that Jewish believers must continue to follow the Jewish traditions and customs. Our Jewish Christians here have been told you are against the laws of Moses, against our Jewish customs, and that you forbid the circumcision of their children. Now what can be done?

"We suggest this: we have four men who are preparing to shave their heads and take some vows. Go with them to the Temple and have your head shaved too. Then everyone will know you approve of this custom for the Hebrew Christians and that you yourself obey the Jewish laws. As for the Gentile Christians, we aren't asking them to follow these Jewish customs—except for the ones we wrote to them about."

Paul agreed to their request, and the next day went with the men to the Temple for the ceremony, thus publicizing his vow to offer a sacrifice seven days later with the others. The seven days were almost ended when some Jews from Turkey saw him in the Temple and roused a mob against him. They grabbed him, yelling, "Men of Israel! Help! This is the man who preaches against our people and tells everybody to disobey the Jewish laws."

The city was electrified by these accusations, and a riot followed. Paul was dragged out of the Temple and the gates were closed behind him. As they were killing him, word reached the commander of the Roman garrison that Jerusalem was in an uproar. He ordered out his soldiers and ran down among the crowd. When the mob saw the troops coming, they quit beating Paul. The commander arrested him and ordered him bound with double chains. When he couldn't find out anything in the confusion, he ordered Paul taken to the armory.

As Paul was about to be taken inside, he said to the commander, "May I have a word with you?"

"Do you know Greek?" the commander asked, surprised. "Aren't you that Egyptian who led a rebellion a few years ago and took 4,000 of the Assassins into the desert?"

"No," Paul replied, "I am a Jew from Tarsus in Cilicia. I request permission to talk to these people."

The commander agreed, so Paul stood on the stairs and motioned to the people to be quiet. A deep silence enveloped the crowd and he addressed them in Hebrew.

"Brothers and fathers, listen to me as I offer my defense. I am a Jew born in Tarsus but educated here in Jerusalem under Gamaliel, at whose feet I learned to follow our Jewish laws and customs very carefully. I became very anxious to honor God in everything I did, just as you have tried to do today. And I persecuted the Christians, binding and delivering both men and women to prison. The High Priest or any member of the Council can testify that this is so. I asked them for letters to the Jewish leaders in Damascus, with instructions to let me bring any Christians I found to Jerusalem in chains to be punished.

"As I was on the road, nearing Damascus, suddenly a very bright light from heaven shone around me. I fell to the ground and heard a voice saying to me, 'Why are you persecuting me? I am Jesus of Nazareth.'

"And I said, 'What shall I do, Lord?' And the Lord told me, 'Get up and go into Damascus, and there you will be told what awaits you in the years ahead.'

"I was blinded by the intense light and had to be led into Damascus by my companions. There a man named Ananias, as godly a man as you could find for obeying the law, came to me and said, 'Brother Paul, receive your sight!'

"Then he told me, 'The God of our fathers has chosen you to see the Messiah and hear him speak. You are to take his message everywhere, telling what you have seen and heard.'

"One day after my return to Jerusalem, while I was praying in the Temple, I fell into a trance and saw a vision of God saying to me, 'Hurry! Leave Jerusalem, for the people here won't believe you when you give them my message. I will send you away to the Gentiles!'"

The crowd listened until Paul came to that word, then they shouted, "Away with such a fellow! He isn't fit to live!"

The commander brought him inside and ordered him lashed to make him confess his crime. As they tied Paul down to lash him, Paul said to an officer, "Is it legal for you to whip a Roman citizen who hasn't been tried?"

The officer went to the commander and asked, "What are you doing? This man is a Roman citizen!"

The soldiers standing ready to lash him disappeared when they heard Paul was a Roman citizen, and the commander was frightened. The next day the commander freed him and ordered the chief priests into session with the Jewish Council. He had Paul brought before them to try to find out what the trouble was all about.

Gazing intently at the Council, Paul began: "Brothers, I have always lived before God in good conscience!"

Instantly Ananias the High Priest commanded those close to Paul to slap him on the mouth.

Paul said to him, "God shall slap you, you whitewashed pigpen. What kind of judge are you to break the law by ordering me struck like that?"

Those standing near Paul said to him, "Is that the way to talk to God's High Priest?"

"I didn't realize he was the High Priest," Paul replied, "for the Scriptures say, 'Never speak evil of your rulers.'"

Then Paul thought of something! Part of the Council were Sadducees and part were Pharisees! So he shouted, "Brothers, I am a Pharisee, as were all my ancestors! And I am being tried today because I believe in the resurrection of the dead!"

This divided the Council—for the Sadducees say there is no resurrection or angels or even eternal spirit, but the Pharisees believe in all of these.

So a clamor arose. Some of the Jewish leaders jumped

up to argue that Paul was right. "We see nothing wrong with him," they shouted. The shouting grew louder, and men were tugging at Paul from both sides. Finally the commander, fearing they would tear him apart, ordered soldiers to take him back to the armory.

That night the Lord stood beside Paul and said, "Don't worry, Paul; just as you have told the people about me here in Jerusalem, so you must also in Rome."

The next morning some forty or more Jews got together and bound themselves by a curse neither to eat nor drink until they had killed Paul! Then they went to the chief priests and elders and told them what they had done. "Ask the commander to bring Paul back to the Council again," they requested. "Pretend you want to ask a few more questions—we will kill him on the way."

But Paul's nephew got wind of their plan and came to the armory and told Paul. Paul called one of the officers and said, "Take this boy to the commander. He has something important to tell him."

The commander took the boy aside and asked, "What is it you want to tell me, lad?"

"Tomorrow," he told him, "the Jews are going to ask you to bring Paul before the Council again, pretending they want to get more information. But there are more than forty men hiding along the road ready to jump him and kill him. They are out there now, expecting you to agree to their request."

"Don't let a soul know you told me this," the commander warned. Then the commander ordered, "Get 200 soldiers ready to leave for Caesarea at nine o'clock tonight! Take 200 spearmen and 70 mounted cavalry. Give Paul a horse to ride and get him safely to Governor Felix."

Then he wrote this letter to the governor:

"From: Claudius Lysias

"To: His Excellency, Governor Felix.

"Greetings!

"This man was seized by the Jews and they were killing him when I sent soldiers to rescue him, for I learned that he was a Roman citizen. Then I took him to their Council to try to find out what he had done. I soon discovered it was something about their Jewish beliefs, certainly nothing worthy of imprisonment or death. But when I was informed of a plot to kill him, I decided to send him to you and will tell his accusers to bring their charges before you."

That night, as ordered, the soldiers took Paul to Antipatris, leaving him with the cavalry to take him on to Caesarea. When they arrived in Caesarea, they presented Paul and the letter to the governor. "I will hear your case fully when your accusers arrive," the governor told him, and ordered him kept in the prison at King Herod's palace.

Five days later Ananias the High Priest arrived with some of the Jewish leaders and the lawyer Tertullus to make their accusations against Paul. Tertullus laid charges against Paul in the following address:

"Your Excellency, you have given quietness and peace to us Jews and have greatly reduced the discrimination against us. And for this we are very grateful. But lest I bore you, kindly give me your attention as I briefly outline our case against this man. We have found him to be a troublemaker who is constantly inciting the Jews throughout the world to rebellions against the Roman government. He is a ringleader of the sect known as the Nazarenes. Moreover, he was trying to defile the Temple when we arrested him. We would have given him what he justly deserves, but Lysias, the commander of the garrison, took him away from us, demanding that he be tried by Roman law."

Then all the other Jews chimed in, declaring that everything Tertullus said was true.

Now it was Paul's turn. The governor motioned for him to rise and speak.

Paul began: "I know, sir, that you have been a judge of Jewish affairs for many years, and this gives me confidence as I make my defense. You can discover that it was no more than twelve days ago that I arrived in Jerusalem to worship at the Temple, and you will discover that I have never incited a riot in any synagogue or on the streets of any city. These men certainly cannot prove the things they accuse me of doing.

"But one thing I do confess, that I believe in the way of salvation which they refer to as a sect; I follow that system of serving the God of our ancestors; I firmly believe in the Jewish law and everything written in the books of prophecy; and I believe, just as these men do, that there will be a resurrection of both the righteous and ungodly. Because of this I try with all my strength to always maintain a clear conscience before God and man.

"After several years away, I returned to Jerusalem with money to aid the Jews and to offer a sacrifice to God. My accusers saw me in the Temple as I was presenting my thank offering. I had shaved my head as their laws required, and there was no crowd around me and no rioting! But some Jews from Turkey were there—but ask these men what wrongdoing their Council found in me."

Felix, who knew Christians didn't go around starting riots, told the Jews to wait for the arrival of Lysias, and then he would decide the case. He ordered Paul to prison but instructed the guards to treat him gently.

A few days later Felix came with Drusilla his wife, a Jewess. Sending for Paul, they listened as he told them about faith in Christ Jesus. And as he reasoned with them about righteousness and self-control and the judgment to come, Felix was terrified. "Go away for now," he replied, "and when I have a more convenient time, I'll call for you."

He hoped Paul would bribe him, so he sent for him from time to time and talked with him. Two years went by in this way; then Felix was succeeded by Porcius Festus.

Three days after Festus arrived, he left for Jerusalem where the priests and other leaders gave him their story about Paul. They begged him to bring Paul to Jerusalem, but Festus replied that since he was returning soon, those with authority in this affair should return with him for the trial. He returned to Caesarea and the following day opened Paul's trial.

On Paul's arrival in court, the Jews from Jerusalem gathered around, hurling many serious accusations. Paul denied the charges: "I am not guilty," he said. "I have not opposed the Jewish laws or desecrated the Temple or rebelled against the Roman government."

Festus, anxious to please the Jews, asked him, "Are you willing to go to Jerusalem and stand trial before me?"

Paul replied, "No! I demand my privilege of a hearing before the Emperor himself. You know I am not guilty. If I have done something worthy of death, I don't refuse to die! But if I am innocent, neither you nor anyone else has a right to turn me over to these men to kill me. I appeal to Caesar."

Festus conferred with his advisors and then replied, "Very well! You have appealed to Caesar, and to Caesar you shall go!"[17]

APOSTLE TO ROME

Arrangements were made to start us on our way to Rome by ship; Paul and several other prisoners were placed in the custody of an officer named Julius, a member of the imperial guard. We left on a boat which was scheduled to make several stops along the Turkish coast.

The next day when we docked at Sidon, Julius was kind to Paul and let him go ashore to visit with friends. Putting to sea from there, we sailed north of Cyprus and passed along the coast of the provinces of Cilicia and Pamphylia, landing at Myra. There our officer found an Egyptian ship from Alexandria, bound for Italy, and put us aboard.

We had several days of rough sailing and finally neared Cnidus, but the winds had become too strong so we ran across to Crete. Beating into the wind with great difficulty and moving slowly along the southern coast, we arrived at Fair Havens. There we stayed for several days. The weather was becoming dangerous for long voyages because it was late in the year, and Paul spoke to the officers about it.

"Sirs," he said, "I believe there is trouble ahead if we go on—perhaps shipwreck, loss of cargo, injuries, and death."

But the officers in charge of the prisoners listened more to the ship's captain and the owner than to Paul. And since Fair Havens was an exposed harbor—a poor place to spend the winter—most of the crew advised trying to go farther up the coast to Phoenix.

Just then a light wind began blowing from the south

and it looked like a perfect day for the trip. So they pulled up anchor and sailed along close to shore. But shortly the weather changed abruptly and a wind of typhoon strength caught the ship and blew it out to sea. They tried at first to face back to shore but couldn't, so they gave up and let the ship run before the gale.

We finally sailed behind a small island where with great difficulty we hoisted aboard the lifeboat that was being towed behind us and then banded the ship with ropes to strengthen the hull. The sailors were afraid of being driven across to the quicksands of the African coast, so they lowered the topsails and were thus driven before the wind.

The next day as the seas grew higher the crew began throwing cargo overboard. The following day they threw out the tackle and anything else they could lay their hands on. The terrible storm raged unabated many days, until at last all hope was gone.

No one had eaten for a long time, but finally Paul called the crew together and said, "Men, you should have listened to me and not left Fair Havens, but cheer up! Not one of us will lose our lives, even though the ship will go down. For last night an angel of the God to whom I belong stood beside me and said, 'Don't be afraid, Paul—for you will surely stand trial before Caesar! What's more, God has granted your request and will save the lives of all those sailing with you.' So take courage! It will be just as he said! But we will be shipwrecked on an island."

About midnight on the fourteenth night of the storm the sailors suspected land was near. They sounded, and found 120 feet of water below them. A little later they sounded again and found only ninety feet. At this rate they knew they would soon be driven ashore, and fearing rocks along the coast they threw out four anchors from the stern.

Some of the sailors planned to abandon the ship and lowered the emergency boat as though they were going to put out anchors from the prow. But Paul said to the soldiers and commanding officer, "You will all die unless everyone stays aboard." So the soldiers cut the ropes and let the boat fall off.

As darkness gave way to early morning light, Paul begged

everyone to eat. "Please eat something now for your own good! For not a hair of your heads shall perish!"

Then he took some hardtack and gave thanks to God before them all, and broke off a piece and ate it. Suddenly everyone felt better and began eating, all two hundred seventy-six of us. After eating, the crew lightened the ship further by throwing all the wheat overboard.

When it was day, they didn't recognize the coastline but noticed a bay with a beach and wondered whether they could get between the rocks and be driven up onto the beach. Cutting off the anchors and leaving them in the sea, they lowered the rudders, raised the foresail, and headed ashore. But the ship hit a sandbar and ran aground. The bow of the ship stuck fast, while the stern was exposed to the violence of the waves and began to break apart.

The soldiers advised their commanding officer to let them kill the prisoners lest any of them swim ashore and escape. But Julius wanted to spare Paul, so he told them no. Then he ordered all who could swim to jump overboard and make for land, and the rest to try for it on planks and debris from the broken ship. So everyone escaped safely ashore!

We soon learned we were on the island of Malta. The people of the island were very kind to us, building a bonfire on the beach to welcome and warm us in the rain and cold. As Paul gathered an armful of sticks to lay on the fire, a poisonous snake fastened itself onto his hand! The people of the island saw it and said to each other, "A murderer, no doubt! Though he escaped the sea, justice will not permit him to live!"

But Paul shook off the snake into the fire and was unharmed. The people waited for him to begin swelling or suddenly fall dead; but when no harm came to him they decided he was a god.

Near where we landed was an estate belonging to Publius, governor of the island. He welcomed us and fed us for three days. Publius' father was ill with fever and dysentery. Paul went in and prayed for him, and laying his hands on him healed him! Then other sick people in the island came and were cured. As a result we were showered with gifts, and when the time came to sail, people put on board all sorts of things we would need for the trip.

Three months after the shipwreck we set sail again, and this time it was in *The Twin Brothers* of Alexandria, a ship that had wintered at the island. Our first stop was Syracuse, where we stayed three days. From there we circled around to Rhegium; a day later a south wind began blowing, so the following day we arrived at Puteoli, where we found some believers! They begged us to stay with them seven days. Then we went on to Rome.

The brothers in Rome had heard we were coming and came to meet us at the Forum on the Appian Way. Others joined us at The Three Taverns. When Paul saw them, he thanked God and took courage.

When we arrived in Rome, Paul was permitted to live wherever he wanted to, though guarded by a soldier. Three days after his arrival, he called together the local Jewish leaders and spoke to them as follows:

"Brothers, I was arrested by the Jews in Jerusalem and handed over to the Roman government for prosecution, even though I had harmed no one nor violated the customs of our ancestors. The Romans gave me a trial and wanted to release me, for they found no cause for the death sentence demanded by the Jewish leaders. But when the Jews protested the decision, I felt it necessary, with no malice against them, to appeal to Caesar. I asked you to come here today so we could get acquainted and I could tell you that it is because I believe the Messiah has come that I am bound with this chain."

They replied, "We have heard nothing against you! We want to hear what you believe, for the only thing we know about these Christians is that they are denounced everywhere!"

So a time was set, and on that day large numbers came to his house. He told them about the Kingdom of God and taught them about Jesus from the Scriptures—from the five books of Moses and the books of prophecy. He began lecturing in the morning and went on into the evening! Some believed, and some didn't.

Paul lived for the next two years in his rented house

and welcomed all who visited him, telling them with all boldness about the Kingdom of God and the Lord Jesus Christ. And no one tried to stop him.[18]

FAMILY OF LOVE

Dear Christian friends at Ephesus: this is Paul writing to you.

How we praise God who has blessed us with every blessing in heaven because we belong to Christ. Long ago, even before he made the world, God chose us to be his very own through what Christ would do for us. He decided then to make us holy in his eyes—we who stand before him covered with his love. His unchanging plan has been to adopt us into his family.

God has told us his reason for sending Christ—a plan he decided on long ago—that when the time is ripe he will gather us from wherever we are, in heaven or on earth, to be with him forever.

Because of what Christ did, all you who heard the Good News and trusted Christ were marked by the Holy Spirit as belonging to Christ; his presence within us is God's guarantee that he will give us all that he promised; and the Spirit's seal upon us means that God has already purchased us.

Ever since I heard of your strong faith in the Lord Jesus and of the love you have for Christians, I have never stopped thanking God for you. I pray for you, asking God to give you wisdom to really understand who Christ is and all he has done for you. I pray that your hearts will be flooded with light so that you can see something of the future he has called you to share. I pray that you will begin to understand how incredibly great his power is to help those who believe him. It is that same mighty power that raised Christ from the dead and seated him in the place of honor at God's right hand far above any other king or ruler or leader. His honor is far more glorious than that of anyone else in this world or in the world to come. And God has made him the supreme Head of the church—which is his body, filled with himself, the Author and Giver of everything everywhere.

E.J q Chp 1

Once you were under God's curse, doomed for your sins. You were just like others obeying Satan, the mighty prince of the power of the air who is at work right now in the hearts of those who are against the Lord. All of us started out bad, being born with evil natures.

But God is so rich in mercy: he loved us so much that though we were spiritually dead and doomed by our sins, he gave us back our lives when he raised Christ from the dead and lifted us from the grave into glory along with Christ—where we sit with him in the heavenly realms.

You have been saved through trusting Christ, and even trusting is not of yourselves—it too is a gift from God. Salvation is not a reward for the good we have done, so none of us can take any credit for it.

Christ has made peace between us Jews and you Gentiles by making us all one family, breaking down the wall of contempt that used to separate us. As parts of the same body, our anger against each other has disappeared for both of us have been reconciled to God. Now all of us, whether Jews or Gentiles, may come to God the Father with the Holy Spirit's help because of what Christ has done for us.

What a foundation you stand on now: the apostles and the prophets; and the cornerstone of the building is Jesus Christ himself! We who believe are joined with him and with each other by the Spirit, and are part of this dwelling place of God.

I, Paul, am in jail for preaching that you Gentiles are a part of God's house. God himself showed me that the Gentiles will have their full share with the Jews in all the riches inherited by God's sons; both are invited to belong to his church, and God's promises of mighty blessings through Christ apply to both when they accept the Good News about Christ. God has given me the privilege of telling everyone about this plan.

When I think of the wisdom and scope of his plan, I fall down on my knees and pray to the Father of all the great family of God—some of them already in heaven and some down here on earth—that out of his glorious, unlimited resources he will give you the mighty inner strengthening of his Holy Spirit. And I pray that Christ will be more and more at home in your hearts as you trust in him. May your roots go down deep into the soil of God's marvelous love; and may you be able to feel and understand, as all God's children should, how long, how wide, how deep, and how high his love really is, though it is so great that you will never see the end of it or fully know or understand it. And at last you will be filled up with God himself!

Glory be to God who by his mighty power within us is able to do far more than we would ever dare ask or even dream of—infinitely beyond our highest prayers, desires, thoughts, or hopes!

I beg you to act in a way worthy of those who have been chosen for such wonderful blessings as these. Be humble and gentle. Be patient with each other, making allowance for each other's faults because of your love. Try always to be led along together by the Holy Spirit, and so be at peace with one another.

We have the same Spirit; there is only one Lord, one faith, one baptism; and we all have the same Father who is over all and in us all.

Christ has given each of us special abilities—whatever he wants us to have out of his rich storehouse of gifts. The Psalmist tells about this, for he says that when Christ returned triumphantly to heaven after his resurrection and victory over Satan he gave generous gifts to men. Notice that it says he returned to heaven. This means that he had first come down from the heights of heaven to the lowest parts of the earth. The one who came down is the one who went back up, that he might fill all things with himself.

Why is it that he gives these special abilities? It is that God's people will be equipped to work for him, building up the church—the body of Christ—to strength and maturity until finally we become full-grown in the Lord—yes, to the point of being filled full with Christ. Under his direction the whole body is fitted together perfectly, and each part in its own special way helps the other parts so that the whole body is healthy and growing and full of love.

If you have really learned the truths concerning him,

throw off your old nature—the you that was a partner in evil ways. You must be a new person—clothe yourself with this new nature.

Stop lying; tell the truth. If you are angry, don't sin by nursing your grudge. If anyone is stealing, he must stop it and begin using those hands for honest work so he can give to others in need. Don't use bad language; say only what is good and helpful and what will give a blessing. Stop being mean; quarreling, harsh words, and dislike of others should have no place in your lives. Instead, be kind to each other, tenderhearted, forgiving one another, just as God has forgiven you because you belong to Christ.

You can be sure of this: the Kingdom of Christ and of God will never belong to anyone who is impure or greedy, for a greedy person loves the good things of this life more than God. Don't be fooled by those who try to excuse these sins.

Take no part in the worthless pleasures of evil, but instead rebuke and expose them. It would be shameful even to mention those pleasures of darkness which the ungodly do. But when you expose them and they see how wrong they are, some of them may become children of light! That is why God says in the Scriptures, "Awake, O sleeper, and rise up from the dead; and Christ shall give you light."

Don't drink much wine; be filled instead with the Holy Spirit and controlled by him. Talk with each other about the Lord, quoting psalms and hymns and singing sacred songs, making music in your hearts to the Lord. Always give thanks for everything to our God in the name of our Lord Jesus Christ.

Honor Christ by submitting to each other. You wives must submit to your husbands' leadership in the same way you submit to the Lord. For a husband is in charge of his wife in the same way Christ is in charge of the church.

And you husbands, show the same kind of love to your wives as Christ showed to the church when he died for her. Since a man and his wife are one, a man is doing himself a favor when he loves his wife! No one hates his own body but lovingly cares for it, just as Christ cares for his body the church.

Children, obey your parents; this is right because God has placed them in authority over you. "Honor your father and mother" is the first of God's Ten Commandments that ends with a promise: a long life full of blessing.

Now a word to you parents. Don't keep on scolding and nagging your children, making them angry and resentful. Rather, bring them up with the loving discipline the Lord himself approves, with suggestions and godly advice.

Slaves, obey your masters; be eager to give them your very best. Serve them as you would Christ. Don't work hard only when your master is watching and then shirk when he isn't looking. Remember, the Lord will pay you for each good thing you do, whether you are slave or free.

And you slave owners must treat your slaves right. Don't keep threatening them; remember, you yourselves are slaves to Christ; you have the same Master they do, and he has no favorites.

Last of all I want to remind you: put on all of God's armor so that you will be able to stand safe against all strategies and tricks of Satan. For we are not fighting against people made of flesh and blood, but against persons without bodies—the evil rulers of the unseen world, those mighty satanic beings and great princes of darkness who rule this world, and against huge numbers of wicked spirits in the spirit world. So use every piece of God's armor to resist the enemy.

To do this, you will need the strong belt of truth and the breastplate of God's approval; wear shoes that are able to speed you on as you preach the Good News of peace with God; in every battle you will need faith as your shield to stop the fiery arrows aimed at you by Satan; and you will need the helmet of salvation and the sword of the Spirit—which is the Word of God.

Pray all the time. Ask God for anything in line with the Holy Spirit's wishes. Remind him of your needs, and keep praying earnestly for all Christians everywhere. Pray for me, too, that I will keep on speaking out boldly even here in prison.

May God give peace to you, my Christian brothers, and

love with faith from God and the Lord Jesus Christ.

Sincerely, Paul[19]

INCOMPARABLE CHRIST

From: Paul, and from Brother Timothy.

To: The faithful Christian brothers in the city of Colosse.

May God our Father shower you with blessings and fill you with his great peace. We have heard how much you are looking forward to the joys of heaven and have been ever since the Gospel was preached to you. Epaphras, our much-loved fellow worker, brought you this Good News; he is Jesus Christ's faithful slave.

We pray that you will be filled with strength so you can keep going no matter what happens, always full of the joy of the Lord and always thankful to the Father who made us fit to share the wonderful things that belong to the Kingdom of light. For he has rescued us out of the gloom of Satan's kingdom and brought us into the Kingdom of his dear Son!

Christ is the exact likeness of the unseen God; he existed before God made anything at all, and, in fact, Christ is the Creator who made everything in heaven and earth, the things we can see and the things we can't; the spirit world with its kings and kingdoms, its rulers and authorities— all were made by Christ. He was before all else began and his power holds everything together. He is first in everything, for God wanted all of himself to be in his Son.

Through what his Son did, God cleared a path for everything to come to him—Christ's death on the cross has made peace with God. As a result, Christ has brought you into the very presence of God, and you are there with nothing left against you that he could chide you for. The only condition is that you fully believe the Truth, standing strong in the Lord, and never shifting from trusting him. This is the wonderful news that is now spreading all over the world! And I, Paul, have the joy of telling it to others.

But part of my work is to suffer, and I am glad, for I am helping to finish up the remainder of Christ's sufferings for his church. I can do it because Christ's mighty energy is at work within me.

I wish you could know how I have struggled in prayer for you, for the church at Laodicea, and for my other friends who have never known me personally. I have asked God that you will be knit together by strong ties of love and you will have the rich experience of knowing Christ with certainty and understanding. For God's secret plan—now at last made known—is Christ himself. In him lie hidden all the mighty, untapped treasures of wisdom and knowledge.

Just as you trusted Christ to save you, trust him, too, for each day's problems. Live in vital union with him—let your roots grow down into him and draw up nourishment from him. Go on growing in the Lord and become vigorous in the truth you were taught. Let your lives overflow with thanksgiving for all he has done.

Don't let others spoil your faith with their philosophies—their shallow answers built on men's ideas instead of what Christ has said. For in Christ there is all of God in a human body; you have everything when you have Christ.

Since you became alive again, so to speak, when Christ arose from the dead, set your sights on the rich treasures of heaven where he sits beside God in the place of honor. Your real life is in heaven with Christ and God, and when Christ who is our real life comes back again you will shine with him and share in his glories.

You are living a brand new kind of life—continually learning more of what is right and trying constantly to be more like Christ who created this new life within you. In this new life, one's nationality or race or education or social position is unimportant; such things mean nothing. Whether a person has Christ is what matters, and he is equally available to all.

Since you have been chosen by God who has given you this new life, and because of his deep love for you, you should practice tenderhearted mercy and kindness to others. Don't worry about making a good impression on them, but be ready to suffer quietly and patiently. Be gentle and ready to forgive; never hold grudges. Remember, the Lord forgave you so you must forgive others.

Most of all, let love guide your life, for then the whole church will stay together in perfect harmony. Let the peace which comes from Christ be always present in your hearts. And always be thankful. Remember what Christ taught and let his words enrich your lives and make you wise. Whatever you do or say, let it be as a representative of the Lord Jesus.

Tychicus, our much loved brother, will tell you how I am getting along. I have sent him on this special trip to see how you are and to encourage you.

Aristarchus, who is with me here as a prisoner, sends you his love; and so does Mark, a relative of Barnabas. Give Mark a hearty welcome if he comes your way.

Dear doctor Luke sends his love. By the way, after you have read this letter will you pass it on to the church at Laodicea?

Remember me here in jail. May God's blessings surround you.

Sincerely, Paul[20]

IN LIFE AND DEATH

From: Paul and Timothy, slaves of Jesus Christ. To: The pastors and deacons and all the Christians in Philippi.

May God bless you all. I am sure that God who began the good work within you will keep on helping you grow in grace until his task within you is finished on that day when Jesus Christ returns.

You have a very special place in my heart: we have shared the blessings of God both when I was in prison and when I was out, defending the truth and telling others about Christ. Only God knows how deep is my love for you—with the tenderness of Jesus Christ.

And I want you to know, dear brothers, everything that has happened to me here has been a great boost in getting out the Good News. For everyone around here, including soldiers at the barracks, knows I am in chains simply because I am a Christian. And because of my imprisonment many Christians here seem to have lost their fear of chains! I know that as you pray for me, this is all going to turn out for my good.

I live in eager expectation that I will always be ready to speak boldly for Christ and that I will be an honor to Christ whether I live or whether I must die. To me, living means opportunities for Christ, and dying—well, that's better yet! Sometimes I want to live and at other times I don't, for I long to go and be with Christ. How much happier than being here! But I can be of help to you by staying; I feel certain I will be staying on earth a little longer.

Does it mean anything to you that we are brothers in the Lord, sharing the same Spirit? Then make me truly happy by loving each other, working together with one heart and mind and purpose!

Your attitude should be the kind shown by Jesus Christ, who, though he was God, did not cling to his rights as God but laid aside his glory, becoming like men. And he humbled himself further, going so far as to die a criminal's death on a cross. Yet because of this God raised him up to the heights of heaven and gave him a name which is above every other name, that at the name of Jesus every knee shall bow in heaven and on earth and under the earth, and every tongue shall confess that Jesus Christ is Lord, to the glory of God the Father.

When I was with you, you were careful to follow my instructions; now that I am away, be careful to do the good things—obey God with reverence; shrink back from all that might displease him. For God is at work within you, helping you want to obey him and then helping you to do what he wants.

If the Lord is willing, I will send Timothy to you soon. He has been like a son to me in helping preach the Good News. I hope to send him as soon as I find out what is going to happen to me here. And I am trusting the Lord that soon I myself may come to see you.

Meanwhile, I thought I ought to send Epaphroditus back to you. You sent him to help me in my need; he risked his life for the work of Christ and was at the point of death while trying to do for me the things you couldn't because you were far away.

All the things that I once thought very worthwhile—now I've thrown them away so I can put my hope in Christ alone. Everything else is worthless when compared with the priceless gain of knowing Christ Jesus my Lord. I have put aside all else, counting it worth less than nothing, in order that I can have Christ and become one with him. I have found it to be the only way to really know Christ, to experience the mighty power that brought him back to life, and to find out what it means to suffer and die with him.

I don't mean to say I am perfect. But I am bringing all my energies to bear on this one thing: forgetting the past and looking forward to what lies ahead, I strain to reach the end of the race and receive the prize for which God is calling us up to heaven.

Our homeland is heaven where our Savior the Lord Jesus Christ is; and we are looking forward to his return from there. When he comes back, he will take these dying bodies of ours and change them into glorious bodies like his own, using the same mighty power that he will use to conquer all else everywhere.

Dear brother Christians, always be full of joy in the Lord; I say it again, rejoice! Don't worry about anything; instead, pray about everything; tell God your needs and don't forget to thank him for his answers. If you do this you will experience God's peace, which is far more wonderful than the human mind can understand.

As I close this letter, let me say one more thing: fix your thoughts on what is true and good and right. Think about things that are pure and lovely, and dwell on the fine, good things in others. Think about all you can praise God for and be glad about. Keep putting into practice all you learned from me and saw me doing, and the God of peace will be with you.

How grateful I am that you are helping me again; I know for a while you didn't have the chance. Not that I was ever in need, for I have learned how to get along whether

I have much or little. I have learned the secret of contentment in every situation, for I can do everything God asks me with the help of Christ who gives me the strength.

Only you Philippians became my partners in giving and receiving; I am generously supplied with the gifts you sent me when Epaphroditus came. They are a sweet-smelling sacrifice that pleases God well. And he will supply all your needs from his riches in glory.

Now unto God our Father be glory forever and ever. Amen.

Sincerely, Paul.

P.S. Say "hello" to all the Christians there; the brothers with me send their greetings too. And all the other Christians here want to be remembered to you, especially those who work in Caesar's palace. The blessings of our Lord Jesus Christ be upon your spirits.[22]

PURE PASTORS

From: Paul, a missionary sent by direct command of God and by Jesus Christ.

To: Timothy.

May God our Father and Jesus Christ our Lord show you his kindness and mercy. Please stay in Ephesus and try to stop the men who are teaching wrong doctrine. I am eager that Christians there will be filled with love that comes from pure hearts, that their minds will be clean, and their faith strong.

These teachers want to become famous as teachers of the laws of Moses when they haven't the slightest idea what those laws really show us. Those laws are good when used as God intended, but they were not made for us whom God has saved; they are for sinners who have rebellious hearts, who do things that contradict the Good News of our blessed God.

How thankful I am to Christ Jesus for choosing me as one of his messengers, though I used to scoff at the name of Christ. I hunted down his people, harming them in every way I could. But God had mercy on me for I didn't know Christ at that time. I long that everyone should know Christ

Jesus came into the world to save sinners—and I was the greatest of them all. God had mercy on me so Jesus could use me as an example to show how patient he is with even the worst sinners.

God our Savior longs for all to be saved and to understand this truth: God is on one side and all the people on the other side; and Christ Jesus, himself man, is between them to bring them together by giving his life for all mankind.

This is the message which God gave at the proper time to the world. And I have been chosen—this is the absolute truth—as God's minister to teach this truth to the Gentiles. So I want men everywhere to pray with holy hands lifted up to God, free from sin. And the women should be quiet and sensible in manner and clothing. I never let women teach men or lord it over them, because God made Adam first and afterwards he made Eve.

If a man wants to be a pastor, he has a good ambition. A pastor must be a good man whose life cannot be spoken against. He must have only one wife, and he must be hard working and thoughtful, orderly, and full of good deeds. He must be gentle and kind, and not one who loves money. The pastor must not be a new Christian, because he might be proud of being chosen so soon—and pride comes before a fall. Also he must be well spoken of by people outside the church.

The deacons must be the same sort of men as the pastors—wholehearted followers of Christ, who is the hidden Source of their faith. They should be given other jobs in the church as a test of their character and ability, and if they do well they may be chosen as deacons.

I am writing these things now though I hope to be with you soon, so that if I don't come for awhile you will know what kind of men you should choose as officers for the church of the living God.

The way to live a godly life is not an easy matter. But the answer lies in Christ, who came to earth as a man and was proved pure in spirit, was served by angels, was preached among the nations, was accepted by men everywhere, and was received again to heaven.

But the Holy Spirit tells us that in the last times some

in the church will turn away from Christ and become followers of teachers with devil-inspired ideas. They will say it
is wrong to be married and wrong to eat meat, though
God gave these things to enjoy.

Explain this to the others, doing your duty as a worthy
pastor who is fed by faith and the true teaching you have
followed. Be a pattern for them in your love, your faith,
and your clean thoughts. Until I get there, read and explain
the Scriptures to the church.

Do you want to be truly rich? You already are if you
are happy and good. After all, we didn't bring any money
with us when we came into the world, and we can't carry
away a single penny when we die. So we should be satisfied
if we have enough food and clothing. People who long to
be rich begin to do all kinds of wrong things to get money,
things that hurt them and make them evil-minded and finally
send them to hell. The love of money is the first step
toward all kinds of sin.

Tell those who are rich not to trust their money, but
their trust should be in the living God who richly gives
us all we need for our enjoyment. They should be rich in
good works, always ready to share with others whatever
God has given them. By doing this they will be storing
up real treasure in heaven—it is the only safe investment
for eternity!

O Timothy, don't fail to do the things God entrusted
to you. May God's mercy be upon you.

Sincerely, Paul[22]

MISSION COMPLETED

From: Paul, sent out
by God to tell men and
women   everywhere
about the eternal life he promised through faith in Jesus
Christ.

To: Timothy.

How I thank God for you, Timothy. I pray for you every
day, and many times during the long nights I beg God to
bless you richly. He is my fathers' God and mine, and
my only purpose in life is to please him.

I know you trust the Lord, just as your mother Eunice

and your grandmother Lois do; and this being so I want to remind you to stir into flame the strength that entered into you when I laid my hands upon your head and blessed you. If you will stir up this inner power, you will never be afraid to tell others about our Lord or let them know that I am your friend here in jail for Christ's sake. You will be ready to suffer with me for the Lord. I am suffering here in jail and I am not ashamed of it, for I know the one in whom I trust and I am sure he is able to safely guard all that I have given him until the day of his return.

Timothy, be strong with the strength Christ Jesus gives you. For you must teach others those things you heard me speak about. Teach these great truths to trustworthy men who will in turn pass them on to others.

Take your share of suffering as a good soldier of Jesus Christ, and as Christ's soldier do not let yourself become tied up in worldly affairs, for then you cannot satisfy the one who enlisted you in his army. Follow the Lord's rules for his work, just as an athlete follows the rules or is disqualified. Work hard, like a farmer who gets paid well if he raises a large crop.

Don't ever forget that Jesus Christ was a man, born into King David's family; and that he was God, as shown by the fact that he rose again from the dead. Because I have preached these great truths, I have been put in jail like a criminal. But the Word of God is not chained. I am more than willing to suffer if that will bring salvation and eternal glory to those God has chosen.

I am comforted by this truth: when we suffer and die for Christ it means that we will begin living with him in heaven. If we think our present service for him is hard, remember that some day we are going to rule with him. When we are too weak to have any faith left, he remains faithful to us and will help us, for he cannot disown us who are part of himself.

God's people must be gentle, patient teachers of those who are wrong; if you talk courteously they are more likely, with God's help, to turn away from their wrong ideas and believe what is true. Then they will escape from Satan's trap of slavery to sin and begin doing the will of God.

You may as well know that in the last days it is going to be very difficult to be a Christian. People will love only themselves and their money; they will be proud and boastful, sneering at God, disobedient to their parents, and thoroughly bad. They will be liars and troublemakers and will think nothing of immorality. They will be cruel, will betray their friends, and prefer good times to worshiping God. And those who decide to please Christ Jesus by living godly lives will suffer at the hands of those who hate him. In fact, evil men and false teachers will become worse and worse, deceiving many—having been deceived themselves by Satan.

But you must keep on believing the things you have been taught. You know they are true, for you know you can trust us who have taught you. You know how when you were a small child you were taught the holy Scriptures, and it is these that make you wise to accept God's salvation by trusting in Christ Jesus. The whole Bible was given by inspiration from God to teach us what is true and to make us realize what is wrong in our lives; it straightens us out and helps us do what is right; it is God's way of making us well prepared at every point, fully equipped to do good to everyone.

And so I solemnly urge you before God and before Christ Jesus—who will judge the living and the dead when he appears to set up his Kingdom—to preach the Word of God urgently at all times, when it is convenient and when it is not.

I won't be around to help you much longer. Very soon now I will be on my way to heaven. I have fought long and hard for my Lord, and through it all I have kept true to him. And now the time has come for me to rest. In heaven a crown is waiting for me, which the Lord, the righteous Judge, will give me on that great day of his return. And not just to me, but to all those whose lives show they are eagerly looking forward to his coming again.

Please come as soon as you can. Only Luke is with me. Bring Mark with you, for I need him. Be sure to bring the coat I left at Troas and also the books, but especially the parchments.

The first time I was brought before the judge, no one was here to help me. But the Lord stood with me and gave me the opportunity to boldly preach a sermon. And he saved me from being thrown to the lions. Yes, and the Lord will always deliver me from all evil and will bring me into his heavenly Kingdom. To God be the glory forever and ever.

Please say "hello" to Priscilla and Aquila and those living at the home of Onesiphorus. Do try to be here before winter. May the Lord Jesus Christ be with your spirit.

Farewell, Paul[23]

PETER'S PLEA

From: Peter, Jesus Christ's missionary.

To: The Jewish Christians driven out of Jerusalem and scattered.

Dear friends, God the Father chose you, and the Holy Spirit has been in your hearts cleansing you with the blood of Jesus Christ; boundless mercy has given us the privilege of being born again so that we are now members of God's own family. And God has reserved for his children the priceless gift of eternal life; it is kept in heaven for you beyond the reach of change and decay. So be glad! There is wonderful joy ahead though the going is rough down here.

These trials are to test your faith as fire tests gold and purifies it. Your faith is far more precious to God than gold; so if your faith remains strong it will bring you much honor on the day of his return. You love him even though you have never seen him; and even now you are happy with the inexpressible joy that comes from heaven itself. Your reward for trusting him will be the salvation of your souls.

This salvation was something the prophets did not fully understand. Though they wrote about it, they wondered what the Spirit of Christ within them was talking about, events which since then have happened to Christ: his suffering, and his great glory afterwards. Now at last this Good News has been plainly announced. It was preached to us in the power of the same Holy Spirit who spoke to them;

so now you can look forward to more of God's kindness when Jesus Christ returns.

Obey God because you are his children. Be holy in everything you do, just as the Lord is holy, who invited you to be his child. He has said, "You must be holy, for I am holy."

God paid a ransom to save you, not mere gold or silver but the precious lifeblood of Christ, the sinless, spotless Lamb of God. God chose him for this purpose long before the world began but only recently was he brought to public view.

You have a new life not passed on to you from your parents, for the life they gave will fade away. This new one will last forever, for it comes from Christ, God's everliving Message. Yes, our natural lives will fade as grass, but the Word of the Lord will last forever.

You have been chosen by God, you are priests of the King, you are God's very own—all this so you may show to others how God called you out of darkness into his wonderful light.

You are only visitors here; your real home is in heaven. Keep away from the evil pleasures of this world, for they fight against your very souls.

Christ is your example: he never sinned, never told a lie, never answered back when insulted; when he suffered he did not threaten to get even; he left his case in the hands of God; he carried the load of our sins in his own body when he died on the cross so that we can be finished with sin. His wounds have healed ours! Like sheep you wandered away from God, but now you have returned to your Shepherd, the Guardian of your souls.

Wives, fit in with your husbands' plans; then if they refuse to listen when you talk to them about the Lord, they will be won by your pure behavior. Your godly lives will speak better than any words.

Don't be concerned about the outward beauty that depends on jewelry or beautiful clothes or hair arrangement. Be beautiful in your hearts with the lasting charm of a gentle and quiet spirit, which is precious to God. That kind of deep beauty was seen in the saintly women of old.

You husbands must be careful of your wives, being thoughtful of their needs and honoring them as the weaker sex. Remember, you and your wife are partners in receiving God's blessings, and if you don't treat her as you should your prayers will not get ready answers.

God has given each of you some special abilities; use them to help each other, passing on to others God's many kinds of blessings.

Dear friends, don't be surprised when you go through fiery trials, for this is no strange thing. Instead, be really glad because these trials make you partners with Christ in his suffering, and afterwards you will have the joy of sharing his glory in that coming day.

Be happy if you are insulted for being a Christian, for the Spirit of God will come upon you. Praise God for the privilege of being called by his wonderful name! The time has come for judgment, and it must begin among God's own children. And if we must be judged, what terrible fate awaits those who have never believed in the Lord? So if you are suffering according to God's will, keep on doing what is right and trust yourself to the God who will never fail you.

With my own eyes I saw Christ dying on the cross; and I will share his glory when he returns. Fellow elders, this is my plea to you: feed the flock of God; lead them by your good example; and when the Head Shepherd comes your reward will be a never-ending share in his honor.

Be careful—watch out for attacks from Satan, your great enemy. He prowls around like a hungry lion looking for some victim to tear apart. Stand firm when he attacks; trust the Lord.

After you have suffered a while, our God will give you his eternal glory.

I am sending this note through Silvanus, a faithful brother. The church here in Rome sends you greetings; so does Mark. Peace be to all of you.

Peter[24]

FISHERMAN'S FAREWELL

From: Simon Peter, a servant of Jesus Christ.

To: All of you who have our faith, the faith that Jesus Christ our God and Savior gives to us. How precious it is.

Do you want more of God's peace? Then learn to know him better. For as you know him better he will give you everything you need for living a truly good life. By mighty power he has given us the blessings he promised to save us from the rottenness around us and give us his own character.

The Lord Jesus Christ has showed me that my days on earth are numbered, and as long as I am still here I intend to send reminders so that you will remember long after I have gone.

We have not been telling fairy tales when we explained the power of our Lord Jesus Christ and his coming again. My own eyes have seen his splendor and glory: I was there on the mountain when he shone with honor given him by God his Father; I heard that majestic voice call from heaven, "This is my much-loved Son; I am well pleased with him."

So we have seen that what the prophets said came true. You will do well to pay close attention to everything they have written, for like lights shining into dark corners their words help us to understand many things that otherwise would be dark and difficult. No prophecy recorded in Scripture was ever thought up by the prophet himself; it was the Holy Spirit within these godly men who gave them true messages from God.

But there were false prophets, too, in those days, just as there will be false teachers among you. Many will follow their evil teaching that there is nothing wrong with sexual sin. These teachers will tell you anything to get hold of your money. But God condemned them long ago and their destruction is on the way. For God did not spare even the angels who sinned but threw them into hell until the judgment day. And he did not spare any of the people who lived in ancient times before the flood except Noah and his family of seven. At that time God destroyed the

whole world of ungodly men with the vast flood. Later
he turned the cities of Sodom and Gomorrah into heaps
of ashes, making them an example for all the ungodly to
look back upon and fear.

At the same time the Lord rescued Lot out of Sodom
because he was sick of the wickedness around him. So
also the Lord can rescue you and me from the temptations
that surround us.

This is my second letter to you, brothers, and in both
I have tried to remind you about facts you learned from
the holy prophets and from us apostles who brought you
the words of our Lord and Savior.

I want to remind you that in the last days there will
come scoffers who will laugh at the truth. This will be
their line of argument: "So Jesus promised to come back,
did he? Then where is he? As far back as anyone can remember, everything has remained as it was since the first day
of creation."

They forget this fact: God did destroy the world with
a mighty flood long after he had used the waters to form
the earth and surround it. And God has commanded that
the earth and heavens be stored away for a great fire
at the judgment day when all ungodly men will perish.

But don't forget, dear friends, that a day or a thousand
years from now is like tomorrow to the Lord. He isn't
slow about his promised return, even though it sometimes
seems that way. But he is waiting—for the good reason
that he is not willing that any should perish and he is giving
more time for sinners to repent. The day of the Lord is
surely coming as unexpectedly as a thief, and then the
heavens will pass away with a terrible noise, the heavenly
bodies will disappear in fire, and the earth and everything
on it will be burned up.

Since everything around us is going to melt away, what
holy lives we should be living! We are looking forward to
God's promise of new heavens and a new earth afterwards
where there will be only goodness.

Our wise and beloved brother Paul has talked about these
things in many of his letters. Some of his comments are
not easy to understand, and there are people who demand

some unusual interpretation—they have twisted his letters to mean something different from what he meant, just as they do the other parts of the Scripture—and the result is disaster for them.

I am warning you ahead of time so that you can watch out and not be carried away by the mistakes of these wicked men. But grow in spiritual strength and become better acquainted with our Lord and Savior Jesus Christ. To him be all glory and honor, now and forevermore. Good-bye.

Peter[25]

JUDE: THE JUDGMENT

From: Jude, a servant of Jesus Christ and a brother of James. To: Christians everywhere—may you be given more and more of God's kindness, peace, and love.

Dearly loved friends, I had been planning to write some thoughts about the salvation God has given us, but now I find I must write of something else instead, urging you to stoutly defend the truth which God gave to his people.

Some godless teachers say that after we become Christians we can do just as we like without fear of God's punishment. My answer to them is: remember that the Lord saved a whole nation of people out of the land of Egypt—and then killed every one of them who did not trust and obey him. And I remind you of those angels who were once pure and holy but turned to a life of sin. Now God has them chained in prisons of darkness waiting for the judgment day. And don't forget the cities of Sodom and Gomorrah and their neighboring towns, all full of lust of every kind. Those cities were destroyed by fire and continue to be a warning that there is a hell in which sinners are punished.

Yet these false teachers go on living immoral lives, degrading their bodies, and laughing at those in authority over them. These men mock and curse at anything they do not understand, and like animals they do whatever they feel like, thereby ruining their souls.

They follow the example of Cain who killed his brother; like Balaam, they will do anything for money; and like Korah,

they have disobeyed God and will die under his curse. They
are like clouds blowing over dry land without giving rain.
They are like fruit trees without any fruit at picking time.
They are doubly dead, for they have been pulled out, roots
and all, to be burned.

Dear friends, remember what the apostles of our Lord
Jesus Christ told you, that there would come scoffers whose
purpose in life is to enjoy themselves in every evil way
imaginable.

But you, dear friends, must build your lives more strongly
upon the foundation of our holy faith, learning to pray in
the power of the Holy Spirit. Stay within the boundaries
where God's love can bless you. Wait patiently for the
eternal life that our Lord Jesus Christ is going to give you.
Be merciful to those who doubt. Save some by snatching
them as from the flames of hell. As for others, help them
find the Lord by being kind, but be careful that you aren't
pulled into their sins. Hate every trace of sin while being
merciful to sinners.

And now—all glory to him who alone is God, who saves
us through Jesus Christ. Yes, splendor and majesty, power
and authority are his from the beginning; his they are and
his they evermore shall be. And he is able to keep you
from falling away and to bring you perfect into his glorious
presence with mighty shouts of everlasting joy. Amen.

Jude[26]

HIGHEST PRIEST— SUPREME KING

Long ago God spoke in
many ways to our fathers
through the prophets—in
visions, dreams, and even
face to face, telling them little by little about his plans.
Now in these days he has spoken to us through his Son,
to whom he has given everything and through whom he
made the world and everything there is.

God's Son shines out with God's glory, and all that God's
Son is and does marks him as God. He regulates the universe by the mighty power of his command. He died to
clear our record of all sin and then sat down in highest
honor beside the great God of heaven.

Thus he became far greater than the angels, for God never said to any angel, "You are my Son, and today I have given you the honor that goes with that name." But God said it about Jesus. Another time he said, "I am his Father and he is my Son." And another time—when his firstborn Son came to earth—God said, "Let all the angels of God worship him." God speaks of his angels as messengers swift as the wind and as servants made of flaming fire; but of his Son he says, "Your Kingdom, O God, will last forever and ever."

God also called him "Lord" when he said, "Lord, in the beginning you made the earth, and the heavens are the work of your hands. They will disappear into nothingness, but you will never change and your years will never end."

So we must listen very carefully to the truths we have heard or we may drift away from them. For since the messages from angels have always proved true and people have always been punished for disobeying them, what makes us think we can escape if we are indifferent to this salvation announced by the Lord Jesus and passed on to us by those who heard him speak? God has shown us these messages are true by signs and wonders and various miracles.

The future world will not be controlled by angels. For in the book of Psalms David says to God, "What is mere man that you are so concerned about him? And who is this Son of Man you honor so highly? For though you made him lower than the angels for a little while, now you have crowned him with glory and honor. And you have put him in complete charge of everything there is."

We have not yet seen all of this take place, but we do see Jesus crowned now by God with glory and honor because he suffered death for us. Jesus tasted death for everyone in the world, and in doing this he was bringing vast multitudes of God's people to heaven; for his suffering made Jesus a perfect Leader.

We who have been made holy by Jesus now have the same Father he has. That is why Jesus says in the book of Psalms, "I will talk to my brothers about God my Father." Since we are human beings made of flesh and blood, he became flesh and blood too, for only as a human being could he die and in dying break the power of the devil who had the power of death. In that way he could deliver those who through fear of death have been slaves to constant dread.

It was necessary for Jesus to be like us so that he could be our merciful and faithful High Priest, merciful to us and faithful to God in dealing with sins. Since he has been through suffering and temptation, he knows what it is like when we suffer and are tempted, and he is wonderfully able to help us.

Think about this Jesus who is God's Messenger and the High Priest of our faith.

Jesus was faithful to God who appointed him High Priest, just as Moses also faithfully served in God's house. But Moses was only a servant; Christ, God's Son, is in complete charge of God's house. And we Christians are God's house—he lives in us!

Jesus, our great High Priest, has gone to heaven to help us. This High Priest understands our weaknesses since he had the same temptations we do, though he never gave way to them and sinned. So let us come boldly to the throne of God to receive his mercy and find grace to help us in times of need.

The Jewish High Priest is merely a man, but he is chosen to speak for all other men in their dealings with God. He presents their gifts to God and offers the blood of animals that are sacrificed to cover sins. No one can be a High Priest just because he wants to be; he has to be called by God in the same way God chose Aaron.

That is why Christ did not elect himself; he was chosen by God. God said to him, "You have been chosen to be a priest forever, with the same rank as Melchizedek."

This Melchizedek was king of Salem and also a priest of the Most High God. When Abraham was returning home after winning a battle against many kings, Melchizedek met him and blessed him; then Abraham took a tenth of all he had won in the battle and gave it to Melchizedek.

Melchizedek's name means "Justice," so he is the King of Justice; and he is also the King of Peace because of the name of his city, Salem, which means "Peace." There is no record of any of his ancestors—he was never born and he never died—his life is like that of the Son of God.

As we know, Christ did not belong to the priest-tribe of Levi, but came from the tribe of Judah. So we plainly see that God's method changed; for Christ, the new High Priest who came with the rank of Melchizedek, did not become a priest by belonging to the tribe of Levi but on the basis of power flowing from a life that cannot end.

The old system of priesthood was canceled because it didn't work; it never made anyone really right with God. Now we have a far better hope, for Christ makes us acceptable to God and now we may draw near to him.

Under the old arrangement, there had to be many priests so that when the older ones died the system could be carried on by others who took their places. But Jesus lives forever and continues to be a Priest, so no one else is needed. He is able to save completely all who come to God through him.

He is exactly the kind of High Priest we need—holy and blameless, unstained by sin, undefiled by sinners, and to him has been given the place of honor in heaven. He never needs the daily blood of animal sacrifices, as other priests did, to cover their own sins and then the sins of the people; for he finished sacrifices once and for all when he sacrificed himself on the cross. Under the old system even the High Priests were weak men who could not keep from doing wrong, but later God appointed his Son who is perfect forever.

When Moses was getting ready to build the Tabernacle, God warned him to follow exactly the pattern of the heavenly tabernacle as shown to him on Mount Sinai. But Christ, as a Minister in heaven, has been rewarded with a far more important work because the new agreement which he passes on to us from God contains far more wonderful promises.

The old agreement didn't work. If it had, there would have been no need for another to replace it. God himself found fault with the old one for he said, "The day will come when I will make a new agreement with the people of Israel and Judah. This is the new agreement: I will write my laws in their minds so they will know what I want them to do, and they will want to obey them. And I will be merciful to them in their wrongdoings, and I will remember their sins no more."

In that first agreement between God and his people, there was a sacred tent here on earth. Inside this place of worship were two rooms. The first contained the golden candlestick and a table with special loaves of holy bread upon it; this was called the Holy Place. Then there was a curtain, and behind the curtain was a room called the Holy of Holies. In that room were a golden incense-altar and the golden chest, called the Ark of the covenant, covered with pure gold. Inside the Ark were the tablets of stone with the Ten Commandments written on them, a golden jar with some manna in it, and Aaron's wooden cane that budded. Above the golden chest were statues of angels called cherubim with their wings stretched out over the Ark's golden cover, called the mercy seat.

When all was ready, the priests went in and out of the first room doing their work. But only the High Priest went into the inner room and only once a year, and always with blood which he sprinkled on the mercy seat as an offering to God to cover his own sins and the sins of the people.

Common people could not go into the Holy of Holies as long as the outer room and the system it represents were still in use. Under the old system, gifts and sacrifices were offered but these failed to cleanse the hearts of the people. The old system dealt with rituals—what foods to eat and drink, rules for washing themselves, and rules about this and that. People had to keep these rules until Christ came with God's better way.

He went into that perfect tabernacle in heaven and once for all took blood into that Holy of Holies and sprinkled it on the mercy seat; with it he made sure of our eternal salvation.

After Moses had given the people God's laws, he took the blood of calves and goats, along with water, and sprinkled the blood over the book of God's laws and over all the people, using branches of hyssop bushes and scarlet wool to sprinkle with. Then he said, "This is the blood that marks the beginning of the agreement between you and God." And in the same way he sprinkled blood on the sacred tent and on whatever instruments were used for worship. In fact, under the old agreement almost everything was cleansed by sprinkling it with blood, and without the shedding of blood there is no forgiveness of sins.

That is why the sacred tent and everything in it—all copies from things in heaven—had to be made pure by Moses in this way. But the real things in heaven, of which these down here are copies, were made pure with far more precious offerings.

For Christ has entered into heaven to appear now before God as our Friend. Nor has he offered himself again and again, as the High Priest on earth offers animal blood each year. He came once for all, at the end of the age, to put away the power of sin forever by dying for us.

Just as it is destined that men die once and after that comes judgment, so also Christ died only once as an offering for the sins of many people; and he will come again but not to deal with our sins. This time he will bring salvation to all those who are eagerly and patiently waiting for him.

In response to all he has done for us, let us outdo each other in being helpful and kind. Let us not neglect our church meetings, but encourage and warn each other that the day of his coming back is drawing near.

Men of God in days of old were famous for their faith. By faith we know that the world and the stars—in fact, all things—were made at God's command from things that can't be seen. By faith Abel obeyed God and brought an offering that pleased God more than Cain's offering did. Enoch trusted God too, and God took him away to heaven without dying.

You can never please God without faith. Anyone who wants to come to God must believe that there is a God and that he rewards those who sincerely look for him.

Noah was another who trusted God. When he heard God's warning about the future, Noah believed him even though there was no sign of a flood, and he built the ark and saved his family.

Abraham trusted when God told him to leave home and

go far away to another land which he promised to give him. He lived in tents like a visitor, as did Isaac and Jacob to whom God gave the same promise.

Sarah, too, had faith, and she was able to become a mother in spite of her old age, for she realized that God would certainly do what he said.

It was by faith that Moses refused to be treated as the grandson of the king, but chose to share ill-treatment with God's people instead of enjoying the fleeting pleasures of sin.

Faith brought the walls of Jericho tumbling down after the people of Israel had walked around them seven days, as God had commanded them. By faith Rahab the harlot did not die with all the others in her city when they refused to obey God, for she gave a friendly welcome to the spies.

It would take too long to recount the faith of Gideon and Barak and Samson and Jephthah and David and Samuel and all the other prophets. These people all trusted God and as a result won battles, overthrew kingdoms, ruled their people well, and received what God had promised them; they were kept from harm in a den of lions and in a fiery furnace. Some through their faith escaped death by the sword. Some were made strong again after they had been weak or sick. Others were given great power in battle. Some women through faith received their loved ones back from death.

But others trusted God and were beaten to death, preferring to die rather than turn from God—trusting that they would rise to a better life afterwards. Some were laughed at and their backs cut open with whips, and others were chained in dungeons. Some died by stoning and some by being sawed in two; others were promised freedom if they would renounce their faith, then were killed with the sword. Some went about in skins of sheep and goats, wandering over deserts and mountains, hiding in dens and caves. And though they trusted God and won his approval, none of them received all that God had promised them; for God wanted them to wait and share the even better rewards that were prepared for us.

Since we have a huge crowd of men of faith watching

us from the grandstands, let us strip off anything that slows us down, especially those sins that wrap themselves tightly around our feet and trip us up; and let us run with patience the race that God has set before us.

Keep your eyes on Jesus, our leader. To keep from becoming weary, think about his patience as sinful men did terrible things to him.

Let God train you, for he is doing what any loving father does for his children. Our earthly fathers trained us for a few years, doing the best for us that they knew how, but God's correction is always right and for our best that we may share his holiness. Afterwards we can see the result—growth in grace and character.

So take a new grip with your hands, stand firm on your legs, and mark out a straight path for your feet so that those who follow you will not fall and hurt themselves but become strong.

Look after each other so that not one of you will fail to find God's best blessings. Watch out that no bitterness takes root among you, for it causes deep trouble.

You have not had to stand face to face with flaming fire, gloom, darkness, and a terrible storm, as the Israelites did at Mount Sinai when God gave them his laws. But you have come right up to the city of the living God, the heavenly Jerusalem; to the church, composed of all those registered in heaven; to God who is Judge of all; to the spirits of the redeemed in heaven, already made perfect; and to Jesus himself and the sprinkled blood which graciously forgives.

So see to it that you obey him who is speaking to you. For if the people of Israel did not escape when they refused to listen to Moses, how terrible our danger if we refuse to listen to God who speaks to us from heaven! When he spoke from Mount Sinai his voice shook the earth, but "Next time," he says, "I will not only shake the earth but the heavens too." Let us please God by serving him with thankful hearts and holy fear and awe. For our God is a consuming fire.

Jesus Christ is the same yesterday, today, and forever. So do not be attracted by strange, new ideas. May he who became the great Shepherd of the sheep by an everlasting agreement between God and you, signed with his blood, produce in you all that is pleasing. To him be glory forever and ever. Amen.

Brother Timothy is now out of jail; if he comes here soon, I will come with him to see you. The Christians from Italy who are here with me send you their love. God's grace be with you all. Good-bye.[27]

DISCIPLE OF LOVE

Christ was alive when the world began— yet I have seen him with my own eyes and listened to him speak. I have touched him with my own hands. We are telling you about what we have seen and heard so you may share the fellowship and the joys we have with the Father and with Jesus Christ his Son. And if you do as I say in this letter, you too will be full of joy!

This is the message God has given us to pass on to you: God is Light and in him is no darkness at all. So if we say we are his friends but go on living in spiritual darkness, we are lying. But if we are living in the light of God's presence, we have wonderful fellowship with each other, and the blood of Jesus his Son cleanses us from every sin.

If we say we have no sin, we are fooling ourselves. But if we confess our sins to him, he can be depended on to forgive us and to cleanse us from every wrong.

My children, I am telling you this so you will stay away from sin. But if you sin, there is someone to plead for you before the Father: Jesus Christ, the one who pleases God completely. He took God's wrath against our sins upon himself and brought us into fellowship with God; he is the forgiveness for our sins and all the world's.

How can we be sure that we belong to him? By looking within ourselves: are we really trying to do what he wants us to? Someone may say, "I am a Christian; I am on my way to heaven," but if he doesn't do what Christ tells him to he is a liar. Those who do what Christ tells them will learn to love God more and more. Anyone who says he is a Christian should live as Christ did.

Dear brothers, I am not writing a new rule for you, for it is one you have had from the start. Yet it is always new and works for you just as it did for Christ; as we obey this commandment to love one another, the darkness in our lives disappears and the light of life in Christ shines in.

Stop loving this evil world and all that it offers you! When you love these things, you show that you do not really love God. These worldly things, these evil desires—the craze for sex, the ambition to buy everything, and the pride that comes from importance—these are not from God. This world is fading away and these forbidden things will go with it, but whoever keeps doing the will of God will live forever.

I am writing to you as to those who can discern the difference between true and false. And who is the greatest liar? The one who says Jesus is not Christ. Such a person is antichrist. A person who doesn't believe in Christ, God's Son, can't have God the Father either. But he who has Christ has God the Father also.

These remarks about the Antichrist are pointed at those who would love to lead you astray. But you have received the Holy Spirit and he lives within you, so you don't need anyone to teach you what is right. He teaches you all things, and he is the Truth.

See how very much our heavenly Father loves us—he allows us to be called his children. Yes, we are God's children right now and we can't imagine what it is going to be like later on. But we do know that when he comes we will be like him. Everyone who really believes this will try to stay pure because Christ is pure.

The person who has been born into God's family does not make a practice of sinning, because God's life is in him; this new life controls him. So now we can tell who is a child of God and who belongs to Satan. Whoever is living a life of sin and doesn't love his brother shows that he is not in God's family. If we love other Christians, it proves we have been given eternal life. Anyone who hates his Christian brother is a murderer at heart; and no one wanting to murder has eternal life within. We know real love from Christ's example in dying for us, and so we ought to lay down our lives for our Christian brothers.

If someone who is supposed to be a Christian has money enough to live well and sees a brother in need and won't help—how can God's love be in him? Let us stop just saying we love people; let us really love them and show it by our actions.

Don't believe everything you hear just because someone says it is a message from God; test it. Does it agree that Jesus Christ, God's Son, actually became man with a human body? If not, the message is not from God but from one who is against Christ, like the "Antichrist" you have heard about who is going to come; his enmity against Christ is already abroad in the world.

If you believe that Jesus is the Christ—God's Son and your Savior—then you are a child of God. Loving God means doing what he tells us to do; every child of God can obey him, defeating sin and evil pleasure by trusting Christ to help him.

Who could win this battle except by believing that Jesus is truly the Son of God? We know he is, because God said so with a voice from heaven when Jesus was baptized and again as he was facing death. And the Holy Spirit says it too. So we have these three witnesses: the voice of the Holy Spirit in our hearts, the voice from heaven at Christ's baptism, and the voice before he died. If anyone doesn't believe this, he is calling God a liar because he doesn't believe what God has said about his Son.

God said he has given eternal life and this life is in his Son. So whoever has God's Son has life; whoever does not have his Son does not have life. I have written this to you who believe in the Son of God so you may know you have eternal life.

We know we are children of God and the world around us is under Satan's power. And we know Christ has come to help us understand the true God. We are in God because we are in Jesus Christ.

Dear children, keep away from anything that might take God's place in your hearts. Amen.

Sincerely, John[28]

PART
12
PARADISE REGAINED

FUTURE UNVEILED

This book unveils the future activities of Jesus Christ. God permitted him to reveal these things to his servant John in a vision; and then an angel was sent from heaven to explain the vision's meaning. John wrote down the words of God and Jesus Christ and everything he heard and saw. If you read this prophecy to the church, you will receive a special blessing from the Lord; those who listen and do what it says will also be blessed.[1]

KING OF THE CHURCH

From: John.
To: The seven churches in Turkey.
Dear Friends:
Grace and peace from God who is, and was, and is to come! And from the sevenfold Spirit before his throne. And from Jesus Christ who faithfully reveals truth to us. He was the first to rise from death to die no more. He is far greater than any king in all the earth. He has gathered us into his Kingdom and made us priests of God his Father. He rules forever!

See! He is arriving, surrounded by clouds, and every eye shall see him—and the nations will weep in sorrow and in terror when he comes. Let it be so!

I, John, a fellow sufferer for the Lord's sake, am writing

this letter to you. I was on the island of Patmos, exiled there for preaching the Word of God and telling what I knew about Jesus Christ. It was the Lord's Day and I was worshiping when suddenly I heard a loud voice behind me saying, "I am A and Z, the First and Last! Write down everything you see, and send your letter to the seven churches in Turkey: Ephesus, Smyrna, Pergamos, Thyatira, Sardis, Philadelphia, and Laodicea."

When I turned to see who was speaking, there were seven candlesticks of gold. And standing among them was one who looked like Jesus, wearing a long robe circled with a golden band across his chest. His hair was white as wool and his eyes penetrated like flames of fire. His feet gleamed like burnished bronze, and his voice thundered like waves against the shore. He held seven stars in his right hand and a sharp, double-bladed sword in his mouth, and his face shone like the power of the sun.

I fell at his feet as dead; but he laid his right hand on me and said, "Don't be afraid! Though I am the First and Last, the Living One who died who is now alive forevermore, who has the keys of hell and death—don't be afraid! Write down what you have just seen, and what will soon be shown to you. This is the meaning of the seven stars in my right hand, and the seven golden candlesticks: the seven stars are the leaders of the seven churches, and the seven candlesticks are the churches themselves.

"Write to the leader of the church at Ephesus:

"I write to inform you of a message from him who walks among the churches and holds their leaders in his right hand.

"He says to you: I know how many good things you are doing. I have watched your hard work and your patience; I know you don't tolerate sin among your members and you have carefully examined the claims of those who say they are apostles but aren't. You have patiently suffered for me without quitting.

"Yet there is one thing wrong: you don't love me as at first! Think about those times and turn back to me again, or else I will remove your candlestick from its place among the churches.

"Let this message sink into the ears of anyone who listens to the Spirit: To everyone who is victorious, I will give fruit from the Tree of Life in the Paradise of God.

"To the leader of the church in Smyrna write:

"This message is from him who was dead and then came back to life.

"I know how much you suffer for the Lord, and about your poverty (but you have heavenly riches!). I know the slander of those opposing you. The devil will soon throw some of you into prison to test you. Remain faithful even when facing death, and I will give you the crown of life. Let everyone listen to what the Spirit is saying: He who is victorious shall not be hurt by the Second Death.

"Write to the leader of the church in Pergamos:

"This message is from him who wields the sharp, double-bladed sword. I am aware that you live at the center of satanic worship, and you have remained loyal to me even when Antipas was martyred among you by Satan's devotees.

"And yet you tolerate some among you who ruin people by involving them in sexual sin. Change your attitude, or I will come and fight against them with the sword of my mouth.

"Let everyone listen to what the Spirit is saying: Every one who is victorious shall eat of the secret nourishment from heaven; and I will give to each a white stone, and on the stone will be engraved a new name that no one else knows except the one receiving it.

"Write this letter to the leader of the church in Thyatira:

"This is a message from the Son of God, whose eyes penetrate like flames of fire, whose feet are like glowing brass.

"I am aware of all your good deeds—your kindness to the poor, your gifts and service to them; also I know your love and faith and patience, and I can see your constant improvement in all things.

"Yet I have this against you: you are permitting that woman Jezebel, who calls herself a prophetess, to teach my servants that sex sin is not a serious matter. I gave her time to change her mind, but she refused. I will lay her upon a sickbed of affliction with all her immoral followers unless they turn again to me, and I will strike her children dead. And all the churches shall know that I am he who searches deep within hearts and will give to each whatever you deserve.

"As for the rest of you in Thyatira, hold tightly to what you have until I come. To every one who overcomes I will give power over the nations. You will rule them with a rod of iron just as my Father gave me the authority to rule them. Let all listen to what the Spirit says.

"To the leader of the church in Sardis write:

"This message is sent to you by the one who has the sevenfold Spirit of God and the seven stars.

"I know your reputation as an active church, but you are dead. Wake up! Strengthen what little remains. Go back to what you believed at first; hold to it firmly and turn to me again. Unless you do, I will punish you.

"Even in Sardis, some haven't soiled their garments with the world's filth; they shall walk with me in white. Everyone who conquers will be clothed in white, and I will not erase his name from the Book of Life.

"Let all who can hear listen to what the Spirit is saying.

"Write to the leader of the church in Philadelphia:

"This message is sent by the one who is holy and true and has the key to open what no one can shut and to shut what no one can open.

"I know you aren't strong, but you have tried to obey and have not denied my Name. Therefore I have opened a door to you that no one can shut. I will force those supporting the causes of Satan while claiming to be mine to fall at your feet and acknowledge that you are the ones I love.

"Because you have patiently obeyed me despite the persecution, I will protect you from the time of Great Tribulation and temptation which will come upon the world to test everyone. Hold tightly to the strength you have—so that no one will take away your crown.

"For the one who conquers, I will make him a pillar in the temple of my God; and I will write my God's Name on him, and he will be a citizen in the city of my God— the New Jerusalem, coming down from heaven; and he will have my new Name inscribed upon him. Let all who can hear listen to what the Spirit is saying.

"Write this letter to the leader of the church in Laodicea:

"This message is from the faithful and true Witness, the primeval source of God's creation:

"I know you well—you are neither hot nor cold; since you are merely lukewarm, I will spit you out of my mouth!

"You say, 'I am rich, with everything I want,' and you don't realize that spiritually you are wretched and miserable and poor and blind and naked.

"My advice to you is to buy pure gold from me, gold purified by fire—only then will you truly be rich. And to purchase from me white garments, clean and pure, so you won't be naked and ashamed; and to get medicine from me to heal your eyes and give you back your sight. I discipline everyone I love, so I must punish you unless you turn from your indifference and become enthusiastic about God.

"I have been standing at the door and I am constantly knocking. If anyone hears me calling and opens the door, I will come in and fellowship with him and he with me. I will let every one who conquers sit beside me on my throne, just as I took my place with my Father on his throne when I had conquered. Let those who can hear listen to what the Spirit is saying to the churches."[2]

KING OF THE COSMOS

Then as I looked I saw a door standing open in heaven, and the same voice I had heard before that sounded like a mighty trumpet blast spoke to me: "Come up here and I will show you what must happen in the future!"

Instantly I was, in spirit, in heaven and saw—oh, the glory of it!—a throne and someone sitting on it! Bursts of light flashed forth from him as from a glittering diamond, and a rainbow glowing like an emerald encircled his throne. Twenty-four smaller thrones surrounded his, with twenty-four Elders sitting on them; all were clothed in white, with golden crowns upon their heads. Lightning and thunder issued from the throne, and there were voices in the thunder.

Directly in front of his throne were seven lighted lamps representing the sevenfold Spirit of God. Spread out before it was a shiny crystal sea. Four Living Beings, dotted front and back with eyes, stood at the throne's four sides. The first of these Living Beings was in the form of a lion; the second looked like an ox; the third had the face of a man; and the fourth the form of an eagle with wings spread out as though in flight. Each of these Living Beings had six wings, and the central sections of their wings were covered with eyes. Day after day and night after night they kept on saying, "Holy, holy, holy, Lord God Almighty—the one who was, and is, and is to come."

When the Living Beings gave glory and honor and thanks to the one sitting on the throne, the twenty-four Elders fell down before him and worshiped him and cast their crowns before the throne, singing, "O Lord, you are worthy to receive glory and honor and power for you have created all things. They were called into being by your act of will."

And I saw a scroll in the right hand of the one on the throne, a scroll with writing on the inside and on the back, and sealed with seven seals. A mighty angel with a loud voice was shouting out: "Who is worthy to break the seals on this scroll and to unroll it?"

No one was permitted to open and read it. I wept with disappointment because no one could tell us what it said.[3]

THE LION-LAMB

But one of the twenty-four Elders said, "Look! The Lion of the tribe of Judah, the Root of David, has proved himself worthy to open the scroll and break its seals."

I looked and saw a Lamb standing before the twenty-four Elders in front of the throne and the Living Beings, and on the Lamb were wounds that once had caused his death. He had seven horns and seven eyes, which represent the sevenfold Spirit of God sent into every part of the world. He stepped forward and took the scroll from the right hand of the one upon the throne. As he took the scroll, the twenty-four Elders fell down before the Lamb, each with a harp and golden vials filled with incense—the prayers of God's people!

They were singing him a new song: "You are worthy to take the scroll and break its seals and open it; for you were slain, and your blood has bought people from every nation as gifts for God. And you have gathered them into a kingdom and made them priests of our God; they shall reign upon the earth."

Then in my vision I heard the singing of millions of angels surrounding the throne and the Living Beings and the Elders: "The Lamb is worthy—the Lamb who was slain. He is worthy to receive power, and riches, and wisdom, and strength, and honor, and glory, and blessing."

And the twenty-four Elders fell down and worshiped him.[4]

LORD OF THE FUTURE

As I watched, the Lamb broke the first seal and began to unroll the scroll. Then one of the four Living Beings, with a voice that sounded like thunder, said, "Come!"

I looked, and there in front of me was a white horse. Its rider carried a bow, and a crown was placed upon his head; he rode out to conquer in many battles and win the war.

Then he unrolled the scroll to the second seal, and broke it open too. And I heard the second Living Being say, "Come!"

This time a red horse rode out. Its rider was given a long sword and the authority to banish peace and bring anarchy to the earth; war and killing broke out everywhere.

When he had broken the third seal, I heard the third Living Being say, "Come!" And I saw a black horse, with its rider holding a pair of balances in his hand. And a voice from among the four Living Beings said, "A loaf of bread for $20, or three pounds of barley flour, but there is no olive oil or wine."

And when the fourth seal was broken, I heard the fourth Living Being say, "Come!" And now I saw a pale horse, and its rider's name was Death. And there followed after him another horse whose rider's name was Hell. They were given control of one-fourth of the earth to kill with war and famine and disease and wild animals.

And when he broke open the fifth seal, I saw an altar and underneath it all the souls of those who had been martyred for preaching the Word of God and for being faithful in their witnessing. They called loudly to the Lord and said, "O Sovereign Lord, holy and true, how long will it be before you judge the people of the earth for what they've done to us?" White robes were given to each of them, and they were told to rest a little longer until their other brothers, fellow servants of Jesus, had been martyred on the earth and joined them.

I watched as he broke the sixth seal, and there was a vast earthquake; and the sun became dark like black cloth, and the moon was blood red. Then the stars of heaven appeared to be falling to earth—like green fruit from fig trees buffeted by mighty winds. And the starry heavens disappeared as though rolled up like a scroll and taken away; and every mountain and island shook and shifted. The kings of the earth, world leaders and rich men, high-ranking military officers and all men great and small, slave and free, hid themselves in the caves and rocks of the mountains and cried to the mountains to crush them. "Fall on us," they pleaded, "and hide us from the face of the one sitting on the throne and from the anger of the Lamb, because the great day of their anger has come and who can survive it?"

Then I saw four angels standing at the four corners of the earth, holding back the four winds from blowing, so that not a leaf rustled in the trees and the ocean became as smooth as glass. And I saw another angel coming from the east, carrying the Great Seal of the Living God. And he shouted to those four angels who had been given power to injure earth and sea, "Wait! Don't do anything yet— hurt neither earth nor sea nor trees—until we have placed the Seal of God upon the foreheads of his servants."

How many were given his mark? I heard the number— it was 144,000 out of all twelve tribes of Israel, as listed here: Judah, 12,000; Reuben, 12,000; Gad, 12,000; Asher,

12,000; Naphtali, 12,000; Manasseh, 12,000; Simeon, 12,000; Levi, 12,000; Issachar, 12,000; Zebulun, 12,000; Joseph, 12,000; Benjamin, 12,000.

After this I saw a vast crowd, too great to count, from all nations and provinces and languages standing in front of the throne and before the Lamb, clothed in white with palm branches in their hands. And they were shouting with a mighty shout, "Salvation comes from our God upon the throne, and from the Lamb."

And now all the angels were crowding around the throne, the Elders, and the four Living Beings and falling face down before the throne and worshiping God. "Amen!" they said. "Blessing, and glory, and wisdom, and thanksgiving, and honor, and power, and might, be to our God forever and forever. Amen!"

Then one of the twenty-four Elders asked me, "Do you know who these are who are clothed in white, and where they come from?"

"No, sir," I replied. "Please tell me."

"These are the ones coming out of the Great Tribulation," he said. "They washed their robes and whitened them by the blood of the Lamb. That is why they are here before the throne of God, serving him day and night in his temple. The one sitting on the throne will shelter them; they will never be hungry again, nor thirsty, and they will be fully protected from the scorching noontime heat. For the Lamb standing in front of the throne will feed them and be their Shepherd and lead them to the springs of the Water of Life. And God will wipe their tears away."[5]

LORD OF JUDGMENTS

When the Lamb had broken the seventh seal, there was silence throughout heaven for what seemed like half an hour. And I saw the seven angels that stand before God and they were given seven trumpets.

Then another angel with a golden censer came and stood at the altar; and a great quantity of incense was given to him to mix with the prayers of God's people, to offer upon the golden altar before the throne. And the perfume of the incense mixed with prayers ascended up to God from the altar where the angel had poured them out.

Then the angel filled the censer with fire from the altar and threw it down upon the earth; and thunder crashed and rumbled, lightning flashed, and there was a terrible earthquake.

Then the seven angels with the seven trumpets prepared to blow their mighty blasts.

The first angel blew his trumpet, and hail and fire mixed with blood were thrown down upon the earth. One-third of the earth was set on fire so that one-third of the trees were burned and all the green grass.

Then the second angel blew his trumpet, and what appeared to be a huge burning mountain was thrown into the sea, destroying a third of all the ships; and a third of the sea turned red as blood, and a third of the fish were killed.

The third angel blew, and a great flaming star fell from heaven upon a third of the rivers and springs. The star was called "Bitterness" because it poisoned a third of all the water on the earth, and many people died.

The fourth angel blew his trumpet, and immediately a third of the sun was blighted and a third of the moon and the stars so that the daylight was dimmed by a third and the nighttime darkness deepened. As I watched, I saw a solitary eagle flying through the heavens crying, "Woe, woe, woe to the people of the earth because of the terrible things that will soon happen when the three remaining angels blow their trumpets."

Then the fifth angel blew his trumpet, and I saw one who was fallen to earth from heaven and to him was given the key to the bottomless pit. When he opened it, smoke poured out as though from some huge furnace, and the sun and air were darkened by the smoke.

Then locusts came from the smoke and descended onto the earth and were given power to sting like scorpions. They were told not to hurt the grass or plants or trees, but to attack those people who did not have the mark of God on their foreheads. They were to torture them for five months with the pain of scorpion stings. They will long to die—but death will flee away!

The locusts looked like horses armored for battle. They had what looked like golden crowns on their heads and their faces looked like men's. Their hair was long like women's and their teeth were those of lions. They wore breastplates that seemed to be of iron, and their wings roared like an army of chariots rushing into battle. They had stinging tails like scorpions, and their power to hurt, given to them for five months, was in their tails. Their king is the Prince of the bottomless pit whose name in Hebrew is Abaddon, and in Greek, Apollyon, and in English, the Destroyer.

The sixth angel blew his trumpet, and I heard a voice speaking from the four horns of the golden altar that stands before the throne of God saying to the sixth angel, "Release the four mighty demons held bound at the great River Euphrates." They had been kept in readiness for that year and month and day and hour, and now they were turned loose to kill a third of all mankind. They led an army of 200,000,000 warriors—I heard an announcement of how many there were.

I saw their horses spread out before me in my vision; their riders wore fiery-red breastplates, though some were sky blue and others yellow. The horses' heads looked much like lions', and smoke and fire and flaming sulphur billowed from their mouths, killing one-third of all mankind. Their power of death was not only in their mouths but in their tails as well, for their tails were similar to serpents' heads that struck and bit with fatal wounds.

But the men left alive after these plagues still refused to worship God! They would not renounce their demon-worship nor their idols made of gold and silver, brass, stone, and wood. Neither did they change their mind about their murders and witchcraft, their immorality and theft.

Then I saw another mighty angel coming down from heaven, surrounded by a cloud, with a rainbow over his head; his face shone like the sun and his feet flashed with fire. And he held open in his hand a small scroll. He set his right foot on the sea and his left foot on the earth, and gave a great shout—it was like the roar of a lion—and seven thunders crashed their reply.

I was about to write what the thunders said when a voice from heaven called to me, "Don't do it. Their words are not to be revealed."

Then the mighty angel standing on the sea and land lifted his right hand to heaven, and swore by him who lives forever and ever—who created heaven and everything in it and the earth and all that it contains and the sea and its inhabitants—that there should be no more delay but that when the seventh angel blew his trumpet then God's veiled plan would be fulfilled.

Then the voice from heaven spoke to me again, "Go and get the unrolled scroll from the mighty angel standing upon the sea and land."

So I approached him and asked him to give me the scroll. "Yes, take it and eat it," he said. "At first it will taste like honey, but when you swallow it it will make your stomach sour!" So I took it from his hand and ate it. And just as he had said, it was sweet in my mouth but it gave me a stomachache when I swallowed it.

Then he told me, "You must prophesy further about many peoples, nations, tribes, and kings."

Now I was given a measuring stick and told to go and measure the Temple of God, including the inner court where the altar stands, and to count the number of worshipers. "But do not measure the outer court," I was told, "for it has been turned over to the nations. They will trample the Holy City for forty-two months. And I will give power to my two witnesses to prophesy 1,260 days clothed in sackcloth."

These two prophets are two candlesticks standing before the God of all the earth. Anyone trying to harm them will be killed by bursts of fire from their mouths. They have power to shut the skies so that no rain will fall during the three and a half years they prophesy, and to send every kind of plague upon the earth.

When they complete the three and a half years of their

testimony, the tyrant who comes out of the bottomless pit will declare war against them and conquer and kill them. For three and a half days their bodies will be exposed in the streets of Jerusalem—the very place where their Lord was crucified. People from many nations will crowd around to gaze at them. And there will be a worldwide holiday—people everywhere will rejoice and throw parties to celebrate the death of the two prophets who had tormented them.

But after three and a half days the spirit of life from God will enter them and they will stand up! Great fear will fall on everyone, then a loud voice will shout from heaven, "Come up!" And they will rise to heaven in a cloud as their enemies watch.

The same hour there will be a terrible earthquake that levels a tenth of the city. Then everyone left will give glory to the God of heaven.

The second woe is past, but the third quickly follows:

For just then the seventh angel blew his trumpet, and there were loud voices shouting down from heaven, "The kingdom of this world now belongs to our Lord and to his Christ, and he shall reign forever and ever."

The twenty-four Elders on their thrones before God threw themselves down in worship, saying, "We give thanks, Lord God Almighty, who is and was, for now you have assumed your great power and have begun to reign. The nations were angry with you, but now it is your turn to be angry with them. It is time to judge the dead, and reward your servants—prophets and people alike, all who fear your Name, both great and small—and to destroy those who have caused destruction upon the earth."

Then in heaven the Temple of God was opened and the Ark of his covenant could be seen inside. Lightning flashed and thunder crashed, and there was a great hailstorm and the world was shaken by a mighty earthquake.[6]

WORLDS' WAR 2

Then a great pageant appeared in heaven, portraying things to come. I saw a woman clothed with the sun, with the moon beneath her feet, and a crown of twelve stars on her head. She was pregnant and screamed in the pain of her labor, awaiting her delivery.

Suddenly a red Dragon appeared, with seven heads and ten horns and seven crowns on his heads. His tail drew along behind him a third of the stars, which he plunged to the earth. He stood before the woman as she was about to give birth to her child. She gave birth to a boy who was to rule all nations with a heavy hand, and he was caught up to God and to his throne. The woman fled into the wilderness, where God had prepared a place for her, to take care of her for 1,260 days.

Then there was war in heaven; Michael and the angels under his command fought the Dragon and his hosts of fallen angels. And the Dragon lost the battle and was forced from heaven. This great Dragon—the ancient serpent called the devil, or Satan, the one deceiving the whole world— was thrown down onto the earth with all his army.

Then I heard a loud voice shouting across the heavens, "It has happened at last! God's salvation and rule and the authority of his Christ are finally here; for the Accuser of our brothers has been thrown from heaven onto earth— he accused them day and night before our God. They defeated him by the blood of the Lamb and by their testimony; for they did not love their lives but laid them down for him. Rejoice, O heavens! You citizens of heaven, be glad! But woe to you people of the world, for the devil has come down to you in great anger, knowing that he has little time."

And when the Dragon found himself cast down to earth, he persecuted the woman who had given birth to the child. But she was given two wings like those of a great eagle to fly into the wilderness to the place prepared for her, where she was cared for and protected from the Serpent, the Dragon, for three and a half years.

Then the furious Dragon set out to attack the rest of her children—all who were keeping God's commandments and confessing that they belong to Jesus.[7]

**DRAGON-
CREATURE**

And now in my vision I saw a strange Creature rising up out of the dead. It had seven heads and ten horns and ten crowns upon its horns. And written on each head were blasphemous names, each one defying and insulting God. This Creature looked like a leopard but had bear's feet and a lion's mouth! And the Dragon gave him his own power.

I saw that one of his heads seemed wounded beyond recovery—but the fatal wound was healed! All the world marveled at this miracle and followed the Creature in awe. They worshiped the Dragon for giving him such power, and they worshiped the strange Creature. "Where is anyone as great as he?" they exclaimed.

Then the Dragon encouraged the Creature to speak great blasphemies against the Lord, and gave him authority to control the earth for forty-two months. All that time he blasphemed God's Name and his temple and all those living in heaven. The Dragon gave him power to fight against God's people and overcome them, and to rule over all nations and language groups throughout the world. And all mankind whose names were not written in the slain Lamb's Book of Life worshiped the evil Creature.

Anyone who can hear, listen carefully: the people of God who are destined for prison will be arrested; those destined for death will be killed. But do not be dismayed, for here is your opportunity for endurance and confidence.

Then I saw another strange animal, this one coming up out of the earth, with two little horns like those of a lamb but a fearsome voice like the Dragon's. He exercised all the authority of the Creature whose death-wound had been healed, whom he required all the world to worship. He did unbelievable miracles such as making fire flame down to earth from the skies. By these miracles he was deceiving people everywhere. And he ordered the people of the world to make a great statue of the first Creature. He was permitted to give breath to this statue and make it speak! Then the statue ordered that anyone refusing to worship it must die!

He required everyone—great and small, rich and poor, slave and free—to be tattooed with a certain mark on the right hand or on the forehead. And no one could get a job or even buy in any store without the permit of that mark, which was either the name of the Creature or the code number of his name. Here is a puzzle that calls for careful thought: the numerical values of the letters in his names add to 666![8]

SONG OR WAIL

Then I saw a Lamb standing on Mount Zion in Jerusalem, and with him were 144,000 who had his name and his Father's name written on their foreheads. And I heard a sound like the roaring of a great waterfall— the singing of a choir accompanied by harps.

This tremendous choir sang a wonderful new song in front of the throne of God and before the four Living Beings and the twenty-four Elders; and no one could sing this song except those 144,000 who had been redeemed from the earth. For they are spiritually undefiled, following the Lamb wherever he goes. They have been purchased from among the men on the earth as a consecrated offering to God and the Lamb.

And I saw another angel flying through the heavens carrying the everlasting Good News to preach to every nation, tribe, language, and people. "Fear God," he shouted, "and extol his greatness. For the time has come when he will sit as Judge. Worship him who made the heaven and the earth, the sea and all its sources."

Then another angel followed him through the skies, saying, "Babylon is fallen, is fallen—that great city—because she seduced the nations of the world and made them share the wine of her intense impurity and sin."

Then a third angel followed them, shouting, "Anyone worshiping the Creature from the sea and his statue and accepting his mark on the forehead or the hand, must drink the wine of the anger of God; it is poured out undiluted into God's cup of wrath.[9]

ARMAGEDDON And I saw in heaven another mighty pageant showing things to come: seven angels were assigned to carry down to earth the seven last plagues—and then at last God's anger will be finished.

Spread out before me was what seemed to be an ocean of fire and glass, and on it stood all those who had been victorious over the Evil Creature and his statue and his mark and number. All were holding harps of God and they were singing the song of Moses the servant of God, and the song of the Lamb:

"Great and marvelous
Are your doings,
Lord God Almighty.
Just and true
Are your ways,
O King of Ages.
Who shall not fear,
O Lord,
And glorify your Name?
For you alone are holy.
All nations will come
And worship before you,
For your righteous deeds
Have been disclosed."

Then I looked and saw that the Holy of Holies of the Temple in heaven was thrown wide open!

The seven angels who were assigned to pour out the seven plagues then came from the Temple. And one of the four Living Beings handed each of them a golden flask filled with the terrible wrath of the Living God. The Temple was filled with smoke from his glory and power; and no one could enter until the seven angels had completed pouring out the seven plagues.

I heard a mighty voice shouting from the Temple to the seven angels, "Now go your ways and empty out the seven flasks of the wrath of God upon the earth."

The first angel left the Temple and poured out his flask over the earth, and malignant sores broke out on everyone who had the mark of the Creature.

The second angel poured out his flask upon the oceans, and they became like the watery blood of a dead man; and everything in the oceans died.

The third angel poured out his flask upon the rivers and they became blood. And I heard this angel declaring, "You are just in sending this judgment, O Holy One, for your saints and prophets have been martyred and their blood poured out upon the earth; and now in turn you have poured out the blood of those who murdered them."

Then the fourth angel poured out his flask upon the sun, causing it to scorch all men with its fire. Everyone was burned by this blast of heat, and they cursed God who sent the plagues.

The fifth angel poured out his flask upon the throne of the Creature from the sea, and his kingdom was plunged into darkness. His subjects gnawed their tongues in anguish and cursed the God of heaven, but they refused to repent of their evil deeds.

The sixth angel poured out his flask upon the great River Euphrates and it dried up so the kings from the east could march their armies westward without hindrance. And I saw three evil spirits disguised as frogs leap from the mouth of the Dragon, the Creature, and his False Prophet. These miracle-working demons conferred with all the rulers of the world to gather them for battle against the Lord on that great coming Judgment Day of God Almighty. And they gathered all the armies of the world near a place called in Hebrew, Armageddon—the Mountain of Megiddo.

Then the seventh angel poured out his flask into the air, and a mighty shout came from the throne of the Temple in heaven, saying, "It is finished!" Then thunder crashed and rolled and lightning flashed; and there was a great earthquake of a magnitude unprecedented in human history. The great city of "Babylon" split into three sections, and cities around the world fell in heaps of rubble; and so all of "Babylon's" sins were remembered and she was punished to the last drop of anger in the cup of the fierceness of his wrath. Islands vanished, mountains flattened out, and there was an incredible hailstorm—hailstones weighing a hundred pounds fell from the sky onto the people below, and they cursed God.[10]

**BABYLON
DETHRONED**

One of the seven angels who had poured out the plagues came over. "Come with me," he said, "and I will show you what is going to happen to the Notorious Prostitute who sits upon the many waters of the world. The kings of the world have had immoral relations with her, and the people of the earth have been made drunk by the wine of her immorality."

So the angel took me in spirit into the wilderness. There I saw a woman sitting on a scarlet animal that had seven heads and ten horns, written all over with blasphemies against God. The woman wore purple and scarlet clothing and beautiful jewelry made of gold and precious gems and pearls, and held in her hand a golden goblet full of obscenities.

A mysterious caption was written on her forehead: "Babylon the Great, Mother of Prostitutes and of Idol Worship Everywhere around the World."

I could see that she was drunk—drunk with the blood of the martyrs of Jesus she had killed. I stared at her in horror.

"Why are you so surprised?" the angel asked. "I'll tell you who she is and what the animal she is riding represents. He was alive but isn't now. And yet, soon he will come up out of the bottomless pit and go to eternal destruction; and the people of earth whose names have not been written in the Book of Life will be dumbfounded at his reappearance after being dead.

"His seven heads represent a city built on seven hills where this woman has her residence. They also represent seven kings. Five have already fallen, the sixth now reigns, and the seventh is yet to come, but his reign will be brief. The scarlet animal that died is the eighth king, having reigned before as one of the seven; after his second reign he too will go to his doom. His ten horns are ten kings who have not yet risen to power; they will be anointed to their kingdoms for one brief moment to reign with him. They will all sign a treaty giving their power and strength to him. Together they will wage war against the Lamb, and the Lamb will conquer them for he is Lord over all lords and King of kings, and his people are the called and chosen and faithful ones.

"The oceans, lakes, and rivers that the woman is sitting on represent masses of people of every race and nation.

"The scarlet animal and his ten horns—which represent ten kings who will reign with him—all hate the woman and will attack her and leave her naked and ravaged by fire. For God will put a plan into their minds, a plan that will carry out his purposes: they will mutually agree to give their authority to the scarlet animal so that the words of God will be fulfilled. And this woman you saw represents the great city that rules over the kings of the earth."

After all this, I saw another angel come down from heaven and the earth grew bright with his splendor.

He gave a mighty shout. "Babylon the Great is fallen, is fallen; she has become a den of demons, a haunt of devils and every kind of evil spirit. For all the nations have drunk the fatal wine of her intense immorality. The rulers of earth have enjoyed themselves with her and businessmen have grown rich from her luxurious living."

Then I heard another voice calling from heaven, "She has lived in luxury and pleasure—match it now with torments and with sorrows. She boasts, 'I am queen upon my throne; I am no helpless widow—I will not experience sorrow.' Therefore the sorrows of death and mourning and famine shall overtake her in a single day and she shall be utterly consumed by fire; for mighty is the Lord who judges her."

World leaders who took part in her immoral acts and enjoyed her favors will mourn for her as they see the smoke rising from her charred remains. Merchants of the earth will weep for her, for there is no one left to buy their goods. She was their biggest customer for gold and silver, precious stones, pearls, finest linens, purple silks, scarlet, every kind of perfumed wood, ivory goods and expensive wooden carvings, brass and iron and marble, spices and perfumes and incense, ointment and frankincense, wine, olive oil, fine flour, wheat, cattle, sheep, horses, chariots, slaves—and even the souls of men.

And the shipowners and captains of merchant ships and crews will stand a long way off saying, "Where is there another city such as this? Alas, for she made us all rich from her great wealth. And now in a single hour all is gone. . . ."

Then a mighty angel picked up a boulder shaped like a millstone and threw it into the ocean and shouted, "Babylon, that great city, shall be thrown away as I have thrown away this stone. She deceived all nations with her sorceries. And she was responsible for the blood of all the martyred prophets and the saints."

After this I heard the shouting of a vast crowd in heaven; "Hallelujah! Praise the Lord! Salvation is from our God. Honor and authority belong to him alone, for his judgments are just and true."

The twenty-four Elders and four Living Beings worshiped God and said, "Amen! Hallelujah! Praise the Lord!"

Then I heard again what sounded like the shouting of a huge crowd or like the waves of a hundred oceans crashing on the shore; "Praise the Lord. For the Lord our God, the Almighty, reigns. Let us be glad and rejoice and honor him; for the time has come for the wedding banquet of the Lamb, and his bride has prepared herself."

And the angel dictated this sentence to me: "Blessed are those who are invited to the wedding feast of the Lamb."[11]

KING OF KINGS

I fell down at his feet but he said, "No! I am a servant of God just as you and your brother Christians are. The purpose of all I have shown you is to tell about Jesus."

Then I saw heaven opened and a white horse standing there, and the one sitting on the horse was named "Faithful and True"—the one who justly punishes and makes war. His eyes were like flames and on his head were many crowns. He was clothed with garments dipped in blood and his title was, "The Word of God." The armies of heaven followed him on white horses. In his mouth he held a sharp sword to strike down the nations. On his robe and thigh was written, "King of Kings and Lord of Lords."

Then I saw the Evil Creature gathering the governments of the earth and their armies to fight against the one sitting on the horse and his army. And the Evil Creature was captured and with him the False Prophet who could do mighty miracles. Both of them were thrown alive into the Lake of Fire that burns with sulphur. And their entire army was killed with the sharp sword in the mouth of the one riding the white horse.

Then I saw an angel come down from heaven with the key to the bottomless pit and a heavy chain in his hand. He seized the Dragon—that old Serpent, the devil, Satan—and bound him in chains for 1,000 years, and threw him into the bottomless pit so he could not fool the nations any more until the thousand years were finished. Afterwards he would be released again for a little while.

Then I saw thrones, and sitting on them were those who had been given the right to judge. And I saw the souls of those who had been beheaded for their testimony about Jesus; they had come to life and now they reigned with Christ for a thousand years.

This is the First Resurrection. (The rest of the dead did not come back to life until the thousand years had ended.) Blessed and holy are those who share in the First Resurrection. For them the Second Death holds no terrors, for they will be priests of God and of Christ and shall reign with him a thousand years.[12]

DEATH'S THROES

When the thousand years end, Satan will be let out of his prison. He will go out to deceive the nations of the world and gather them together, with Gog and Magog, for battle. They will go up across the broad plain of the earth and surround God's people and the beloved city of Jerusalem on every side. But fire from God in heaven will flash down on the attacking armies and consume them.

Then the devil who had betrayed them will again be thrown into the Lake of Fire burning with sulphur where the Creature and False Prophet are, and they will be tormented day and night forever and ever.

And I saw a great white throne and the one who sat upon it, from whose face the earth and sky fled away, but they found no place to hide. I saw the dead, great and small, standing before God; and The Books were opened, including the Book of Life. And the dead were judged according to the things written in The Books, each according to the deeds he had done. Oceans surrendered the bodies buried in them, and the earth and the underworld gave up the dead in them. Each was judged according to his deeds. And Death and Hell were thrown into the Lake of Fire. This is the Second Death. And if anyone's name was not found recorded in the Book of Life, he was thrown into the Lake of Fire.[13]

NEW WORLD

Then I saw a new earth and a new sky, for the present earth and sky had disappeared. And I, John, saw the Holy City, the new Jerusalem, coming down from God out of heaven. It was a glorious sight, beautiful as a bride at her wedding.

I heard a shout from the throne, saying, "Look, the home of God is now among men, and he will live with them and they will be his people. He will wipe away all tears and there shall be no pain. All of that has gone forever."

And the one sitting on the throne said, "See, I am making all things new!" And then he said to me, "Write this down, for what I tell you is trustworthy and true: 'It is finished! I am the A and the Z—the Beginning and the End. I will give to the thirsty the springs of the Water of Life—as a gift! Everyone who conquers will inherit all these blessings, and I will be his God and he will be my son. But cowards who turn back from following me, and those who are unfaithful to me, and the corrupt, and murderers, and the immoral, and those conversing with demons, and idol worshipers and all liars—their doom is in the Lake that burns with fire and sulphur.'"

Then one of the seven angels who had emptied the flasks containing the seven last plagues came and said to me, "Come with me and I will show you the bride, the Lamb's wife."

In a vision he took me to a towering mountain peak and from there I watched that wondrous city, the holy Jerusalem, descending out of the skies from God. It was filled with the glory of God and flashed and glowed like a precious gem, crystal clear like jasper. Its walls were broad and high, with twelve gates guarded by twelve angels. And the names of the twelve tribes of Israel were written on the gates. There were three gates on each side—north, south, east, and west. The walls had twelve foundation stones, and on them were written the names of the twelve apostles of the Lamb.

The angel held in his hand a golden measuring stick to measure the city and its gates and walls. He found it was a square as wide as it was long; in fact, it was in the form of a cube, for its height was exactly the same as its other dimensions—1,500 miles each way.

The city itself was transparent gold like glass! The wall was made of jasper and was built on twelve layers of foundation stones inlaid with gems: the first layer with jasper; the second with sapphire; the third with chalcedony; the fourth with emerald; the fifth was sardonyx; the sixth layer with sardus; the seventh with chrysolite; the eighth with beryl; the ninth with topaz; the tenth with chrysoprase; the eleventh with jacinth; the twelfth with amethyst. The twelve gates were made of pearls—each gate from a single pearl! And the main street was pure, transparent gold.

No Temple could be seen in the city, for the Lord God Almighty and the Lamb are worshiped in it everywhere. And the city has no need of sun or moon to light it, for the glory of God and of the Lamb illuminate it. Its light will light the nations of the earth, and the rulers of the world will come and bring their glory to it. Its gates never close; they stay open all day long—and there is no night! And the glory and honor of all the nations shall be brought into it. Nothing evil will be permitted in it—no one immoral or dishonest—but only those whose names are written in the Lamb's Book of Life.

And he pointed out to me a river of pure Water of Life, clear as crystal, flowing from the throne of God and the Lamb, coursing down the center of the main street. On each side of the river grew Trees of Life, bearing twelve crops of fruit with a fresh crop each month; the leaves were used for medicine to heal the nations.

There shall be nothing in the city which is evil, for the throne of God and of the Lamb will be there and his servants will worship him. They shall see his face, and his name shall be written on their foreheads. And they shall reign forever and ever.

Then the angel said, "These words are trustworthy: 'I am coming soon!' God, who tells his prophets what the future holds, has sent his angel to tell you this will happen soon. Blessed are those who believe it and all else written in the scroll."

I, John, saw and heard all these things and fell down to worship the angel who showed them to me; but again he said, "No, don't do that. I, too, am a servant of Jesus as you are, as well as all those who heed the truth stated in this Book. Worship God alone."[14]

"COME!" "I am the A and the Z, the Beginning and the End, the First and Last. Blessed are all who wash their robes to have the right to enter in through the gates of the city and to eat the fruit from the Tree of Life. I, Jesus, have sent my angel to you to tell the churches all these things. I am both David's Root and his Descendant. I am the bright Morning Star."

The Spirit and the bride say, "Come." Let each one who hears them say the same, "Come." Let the thirsty one come—anyone who wants to; let him come and drink the Water of Life without charge.

And I solemnly declare to everyone who reads this book: if anyone adds anything to what is written here, God shall add to him the plagues described in this book. And if anyone subtracts any part of these prophecies, God shall take away his share in the Tree of Life and in the Holy City.

He who has said all these things declares: "Yes, I am coming soon!"

Amen! Come, Lord Jesus![15]

NOTES

PART 1/PARADISE—LOST

1. Genesis 1:1–6, 8–20, 22–24, 26; 2:7.
2. Genesis 2:8–18, 21–23, 25; 1:27—2:3.
3. Proverbs 8:1, 14, 17–25, 29, 35, 36; Psalms 24:1; 104:24, 30; 93:3; 103:20–22.
4. Genesis 3:1–24.
5. Isaiah 14:12–15; Ezekiel 28:12–16.
6. Genesis 4:1–22, 25, 26; 5:1, 3–32.
7. Genesis 6:1–10, 12–22; 7:1–6, 11, 12, 18, 19, 21, 23, 24; 8:1, 3–5; 9:8–13.
8. Genesis 9:1–6; 10:1–6, 8–11, 15–19, 22, 24, 25, 32.
9. Genesis 11:2–9.
10. Job 1:1–21; 2:1, 3–13; 3:1, 4, 10, 23; 4:1, 3–5, 7, 8; 5:6–8; 8:1, 3–6, 10, 11, 20, 21; 11:1, 6, 13–16; 12:1; 13:13–15, 18–22; 14:14, 15; 16:8; 17:7, 8; 19:6, 8, 14–18, 20, 25–27; 23:2–5, 8; 29:2–7, 11, 12, 15, 16, 18; 30:16–19, 30, 31; 32:1, 2, 5, 6, 8; 33:1, 8–10, 12, 13; 34:2, 4–7, 10, 11, 13–15, 31–33; 35:9–14; 36:22–24; 37:21–24; 38:1–5, 8, 12, 14, 17–20, 25–27, 31–32; 40:2–10, 12, 14; 42:1–3, 5–13, 15–17.

PART 2/COVENANT PEOPLE

1. Genesis 11:10, 12, 14, 16, 18, 20, 22, 24, 26–29, 31; 12:1–20; 13:1, 3–12, 14–16, 18; 14:1, 2, 4, 5, 8, 9, 11–20.
2. Genesis 16:1–11, 13, 15.
3. Genesis 17:1–5, 7, 8, 10, 13, 15, 16, 19–21, 23.
4. Genesis 18:1, 20, 21, 23, 24, 26–38; 19:1–15, 17, 18, 20–26, 30–38.
5. Genesis 20:1–15.
6. Genesis 21:1–3, 6–31, 34.
7. Genesis 22:1–19; 23:1–6, 8–10, 14–19.

8. Genesis 24:1–7, 9–20, 22–38, 42–47, 49–58, 61–67; 25:5, 7, 9, 10, 12–18.
9. Genesis 25:20–34; 26:1–6, 12–18, 23–26, 28–35; 27:1–22, 25, 27–46; 28:1–4, 6–9.
10. Genesis 28:10–13, 15–22; 29:1, 2, 4–6, 9–23, 25–28, 30–35; 30:1–14, 16–25, 27, 28, 32, 34, 37, 40, 43; 31:1–3, 17, 20; 32:3–19, 21–24.
11. Genesis 32:24–31; 33:1–14, 16–20; 35:1, 5, 9, 11–14, 16–21, 27–29.
12. Genesis 37:1–8, 12–35; 39:1, 2, 4–17, 19–22; 40:1–23; 41:1–4, 8–16, 25–27, 31, 33–42, 45–52, 54, 56, 57.
13. Genesis 42:1–11, 13, 18–26, 29, 36, 38; 43:1, 2, 11, 13–16, 24–34; 44:1–7, 9–14, 16–18, 30–34; 45:1–5, 7–10, 14, 15, 21, 22, 25–28; 46:1–5, 26–30; 47:1–7, 27–29; 49:1, 3–10, 13–17, 19–27, 29–30, 33; 50:12–14, 22–26

PART 3/CHOSEN NATION

1. Exodus 1:8–12, 15–17, 20, 22.
2. Exodus 2:1–22.
3. Exodus 3:1–4, 6, 7, 10–15, 17; 4:1–5, 10–16, 27–31.
4. Exodus 5:1–9, 13, 14, 22, 23; 6:1–4, 6–8; 7:5, 7–13; 8:20–22, 24–32; 9:13, 14, 18–25, 27–28, 33, 34; 10:21–26, 28, 29; 11:1; 12:2–8, 10–14, 17, 21–23, 28–30, 31, 32, 37, 40–42; 13:3, 14, 16, 19–22; 14:1–7, 9, 10, 13, 14, 19–23, 26–28, 31; Psalm 90:1–8, 10–17; Exodus 15:22, 27; 16:1–6, 8, 13 16, 19, 21–24, 27, 31, 35.
5. Exodus 19:1–20; 20:1–5, 7–17; 24:3 8, 12–18.
6. Exodus 25:1, 8–14, 16–20, 22–24, 29–33, 37, 40; 26:1–7, 9, 15, 26, 28, 29, 31, 33, 35–37; 27:1–7, 9, 11–13, 20, 21; 28:1–9, 12, 15–22, 29, 33–37, 39–41; 29:38, 39, 42, 43; 30:1–3, 6–8, 17–20; 31:1–3, 6–11, 18.

7. Exodus 32:1–13, 14, 15, 19, 20, 30–33, 35; 34:1, 4–14.
8. Leviticus 25:1–10, 14–27, 29–31, 35, 36, 39–41; 26:3, 4, 6, 7, 9, 12–17, 27, 28, 30, 31, 33–35, 40–42, 44; Genesis 34:28, 29.
9. Exodus 35:1, 5–16, 19–21; 36:2–7; 38:24, 25, 29; Numbers 3:5–13; Exodus 39:32; 40:17, 18, 29, 33, 34, 36–38.
10. Leviticus 1:1–9, 14; 2:1–3, 13; 3:1, 6; 6:25, 26, 30; 5:15; 7:1–3, 7, 11–13, 22, 23, 26, 27; 10:8–11; 18:1–3, 6, 21, 22, 24; 19:1, 9–10, 13, 15–18, 31–36; 23:1, 2, 5–19, 23–27, 29, 33–36, 40, 43, 44; Numbers 1:1–4, 17, 18, 20–47, 50, 52; 10:1–4, 8–12, 14–27, 33; 11:4–8, 10, 11, 13, 15–20, 24, 25, 30–35; 12:16.
11. Numbers 13:1–23, 25, 27–33; 14:1–10.
12. Numbers 14:11, 22, 23, 30, 33; 16:1–7, 18–32, 35, 40; 17:1–10; 20:1–12.
13. Numbers 20:14–18, 20, 23–29; 21:4, 10–13, 16, 18–24, 32–35; 22:1; 32:1–6, 15–17, 28, 33; 27:12, 13, 15–23.
14. Deuteronomy 1:1–3; 4:32–35; 6:4–7, 10–12; 7:1–8, 21, 22; 8:2–5, 7–9, 12–16, 18–20; 10:17–19; 13:1–3; 17:14–20; 18:9–12, 14, 15, 17, 19; 19:15, 16, 19, 20; 27:12–26; 28:15, 20, 22–25, 32, 33, 35–37, 45; 30:1–6, 19, 20; 31:1–3, 6; 34:1–6, 8, 10–12.

PART 4/PROMISED LAND

1. Joshua 1:1–5, 7, 8, 10, 11.
2. Joshua 2:1–6, 8–15, 17, 18, 22–24; 3:1–6, 9, 10, 14–16; 4:1–4, 8, 18–24; 5:10–12.
3. Joshua 5:13, 14; 6:2–6, 11–18, 20–24; 9:1–9, 11, 14–16, 22–27; 10:1–14, 40, 43; 11:1–8, 10, 12, 16–18; 12:24.
4. Joshua 13:1, 7, 8; 18:1–4, 9, 10; 19:51; 20:1–4, 6–9; 21:1–3; 23:1–8, 10, 12–16; 24:1–5, 7, 8, 11–18, 25, 26, 28–30, 32, 33.

PART 5/HEROES; HUMILIATIONS

1. Judges 1:1, 2, 4, 8–10, 18, 20–23, 27, 30–34; 2:9–11; 3:5–21, 23, 26–30.
2. Judges 4:1–17, 20, 21; 5:31.
3. Judges 6:1–4, 6, 7, 11–22, 24, 33–38; 7:1–9, 16–23; 8:28, 32.
4. Judges 13:2–5; 14:1–19; 15:1–15, 20; 16:4–6, 16–31.

5. Ruth 1:1–11, 13, 14, 16, 18–20; 2:1–20, 22, 23; 3:1–9, 12, 13, 16–18; 4:1–6, 9–13, 16, 17.
6. 1 Samuel 1:1–6, 9–28; 2:11, 12, 17–25, 27–31, 34, 35; 3:1–13, 15–20; 4:1–14, 18; 5:1–4, 6–11; 6:1, 2, 6–10, 12, 13, 15, 21; 7:1–13, 15–17; 8:1–14, 17–20, 22.

PART 6/KINGDOM GLORY

1. 1 Samuel 9:1–6, 10–12, 14–19, 22–27; 10:1–10, 17–21, 24, 25.
2. 1 Samuel 11:1–11, 14, 15; 14:47–52; 15:1–5, 7–24, 27–29, 34, 35; 16:1–13.
3. 1 Samuel 16:14–19, 21–23; Psalm 23:1–6; 19:1–3, 7–14.
4. 1 Samuel 17:1–8, 10, 12–15, 17, 18, 20, 22, 23, 25, 26, 30–35, 37–43, 45, 46, 48–53.
5. 1 Samuel 18:2–9, 17–21, 25–30; 19:1, 4–10, 18–20; 20:1, 4–7, 12–17, 27–35, 41, 42; 22:1, 2; Psalm 31:1–5, 15, 16, 19–21.
6. 1 Samuel 23:1–9, 13–18; Psalm 40:5–8, 13, 17; 1 Samuel 25:1; 26:1–22, 24, 25; Psalm 139:1–3, 6–18, 23, 24.
7. 1 Samuel 28:1, 5–22, 25; 29:1, 2, 11; 31:1–6; 2 Samuel 1:11, 12, 17; 2:1–8, 10–13, 17–23, 29, 32; 3:1–10, 17–28, 31, 37; 4:1–3, 5–9, 11, 12; 5:15.
8. 2 Samuel 5:6–8; 1 Chronicles 11:6–9; 2 Samuel 5:11, 12; Psalm 34:1–16, 18–22.
9. 2 Samuel 5:17–20, 22–25; 1 Chronicles 14:17; 13:1–8; 2 Samuel 6:6–11; 1 Chronicles 15:1–3, 14–16, 28; 16:1, 4, 7–11, 23–36.
10. 2 Samuel 7:1–22, 27–29; Psalm 8; 2; 110:1; 2 Samuel 8:1–6, 9–12, 15–18; 9:1–3, 5–12.
11. 1 Chronicles 20:1; 2 Samuel 11:2–12, 14–18, 22–27; 12:1–23.
12. Psalm 51:1–8, 10, 12–17, 19; 2 Samuel 12:24–30.
13. 2 Samuel 13:1–19, 21–25, 27–33, 37–39; 14:1–8, 12, 13, 17–21, 24, 28, 29, 32, 33.
14. 2 Samuel 14:25; 15:1–18, 23, 24, 26–36; Psalm 42:1–8, 11; 2 Samuel 15:37; 16:16–18, 20; 17:1–4, 7–16, 23–26; 18:1, 2, 5–11, 14, 16, 17, 21, 31–33; 19:9–12, 14, 15, 18; 20:2; Psalm 27:1–6, 8–10, 13.

15. 2 Samuel 21:15–17; 1 Chronicles 21:1; 2 Samuel 24:2–4, 8–11; 1 Chronicles 21:10–13; 2 Samuel 24:15–25; Psalm 103:1–5, 7–18.

16. 1 Kings 1:1, 5–7, 9–20, 22–25, 27–43, 49; 1 Chronicles 28:1–9, 11, 13, 19, 21; 29:1–3, 5–12, 18–22; 1 Kings 2:1–3; Psalm 72:1–4, 6–8, 10, 11, 18, 19; 1 Kings 2:10; 2 Chronicles 1:1–3, 5–15; 1 Kings 4:21, 25, 29–34.

17. Proverbs 1:1, 2, 7, 20, 21; 2:1–10, 20–22; 3:4–6, 13–15, 18, 21, 24–26; 5:15, 18, 19; 6:6–11, 20, 21, 24, 26–29, 32; 10:28–32; 11:11, 18, 19, 22, 24, 25; 15:1, 4; 21:21; 22:2, 6; 20:1; 23:29–32; 29:17, 19, 23.

18. 2 Chronicles 2:1–5, 7, 8, 11–14, 16; 3:1–15; 4:1–3, 5–9; 5:1–5, 7, 11–14; 6:12–14, 20, 21, 26, 27, 32–34, 36–41; 7:1–3, 8–10, 12–20; 1 Kings 7:1–4, 6–9.

19. Psalm 127:1–5.

20. Song of Songs 1:1; 2:8–13, 16, 17; 4:1–6, 12, 13, 15; 5:10–16; 8:4.

21. 2 Chronicles 8:1, 2, 6, 17, 18; 9:1–3, 5, 6, 8, 9, 12; 1 Kings 11:1–4, 7–9, 11–13; Ecclesiastes 1:1; 3:1–8, 14; 7:29; 11:9; 12:1, 3, 4–7, 13, 14.

PART 7/KINGDOM CALAMITIES

1. 1 Kings 11:26–31, 33–38, 40; 2 Chronicles 9:30, 31.

2. 2 Chronicles 10:1–14, 16, 18; 11:1–10.

3. 1 Kings 12:25–33; 13:1–6, 33; 14:1–10, 21–24; 2 Chronicles 11:18, 20–22; 12:2, 3, 5–9, 12–14, 16; 13:2–6, 9–15, 18–20; 1 Kings 14:20; 15:6–9, 11, 12, 14, 25–27, 29, 32, 33; 16:8–10, 15–18, 23–25, 28, 29; 2 Chronicles 14:8, 9, 11–13; 15:1, 2, 5–8, 16; 16:12–14; 17:1, 3, 5, 7–13.

4. 1 Kings 16:29–33; 17:1–16; 18:1–8, 16–21, 23–40; 19:1–16, 18–20; 2 Chronicles 18:1–8, 14, 16, 17, 25–31, 33, 34; 1 Kings 22:51, 52; 2 Kings 1:1–4, 17; 2 Chronicles 21:1, 4–6, 11–19.

5. 2 Kings 2:1, 6–15; 5:1–15; 6:8–23; 2 Chronicles 22:1; 2 Kings 8:26–29; 9:1–7, 11–13, 16, 17, 21–24, 27, 28, 30–33; 10:31, 35.

6. Joel 1:1–3, 5–10, 17, 18, 20; 2:1–5, 10–15, 17–20, 23–25, 27–32; 3:1, 2, 7, 9–11, 14, 16, 17.

7. 2 Kings 11:1–3; 2 Chronicles 23:1–3, 9–16, 18, 20, 21; 24:7–13, 15, 17–21, 23, 25, 27; 25:1, 3, 17–24; 2 Kings 14:16, 23–25, 29.

8. Amos 1:1, 2; 2:6; 3:1–3, 6, 7, 10, 11, 14, 15; 4:6, 8, 9, 11–13; 5:4, 5, 8, 14, 15; 6:4–8, 14; 9:8, 9, 11, 12.

9. Hosea 1:1; 4:1–3, 6, 9, 11–14; 5:3, 4; 6:6; 9:3; 14:1–7, 9.

10. Jonah 1:1–17; 2:1, 3, 4, 6, 8–10; 3:1–5, 7–10; 4:1, 2, 5–11.

11. 2 Chronicles 25:25, 27, 28; 26:1, 4–11, 14–21, 23.

12. Isaiah 1:1–5, 18, 20, 21, 23; 3:15; 6:1–8.

13. 2 Chronicles 27:1, 3–5, 8, 9; 28:1–3, 5; 2 Kings 15:9, 10, 14, 18–20, 22.

14. 2 Kings 15:24, 25, 28–30; Isaiah 7:1–4, 7–16; 8:16; 9:2, 3, 6, 7.

15. Micah 1:1–3, 5, 6, 9; 3:9–12; 4:1–4; 5:2, 3, 7.

16. 2 Kings 17:3–6, 23, 24, 27–29; 2 Chronicles 28:16–18, 20–25, 27.

17. 2 Chronicles 29:1–12, 15–21, 25–27, 29, 31; 30:1, 6, 9, 10, 12–15, 22, 23, 26, 27; 32:1–3, 5–11, 13–15, 18; Isaiah 37:14–22, 24, 26, 28–31, 33–38; 38:1–10, 12, 13, 14–17, 19, 20; 39:1–7; 2 Chronicles 32:27–30, 33; 33:1–6.

18. Isaiah 13:1, 14, 17–19; 47:1, 3, 6–8, 11–14; 45:1–5; 11:1–5; 40:3, 5, 6, 9, 11; 42:1–9; 53:1–12; 61:1–4, 6–9; 11:6, 8, 9; 2:2–4; 55:6–11.

19. 2 Chronicles 33:10–16, 20–25.

20. Jeremiah 1:1–11, 13–16; 2:13; 7:16, 18, 20–26, 28; 9:23–26, 28; 9:23–26; 13:23, 24.

21. 2 Chronicles 34:1, 3, 4, 7–11, 14–16, 19–24, 26–32; 35:1–6, 10, 11, 13, 17–19; Psalm 100; 2 Chronicles 36:1–5.

22. Habakkuk 1:1, 5, 6, 11–13; 2:2–6, 12–16, 18–20; 3:1–6, 16–18.

23. Jeremiah 27:1, 3–8, 11; 36:1–6, 8, 9, 11, 12, 14–16, 19–21, 23, 27–31; 25:1–3, 8, 9, 11, 12, 14.

24. Daniel 1:1–3, 5–8, 10–17; 2:1, 2, 5–28, 31–49; 2 Kings 24:1, 2; 2 Chronicles 36:7; Jeremiah 27:19–21; 2 Kings 24:10; 2 Chronicles 36:10.

25. Ezekiel 1:1–11, 13–17, 19–28; 2:1, 2, 10–19; 8:1–14, 16–18; 9:1–7; 10:1, 2, 6–10, 12, 13, 15, 18, 19; 11:1, 2, 4, 5, 9, 12, 14, 16–18, 22–25; 34:1–6,

21. John 13:31–35; Luke 22:28–32; Matthew 26:31–35; John 14:1–6, 8, 9, 15–17, 21–23, 25, 26, 30, 31; 15:1–4, 8–10, 12–14, 20, 21, 23, 25; 16:1, 2, 5, 7, 8, 12, 14, 15, 27–33; 17:1–6, 8, 11, 17–21, 23, 25, 26.

22. John 18:1, 2; Mark 14:32–40; Matthew 26:44; Luke 22:43–45; Matthew 26:45–49; Luke 22:47–51; Matthew 26:53–56.

23. John 18:12–24; Matthew 26:59–66; Luke 22:63–65; Matthew 26:69; 27:1, 2; Luke 23:2, 3; John 18:36–38; Luke 23:5–11, 13–16; Mark 15:6–9, 11–13; Matthew 27:19; Luke 23:17, 18; Mark 15:15–19; John 19:4–16; Matthew 27:3–5.

24. Luke 23:26–34; John 19:19–24; Matthew 27:39–41; Luke 23:39–43; John 19:25, 26; Luke 23:44; Matthew 27:46–49; John 19:28; Luke 23:46; Matthew 27:51, 52; Luke 23:47–49; Mark 15:40; John 19:31–37; Mark 15:43–45; John 19:39–42; Matthew 27:60; Mark 15:47; Matthew 27:62–66.

25. Matthew 28:2–4; Luke 23:55; 24:1–8; Matthew 28:11–13, 15; Mark 16:9; John 20:1–8, 10, 11, 14–17; Matthew 28:8–10; Luke 24:13–48; John 20:21, 22, 24–29; Mark 16:15, 16; John 21:1–25.

26. Acts 1:3–8; Matthew 28:18–20; Acts 1:9; Luke 24:50, 51; Acts 1:10, 11; Luke 24:52, 53.

PART 11/THE NEW PEOPLE

1. Acts 2:1–11, 13–33, 37–39, 41–47.

2. Acts 3:1–13, 15, 17–22, 24–26; 4:1–10, 13, 15–21, 23–27, 29–32, 36, 37; 5:12, 14–35, 38–42.

3. Acts 6:1–3, 5–9, 11–13; 7:1–6, 8–10, 14, 18–24, 29–32, 34, 36–39, 42, 43, 51, 52, 54–60; 8:1, 3–7, 14–17, 25–39; 9:1–30.

4. Acts 9:31–43; 10:1–20, 23, 24, 27–45, 47, 48; 11:19, 22–26.

5. Acts 12:1–19, 25; 13:1–6, 13–23, 26, 27, 29–33, 38, 39, 42, 44–48, 50, 51; 14:1–28; 15:1, 2, 4–16, 19–22, 30–34.

6. Galatians 1:1, 2, 6–8, 11, 12, 17–19, 21; 2:1–3, 6–9, 19–21; 3:1–3, 6–8, 11, 14, 17, 19, 24, 26–29; 4:1, 3–11, 21–28, 30, 31; 5:10, 13, 14, 16, 17, 19–23, 25; 6:7, 8, 18.

7. James 1:1–7, 12–17, 26, 27; 2:1, 4–9, 14–18, 20–23, 26; 3:1, 5, 6, 10, 13, 15, 17, 18; 4:1–8, 13–15, 17; 5:7, 9–11, 13–20.

8. Acts 15:36–41; 16:1, 3–40; 17:1–19, 22–28, 30–34; 18:1–11.

9. 1 Thessalonians 1:1–10; 2:13, 14; 4:13–18; 5:2–5, 9–10, 16–18, 23, 27, 28.

10. 2 Thessalonians 1:1, 3, 4–10; 2:2–5, 7–12, 16, 17; 3:1, 2, 6, 12, 17, 18.

11. Acts 18:12–16, 18–28; 19:1–6, 8–10.

12. 1 Corinthians 1:1, 2, 4, 5, 10–14, 16–18, 22–25; 2:7–10, 13; 3:5, 6, 9–13; 5:11–13; 6:1, 2, 7, 12, 13, 15, 16, 18–20; 7:1–4, 6, 7, 10–14, 17; 11:17, 18, 23–28; 12:1–13, 29–31; 13:1–13; 14:1, 37; 15:1, 3–10, 12–15, 19–24, 29, 30, 32, 35–45, 47, 48, 50–52, 54–58; 16:19, 23.

13. 2 Corinthians 1:1, 2, 8–11; 2:14–16; 4:3, 4, 6–10, 16–18; 5:1, 4–10, 14, 17–21; 6:3–6, 8–18; 11:2–4, 14, 15, 22–29; 12:1–4, 7–10; 13:5, 6, 9, 11, 13, 14.

14. Acts 19:11–20.

15. Revelation 22:13, 14, 16–20.

15. Romans 1:1–10, 13, 16–21, 23, 25–32; 2:5–8, 12–14; 3:9, 10, 12, 19–25, 27, 31; 4:16–25; 5:12, 14, 17, 21; 6:1–3, 13, 17, 23; 7:1, 2, 4, 18, 22–25; 8:1, 2, 4, 14, 17–23, 26, 28–32, 35–39; 9:1–7, 13–15, 17, 18, 21–24, 30–33; 10:2, 4, 8, 9, 13–16; 11:1, 3–5, 15, 22, 25–32; 12:1, 2; 13:1, 3, 6, 8, 9; 15:14–16, 19–26, 28, 30–32; 16:25–27.

16. Acts 19.21–32, 35–41; 20:1, 3, 4, 6–12, 16–25, 28–32, 36–38; 21:1–4, 7–14.

17. Acts 21:15–28, 30–34, 37–40; 22:1, 3–8, 10–15, 17, 18, 21, 22, 24–26, 29, 30; 23:1–17, 19–33, 35; 24:1–20, 22–27; 25:1–12.

18. Acts 27:1–44; 28:1–24, 30, 31.

19. Ephesians 1:1, 3–5, 9, 10, 13–23; 2:1–6, 8, 9, 14, 16, 18, 22; 3:1, 3, 6, 7, 14–20; 4:1–10, 12, 13, 16, 21–26, 28, 29, 31, 32; 5:5, 6, 10–14, 18–23, 25, 28–30; 6:1, 2, 4–6, 8–20, 23.

20. Colossians 1:1, 2, 4, 5, 7, 11–13, 15, 17, 19, 20, 22–24, 29; 2:1–3, 6–10; 3:1, 3, 4, 10–17; 4:7, 8, 10, 14, 16, 18.

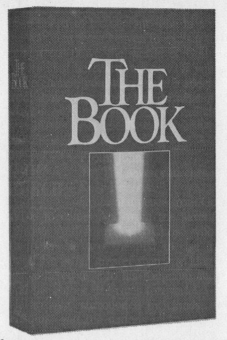

If you enjoyed THE STORY, you'll love THE BOOK. Pick up a copy wherever books are sold and discover why millions of people have selected THE BOOK as the world's easiest to read and understand Bible.